Preface to the Third Edition

There have been a number of changes in South America since the First Edition of this book was published in 1979. I made some alterations for the Second Edition and further changes have been made for this new version. My own ideas have matured with respect to some themes and I have been able to glean some more information on others.

The chapter layout of this edition is made a little more logical and simple by having only two parts, systematic and regional.

There is a new chapter on Politics and Territory, examining the three themes of territorial disputes, including the Falklands, geopolitics and regionalism. The chapters on agriculture and on economic development have both been rewritten completely.

Most of the systematic chapters have substantial modifications. In Physical Geography there is new material on ecological problems and natural hazards. In Industry there is more emphasis on the process of industrialization and on location factors. In the Population chapter there is a substantial discussion of urban growth processes and models.

Some new developments in specific regions are covered in the regional chapters. For example, there is the conversion of the upper R. Negro in Argentine Patagonia to a chain of lakes with hydroelectric power plants. There is also the Brazil/Paraguay border region and its colonization with soya bean farming. Included as well are the problems of massive developments in Brazil's Amazonia, at Carajas, at Tucurui, and on the Jari river.

Elsewhere there is general updating of the text, and a revision of all maps and diagrams.

Acknowledgments

The author and publisher wish to thank the following for permission to reproduce the illustrations in this book:

Booker McConnell Ltd., plates 35 and 26; the Brazilian Embassy, plates 5, 6, 7, 30, 31, 33 and 34; Christian Aid, plates 14, 20 and 21; Spectrum Colour Library, plates 3 and 22 (photographs by C.E.C. Gannon); John Topham Picture Library, plates 1, 37, 38, 41 and 43; David Wickers, plates 8, 9, 12, 13, 17, 23, 25 and 40.
Cover photo: Rob Cousins

The remaining photographs were taken by the author.

Cartography by Michael C. Shand and Kaẑia Kram

The following maps were based partially on these sources:
Fig. 1 — maps by J. J. Scholten in Soil Map of South America (see Ch.1 bibliography)
Fig. 6 map of agricultural regions in Goodes World Atlas (1967), p. 24
Fig. 32 — maps in J. M. G. Kleinpenning, T.E.S.G. (1984)
Fig. 36 — map in J. Bähr and R. Riesco, Revista de Geografía Norte Grande (1981)

Preface

It is common for Northern Hemisphere readers to think of all
South America as a fairly homogeneous unit, all of it belonging
to the Iberian languages and civilization, all in the Third World
category, nearly all of it characterized by simple economies,
including subsistence agriculture and the production of one or
a few items for export. The present text is intended to correct
such views, by demonstrating the diversity of landscapes,
societies and economies in the continent. In addition to presenting the physical, economic and other patterns, some attempt is
made at analysis, based on the author's firmly held view that
the best mnemonic for a geographical pattern is understanding
of the underlying processes.

As the book is intended for readers not familiar with Spanish
or Portuguese, only a limited number of foreign terms are
used, with italics and accent marks except where an English
form is well known. A glossary is included in the appendixes.

Any regional text in geography is inevitably, to a considerable extent, indebted to a wide variety of authors and to practical help from many sides. I cannot list here all those Latin
Americans who have aided me while I was in the regions or my
colleagues who have helped in many ways over the years. They
must accept this non-specific note of my gratitude. I must par-
ticulary thank Mr I. Tilbrook of Chipping Campden and Dr
R. P. Beckinsale of Oxford who taught me geography, and the
latter especially for suggesting this book. My wife also deserves
credit for forbearance, and for designing the maps.

Contents

Plates

Maps and Diagrams

MAPS AND DIAGRAMS

Introduction

The weight of South America in world affairs is relatively slight. It is a continent of substantial size, with area comparable to that of North America, but its *oecumene*, the inhabitable area at the present stage of technological progress, is quite restricted. Areas of very slight population include the cold deserts of the mountain tops and middle-latitude Patagonia; hot deserts, especially along the west coast; and the upland parts of the hot and humid Amazon Basin, where alluvium is not provided by rivers and soils are infertile. Collectively these areas cover more than half the continent, and have defied man's attempts at permanent settlement to date. Thus the impression of the continent as a region of wide open spaces awaiting the settler is not accurate. Population figures of 219 million in 1975, compared to a resident population of nearly 213 million in the United States alone, should not lead us to suppose enormous possibilities for growth.

Nevertheless, the importance of the continent is growing. It is a part of the Third World, which also includes most of Africa, the Middle East and South-East Asia. As such, it is a region which attracts increasingly the attention of the developed countries, for a variety of reasons. First, there is competition amongst the major powers for political influence among these countries, which can give their support to big-power policies in international assemblies and litigation as well as in war.

Second, there is an economic interest in these countries of Latin America, on the part of industrial powers which need their contribution of raw materials and foods in order to supply their manufacturing and processing enterprises. Japan, North America and Western Europe all rely on South American contributions of food and materials. On the other hand, these same industrial countries plus the Soviet bloc all seek to promote their own industrial products as exports to the continent, wherever possible exporting directly from home to a South American market, and if not permitted to do so, penetrating it by setting up subsidiaries on the continent.

Finally, much of the renewed interest in the region must derive from its evidence of internal change. There are all signs, social, economic and political, of a people in the process of development, a process more all-embracing than economic development, involving a challenge to old ideals and attitudes on class, religion and the State.

The violent political revolutions which have affected Bolivia (1952) and Cuba (1959) are indices of the forces for change, which are currently repressed to some extent in almost every country by military governments. Chile, with something of a democratic tradition, and Uruguay, where democracy had brought some aspects of the welfare state into being early in this century, have both had their floodtide of change abruptly stopped in recent years by military take-overs. To the pessimist this might seem merely a continuation of the secular situation of governmental disorder and impermanence, but there is evidence that dictatorial governments are having greater tasks because of the spread of political consciousness, and cannot continue indefinitely without popular support.

This political consciousness is itself a function of the rise in education, health and other welfare standards over the continent, which stimulates interest in a better life, the so-called revolution of rising expectations. It is also a function of urbanization, a universal phenomenon but one which has particular force in Latin America because of the rapidity of its occurrence. Within a generation, many families have pulled up their roots and moved from completely rural to urban communities; the factory, or unemployment, has replaced work on a farm; the radio and newspaper replace illiteracy; concern for personal status replaces an unthinking acceptance of humble positions in a strongly stratified rural society.

To systematize the interrelated phenomena of this society in motion, and the physical and human factors involved in its varied face from one country and from one region to another, is the intent of the following chapters.

1 Lake Calima is a reservoir created by the Alto Anchicayá dam. This provides a source of power for Cali industries. It also serves to control flooding on the Cauca River

1. Physical Geography

The continent of South America occupies 17.85 million sq km, making it slightly smaller than North America but still a great land mass, far larger than Europe west of the Urals, which covers 10 million sq km.

STRUCTURE

In tectonic and structural terms this is an important continental block, and one exhibiting considerable activity, for its nearest relative, as predicted long ago by Wegener and recently substantiated by a variety of lines of evidence, is the shield block of Africa, from which it was separated in the Mesozoic era. The central unit of the South American continent is the Brazil—Guiana shield, occupying half the continent and most of Brazil and the Guianas, covered often with thin sediments or volcanic sheets, but not undergoing any kind of folding after the Assynt orogeny of late pre-Cambrian and early Cambrian time.

This shield is relatively young compared with the African and North American ones, and radioactive decay dating places most of its rocks as less than 1000 million years old. It seems to have grown from an ancient core in the Bolivian frontier region of Chiquitos, and to have added mountains in the pre-Cambrian, including the Espinhaço and original (now re-uplifted) Serra da Mantiqueira mountains, in the southeast of Brazil. To the south of Brazil there is another great shield unit, no doubt related to it, the Patagonian block, also locally covered with sediments and volcanics. In the north, the Guiana

section of the shield is separated by the rift valley of the lower Amazon, opened out in Tertiary time.

The Andes

Flanking the shield to west and north are high mountains. The Andes are the world's greatest range of continuously high (over 3000 m) mountains, along a line which extends from Tierra del Fuego, to Venezuela and through Colombia into Central America, linking to the North American systems. These mountains are of varying age, ancient remnants dating back to the early Palaeozoic, but the present height of the range and its latest immense fold—fault system are of recent origin. Fold movements producing mountains in the location of the present ranges have their beginnings in late Mesozoic time, probably related to the initial separation of America and Africa, and they continue well into the Tertiary, pushing up high mountains to the west of the roots of older Palaeozoic ones. At this same time, the strains on the earth's crust of continental drift were relieved by basalt outpourings over $2\frac{1}{2}$ million sq km of the Paraná Plateau, in Brazil and neighbouring parts of Paraguay and Uruguay.

In late Tertiary time, after a period of relative quiescence, the mountain system was subject to massive uplift without much folding, to produce finally the present high mountains, fault-flanked horst blocks rather than fold mountains. Some of the recent uplift is shown in the high level marine terraces, now lying more than a thousand metres above present sea levels though only recently cut by the sea, along thousands of kilometres of the Pacific coast.

Pleistocene glaciation was highly localized and did not produce ice sheets as in the Northern Hemisphere, but valley glaciers over most of the Andes. In the far south a fairly large glacier system in the Patagonian Andes was able to expand and form broad piedmont glaciers occupying the southernmost Patagonian plateau and reaching the Pacific to the west. Morainic material is abundant in central and southern Chile, from the several glaciations, and terminal moraines hold back the glacial lakes of the Argentine Patagonia, lakes Viedma, Argentino, Buenos Aires and San Martín. To the present day, a combination of low temperature and heavy precipitation in the southernmost Andes permits a discontinuous icecap of more than 10 000 sq km, between 46°S and 51°S latitude, on the Chilean side of the mountains. The fact that there are moraine dams west of the main line of mountains means that there is a difference between the peak line and the drainage divide, creating room for problems between the two frontier countries, Argentina and Chile.

Further north in the Central Andes, there is evidence of Pleistocene glaciation, down to 3200 metres in Ecuador, except where active volcanoes like Cotopaxi have covered the moraines over with ash. In the Northern Andes, moraines reach down to 3000 m and some valley glaciers down to 2600 m in Venezuela, 2200 m in the Sierra de Santa Marta (Parsons, 1982). Cirque lakes are common at about 3500 m from Ecuador northward.

Tectonic activity has not come to an end in the continent. All along the Andean line, from the Chile icefields north into Venezuela, there is volcanic activity, occasionally causing damage through hot ash deposits on farmlands. More important by far are the earthquakes which have devastated many Andean towns more than once, either by direct shock waves, or as in the dramatic Peruvian quake of 1970, through dislodging pieces of ice and rock which then form landslides.

Topographically, the Andes do not form a single line of mountains. Three or more lines, subparallel to one another, are common. Between them are high basins, filled in with masses of detritus from the surrounding slopes, and forming flat land areas which can be of great human significance. The altiplano of Bolivia and Peru is the largest of these upland basins, but there are many others on a smaller scale, and the advanced civilization of eastern Colombia, the Chibchas, occupied as centre, a series of small altiplanos formed in similar fashion on the eastern Cordillera of that country. In Colombia too, where the cordilleras open out more and present access to the Caribbean, major rivers occupy the intermontane valleys, the Cauca and Magdalena.

The plains

Between the Andes and the Shield there are broad expanses of plains country where the surface is of loose sediments of Tertiary or Recent origin, swept into the depression of the Shield adjacent to the mountains. Stream action and sheet floods form here an enormous flat surface, where there are indeed regional slopes to the east, though invisible to the human eye and creating the impression of a completely level plain. The Paraná—Paraguay system belongs to this region, as well as the Orinoco and Upper and Middle Amazon basin. The lower Amazon is of somewhat different nature, formed essentially as a rift valley, fault-lined, between the shield blocks.

In some places, the plains are broken by islands of old rock, either of the Shield or related to Andean structures. In the central part of the Bolivian Oriente, the thinness of the sedimentary fill allows low projections of ancient rocks in the Chiquitos uplands, and in northwest Argentina a series of fault blocks produces a basin and range topography something like that of the United States Southwest in the Sierras Pampeanas — literally the 'hills of the plains' — the mountain blocks parallel to but older than the Andes to the west of them; in the driest areas the basins have salt lakes and no drainage to the exterior.

Geomorphic processes

Landscapes in a largely tropical continent are often distinct from those of temperate lands. The rivers, for example, flood relatively easily over their floodplains, for the ultimate product of tropical weathering is clay particles, not silt or sand size particles in any quantity, so that levees are not built up in the same way as in middle latitudes for want of a heavy fraction, and the rivers soon swell beyond their beds. It has been claimed that meanders are less frequent on this account, though no proof of this can be adduced. Tropical weathering is also probably responsible for the frequency of falls and rapids on the rivers, as opposed to the more usual middle-latitude graded courses of streams.

The processes of tropical weathering down to clay account for the typical tropical sugar-loaf mountains, rounded or chunky mounds standing above a general level. These are the result of very deep weathering, penetrating up to a hundred metres, of a chemical nature, followed by erosion which eats out in selective fashion the mass of rock waste, penetrating deep where joints have allowed water to penetrate and act chemically, and leaving behind hills which are giant joint blocks into which the ground water has not been able to run. Mass movement in landslides is the main form of wearing down of the rounded bosses themselves, and occurs frequently with devastating results in such areas as the Rio de Janeiro district of Brazil, where the sugar-loaf hills, the *morros*, have been colonized by shanty-town populations.

CLIMATE

South American climate is everywhere dominated by the oceanic circulation cells, giving no room for separate continental cells; although the continent is large, it has no great width in middle latitudes where continental air masses might be generated by the greater cooling of land during winter seasons.

On the other hand, lack of a forceful continental circulation in summer or winter allows the middle-latitude dynamic forces produced by the encounter of tropical and arctic air to have considerable penetration into the tropics, so that depressions originating in the South Pacific may curl round Cape Horn or over the lower Southern Andes to move far north and form the Argentine *pamperos* which sometimes reach into the Chaco and cause cold waves as far north as the Amazon. The depression eye usually moves along the coast, causing year-round but particularly spring and autumn rainfall in the Pampas, and into southern Brazil as far as the São Paulo — Rio region, though also at times on to the shoulder of Brazil and Cape São Roque.

Some further special factors may be noted here. First, climatic types are all closer to the Equator than their Northern Hemisphere equivalents, partly because the world's heat equator is in the north, forming the base line for climatic zonation. Second, with only a small mass of subtropical land, there is nothing comparable to the Indian monsoon or even that of the Southeast United States.

Another important climatic factor is the strong northward-setting ocean currents, operating on both sides of the continent, and contributing to the northward displacement of climatic regions. The Humboldt current, a veritable river in the sea which moves millions of tonne/kilometres of water daily, is a determinant of the coastal desert which occupies the west coast from 30°S to near the Equator. Its cold water is due to both its origin and to upwelling of water along the coast, due to offshore winds and to a differential Coriolis effect on heavier, colder water.

This cold water cools the base of an already stable South Pacific anticyclonic airmass, forming ultrastable air all along a coast which curves round to the west, following the average anticyclone shape itself and helping in its prolongation northwards. On the other side, the Falklands current is equally cold, but can have less effect since it lies downwind of the continent. It is however true that the driest part of the Patagonian desert is adjacent to this coast.

The mountains themselves have their own climatic effects; forming such a high wall, they separate in good measure the circulation patterns on either side, allowing in particular little transfer of moisture from one side to the other. From the human utility point of view, the mountains are of the highest importance, for they penetrate into cool zones where moisture may be preserved as snow for the lowlands irrigation, and in the tropics they provide the oecumene for all man's activity.

REGIONAL CLIMATES

Amazon Basin

A continuous inflow of warm and humid air from the Atlantic in the easterly trades maintains an equatorial climate typified by thunderstorms at frequent intervals and little seasonality. However, there are dry spells everywhere of different length, and probably only the eastern Peru—westernmost Brazil zone has a year-round high level of rainfall. Cold waves from the south also serve to provide occasional variety in temperature. Georgetown, Guyana, provides an example of the coastal, central phase of this climate, while Belem, near the Equator, shows a Southern Hemisphere seasonality reflecting the fact that heat equator and intertropical front remain north of the geographical equator for most of the year.

On the western edge of the Amazon Basin, rainforest continues under a slightly less equatorial temperature regime, in the eastern mountain fringe of Peru and Bolivia. Rainforest of a similar nature occupies the coast of Brazil in Ilheus, Rio and Sao Paulo, fed by constant rains and having equable maritime temperatures.

Pacific Coast equatorial climes are similar to those of the Amazon Basin, though the main source of moisture is now no longer the easterlies, but winds blowing in from the Pacific, which give enormous annual totals of rainfall, over 3000 mm, to the coast and mountains which face them directly in Colombia and Ecuador.

Equatorial highlands

Rimming the Amazon Basin to north and west are high mountains with a complete set of climatic zones, equatorial to subarctic, though with special features because of their tropical location. The climatic differences are recognized in local usage, in most places denominated as *tierra caliente, tierra templada, tierra fría* (with European temperatures averaging around 15°C), and *páramos*, lying above the treeline and thus generally over 3500 m in altitude. *Tierra fría* and *tierra templada* are often considered to be optimal climatic locations, having the reputation of lands of eternal spring, because their seasonal variation, as in the neighbouring lowlands, is very slight, and the average temperatures very pleasant. This lack of seasonal variation is true even up into the *páramos*, as the figures for Cruz Loma, only three kilometres from Quito but 1000 m higher, indicate.

In fact one month is quite similar to any other in temperature, but diurnal temperature variation is great, with the rapid outward radiation of heat permitted by a thin cap of atmosphere, and comparatively little water vapour in this cap. Indians of the Ecuadorian altiplano wear woollen shawls and with good reason, for their nights are cold, regularly reaching freezing point at 3000 m altitude.

2 *In the* páramos, *from Bolivia to Venezuela, unusual plant types are found. Espeletias, woolly-leaved and with bright yellow flowers, shown here in the Andes of Mérida, Venezuela, are common in the Northern Andes*

Tropical woodlands climates

Away from the permanent proximity of the inter-tropical convergence there are lower totals of precipitation and definite dry seasons, thus producing a less luxuriant forest cover or even grass and parkland landscapes. There are also larger seasonal variations in temperature, excluding some of the plant life of the equatorial belt which is not cold-tolerant. Cuiabá (see table) is typical of this climate, though it covers a large part of central Brazil and has many local variations on the central theme of seasonality.

The dry lands

A large dry zone occupies the whole northeast shoulder of Brazil; it has no single name, for it merges gradually with other zones and to the Brazilians is merely part of the backcountry, the *sertao*, of interior Brazil. Nor is it always very dry, receiving an irregular amount of rainfall of perhaps 500–700 mm per annum, though rain usually comes in the form of brief heavy showers

CLIMATIC DATA FOR REPRESENTATIVE STATIONS

Type and Station Lat. and elevation		Jan	Feb	Mar	Apr	May	Jun	Jul	Aug	Sep	Oct	Nov	Dec	Year
Equatorial Rainforest														
Belém, Brazil	T	25.2	25.0	25.1	25.5	25.8	25.8	25.8	25.9	25.8	26.1	26.3	25.9	25.7
1° 28′S, 24 m	P	339	408	436	343	288	175	145	127	118	92	86	175	2732
Georgetown, Guyana	T	26.3	26.4	26.8	27.1	27.0	26.7	26.7	27.2	27.7	27.7	27.4	26.7	27.0
6° 48′ N, 2 m	P	251	122	113	178	296	346	281	185	88	98	147	313	2419
Tropical Forest and Campo Cerrado														
Cuiabá, Brazil	T	26.4	26.2	26.2	25.9	24.3	23.0	22.5	24.8	26.6	27.0	26.8	26.5	25.5
15° 35′ S, 171 m	P	213	200	222	106	46	14	9	27	48	124	161	208	1378
Equatorial Highlands														
Quito Ecuador	T	13.0	13.0	12.9	13.0	13.1	13.0	12.9	13.1	13.2	12.9	12.8	13.0	13.0
0° 13′ S, 2818 m	P	124	135	159	180	130	49	18	22	83	133	110	107	1250
Cruz Loma, Ecuador	T	6.1	6.5	6.7	6.8	6.4	6.2	6.1	6.0	6.1	6.4	6.7	6.4	6.4
0° 13′ S, 3950 m	P	198	185	241	236	221	122	36	23	86	147	124	160	1780
West Coast Desert														
Lima, Peru	T	21.5	22.3	21.9	20.1	17.8	16.0	15.3	15.1	15.4	16.3	17.7	19.4	18.2
12° 30′ S, 11 m	P	1.2	0.4	0.6	0.1	0.5	0.8	2.0	2.3	1.2	0.4	0.1	0.4	10.0
La Serena, Chile	T	18.2	18.4	16.9	14.9	13.4	12.1	11.7	12.0	12.7	14.0	15.5	17.0	14.7
29° 54′ S, 35 m	P	0.1	0.8	0.6	2.6	21.9	43.7	29.7	23.2	6.0	3.7	0.7	0.3	133
Argentine Deserts														
Trelew, Argentina	T	20.6	20.0	17.3	13.2	9.6	6.1	6.0	7.6	10.2	14.0	17.3	19.3	13.5
43° 14′ S, 39 m	P	6	14	17	11	19	11	15	13	14	17	13	14	165
Mendoza, Argentina	T	23.6	22.5	20.2	15.6	11.5	8.1	7.6	10.2	13.9	16.7	20.4	22.7	16.1
32° 53′ S, 769 m	P	28	21	22	10	11	8	7	10	14	23	20	23	197
Humid Pampas														
Bahía Blanca, Arg.	T	20.6	20.5	17.8	15.0	11.1	8.3	7.8	7.7	11.2	13.9	17.0	17.7	14.3
30° 00′ S, 10 m	P	40	67	80	65	52	25	30	31	77	45	66	43	621
Córdoba, Arg.	T	24.2	23.2	20.7	16.8	13.8	11.0	10.6	12.3	15.1	17.9	20.8	23.1	17.4
31° 24′ S, 425 m	P	101	88	93	39	24	10	8	15	29	77	88	108	680
Artigas, Uruguay	T	26.6	26.1	23.6	19.1	16.2	13.9	13.6	15.4	17.0	19.2	22.6	25.2	19.9
30° 24′ S, 117 m	P	115	102	122	139	103	127	81	64	123	149	81	118	1325
Middle Latitude West Coast														
Valdivia, Chile	T	17.0	16.4	14.5	11.8	9.7	8.2	7.7	8.0	9.3	11.5	13.3	15.3	11.9
39° 48′ S, 9 m	P	65	69	115	212	376	414	374	301	214	119	122	107	2489
Subtropical Uplands														
Curitiba, Brazil	T	20.1	20.1	19.2	17.1	14.3	12.9	12.1	13.4	14.5	15.9	17.7	19.3	16.3
25° 26′ S, 949 m	P	183	149	106	75	88	104	69	85	124	122	120	138	1363

NOTES: Temperature in degrees centigrade, precipitation in millimetres.
 Both temperature and precipitation are in the form of monthly means.

3 Arid landscape. Desert scrub on the Bolivian altiplano, with bunch-grass cover on the hills behind

which are of little benefit to plants, for they are soon dissipated, lost by runoff and evaporation from open soil surfaces.

For six months of the year the region is under the South Atlantic anticyclone, which retreats away in summer to allow the inter-tropical convergence zone disturbances to move in, but anticyclonic departure may be delayed thus provoking droughts of an extremely damaging kind, because this is a region of dense agricultural population, as it has been since the time of colonial plantations.

The West Coast subtropical desert is of somewhat different type. Here the anticyclone is stronger, reinforced in the east Pacific by the flanking action of the Andes and by cold water alongshore. The result is complete desert, with no recorded rainfall at some points in the

Atacama, and brief storms accounting for most of the record further north and south. At either end, the desert has its transition, rapidly to the north in Ecuador, more gradually in Chile in the Mediterranean and subtropical steppe zones of that country. Lima, Peru, is an example of the climate of the central desert; La Serena, at 30°S, of the transition through steppe to the Mediterranean climate north of Santiago.

East of the Andes there are other desert or semi-desert zones in the west of Argentina, with 200–500 mm of rainfall. Here the Pacific anticyclone is not active but the mountains themselves provide a substantial rainshadow, not from the immediate west but from the southwest where South Pacific depressions might otherwise enter. The region also holds an interior position with respect to the Atlantic depressions. A lee effect from the Andes continues on into Patagonia, which is also largely desert, from the Andean foot to the Atlantic. Foehn winds are present all along the mid-latitude Andes, most noticeably in central western Argentina, where the sucking in of small quantities of hot and dry air in the Zonda to form a shrivelling northern wind may cause complete crop loss in the agricultural oases of Mendoza and San Juan. Examples of the Patagonian and interior desert climates are given in the figures for Trelew and Mendoza.

A last dry zone is that along the north coast, starting in Venezuela with the region of Cumaná, and continuing along the northward-projecting pieces of Venezuelan coast and the offshore islands of Curaçao and Bonaire, into the Guajira peninsula of Colombia. The cause of drought here seems to lie in the divergent nature of the tradewinds along this coast, aided by differential friction of land and sea on winds which are sub-parallel to the coast.

Pampas climates

The Argentine Pampas, Uruguay and to some extent Paraguay and Southeast Brazil, are all affected by similar airmass systems. Through most of the year, the predominant influence is that of depressions moving along the ocean front, into Brazil's coastal region and as far north as Rio de Janeiro and Bahia. These give rainfall throughout the winter half of the year, and are balanced by summer thunderstorm rainfall. Bahia Blanca and Córdoba are examples of the fringes of the Pampas to the south and west, where the winter depressions carry little moisture, and Artigas in Uruguay, an example of the northern edge, where the depressions are dominant and cause equinoctial maxima, unusual in this latitude where the world pattern would suggest a simple summer maximum of rainfall.

Typical middle-latitude depression features are well known from this region. The *pampero* is a wind resulting from the passage of a cold front northwards at the rear of a depression, and causing dust storms when strong and when the soil is dry and loose. During the summer, the region may be more influenced by tropical air from the South Atlantic or even from the Amazon basin, since a general low pressure cell develops within the Chaco of northern Argentina.

Middle-latitude forest climates

An important area of southern Chile has climate similar to that of British Columbia or coastal Northwestern Europe, with a high frequency of depressions throughout the year, and high rainfall with constant cloud cover and moderate temperatures. This incidence of Polar front depressions is responsible for precipitation of around 2500 mm annually at such stations as Valdivia, providing for rapid forest growth. Further south, the climate continues wet, but deteriorates in temperature and increases in wind force to give one of the world's most inhospitable climates to the Chilean section of Tierra del Fuego.

Another midlatitude forest climate is found in southern Brazil, where the Paraná Plateau basalts lie at levels around 1000 m and support a coniferous vegetation dominated by the Paraná pine, *Araucaria angustifolia,* related to the Chilean pine, *Araucaria araucana,* a member of the Chilean forest assemblage. This forest is best developed in the provinces of Paraná and Santa Catarina; the plateau receives regular winter frost and snowfall is often possible in the southern parts, precipitation totalling from 1200 to 1700 mm. Curitiba, for example, has 1360 mm annually. The source of the through-year regular precipitation is the South Atlantic, though the rainfall mechanism may be thunderstorm or depression in type.

SOILS AND VEGETATION (fig. 1)

Soil types exhibit variations in correspondence with vegetation, climate and topography—geology forming with these elements a unified physical system. In South America there are large areas where this system has been left to act with little modification by man. Over the most favourable agricultural land however, and in an increasingly large number of tropical forest locations where only temporary agricultural use is made of the soil, man has destroyed the cycle of soil and vegetation, taking out important consituents such as potash, phosphorus and nitrogen from the soil by burning and cultivating, opening the soil to the sun's direct rays,

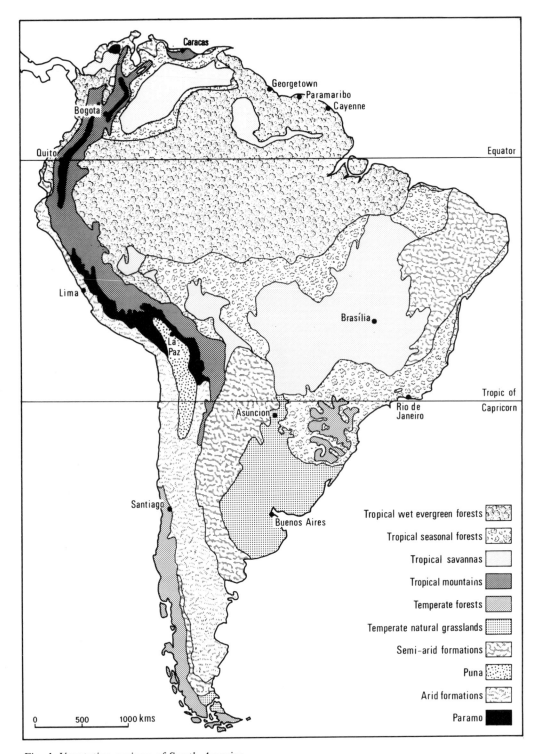

Fig. 1 Vegetation regions of South America

Legend:

- Tropical wet evergreen forests
- Tropical seasonal forests
- Tropical savannas
- Tropical mountains
- Temperate forests
- Temperate natural grasslands
- Semi-arid formations
- Puna
- Arid formations
- Paramo

0   500   1000 kms

Caracas
Georgetown
Paramaribo
Cayenne
Bogota
Quito
Equator
Lima
Brasília
La Paz
Tropic of Capricorn
Asuncion
Rio de Janeiro
Santiago
Buenos Aires

destroying the vegetation, and in sum causing soil breakdown and replacement of the climax vegetation by other types which are usually of less luxuriance and variety.

The humid tropics

Much of the Amazon Basin has selvas vegetation, a superb forest of very tall, large trees over 40 m high, mostly evergreen hardwoods, often supported by giant buttress roots, and substrata and lower levels of giant palms and bamboos, shade-tolerant hardwoods, and very little surface cover because of the dense shade conditions, so that the surface is quite open, giving a cathedral-like, vaulted aspect. Lianas and epiphytes of many kinds are common, a function of the need for light which drives plants up in search of the sun. Enormous variety of plant life is found, including at least 2500 species in the Amazon basin. Locally one giant tree type is fairly common, as in the Mora or Greenheart forests of Guyana, but more typical is a very wide species mix.

There are variants of the Amazonian rainforest in two coastal regions: the Pacific coast of Colombia, and the Bahia section of coastal Brazil.

Tropical seasonal forest

Around the rainforest proper, to north and south there are tropical seasonal forests, sometimes called semi-evergreen or monsoon forest. Here a dry season begins to make its impact, giving a vegetation cover which is less rich in number of species; some trees also lose their leaf cover regularly during the dry period. The rim around the Orinoco Llanos constitutes one such area. Another is the strip running from eastern Bolivia through northern Mato Grosso to Goias. A third is in the hills of southeast Brazil, its content very variable, depending on altitude and exposure; one of its representatives is the Brazilwood tree, the country's first resource and origin of its name. A fourth zone is Maranhao and Piaui in north Brazil, where palms are conspicuous, especially *babaçu* (*Orbignya martiana*) and *carnauba* palms (*Copernicia cerifera*) in the wet soils of river valleys. *Babaçu* oil is produced from the seed, and *carnauba* leaves produce a wax used in polishes and soaps.

Tropical savannas

As the dry season grows longer, the Seasonal Forest is replaced by grasslands, with or without trees intermixed, both types being covered by the Amerindian word 'savanna'. In the Orinoco plains, much of the landscape is open grassland without any trees, and seasonal flooding of huge areas helps to kill off any tree seedlings in this environment, so that it may be regarded as grassland due to both climate and drainage. Trees grow locally along rivers, on the higher rich soil of the levees, forming what is termed gallery forest; an important member of this formation is the *moriche* palm (*Mauritia sp.*). Similar grasslands on poorly drained plains with patches of tree cover occupy the Rio Branco basin in Roraima territory, Brazil, in the Guianas, in northern Colombia, and in a belt through the eastern Mojos plains of Bolivia with an outlier in the Gran Pajonal of Peru. An exceptionally marshy area is the Pantanal, the upper Paraguay basin, which is widely flooded in the wet season from December to May, and forms a major wetland with distinctive wildlife, one which will prove difficult to preserve as the farming frontier advances. The Pantanal has gallery forest and woodland blocks on the drier marginal areas.

Distinct from these drainage-controlled grasslands are those of tropical uplands. There are two main areas: the Guiana uplands and the *cerrado* of the Central Brazilian plateau. *Cerrado* is the name generally given to the largest block of tropical grassland; it is variable, from *campo limpo* (open grassland) through *campo sujo* (grass with small shrubs) and *campo cerrado* (grasses with an open canopy of low trees), to *cerradão*, where the tree growth is fairly continuous. Based on rainfall amounts (1100–1600 mm annually) a forest vegetation might be expected; the grass cover was formerly thought to be due to the strength of the dry season, or to fires set by man. More recently (M.M. Cole, 1960) the *cerrado* vegetation was interpreted to be a result of geomorphology. Monica Cole discovered that *cerrado* vegetation corresponded with the old planation surfaces of Tertiary age, while forest grew in the valleys cut into these surfaces. The most recent argument (R. Goodland, 1970) is that the controlling factor is soil, which is in fact closely related to geomorphology. On the ancient planation surfaces, the tropical red soils have undergone a very long leaching process and are very poor, as well as suffering toxicity for plants from their high aluminium content.

River cutting through this leached layer allows forest cover on the more fertile material exposed in valley sides. The *cerrado* has usually been thought of as a transitional, fluctuating type; with increasing knowledge of its adaptations and age as a formation, it is regarded now as a stable vegetation, resistant to climatic changes and to man's attack on it.

Tropical mountains

On the mountain slopes of the northern and central Andes, there is a rapid variation from subtropical forest in the lower levels, through cloud forest at 1500–3000 metres, to the shrubby levels near the tree line at 3500 m. Within the Andes there are many enclosed basins or longitudinal valleys, which have a dry climate and soils and vegetation characteristic of semi-arid lands. In the central Andes in Peru and Bolivia, of ancient human occupation, much of the tree cover has been eliminated and replaced by *paramo* vegetation. Even on the steepest slopes, and in the remotest areas, this tropical mountain formation is under attack from shifting cultivators who clear huge areas of land by cutting and burning.

Puna and paramo

In the Central Andes from Lake Titicaca south to northwest Argentina, there is a dry cold grassland above the treeline which lies at 3000–3500 m, extending up to the limits of vegetation at 4500 m, above which lies a cold desert before the permanent snow line is reached at 5000 m. The *puna* is a bitterly inhospitable environment, with little seasonal change of temperature but wide diurnal changes. It supports poor bunch grass (*ichu*) and isolated bushes of *tola* (*Lepidophyllum sp.*). Locally there is bogland where runing water is available, and this forms grazing lands for the alpacas and llamas which roam here.

Further north and in wetter country, there is a formation called *paramo* above the treeline, with dense tussock grasslands and, locally, woods in sheltered spots, of *quinuar* (*Polylepis sp.*) and *buddleia*. In Colombia and Venezuela the *paramo* is often covered in kinds of giant groundsel, the *frailejones,* along with scattered bushes. In much of the *puna-paramo* area the formations mentioned have been extended by tree-cutting for fuel or construction purposes, so that their 'natural' extent is hard to determine.

Temperate forests

In the northern hemisphere the temperate deciduous and evergreen forests occupy a large part of the continents between 45′ and 60′ N. In South America the suitable cool temperate climates are limited to a small area, mostly in southern and central Chile and in Brazil.

A first area is the evergreen woodland of central Chile, dominated by small xerophytic trees, from 31 to 37′ S, comparable in its structure to the natural vegetation of the northern Mediterranean countries. In south-central Chile this is followed by a transitional area of roble-rauli forest, dominated by the deciduous southern beeches, roble (*Nothofagus obliqua*) and *rauli* (*Nothofagus obliqua*), both commercially valuable timbers. Inland from this in the Andean foothills at 600–1600 m lies a forest often of pure stands of *Araucaria araucana,* the monkey-puzzle tree, on both Chilean and Argentine sides of the border. Further south along the coast is the Valdivian forest, reaching up to the treeline at 1600–1900 m, with southern beeches, and the commercially useful southern larch, (*Fitzroya patagonica*). In the far south the southern beeches are still dominant, but there are other more resistant species, and the extreme wind exposure brings the treeline down to 200 metres in Tierra del Fuego.

A separate area is the Paraná pine (*Araucaria angustifolia*) forest on the Parana plateau, occupying the good soils derived from the lava flows of the region. Besides the pines, there are Podocarpus and the *yerba mate* tree (*Ilex paraguayensis*) in the understorey. The value of the soil and moderate climate have attracted farm settlers, and the forest has largely been cleared. Sawmills have now disposed of nearly all the large stands of pine and *Podocarpus* commercial timber.

Temperate grasslands

Through much of eastern Argentina, together with Uruguay and Rio Grande do Sul in Brazil, there is natural grassland. It is warm enough in winter to support cattle through the year, and is based on a deep black chernozem soil, optimal for temperate agriculture. This is the world's best remaining example of this kind of soil, since farming has not yet destroyed or eroded it. Fires are probably responsible in part for maintaining the grass cover in the past, for trees grow well if given initial protection from fire and grazing animals. An outlying patch of good grasslands is in eastern Tierra del Fuego, with its cool, dry and sunny climate.

Semi-arid Lands

In northeast Brazil a large area with under 700 mm annual rainfall has soil and vegetation adjusted to a climate of long seasonal droughts. The central driest part is the *caatinga,* a scrubland and thorny woodland with large cacti and deciduous thornbushes with various adaptations to drought — 'fat-bellied' trees which store water in their trunks, leaf loss in dry seasons, waxy leaves, and the physiological adjustment of reducing transpiration by day. On the eastern margins of the *caatinga* a transitional band, the agreste, with 700–1000 mm annual rainfall, has a natural vegetation of open deciduous forest, again largely cleared now for farming.

Other semi-arid areas are the Manabi zone of coastal Ecuador, dominated by *ceibo* (the kapok tree) open forest, and a Caribbean coastal strip in Venezuela and Colombia. There is also the thorn scrub around the Pampas, dominated by leguminous shrubs and trees such as Prosopis, acacia, and mimosa. The largest region is the Gran Chaco, in Argentina, Paraguay and Bolivia, where the drought-resistant algarrobo tree, *Prosopis alba* and *P. nigra,* frequently occurs, as well as the tannin-yielding quebracho (*Schinopsis sp.*), palm savannas in areas with poor drainage, and salt flats.

Arid lands

The extremely low rainfall of the Chilean coastal desert means it has large areas of no vegetation and saline or alkaline soil material. In southern and central Peru there are areas of 'Lomas' vegetation at 150–800 m, induced by the moisture of sea fogs formed over the cool Humboldt current. In favourable sites this may include even trees, but the vegetation is mostly short-cycle ephemerals. The desert extends up into the Andes and through northwestern Argentina to link with the Patagonian steppes, where tussock grass and low shrubs are common. Through the Argentine deserts, strong winds are an additional desiccating factor which has affected the development of irrigation agriculture in the several large oases fed by Andean snow-melt rivers.

Natural Hazards

Some of the most spectacular natural catastrophes occur in South America, the best-known being those associated with Andean tectonic movements, including earthquakes, and the landslides they set off, as well as volcanic eruptions. Less well known but equally important for social and economic effects are the floods which cause damage to very extensive land areas, and the droughts which are a plague on several major regions. Cold is not usually such a hazard, but cold waves moving north along the Atlantic seaboard are a problem in southern Brazil today.

Volcanic Phenomena

The reason for earthquakes and volcanoes along the Andean front is that it lies along the boundary between major tectonic plates, where adjustments between two adjacent plates occurs as one slides over the other. For S. America it is the Nazca oceanic plate which runs underneath the South American continental plate as the latter pushes westwards. The subducted oceanic plate edge is melted and some forces its way back to the surface as volcanic material, often spectacular cone volcanoes in the Andes which are mostly ash and cinders, rather than the lava which is more typical of the opposite kind of plate-edge, the mid-oceanic ridge.

The volcanic eruptions are often made more catastrophic because the high cones lie well in the snow zone, so that small lakes formed by glacial action or ash from the volcano itself may suddenly discharge large amounts of water as their walls are cracked by earthquakes or as meltwater suddenly cascades into them. The heat melting snow causes river flooding in any case, and the snow may combine with mud to form very high speed avalanches. The November 1985 eruption of the Nevado del Ruiz (5578 m.) in the Central Cordillera of Colombia, caused rapid melting of the permanent snow-cap; the water streaming off brought down a very heavy ash and silt load from the high unvegetated slopes above 4000 m, broke through a temporary dam which had been forming above the town of Armero due to silt brought down over the previous six months' of mild volcanic activity, and ended as a sea of mud often ten feet deep, killing over 20,000 inhabitants of the region.

In Ecuador, Cotopaxi's beautiful ash cone at 5900 m caused similar damage in 1877, the hot ash from an eruption causing flash floods which terminated as mudflows in valleys up to 200 miles away. On another occasion in the 1890s, Cotopaxi produced hot flaming gas flows which flowed at over 100 mph to devastate the town of Latacunga over 20 miles away.

Volcanoes are not evenly distributed down the backbone of the continent. There are major gaps, from 33–24′ S and from El Misti at 17′S in southern Peru, to Sangay in Ecuador at 2′S, one of the world's most active volcanoes. Activity is also absent north of the Nevado del Ruiz, at 5′N. In the southern Andes too, the volcanoes are less damaging to human life because the Argentine and Chilean high mountains are desert with scanty population, and being very dry have less snowmelt to help form avalanches. Earthquakes are much more widespread. Virtually anywhere in the vicinity of the Andes one may feel tremors which will rattle glasses or furniture, but nothing more serious. Major quakes cause damage by breaking water, power or gas lines, destroying buildings, and on the coast causing tidal waves. Throughout the Andean countries earthquakes are so frequent that until recently laws expressly forbade construction of buildings more than one or two storeys high. Modern buildings are commonly required to be 'anti-seismic', which means construction is of reinforced concrete or uses an interlocking steel frame with joints that allow some movement.

The most devastating earthquakes are those which occur in combination with other accidents, such as flooding or landslides. A good example from recent times is the Huaylas earthquake of 1970. A powerful earthquake, force 6 on the Richter scale, caused some immediate damage to the town of Yungay; within two minutes, a snow-mud mixture moving at 320 km/h (200 mph) buried the town entirely and killed 20–25 thousand people, in villages along the slide's path and in Yungay itself. The Huaylas valley had already been hit by a mudslide in 1941, which buried the town of Huaraz, and in 1962 a rock-ice slide went through high villages, killing 3500. The whole Huaylas valley, 320 km north of Lima, is liable to avalanche damage because its eastern flank, the Cordillera Blanca, has very steep slopes and high precipitation, with temperatures oscillating quickly between freeze and thaw.

Another kind of earthquake damage is exemplified by southern Chile's 1960 quakes. The first movements brought down one-third of the houses of Concepcion. Other cities badly hit were Valdivia and Puerto Montt, both of which had residential areas built on loose fill which experienced much more powerful shock waves than the solid rock. Then *maremotos*, powerful tidal waves, flooded many fishing villages and the town of Ancud on Chiloe Island. The Chilean government was forced to resurvey its navigation charts for the region because of changes in sea level which had produced a new coastline. Another indirect effect was the formation of dams of loose material which had slumped into the San Pedro river, forming an unstable dam wall to new lakes. Engineers tried to make them into firm dams by building bypass canals and reinforcing the walls with cables and timber, but two months later the dams gave way and villages down the valley were flooded, with a loss of 1000 lives.

One very large-scale climatic phenomenon is of interest. From time to time the easterly trade winds in the Pacific lose their strength and the major ocean currents are seriously affected. The Peru current, driven by the SE trades flowing round the S. Pacific anticyclone, weakens and is replaced by a warm equatorial current, especially in the southern summer when the anticyclone is at its weakest. Instead of the oxygenated life-favouring current enriched by powerful upwelling along its course and teeming with fish, there is the oxygen-poor, low-plankton tropical current, called El Niño (the Christchild) because of its appearance around Christmastime off Peru. Such a current change causes no dramatic effects like an earthquake, but its long-term economic effect is enormous. On land it is associated with periods of heavy rain that may cause floods in the arid valleys of northern Peru. At sea the 1971–72 El Niño caused a massive decline in the fish catch, from 12.5 million tons to 4.5 million, comparing 1970 and 1972 data. This was a catastrophe for fishermen, for packing and freezing plants, and for the Peruvian government, which had anchovy processing into fishmeal as a major export industry. It is of course true that this disaster was compounded by overfishing through the 1960s off Peru.

ECOLOGY AND CONSERVATION

In both rural and urban areas of South America there is a need for more attention to the way in which man affects native flora and fauna, soils and water courses, and the reciprocal effects of nature on man's activities. Ecology is the study of relationships between different elements of the biosphere, tending to concentrate on the point of view of man and his specific relationship with the environment. Conservation signifies the rational use by man of the environmental resources, native and non-native, so as not to destroy them while using them. We may discuss separately for convenience, rural and urban aspects of the problem, though there are of course major overlaps between them.

Rural areas

Human use of the land of South America has extended over perhaps 50 000 years, and has therefore produced major changes in the natural environment of the most intensely occupied areas. In the present century however, the pace of exploitation and change has accelerated drastically and the effects are more fundamental.

One area of intense human use is in the Andean uplands. Here tillage and cattle farming on steep slopes with dry soils, often sandy or of loose volcanic ash, tree-felling for construction, fuel or land clearance, have resulted in a tree-less windblown landscape and parched, eroded soils. We have no information on the former extent of forest, but the ease with which blue gum (*Eucalyptus globulus*) and Monterrey pine can now be grown at heights of up to 4000 m suggest that the valleys between the mountains, from Chile to Colombia, and even the lower *páramos*, were once tree-covered.

Today tree-cover is being maintained or increased in these areas, mostly with the species cited, but this leaves large areas unprotected from further degradation, especially where there are intensively worked farms. Fields are ploughed parallel to the slopes instead of across them, few animals are kept and there is little manure especially on the marginal fields, which can only be cultivated once every few years. In wetter areas this cultivation is preceded by burning off brush and coarse grasses, which causes a long-term loss of nitrogen from the soil. Correction of this situation requires farmer education, afforestation, and withdrawing of the worst areas from farming altogether, but most of all agrarian reform to give farmers an incentive for change.

Conservation is readily combined with agriculture, given good management and education. Unfortunately, the main direction of effort in reforestation has been towards commercial plantations, which are monocultures that keep out agriculture. In Ecuador, for example, the province of Loja has a regional agency, PRE-DESUR, engaged in the promotion of tree planting for timber as well as erosion control in a semi-arid area which has steep slopes and a history of overuse. The trees for planting are however only to be planted as solid blocks, for exploitation as woodpulp or structural timber — eucalyptus, and fast-growing pines, which can be cut at 20 years. These species tend to allow no undergrowth, as their leaf-fall is toxic to other species; nor do the trees provide much employment — perhaps only two men for one hundred hectares of forest. Thus neither soil conservation nor a stimulus to the local economy is provided. Finally, the trees compete for scarce water resources in the area, extracting from the soil some of the water required for irrigation systems.

A more suitable 'afforestation' here might be the planting of terrace edges with fruit trees, which provide some shade, erosion control and a useful crop; or the planting of acacias and similar leguminous trees and thus help to fix nitrogen in the soil. On windy sites shelter belts are needed, and near houses plots for firewood provision. By contrast, on the high and wet paramos where there is virtually no population or competition for water, blocks of commercial trees for timber or pulp would be acceptable.

A completely different environment is that of the Amazon selva, an area of 4.5 million sq km. It has been only lightly exploited before this century, and then only on the richer *varzea* soils. In this forest, the natural balance achieved is one now recognized as fragile, in which any major changes are likely to be non-reversible. Although the soils are inherently infertile on the *terra firme*, and carry little nutrients, the forest has various adaptive mechanisms. It has a storied canopy which reduces raindrop impact on soil and keeps out the sun's direct rays which would burn up humus. Epiphytes and forest trees can extract nutrients from the rainfall directly, thus relying less on the soil storage mechanism. Fungi in the soil feed on dead vegetation and the tree feeds on them, cutting out much of the need for nutrient solutions in the soil.

However, once the forest is removed these mechanisms are destroyed and the yield of any crops planted diminishes rapidly. Areas such as Bragantina in North East Brazil (see Chapter 16), where clearance took place a hundred years ago along the railway, have long become lands of shifting cultivation in secondary forest.

Not all forest use is destructive, however, and the selva does have good powers of regeneration if it is not repeatedly destroyed. In the Peruvian selvas, selective logging has long been practised by settlers without any major disturbance to forest balance. Along the Urubamba, Spanish cedar and mahogany are extracted, but cause no loss because these are light-seeking species which tend to fill in any gaps made by loggers. In any case, only trees along stream courses which provide a means of transport are being cut, leaving a constant reserve in the interfluve areas (S. White, 1978).

Outside the immediate area there are broader implications of selva clearance. At the regional level flooding is more acute when forest is cleared to give rapid runoff. At a world level, there are unknown changes possible from major forest clearance, including global cooling and the reduction of carbon dioxide, oxygen and atmospheric moisture. Amazon rainforest exploitation is of course not as advanced as in the Andes — most of the Amazon remains as forest today despite rapid advances in colonization along new roads. The action appropriate here is thus more truly conservation, whereas in the Andes it is rehabilitation. But how far can the forest environment be conserved? Scientists suggest that *silviculture*, whereby the forest is not entirely cut over, but cut selectively so as to encourage the more useful species, is one answer. Another is *agri-silviculture*, forest clearance followed by annual crops, then shrubs like coffee or cocoa, then slower-growing useful trees, in a sequence which gradually restores a modified forest. A variation of this is to rotate crops, ranching, and forest, in one area, over a period of up to fifty years. Different policies stressing conservation above economic use are the creation of forest parks, forest reserves, and Indian reserves.

Some countries, such as Ecuador and Brazil, require a percentage of forest left in new extensions of farmland, but this is difficult to super-vise and does not ensure of itself that only the most appropriate soils, those of rich alluvium, are used for agriculture. Obviously careful soil and vegetation surveys are needed prior to settlement in order accurately to designate land uses of newly colonized areas.

Lakes

A great problem in tropical areas is the management of freshwater lakes, whether man-made or natural. An example of the latter is Lake Valencia in Venezuela (A. Bockh, 1973), the largest lake in S. America after Lake Titicaca, with which it contrasts ecologically. Titicaca's shores are in a cool, temperate zone and are subject only to subsistence farming on terraced lands, with few towns of any size nearby. Soil erosion and nutrient from fertilizers are unimportant in such conditions, and so is urban waste disposal. Valencia on the other hand has an urban population of two millions in the lake's vicinity, notably in the cities of Valencia and Maracay on either side of the lake. Urban and industrial wastes are collected in the lake, while farming has led to soil erosion in the tropical climate, and water has long been diverted for irrigation schemes. Since about 1720, this water diversion has meant the lake has changed from one of external drainage to an internal lake with no outlet, thus gradually increasing its mineral and salt content, so that it has become increasingly polluted. The water level is still falling so sharply that waterside facilities built a few years ago have been left far from the present shoreline.

The problems of man-made lakes are comparable, but here the most acute concerns are over eutrophication of lake waters, and rapid silting of the reservoir so as to make it unusable within a few years. The chapters on Ecuador, peripheral Brazil and Guiana, with their references to the Daule–Peripa scheme, the Tucurui dam and that of Brokopondo, illustrate this matter.

The Orinoco Llanos

In the Amazon a fairly capital-intensive programme may be able to exploit and still conserve the environment. In many areas the best strategy for land management may be one of low capital investment and minimal interference even where abundant money resources are available. Such are the cases where there occur major natural catastrophes such as landslides, volcanic eruption, or flooding.

One example of the latter is the Venezuelan Llanos where the main hazard is floods. The Lower Orinoco runs through the Colombian and Venezuelan Llanos and is partially dammed in by the salient of the Guyana massif north of Cabruta. This plus the slight gradient from San Fernando (45 m to the sea at 1000 km distance, means flood liability all along the river but especially in the lower Apure. Floods covering thousands of square kilometres occur at intervals of about 10 years here in an area of savanna grasslands.

In 1976 this area was extensively flooded (Fig. 55) over July–August, to a total area of 65 000 sq km according to estimates from aerial photographs. Losses of life were minimal but roads and cattle and the small crop area were badly affected.

Apart from the basic drainage problem, new factors were noted as inducing exceptional floods. Forest destruction on the slopes around the basin helped, though most of the floodwater was pluvial, not fluvial, in other words the result of heavy rainfall on the plain itself and not brought down from the upper river. Engineering works also increased run-off and flood liability, since roads had been built across the Llanos on high embankments to keep them well above the floods; these embankments acted as effective dams for the floodwater, as on the road from San Fernando west to Mantecal, or that from San Fernando north to Calabozo, and increased the flooding behind them. Some ranches also aggravate flooding because they have perimeter banks built to keep out floodwater, which puts a greater flood load onto neighbouring property. Agricultural colonization schemes such as the Guanare–Masparro north-west of San Fernando, have also increased flooding though clearing vegetation and improving drainage.

In the Guanare-Masparro area dams were sited wrongly, according to J.C. Dickinson (1982). Firstly, for these multipurpose dams the flood control function was slight, as the only good farm lands are not the flood-liable ones, apart from some further downstream which could not be protected by the dams. Secondly, irrigation use of the dams could not be expected — current schemes in the Llanos are already underutilized. Finally, use of the water for drinking supplies

was a poor idea. Shallow water in the reservoirs, abundant nutrients washed down with the silt, and a very sinuous shoreline, were all features that aided eutrophication, choking the reservoirs with aquatic weeds.

Because of these negative effects of human intervention a policy of adaptation rather than control is now being advocated. Dams on the river are specifically rejected as a solution. It has already been noted that most flooding in 1976 was from rainfall in the plains area, uncontrollable by river dams. Dams and massive levées tend to hold back this kind of 'pluvial flood' and prevent it from draining into the rivers. In any case the large dams built at El Guri, Camatagua, Guárico and elsewhere control only 5% of the Orinoco's flow and protect 5% of its basin in Venezuela. Over 30% of the basin is outside all control, in Colombia.

Instead, the recommended strategy includes use of a warning system to protect urban populations at floodtime and allow planned evacuation; elimination of all obstructions to flow on the floodplain near the river, such as buildings, bridges, and roads, which might hold back natural drainage; use of the traditional custom of transhumance of cattle from low meadows to higher terraces, and temporary cultivation for crops of *vegas*, fertile lowlands which are then abandoned in the wet season; general adoption of non-intensive land uses on the floodplain; and preservation of forest where possible. Such strategies might well be adopted elsewhere with variations to suit the case. A comparable flood area is in central Buenos Aires province, where massive floods of the Salado trough occurred last in 1979 and 1980. These floods were aggravated by the north–south alignment of the main road and rail lines between Buenos Aires, Mar del Plata, and Bahía Blanca, blocking natural drainage.

Parks and reservations

One important aim of conservation is to preserve intact the native flora and fauna in their natural surrounding, especially in areas of scenic value, historical or archaeological interest. National Parks had their origin in 1872 in the US Yellowstone Park. In South America, despite the presence of a tropical rainforest with a larger number of animal and vegetable species than all corresponding areas of the Old World, and a rapid rate of destruction of that forest, despite the existence of places such as the Galapagos Islands with their unique fauna, little was done before the 1940s, and even now the effort is uneven. Argentina has eight national parks occupying 2.3 million hectares, but largely restricted to the Patagonian Andes. These parks are protected from exploitation except for tourist use. Chile created national parks from 1931 and they occupy nearly a million hectares, again largely in the southern Andes. In this country however, farmers have been allowed to come in and settle on good lands in the parks. This is a problem which must also be faced by colonizing countries such as Brazil: the need to compromise between park creation and colonists' needs for land on a farm frontier — such conflicts are not found in old-settled lands such as western Europe.

Bolivia lacks national parks but Peru has created several small ones to conserve archaeological and faunal curiosities, plus a larger one in the Cordillera Blanca. Ecuador's park system began with the Galapagos Islands, protected since 1964 because of their unique zoological values. On the mainland, parks and nature reserves date from 1970 and most are only a few years old. Of the twelve national parks, several are relatively protected by their isolation — Sangay volcano in the Eastern Cordillera, Yasuni in the eastern plains. The Galapagos are protected because of their international fame. Others, in Manabi, Cotopaxi, Cajas near Cuenca, are under constant pressure from dense farming populations in the vicinity who burn the grass, cut available trees for firewood, graze animals or even cultivate the land. In no case are there marked limits to the park area and usually no park guards.

Venezuela has a number of large parks covering in all 500 000 ha, begun in 1937 with the Pittier park in the mountains north of Maracay. The Mérida mountains have another, and one lies between Caracas and the Caribbean, its most important function being possibly the restriction of urban growth onto the steep slopes of Mount Avila adjacent to the city.

Brazil's first National Park dates from 1937, and the large Iguassu Falls park from 1944, but most are much later, the biggest being at Bananal Island on the middle Araguaia river, with 460 000 ha and dating to 1973, and Amazonia, created at the same time in 1 million hectares of western Para state. It is noteworthy that Brazil's national parks are very largely in the southeast where there is more demand for recreation and more conservation awareness. The poor northeast, despite its population, is not provided. There are over 2 million hectares of National Parks in Brazil, plus over 1 million hectares of State Parks. A fundamental problem, here as elsewhere, is control over land use in parks occupying sparsely-populated and little-known regions.

Other parks are created with special functions. In 1966 Peru, followed by Bolivia, Argentina and Chile, created parks to protect the *vicuña* which had been almost exterminated through hunting for its fur-like wool. This action, helped by bans on export of *vicuña* wool from these countries and import bans in former markets, has been successful in saving this species.

Urban areas
In previous centuries the amount of land used by cities, their population size, and their capacity for pollution, were all much lower. In the last twenty years, South America has had not only many cities, but several of megalopolis size, creating demands on services such as water and sewage disposal which are not just larger but demand radically new technology.

In the big cities man has replaced large areas of vegetation with concrete and tarmac, and tunneled through the subsoil to a depth of 50 metres in places. Consequences are more rapid run-off to river, a special urban micro-climate, and a lowered water table. Cities also create noise, air, visual and water pollution to the point where they constitute major health hazards. Water pollution may be crucial where big cities are on small rivers. Caracas, with 3 million inhabitants, is on the little Guaire, which is consequently heavily loaded with silt from steep unprotected slopes round the city, and heavily contaminated as well, especially during the dry season. Other ultra-polluted waterways are the Riachuelo of Buenos Aires, the Machángara in Quito and the Rimac at Lima in Peru.

The Machangara at Quito is a medium-sized river, deeply incised into the plateau and with a good slope allowing turbulent flow and rapid oxygenation of its water. The steep river slopes, however, kept free of standard housing because of their danger from landslides and the high cost of any construction, have been colonized by shanty towns which send effluent directly into the river, from humans and countless chickens, pigs and other domestic animals. There is also industrial waste from a suburb on the north side. High rates of erosion of the dry ash-based soil make for heavy sedimentation in the river. Present analyses of the river show no dissolved oxygen, but the presence of nitrites and nitrates, ammoniac, phosphates, sulphates and a heavy load of fungi and bacteria. This same water is used close to Quito to irrigate market gardens and orchards, thus completing a cycle of infection through the consumers of these products.

Atmospheric pollution is particularly important at the west-coast cities which, like Los Angeles in California, enjoy stable subtropical high pressure weather most of the year and occupy basin sites. Santiago in Chile, Lima in Peru, enter this category. Basin sites such as that of Caracas are less problematical because of a constant wind, here the Easterly trades. Buenos Aires and São Paulo, the largest cities, usually have some wind but when it fails suffer greatly from air pollution, much of it from the street traffic rather than industrial sources. Along with air pollution, noise pollution from the same traffic is of a higher intensity than in Europe. This problem affects small cities as well as large, as does the visual pollution produced by countless billboards and hoardings, telephone, power and other cables, and architectural horrors.

There are solutions to these problems, some involving great cost and imported technology (underground railways for example), others the simple remedy of tree-planting wherever possible to moderate city climate and pollution. Urban planning can do much but has not traditionally been strong in these countries.

One major effort has been in Buenos Aires, where the primary problem was air pollution, visible from many miles away as a dense pall of smog over the city. Some of this came from the burning of refuse. In 1969 burning was prohibited in the city, but this merely exported the problem out to the more than 150 dumps outside the city which became foci of rats and disease. Within the city, another problem was lack of parks and green areas. The solution which has been reached is the creation of a Green Belt, the Metropolitan Ecological Belt, on 300 sq. km of land round the city, reaching from the existing green area of the Parana Delta, through the open land of Ezeiza northwest of the city, to Pereyra Park on the south. This project includes filling in the swamplands around the city with refuse and thus eliminating the swamps, and also planting trees to given an urban lung and provide a space which will be used to locate schools, hospitals and recreational areas.

2. Historical Aspects

BEFORE THE CONQUEST

Nineteenth-century archaeologists originally maintained that the Americas have been inhabited by man for a long time. On finding that early dates could not be proved, the opposite point of view, that settlement was very recent, became fashionable. Nowadays there is a trend to acceptance of a substantial antiquity for New World man, who is thought to have entered during a low sealevel period of the Pleistocene, perhaps as a hunter of mammoth and other big game, coming across a landbridge in the Bering Straits regions which may have connected Siberia and Alaska. The date of entry is still uncertain, but lies more than 20000 years ago, for evidence of human occupation dating from that time has been found in caves near Ayacucho in upland Peru. The oldest finds, here and elsewhere in the continent, are of flint and obsidian choppers and scrapers used by hunters of extinct animals, mammoth, wild horses, animals related to the modern llama, and a giant sloth. Later hunters used more finely executed spearheads and blades. Their principal hunting grounds appear to have been cold grasslands, near the altitudinal limits for vegetation.

Changes away from this kind of life were only gradually achieved, with the introduction of gathered, then of cultivated plants into the diet. From 3600 BC onwards settled forms of life are known from the Peruvian southern and central coasts, based on both crops and shellfish. How and where agriculture began in the Americas is still in dispute, but its earliest locations were probably not on the coast, where most early remains are known because of the excellent conditions for preservation, but in other areas; one such is the Peruvian Sierra, another is southern Mexico, another on the southern shores of the Caribbean. In each of these regions a variety of environments, according to Carl Sauer, would have allowed the domestication of many species of plant, especially those which can be cultivated using vegetative reproduction (plant division as opposed to seeds), such as the potato and yam, requiring only a minimal level of technical expertise. However domestication came about, the effects were the same in all parts, the advent of settled village life, allowing much more of the paraphernalia of tools and equipment of modern man than ever could be used by nomadic man. Crafts such as cotton cloth making, which have been identified from the deserts of north Peru as over 5000 years old, and the making of pottery, were now possible. It has been suggested, largely from Mexican evidence (MacNeish, *vide* Bibliography), that there was a Neolithic Evolution rather than a Revolution, and this may also be true of South America. Plant domestication in Mexico dates back to 5000 BC, but villages did not follow until 3000 BC and pottery only in 2300 BC. For some unknown reasons the pace of innovation seems to be slower than in the Old World.

Stages of social evolution

In the Old World, prehistoric stages of man's development are based mostly on technology,

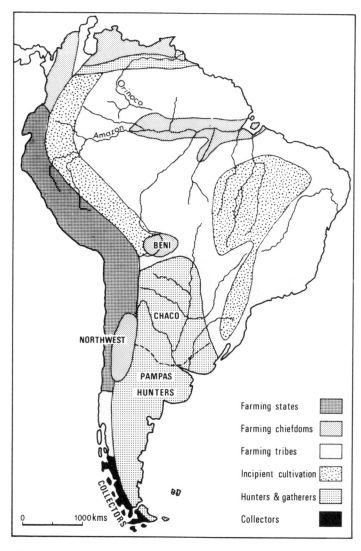

Fig. 2 Culture types in South America about AD 1500

from the Stone Ages through the Chalcolithic to the Bronze and Iron Ages. This sequence does not easily fit the American experience, for the key materials are not the same — no iron was used, for example — and civilizations had different relations between social advance and technical advance. Instead, it is more meaningful, following Sanders and Marino (fig. 2) to order society into bands, tribes, chiefdoms and ancient states. Of these, *bands* were always the most widespread, as kinlinked groups of under 100 persons with relatively slight organization. Above them, *tribes* might have several thousands, and permanent settlements based on farming rather than the bands' hunting and collecting; they also had some social division into classes. Above these again in social complexity, the *chiefdoms* with 5000–20 000 persons, had hereditary chiefs, a definite power hierarchy and considerable division of labour, often also ceremonial centres and palaces. *Ancient states* saw the final displacement of kinship links by organized control of territory as the social bond, and the rudiments of a commercial marketing system.

Tribes and a sedentary village life lasted without alteration until at least 2000 BC. From then, chiefdoms with their specialized urban centres of craft, administration and religion began to appear, earlier in the Peruvian culture hearth than anywhere else in America. The most colourful and splendid of the chiefdoms came later with the Chavín culture of 1200–750 BC, chronologically and socially the equal of the Olmec culture in southern Mexico, the other cradle of American civilization. Chavín is in the Northern Highlands of Peru, and has a stone-built temple and palace complex, together with a large residential sector adjacent to it, implying not just a ceremonial centre here but also organized agriculture producing regular surpluses for the urban population.

Ancient states

Chiefdoms are followed in time by the first ancient states, such as the Mochica state of AD 1–800, with its elaborate irrigation-based agriculture and fine development of arts and technology, exemplified in metal working using a variety of techniques, in gold, silver and copper; these people were followed by the Huari—Tiahuanaco culture in the culture-hearth area, and then by the Incas. The Tiahuanaco culture has recently been proved to have substantial depth at its name-site on the Bolivian altiplano above La Paz. Here the buildings show an evolution spread over a period from 1200 BC to AD 1000. Pyramids and temples dating from shortly after Christ are built with a high level of engineering competence, for, despite its burial in wet alluvial mud for many centuries, the architecture has not suffered much deterioration, having an excellent drainage system to keep the whole dry.

After AD 1200 the Inca empire grew up, first occupying a small area near Cuzco, then in the last century before the Conquest, spreading over an area which extended over 3000 km from north to south (fig. 3). More than a million people owed allegiance to the Inca, as visible ruler and deity. The Incas achieved remarkable attainments in stone architecture, using few mechanical aids — the wheel for example was not apparently known, though used in miniature form for toys — and uncemented, and a variety of engineering works such as castles, irrigation canals and terraces are ascribed to them, though much must have been copied, extended, or merely taken over from earlier civilizations. The Incas' relation to their predecessors was probably like that of the Romans to the Greeks, that of a practical, militaristic, hierarchically more organized people, who invented little but used the astounding discoveries of their fore-bears to good purpose.

There have been conflicting views of the Inca organization of life. One older view was that it was a highly democratic welfare state, from the evidence of large storehouses along the royal roads, and the system of redistribution of gifts from the central government to local communities. More likely is the thesis of an autocratic militaristic state, using its roads and warehouses to move and feed large armies, and its redistribution to reinforce bonds of loyalty with local chieftains. The thousands of miles of roads and the bridges constructed of agave ropes, the maintenance of terraces and canals, building of public buildings, had to be done, not by a slave force but certainly by compulsory labour in the *mita,* which was taken over as a system by the Spanish.

Much recent attention has been focussed on the finding that the Incas exploited different physical environments, different 'ecological niches', in the Andean fringe zone, from tropical to frigid, in order to provide themselves with all sorts of supplies. Instead of long-distance trade, which was more common in the Maya and Aztec areas of Central America, the Incas had a system of control over small patches of land at different levels, through colonists sent there to produce for them. They gained maize, main feedstuff for the armies, from subtropical levels, coca from the tropical margins, medical resources from tropical leaves or bark of trees. The colonists sent into lowland areas would be from groups already adapted to tropical living, for, in the lowlands, highland Indians could succumb to tropical disease. They were for example apparently prevented from permanently occupying the coca lands of the Urubamba valley, near Cuzco, by virulent leishmaniasis which is carried by sand flies in the area below 1800 m and causes disfiguring lesions to the face or even kills its victims.

As a military empire their geographical limits were fairly well defined; they could occupy only the open grass-covered uplands, with some minor exceptions, and to east, north and south were delayed and halted by swamps and forests, where guerrilla warfare could indefinitely hold back an organized army. To the south they thus came no further than central Chile, and to the north to central Ecuador, while in the east their limits were those of the eastern cordilleras. In the southeast, they did not have a forest front, but a plains one, and seem to have shunned the Argentine Chaco simply because it was unattractive to them and held no resources.

Outside the Inca empire, large regions were occupied by chiefdoms, societies of a smaller total size and with less complex organization, in particular without the class structure that characterized the Incas. Figure 2 shows that one of these regions, occupied by many chiefdoms, was that of Ecuador–Colombia, on the north front of the Incas and no doubt influenced by the older upland civilizations. The Chibcha were perhaps the best organized of these chiefdoms, a group lying on the upland savannas of the Colombian Cordillera Oriental, with organized trade in textiles, salt and farm products. At a probably lower economic but similar social level, there were the people of the San Agustin culture of southern Colombia, responsible for elaborate ceremonial architecture in stone known from over thirty major sites, with features reminiscent of the Chavín culture formerly dominant in the south. The Beni region of northeast Bolivia also had chiefdoms with organized power of a military nature, and built causeways and canals across the seasonally flooded savanna.

Beyond empires and chiefdoms, Indian tribes practising slash and burn agriculture, which had gradually replaced an older gathering and hunting economy, occupied the tropical forest lowlands, while the Pampas were still the domain of wandering hunters, and hunters and gatherers lived in the Chaco, as they have done until the very recent past.

THE IBERIAN ORIGINS OF THE CONQUEST

Inevitably, the history of the Iberian peoples has had much influence on the course of American history. In particular, the secular battle against the Moors, over the harsh environment of the Meseta, quite different from anything else in Europe, could not but mould American events. Isolation of the peninsula made Iberia socially more traditional than most of Europe, so that while the Conquest of the New World belongs to Renaissance time, Iberian, and particularly Spanish, attitudes to life and the afterlife were medieval rather than Renaissance; faith in God rather than belief in human potential for achievement was the motif of the early years of the Conquest. The overseas empires grew up with many features of feudal, Church-dominated medieval Europe, despite the new environment of the New World, which could have permitted innovations and change.

Spanish — Portuguese differences

Although both Spain and Portugal grew out of the Reconquista, the advance against the Moors, they evolved in different ways, which were reflected in differences in their New World possessions. First, the Portuguese were much earlier in forming a stable independent state, finally expelling the Moors from their south in 1249, whereas Spain did not oust the Moors from Granada until 1492, the year in which Columbus discovered America, so that for Spaniards, the fight for America was to some extent a continuation of the fight for Spain itself.

By 1500, the Portuguese were comparatively experienced in colonial rule, from their explorations and acquisitions in Africa; Spain had also expanded to Africa, but was less committed or interested in foreign parts in the fifteenth century while she still had enemies on home territory. Portugal had also become a cosmopolitan society, with many Negroes and Moslems incorporated and accepted in the country, contrasting with Spain's intolerance, later to express itself forcibly both at home and abroad.

In America then, the Spanish came with little experience of governing, and with a mixture of motivations among the young conquistadors that is quite surprising to modern minds. They had something still of the medieval Christianizing fervour and search for honour inherited from their battles in Spain, mixed with a greed for personal gain that was more consistent with the rest of Renaissance Europe. Portuguese colonists, though there were a few idealists

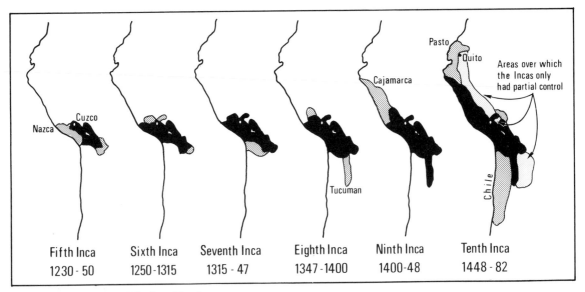

Fifth Inca   Sixth Inca   Seventh Inca   Eighth Inca   Ninth Inca   Tenth Inca
1230 - 50   1250-1315   1315 - 47   1347-1400   1400-48   1448 - 82

Fig. 3 The expansion of the Inca Empire

among them, came with more strictly material-istic ideas of the possibilities of the New World.

The medieval endowment: feudalism and fantasy
In the late stages of the Spanish advance across the Castilian Meseta, especially in the thirteenth-century push south from the Tagus, the Spanish king adopted the policy of granting titles of nobility and land to the soldiers and religious—military orders who led the attack. Land and people were placed under the feudal protection of the new lords. This policy was effectively continued into the New World, with donations of great land areas and their depen-dent population to the leaders. Such a practice was not followed in Brazil, nor could it be with the lack of Indians and cultivated land worth giving to soldiers; but a similar land policy, following that used in Madeira and Africa, was adopted: this was the granting of great tracts of land with seignorial rights of taxation and land for the nobles who took control of it under the crown.

Another strain of medieval influence was that of fantasy: legends of unknown lands or cities and fabulous beings, most of them originating in European writings with no empirical foundation, pursued the Spaniards into the New World. They included those of the Amazons, tribes of warlike women, thought to have been seen in California

as well as on the river Amazon; the legend of El Dorado, the gilded king, whose subjects regu-larly adorned him in gold paint, a legend which motivated exploration over the whole northern half of the continent; and the mysterious seven cities of Cíbola, placed anywhere from the Mississippi valley to Argentina.

The Conquest
The Spanish gained the upper hand in America, over all other potential colonizers. They were given rights to land west of 100 leagues from Cape Verde in a Papal Bull of 1493, amended to 370 leagues west in the Treaty of Tordesillas in 1494. After a relatively slow start in the West Indies, they expanded rapidly onto the continent from 1519, with Cortés' exploration into and conquest of the Mexican empire, followed by Pizarro's adventure into Peru, begun in 1530, which obtained at one dramatic stroke the accumulated wealth of centuries of civilization, including gold, fertile land, and dense settle-ments of peaceful Indians. The Portuguese had no similar fortune to await them in their legally allotted section of the continent. In Brazil there were no densely settled Indian populations, nor mineral riches, as far as could be ascertained, and precious little fertile land in cultivation or awaiting the plough.

The geography of conquest was simple in outline. Closest to South America of the Spanish bases in the Indies was Panama. From here, Pascal de Andagoya sailed 320 km down the Colombian Pacific coast and explored the Rio San Juan in 1522. In 1524, Francisco Pizarro led a first trip with 80 men and four horses, and in 1526, a second one with 160 men, disastrous in its losses of men and goods, but serving to show for the first time the wealth of a civilized people living to the south, from the evidence of pottery, metal-working, clothing and domesticated animals.

In 1530, Pizarro launched a third expedition, with finance and men he brought from Spain. Moving slowly south from a landing in Ecuador he at last struck inland in 1532 with 170 men. His timing was lucky for the Inca* Atahualpa and a large army of perhaps 80 000 men were nearby at Cajamarca. To this town he went, occupied the square which is still modern Cajamarca's central plaza, and invited the Inca to a parley. Atahualpa accepted the invitation and entered the town with as many men as could squeeze into the square. He was surprised not to see any Spaniards, but these were in fact lying in wait in the houses around the square with their horses and cannon. First Pizarro's priest approached to read the Requirement, an impractical Spanish document intended to be read to natives and asking them to accept Christian faith and Spanish sovereignty or be massacred. On finding little reaction to this, a Christian breviary was shown to the Inca who at first could not even open it, let alone understand it, and threw it down. This was the signal for attack. The Indians, massed into the square, panicked at the sound of cannon and the sight of horses, and vast numbers of them were slaughtered immediately. The Inca was captured, and the breakdown of the Empire, following a pattern established by Cortés in Mexico, had begun.

Everywhere Spanish arms held the advantage of horse against foot soldiers, armour against the cotton quilting used by the Indians, and firearms against wooden clubs, or bows and arrows. Following the conquest of Cuzco and most of Peru, lieutenants of Pizarro were sent out to finish the task of subjection. Jimenez de Quesada entered the Magdalena valley from the

Caribbean and arrived at the Chibcha centre of Bogotá before Sebastian de Belalcazar from Quito and the German Federmann from Venezuela. Chile was conquered directly by Diego de Almagro from Peru.

Thus the Andean lands were brought into subjugation. In the river Plate the impetus for settlement came initially in the search for a western passage to the Spice Islands, a search continued long after it was discovered that America did not reach to Asia or adjoin it. Juan de Solis made a first landfall in the Plate estuary in 1513, though from contemporary maps it seems he was anticipated by undocumented Portuguese voyagers. On a second trip in 1515, Solis was killed on the Uruguayan shore by hostile Indians. He was followed by Magellan, though no settlement was made then, for the search for western sea routes was still uppermost in Spanish minds.

Settlement on the Plate only came with the large group brought by Don Pedro de Mendoza, which ended in near disaster because of famine and Indian attacks. It was learnt early that settlement was only possible where settled Indians could be made to work for their parasitic conquerors. Where, as in the Plate, they could not, the conquerors had to move on, in this case to the upper river, at Asunción, among the Guaraní farmer Indians.

In Portuguese America the tale of conquest was perhaps less dramatic but it was equally brutal and the results, for the native peoples, equally disastrous, resulting again in the total breakdown of native cultures. For the first 30 years the Portuguese engaged only in trade, like the French on the same coast. But thereafter, and for the remainder of the sixteenth century, they were engaged in a colonization policy which established permanent settlements only after all-out wars against the Indians. These wars usually ended in the almost complete elimination of the Indians, through the immediate war losses and burning of their villages, their flight out of the coast lands into the interior forest for protection, and through European diseases, which decimated them, smallpox and dysentery being important early killers. The Portuguese found it only easy to settle among and conquer the Tupi tribes of the coast between Bahia and Pernambuco. Further north they were hard pressed by the French and by a well-organised Tupi group of tribes; further south they faced

---

* The name Inca was strictly that of the king or one of his family, but was applied later to the whole civilization.

non-Tupi tribes, at a more primitive level, without large villages or permanent residences of any kind, who fought a guerilla war against them, making colonization almost impossible. The Portuguese settlers and government were substantially aided by the Jesuit missionaries who in creating villages and in teaching the Indians also made them more controllable and totally dependent. Concentration in villages also probably helped spread European diseases more quickly.

Neither Spanish nor Portuguese advanced into the interior in the way that North American settlers were later to do. The Spanish especially were not farmer—settlers looking for land but knights on horseback, founding cities and claiming land without actually occupying it themselves. Only in the southern grasslands of the Pampas was there a frontier. Here wild raiding Indians were a reality, pressing on the frontier of military forts and tightening it, and making an impression on Spanish settlers, who were forced to occupy the land themselves for want of Indian farmers to do so for them. There was however none of the frontier experience of the North Americans, for the Pampas frontier was thinly peopled and static until the latter part of the nineteenth century. Latin Americans never experienced the socially democratizing influence of a small-farmer frontier.

COLONIAL ECONOMY AND SOCIETY

Land tenure

Arrangements for Spanish—Indian relations in America were complicated by the fact that the sovereigns who published laws of a humane nature governing the 'Indies', as they continued to be called, did not see them put into practice. Thus, while Spanish monarchs genuinely desired the wellbeing of their new American subjects, and would never permit their enslavement, in practice the Spanish overlordship was often terribly harsh. One institution set up was the *encomienda*, for the protection and conversion of Indian peoples put under an *encomendero*; the term implies the commending of Indian souls to the teaching of their Spanish master, but more

than this was involved — a regal ordinance of 1573 describes one facet that could lead immediately to exploitation of Indians:

> The Indians who offer us obedience and are distributed among Spaniards are to be persuaded to acknowledge our sovereignty over the Indies. They are to give us tributes of local produce in moderate amounts, which are to be turned over to their Spanish *encomenderos* so that the latter may fulfill their obligations [to the Crown], reserving to us the tributes of the principal villages and the seaports, as well as an amount adequate to pay the salaries of our officials.
>
> *cited in Lewis Hanke (ed.),* History of Latin American Civilization *(Methuen, 1969), p. 152.*

In fact many *encomiendas* were treated as land grants together with a serf Indian population to be used for labour. A highly stratified social relationship developed in the Inca territories, with Indians, imported slaves and *mestizos*, all set below the Europeans and *criollos*, Europeans born in America. True land grants, *donaciones* and *mercedes,* were also made, of so great a size that often the local Indians had to become serfs on them, for want of other land to work in the vicinity. Alternatively, they might move to new lands, but over the colonial period these were increasingly the marginal lands, away from valley floors and alluvial soils which were occupied by the estates. The *mercedes* were supposed to be for one generation only, but in fact tended to remain within the family granted them rather than reverting to the Crown.

The *encomienda* system broke down at different rates in different areas, in its transformation into the *haciendas*. These latter were large estates privately owned by Spaniards using Indian labour. They were introduced rapidly in such areas as the Peruvian coast where Indian population declined rapidly in the sixteenth century, less rapidly in the Sierra because a large Indian population could still be exploited under the old system. *Encomiendas* also declined because they were insufficient in number to support the demands of an increasing number of Spanish immigrants and their sons. *Haciendas* grew as the European system of private holdings replaced the communal ownership of most land in the old civilisations of Latin America. As communal holding was not recognized by Spanish law, communal lands could be taken readily in legal actions against it when there was no ready defender.

New crops and animals

The structure of farming was changed away from subsistence or semi-subsistence farming towards commercial farming. Important in these changes were the animals and crops introduced from Europe. The New World was not rich in domesticated animals, for, apart from the dog, it had only poultry, guinea pigs, llamas and alpacas as important domesticates. The introduction of sheep, cattle, pigs and goats to the region put a new value on unused pasture lands. The horse, mule and donkey brought a virtual transport revolution to the land. Llamas had been used for carrying burdens but they were weak compared with donkeys, and there was nothing to match the horse, as carrier of man or puller of the plough, which was here, as in the Old World, a symbol of its owner's prestige and power.

For crops, the Americas were richer and could even provide Europe with new commodities, such as tomatoes, maize and potatoes; but the middle-latitude grains — wheat, barley and oats — were an important innovation, replacing and supplementing the old crops of quinoa on the cold uplands and temperate south. Vines and olives were also important in these temperate lands. Sugar was easily transplanted and became an early export crop, associated with particular forms of society and farm organization, as is shown in later chapters. Citrus fruits also came to the tropics and subtropics at an early date, and spread so rapidly that it has been asserted until the present that there must have been a native, wild variety of orange.

Brazil

The Portuguese, after an initial period of interest only in trade with the coastal natives in manufactured trinkets which were exchanged for great logs of brazilwood, established their own land-holding system, a little different from the Spanish, in fact comparable in form to the colony system used for the first North American colonies. Grants, *donatárias,* were made by the crown to nobles or rich men to exploit, in return for a tenth of harvests or a fifth of metals extracted. The lands granted were placed under the *donatário* for the purpose of internal taxation

and lawmaking, and he received in addition half the income from brazilwood and a fifth of the land in his domain.

This system was intended to promote colonization; it had already done so in Madeira, the Azores and the Cape Verde islands. Here in Brazil it was more difficult to advance; Duarte Coelho, *donatário,* says in a letter to the king: 'We are obliged to conquer by inches, the land that your Majesty has granted us by leagues' (cited in Roberto Simonsen, *História Económica do Brasil* (São Paulo, 1957), p. 85).

A tropical climate, the hostility and the very lack of Indians, competition from French and Dutch to which the Spaniards were not exposed, all slowed down the process of expansion. For lack of a labour force, the Portuguese were forced to bring in slaves from their West African possessions, establishing the plantation system that lasted until the nineteenth century. The Dutch did similarly in their own sugar plantations in Guiana, finding few Indians willing to work for them on the coast.

The Church

Distinctive forms of tenure and production were occasionally established by the Catholic Church in America. Large land holdings all over the continent were owned by the Church, many of them bequests by repentant landlords on their deathbed. Some of the largest *latifundia* in the continent came into being in this way, to be expropriated finally by the state in nineteenth-century independence reforms.

While most church holdings were operated as ordinary cattle *haciendas* or crop farms, with the clergy exerting no influence on the form of economy, the Jesuits set up what amounted to complete economic and social enclaves in South America, in the Amazon valley, in eastern Bolivia and in eastern Paraguay and adjacent parts of Brazil (fig. 4). Their method was to build *aldeias* or *reducciones,* villages occupied only by the Indians with a Jesuit director, to produce goods for sustenance and sale, at the same time converting the Indians and controlling their whole way of life.

In the Amazon, the economic base was spices and cocoa, gathered or cultivated by the Indians and exported to Europe without paying tax. In Bolivia, cotton and craft products were sent to the altiplano from the *aldeias* while the Paraguayan *reducciones* produced yerba mate, tobacco, sugar and cotton for export. The Jesuits must be seen as a major force in colonial South America, organizing the Indians into villages, protecting them from slave attack or at least from the shocks of adaptation to lay European culture. They also served a strategic purpose, providing a buffer state or no-man's-land between Portuguese and Spanish territories, and even provided a good economic example to the rest of society. Jesuit rule has been criticized as domineering and autocratic; but this was also its strength, and what allowed it to become economically successful. It must also be remembered that Indians willingly entered the *reducciones* and welcomed their protection from the slave-catchers.

TRADE

Both Spanish and Portuguese economic policies were what may be called mercantilist, whereby the colonies were forced to trade with the mother country alone, to produce only raw materials and items of immediate consumption, and were not allowed to engage in manufacturing to compete with the mother country. In addition, most South American trade was channelled through the ports of Lima and Cartagena, if destined for Spain's colonies in the subcontinent. A convoy system was set up, ships travelling under naval escort across the Atlantic to the Outer Antilles, where the fleet split up into two, the northern part going to Veracruz in Mexico, the southern to Venezuela, Colombia and Panama, where it met a similar fleet from Peru travelling up the Pacific coast.

Further restrictions were the crown monopolies, in Spanish territory of tobacco and alcohol, in Brazil of brazilwood and salt; besides these there were many different taxes on trade transactions, which helped to raise, for example, the price of imported Spanish cloth from fivefold to eightfold between Lima and Buenos Aires. Such monstrous impositions encouraged corruption and contraband trade on a large scale.

The map (fig. 4) shows the major trade items and directions of movement in the early eighteenth century. Lima was the obvious focus of the Spanish South American economy, receiving goods via the Panama isthmus in the annual fleets which brought textiles, metal goods and luxury items such as fine furniture, and sending back gold, silver, and such durable products as hides and tallow. Lima received her stock of these goods from an enormous hinterland, within which only a few producing areas contributed the greater part.

MANUFACTURING AND DEPENDENCE

Before the eighteenth century, some of the tributary areas had produced much more by way of manufactures themselves; textiles in Chile and New Granada's Quito district, the upland region of present Ecuador; leatherwork, such as saddles and harnesses, carpentry, carts and carriages, in northwestern Argentina and eastern Bolivia; iron and other metal goods for farmers in many isolated regions.

After 1750 the Industrial Revolution and European manufacturing began to strangle this craft industry and reduced the peripheral areas to the status of raw material producers. A curious process of relative underdeveloping, holding back development while other areas went ahead, was put into operation. The Jesuit-controlled areas fared better, for their independence in economic matters meant that their surpluses could be chosen, and they were never hampered by trade restrictions. The Caribbean and river Plate also did better in trade than their remote positions would suggest, for contraband trade kept them busy with British and French buccaneers.

Brazil had similar mercantilist restrictions imposed by Portugal but it did not have the high-value trade items which permitted trade concentration at one great market as in Spanish America. Trade was rather of more bulky products, which necessarily moved out to Europe from the nearest port, and so went from a whole range of locations along the coast, not from one great port. Sugar, brazilwood and even cotton required ready access to sea routes. Probably the most significant imports to Brazil, in terms of value, were the West African slaves. To the north of Brazil, another trading region was that of the Guianas, especially the coastal fringe of present-day Surinam and Guyana, which were under Dutch control and sent sugar out to Europe from slave plantations. The Guianan economic geo-

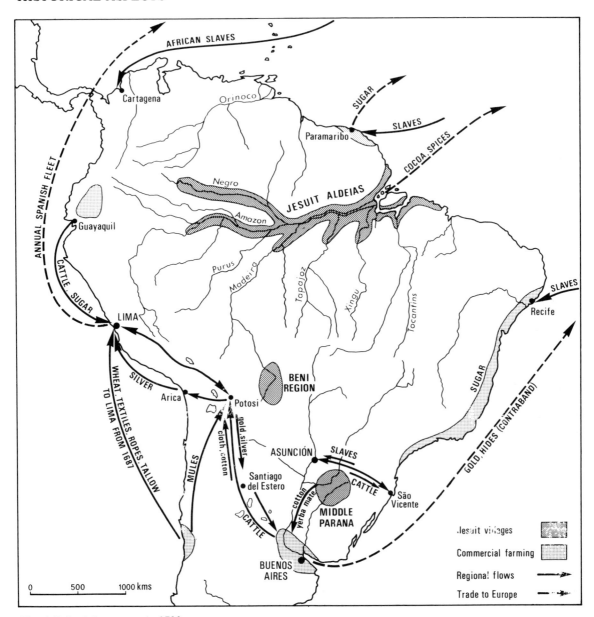

Fig. 4 Colonial economy in 1700

graphy was similar to that of Brazil, with emphasis on the coast and relations to Europe.

POLITICAL ORGANIZATION

The administrative machinery of the Spanish American Empire was strongly hierarchical, and very important in most aspects of life, with independent structures for towns, large regions and for legal matters. The basic division was into several viceroyalties, of which the most important in South America was that of Peru. Lima held great power as centre to South America, exercising some authority over most of the inhabited land of the continent. Within its viceroyalty, several units preserved some separate administrative identity. The Captaincy-General of Chile, the presidencies of Charcas,

Cuzco, Quito and Caracas, were all early units which had separate legal definition in the Audiencias of their district.

In the eighteenth century, Bourbon Spain attempted reforms in its Empire, and split off the northern and southern wings of the Peruvian Viceroyalty, as the new Viceroyalties of New Granada, first established in 1717, and of La Plata, 1776 (fig. 5), recognizing the real differences in interest and structure of economy between these lands.

Between these colonies and the Viceroyalty of Brazil, there was a *cordon sanitaire* of remote Indian settlements, under Jesuit domination until the expulsion of this order in 1767-8. Brazilian colonies were captaincies, under the nominal leadership of Bahia (Salvador), but, in correspondence with the economic facts of life, having no high degree of centralized power as in Spanish America. The northern region of Maranhão was for some time in danger of splitting off as a separate colony.

CULTURE AND SOCIETY

Given the feudal structure of the latifundia and the still more rigid division of labour on the plantation, social divisions were necessarily strong between different classes of society in Spanish America. To some extent, division was along racial lines: the slaves were Negroes, the Indians were a servile population, the Spaniards and *criollos* formed an urban élite. Mestization permitted some breaching of the division, though mestizos tended to form yet another group, intermediate between whites and Indians.

Regional differences in culture were apparent across the continent, as was natural given the isolation of one centre from another, separated by hundreds of kilometres of near deserted territory. An index is language; Spanish as spoken by high-class Colombians was regarded as among the best Spanish spoken in the world, and was quite different from that of Argentina. In the altiplano of Peru, most Indians were maintained outside the Spanish-speaking community and spoke their native languages. In other countries where mestizos were more important, Spanish was spoken by nearly all the population. Only in one country, Paraguay, did an Indian language

take over as the leading one. Guaraní language is still spoken today by all Paraguayans, and its prevalence indicates the deep penetration of Indian culture in this region.

South America is more notable now for cultural homogeneity than distinctiveness of regions; one colonial factor in this state of affairs was the refusal to allow other than Spanish and Portuguese immigrants into the area. Only in the Guianas, under North European rule, did different policies prevail. Another factor for unity was the Church, far more powerful than today, and influencing Indian as well as European. Old Indian religious beliefs and customs were adapted and moulded into Christian frames rather than completely suppressed; into the Baroque ecclesiastical architecture of Brazil and Peru, motifs such as snakes and monkeys, sacred to the Indians, were incorporated by clever Indian masons. Former holy days were given Christian saints' names, former holy places given legal existence as places holy to Our Lady or to a patron saint of the Christian calendar.

THE NINETEENTH CENTURY

It has often been asserted that the breakup of the Spanish Empire was due to internal decadence. Nowadays it is recognized that eighteenth-century Spain was not as much in decline as might be supposed; both economically and politically, Spain and her colonies made something of a recovery over the latter part of the century. Breakup was probably due more to external pressures, the rise of northern Europe and North America, than to internal problems. New ideas on politics, economy and society were beyond the control of Spain, and must eventually have wrought great changes even if Spain were to retain control. As it was, small groups of intellectuals, then the *criollos* of colonial cities, a disaffected group because they were kept out of high administrative office by Spanish rule, began to read the revolutionary writings of Rousseau, Locke and others, and foci of rebellion sprang up in Buenos Aires, Caracas, Bogotá and Santiago. These provincial centres, after the wars of independence, became the capitals of new states, each with their own political leaders and administrative machines, developed in the late eighteenth century and revolutionary period.

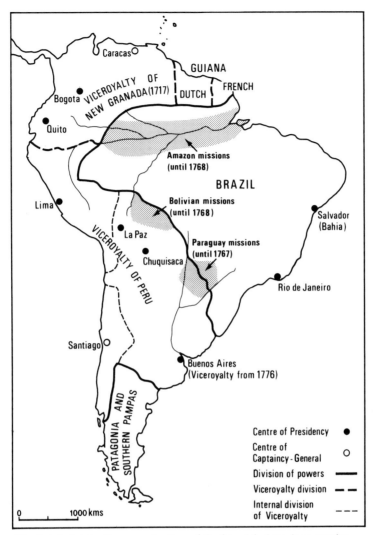

Fig. 5 *Administrative organisation of the Spanish American empire*

Since the middle-class *criollos* were the mainstay of revolution, little was changed in the social order by Spain's overthrow, and the same social system as in colonial time, with some modifications, was carried over into Independence. Slavery was gradually abolished in the course of the century, though the released slaves were not always given an easier lot. Church holdings throughout Latin America were expropriated, but were taken over by *criollos* and other wealthy landowners, leading to no democratization of land holding. Prohibition on settlement by other than Spaniards or Portuguese was abolished, and

this meant something of a change for the temperate countries, Argentina, Uruguay and Chile.

Independence and a new dependence
Freedom from Spain thus brought social change to only a few areas; economic change was similarly restricted, for the same kinds of exports and imports were maintained, ultimate control of trade merely moving from the Spanish metropolis to the English. This was a move which had begun in the previous century with the freeing of ports in the New World to more open trade. Now a strong English manufacturing sector was able

to penetrate all parts of the continent, bringing cotton cloths from Manchester, knives and forks from Sheffield or Birmingham and furniture and other luxury items from northwestern Europe generally.

The entry of cheap manufactures finally doomed the old craft industries of areas such as Santander—Boyacá in Colombia, Mendoza and the northwest of Argentina, where cloths and metal and leather goods had continued to be made. Penetration of European goods was facilitated by gradual improvements in transport means; steamboats up the rivers helped, though there are few easily navigable waterways in the continent; more important were the railways, especially after 1880, and notably in Argentina, Peru and Colombia, lowering the real cost of transport four- or five-fold over mule packing, the previous norm in mountainous country.

Nineteenth-century Brazil

Brazilian transfer of power was peaceful, beginning with the removal of the whole Portuguese court and royalty to Brazil as a consequence of Napoleon's takeover in 1808. Effectively, Brazil could begin to turn her back on Portugal without losing her traditional respect for royal authority, in contrast to Spanish colonies where this duality of affections slowed down the Independence movements. From 1808 there were relaxations of colonial rule, with Brazil the centre of the empire. Manufacturing was now permitted, trade completely freed, and a period of economic prosperity ushered in.

A question sometimes posed by historians on Brazilian evolution is how such a large country could hold together despite tendencies towards separation throughout colonial times and tenuous connections along the coast between the various rival centres. One reason for this keeping together into modern times may have been the presence of the king in the country, an important symbol of unity. Another reason was the very primitiveness of the country, with few centres of intellectual activity to compare with those in Buenos Aires, Bogotá and elsewhere in Spanish America. For revolution to occur, as has been observed in this century, a certain degree of economic and social development is necessary. Finally, we should note that the economy of Brazil over the colonial period focussed in one region at a time; first on the coast, then in the northeast, then in the southeast, so that economic unity and a single core was maintained.

Nineteenth-century Brazilian economic evolution proceeded much as in Spanish America, with dependence on Portugal transferred to Britain. In fact dependence had moved, in this case too, to England in the eighteenth century, when Portugal had become to some extent an economic colony of the northern state, exchanging military protection for unequal trade terms; under the Methuen Treaty of 1703, amplified by later measures, Portugal gave free entry to English textiles, and English manufactures or displaced Portuguese manufactures had to look for markets in Brazil and elsewhere. Direct entry of British goods became important in the nineteenth century.

Immigration of new European blood was slight until the late nineteenth century, coming first into Rio Grande do Sul and Santa Catarina, from 1840, then on a grander scale into Sao Paulo in the 1880s and 90s, with the rise of coffee. Slavery did not come to an end until the 1880s, forestalling labour problems for the sugar plantations and deterring what slight immigration might have occurred into the tropical regions. Formal declaration of a republic was also delayed until the 1880s, when the Emperor Don Pedro II was quietly replaced in a palace revolution of 1889, followed by the optimistic creation of a United States of Brazil, with a constitution based on that of the United States of America, giving strong rights to the state governments, though in fact centralized government was to be the norm.

TERRITORIAL ADJUSTMENTS

Colonial boundaries between the various colonial territories had not often been precisely defined, still less surveyed on the ground, so that there was room for considerable jostling between the newborn states, changing the political map during the nineteenth century. In the centre, Paraguay, controlled by a dictator with expansionist aims, made war on all its neighbours in the War of the Triple Alliance (1865-70). This war devastated the country, and caused it to lose land to Brazil and Argentina. The boundaries on the open plain of the Chaco, with few natural markers to use as limits, were still unsettled, and in the 1930s Paraguay again went to war, with disastrous results, in the War of the Chaco, fought partly for the economic interests in potential oil supplies.

Economic interests were also uppermost in the War of the Pacific from 1880 to 1884, interest focussing in this case on the nitrates of the Atacama, developed by Chilean entrepreneurs. In the war both Bolivia and Peru lost their claims to the nitrate lands. Other economic interests were present in the shifts of boundary pressed on Bolivia by Brazil during the century. The upper Amazon valley acquired a new value for its wild rubber trees, and Brazil found it easy to exert pressure on Bolivia for these lands, holding the transport key to trade, in the great river leading to the Atlantic and Europe. Brazil similarly expanded to take over Amazon territory in Colombia, Venezuela and Ecuador, in each case Brazilian occupation of the zone allowing a claim of de facto control. Brazilian *caboclos* moved in from the east, upriver, in a natural and unrecorded advance of the frontier, while the Andean states, with no tradition of lowland forest settlement and with no occupants for the frontier zones, found it difficult to enforce any claims to the Amazon lands. A common thread unites these territorial disputes or wars; while the excuse for battle was dispute over the true lines of demarcation between countries, the real interests were vital economic ones, pressed not by farmers on the frontier but by urban administrators and middle-class landowners or merchants who stood to gain most.

CONCLUSIONS

Two themes seem worth recalling in the history of the continent. One is the continuity of human patterns, another is its broad unity, increasing rather than diminishing over time. Continuity is apparent despite upsets and distortions produced by revolutions and wars. Part of this continuity is a reflection of environmental dictates, most notably the climatic and other effects of the mountain areas. These lands provided veritable islands of temperate climate in the tropics and open, relatively fertile land above the dense forests. Here the ancient civilizations developed to their highest levels, and here the Spanish found it easiest and most rewarding to impose their rule. To the present day the oecumene of the continent within the tropics is partially confined to the mountains, following old patterns, despite expansionary movements into the lowlands, which serve to occupy the mountain fringe, but not the main body of tropical lowland. Brazil provides the best exceptions to this rule, with a throbbing economic core in the Southeast, although this is only marginally tropical, in an area where no ancient civilization seems to have grown up. And the Brazilian Northeast has long had a dense lowland population and active economy, albeit based in good measure on African, not European, blood.

Economic and social patterns also have historical antecedents. Inca civilization involved strong class distinctions, which were taken up and utilized with racially determined groupings. On the economic front, continuity is found in the state of subordination to foreign powers, begun in the sixteenth century and remaining to the present despite political changes which have brought independence to nearly all parts of the continent.

Unity is as impressive as continuity in South America. Given control by the two Iberian nations alone over a period of more than three centuries, this is perhaps not surprising, but its special force must be ascribed to the power of the Church, in matters both spiritual and temporal, and to the strictness of Spanish and Portuguese colonial policy, allowing no other nation to influence their American wards, or to send settlers to the region with new ideas. Over a continent, similar language, culture and economy were imposed, similar relations to a mother country which insisted on uniform methods of government and administration throughout its domains.

3. Agriculture

An outsider's view of South American agriculture is typically of lands producing plantation crops such as coffee, cocoa, bananas and sugar for export from the tropical regions; beef, wool and wheat from the temperate Pampas. This picture is not so much wrong as incomplete. Besides the commercial farming there is subsistence or near-subsistence farming over wide areas, producing different crops by different methods and for distinctive markets. South America does have large open areas, and a slight population density compared to Southeast Asia or Africa, giving her the physical resource for producing export crops instead of having to concentrate on feeding her own people; but in some areas there are very small farms which provide only subsistence crops for their owners. Famine is infrequent, but malnutrition common enough. Although the physical productive base is good enough for current populations, historical factors have given rise to structural problems of farm size and farm tenure that have not yet been solved.

MAIN CROPS

Basic food crops
For Latin America, food supply is adequate, and local or regional shortages can normally be overcome with supplies brought in from other regions. This happy overall position has not been reversed by the rapid growth of population over the last thirty years, as the table shows. It is less impressive an achievement if we note that most of the increase over these years in some countries is due to expanding frontiers and increased areas under cultivation.

Bolivia's, Brazil's and Venezuela's figures nevertheless look impressive, especially given the rapid increase of population in these countries; the southern cone countries did much more poorly, barely keeping abreast of a more slowly rising population. Expansion of land under arable and permanent crops is particularly notable in Paraguay and Brazil, where the 1975–1983 years alone saw an increase of 57.3% and 23.1% respectively in these countries. By contrast, Venezuela managed to make her increases mostly from higher yields, while Chile and Peru had disastrous records, with increased areas under cultivation but lower per capita production.

Commercial crops
The southern cone countries, Argentina, Chile and Uruguay, had important parts of their development predicted on the export of agricultural commodities. Argentina still has maize (corn), wheat and beef, though they now only contribute 30% of the export total. Uruguay has beef and wool, though again in limited supply. Chile was an important wheat supplier in colonial time and still produces the crop on large and medium-sized commercial farms. Elsewhere wheat was not the traditional staple crop, for it was a European introduction, and other grains and tubers took its place. Marginal wheat lands

BASIC FOOD PER CAPITA PRODUCTION

	Uruguay	Argentina	Chile	Bolivia	Brazil	Colombia	Ecuador	Paraguay	Peru	Venezuela
1952	96.7	106.3	93.3	105.4	92.1	101.9	77.0	103.1	94.9	92.1
1955	100.0	100.0	100.0	100.0	100.0	100.0	100.0	100.0	100.0	100.0
1960	83.8	90.6	94.2	148.4	106.9	93.0	116.6	95.0	100.9	107.6
1965	94.8	94.7	89.4	158.1	119.5	92.9	136.7	101.0	98.9	124.1
1970	94.5	105.2	96.1	164.0	126.0	93.9	120.8	105.1	107.0	139.1
1975	90.1	106.3	89.5	186.6	139.6	105.4	133.6	97.0	98.5	141.7
1980	89.1	115.6	87.6	170.4	158.2	113.0	133.6	117.4	81.7	145.8

Source: Statistical Abstract of Latin America, *Vol. 23, pp. 754–55.*   Index: 1955 = 100.

such as the highlands of Colombia and Venezuela have also tended to disappear because they cannot compete with the world's major wheat producers. In the tropical and subtropical climates, maize becomes important as the staple food crop, though it has limitations, requiring fertile well-watered soils with plenty of nitrogen. It may be grown as a commercial crop or as a peasant's subsistence crop. In areas of poor soil in the tropics it is replaced by cassava or manioc, notably in the interior of Brazil on the poor plateau soils, and in Paraguay, but it does not enter much into trade. Rice is another tropical alternative, used where water is abundant; it enters widely into trade from the intensive irrigated regions, such as the north coast of Peru and the Guayas valley in Ecuador.

Elsewhere in the tropics tree crops are the basis for commercial agriculture. Bananas are the best-known example, widely exported from the Guayas valley and from the Magdalena lowlands of Colombia. Coffee is a very widely produced subtropical crop, important in southern Brazil, the world's largest producer, and throughout the Andean countries on the Andean fringes at a level of about 1000 metres, but most especially in Colombia. Sugar is also widely grown, the largest producers being Brazil and Colombia; it is not competitive in the southern cone countries, but is maintained by high price structures in the northern Argentine provinces. For Guyana it is the principal export.

Throughout the southern cone countries there are regional specialities commercially farmed — in northernmost Argentina, tobacco, citrus fruit, yerba mate, tea, cotton; in temperate Argentina and south-central Chile, dairy products; in Patagonia, sheep for wool and apples from orchards in the valleys.

Adding up these different contributions, we could draw a map of commercial farming areas — almost all of Argentina would be included in one, together with Uruguay and Chile. Further north, the coast region of Peru is another highly commercial region, producing cotton, rice and sugar cane from a few intensively farmed valleys. This region extends beyond the frontier, into the coast region of Ecuador, especially the Guayas valley, with its bananas, rice and oil palms in recent years. Another major commercial region is around the urban centres of southeast Brazil, Rio and São Paulo. Here the crops are coffee, sugar cane, maize, and a newcomer in the last fifteen years, soyabeans. Elsewhere on the continent, commercial, market-oriented crops occupy smaller patches of ground, often integrated with forms of subsistence farming which feed their labour force, or merely rings around individual large city markets (fig. 6).

Subsistence crops

Outside the main commercial crop regions, and sometimes interwoven with them, there are areas where only subsistence farming is practised, feeding the farmer and his family with only occasional or limited surpluses for sale. In the Andes, from northernmost Argentina through to Venezuela, there is a wide variety of crops, often forming intricate patterns to match the diversity of physical locations, slopes, climates, soils, drainage, all varying rapidly within a few kilometres. They are varied also because subsistence agriculture is not generally a monoculture (growing only one crop).

Root crops are the most important, principally potatoes, of which there are eight species and thousands of varieties known, but also other tubers, such as *añu* or *oca* (*Oxalis tuberosa*), *ulluco* or *melloco* (*Ullucus tuberosus*) *mashua* or *isañu* (*Tropaeolum toberosum*), which have never been adopted outside the Andes. These seem to be the most ancient of Andean crops, and their variety allows them to penetrate upwards to the highest limits of cultivation, above 4200 metres in Peru, where they can be combined with the rearing of llamas, alpaca and sheep.

There are few grains grown; maize, an American crop, is produced wherever good level land can be found at up to about 2800 metres, and this has been important since the time of the Incas. An important high-altitude grain is *quinoa* (*Chenopodium quinoa*), related to the weed known in Europe as goosefoot, which is widely grown from Bolivia to Ecuador, though always on a small scale as a garden patch crop. A related crop is *cañihua* (*C. pallidicaule*), grown in the same area. Amaranths (*Amaranthus caudatus*), which in Britain is known as a garden flower, love-lies-bleeding, give a small grain of exceptional interest today. This grain has a protein content of 14–18%, higher than corn or barley, and with a better amino-acid mix for human consumption. It is grown as a garden crop from northern Argentina to Ecuador.

As minor crops, beans, peas and other vegetables are grown, as well as lupins, another legume from which an edible variety has been cultivated.

All the above refers generally to the subsistence crops of the Andes; in the plains of the tropical areas there may also be subsistence farming, based on a poorer and more primitive native set of crops, with cassava as the principal source of carbohydrate, and with bananas or plantains as an alternative.

FARMING SYSTEMS

Rather than the cultivation of single crops, it is necessary to see farming as a system combining various activities and products. There are many of these and many transitional types, but a few major ones may be mentioned.

Andean subsistence farming
In the remoter and less advanced areas there is something approaching a true subsistence system, producing for domestic consumption or that of the immediate community. Crops are closely interrelated, even in one field, so that a maize field may have lupins growing amongst the maize to provide nitrogen, squash covering the ground below and protecting it from erosion, and thus there may be three crops from one field. This polyculture system has the aim of survival, not profit, so that it does not concentrate on the highest-yielding crop alone. The multiplicity of crops spreads the farm work out over the year, and the failure of any one crop does not spell disaster. Mixing of the crops reduces the incidence of pest and disease attack.

In the highlands, the robustness of the system is extended by the farmer's use of a vertical set of ecological niches at different altitudes. On the *páramos* at 3500 metres, he has access to common land where he may graze his sheep or llama herd. Down at 3000 metres are his private lands where grains and tubers are grown, with vegetables in the garden by his house.

The protein supply gained for consumption is apparently slight, but *quinoa* is a high-protein grain, as is amaranth; in addition, the farmer keeps a dozen or so guinea pigs in his house, more or less confined to a straw-covered enclosure on the earth floor but living off household food scraps. These animals are eaten when full-grown. Chickens and ducks may be kept in the kitchen garden by the house. One of his neighbours is likely to keep several pigs, and he probably exchanges some of his maize for an occasional pig. Wool is spun by his wife and then woven, to supply some of the clothing needs. Near the house there are probably a few eucalyptus trees growing for firewood or to be used as roof timbers.

This kind of production system is of course not simply an economic system. It lives on because of its deep historical roots, as part of the Andean culture which has not been totally suppressed by colonial intervention. It is best preserved among those groups, frequent in Bolivia and the southern Peruvian Sierra, which are of Amerindian stock, rather than the *mestizo* who is more common elsewhere. In the purest form, land is owned and agriculture is conducted, communally, by the *ayllu* or traditional community, but more frequently the communal ownership has disappeared from the best lands, as they have been swallowed up long ago by *haciendas*, leaving only high pastures as the common land. What has often survived is labour cooperation amongst the community. In regions as far apart as the Mérida highlands of Venezuela, and the dry altiplano of Potosí, Bolivia, this writer has seen groups of peasants working together to harvest a field, to dig a drainage ditch, or to build a house. In the sharing of work there is a further element of security, since success is not dependent on one person's good health, and the harvesting of a crop can be ensured at the correct time.

The hacienda

The other main element in Andean agriculture is the *hacienda*. This is typically a large farm of more than 1000 hectares, used as a cattle ranch; in some areas it may be mostly in arable land, and in such cases could be much smaller, say 300 hectares. In this system the hacienda is worked at a low intensity and divided into two parts, the home farm, which is worked for the owner by tenants as a labour rent, and the remainder, which is the land used by the tenant farmers for themselves. The proportions between these vary. Given high population pressure, with lack of interest by the absentee owner, with relatively good land for arable farming, most of the hacienda might be divided into *minifundio* blocks; on poor windswept uplands with low population densities, the whole might be a single cattle ranch managed as one unit. This type of unit, as we shall see in the section on agrarian reform, has been a primary target for reform and expropriation. Where there is a higher population density the *hacienda* is typically one half of a symbiosis between *latifundio* and *minifundio,* a large farm worked at low intensity, with peasants living on small intensively worked plots adjacent to it. The obvious inequality of the system makes it open to reform. It is also liable to change simply because of its inefficiency, lack of capital investment and limited profitability.

Variants on the hacienda type of traditional estate may be found in other well-populated parts of the continent, as in northeast Brazil's interior. In tropical lands with a lower population, the system tends towards a simple ranch unit, worked by paid hands, as found in lands peripheral to the Argentine Pampas, the Chaco in northern Argentina and western Paraguay, or the Orinoco Llanos of Venezuela and Colombia.

These are *latifundios* but without the attendant *minifundio*, as arable agriculture is not a possibility.

Modern commercial farming (fig. 6)

In some parts of the continent a transition has been made from the traditional types to modern farming. In the southern cone countries, such farms are the norm. Argentina's *estancias,* in the main humid Pampas region and in Patagonia and Tierra del Fuego, are modernized units, having evolved out of the traditional range type just described. A typical estancia today of 1000 hectares will have a manager, a *tractorista* to plough and cultivate the 100 ha of arable land that is shifted regularly round the estate, and a pair of cowboys who are employed part-time. The natural grassland of the area will have been improved by cultivation every ten years, and the grass upgraded with alfalfa plantings. Store cattle are brought in from the dry lands to the west and fattened on the grass, with additional grain feed from the cultivated land; they are then sent to Buenos Aires to the big meat-packing centres (*frigoríficos*) where they are converted into prime beef.

Locally within the Pampas there are more intensively farmed regions and farms of 20–50 ha; around the cities of Montevideo and Buenos Aires are dairy regions producing dry milk, cheese, butter. In the Balcarce region is a concentration of commercial potato production. In Chile too, the Little South region from Concepción to Puerto Montt has commercial farming on 50 ha units with a mixed farming system of dairying and arable land, often with woodlots for timber. All these regions have benefited from the arrival of immigrants during the nineteenth century, bringing their traditions of intensive European farming, which have constantly been at war with the older ranching or *hacienda* traditions.

In Brazil a similar type has come into the state of Santa Catarina, producing tobacco, maize used for pig production, and dairying, again based on European immigrants. In the present century similar intensive small farms have been set up in São Paulo state by Japanese immigrants. Coffee farms in Paraná State and São Paulo, and in Antioquia within Colombia, are also of this kind, though not so diversified. All these commercial farms use as much machinery as they can afford. For the most part they are owner-operator farms, relying on the farmer's own family for labour, though some may be tenanted, albeit with normal money rents rather than the traditional rents in kind or labour of the *hacienda*. They rely on reasonable access to the urban markets, where their products are sold, and where many of their children may be educated.

Plantations

Today plantations are run as modern commercial farms, but their organization is sufficiently different from *haciendas* to merit special mention. They are almost all in the tropical areas, and for the most part located near the coasts, relying on good transport to export their products. They grew up in the colonial period, based on slave labour. The most representative are the sugar cane plantations of the Guianas, of northeast Brazil, of Colombia's Caribbean coast, and of northeast Venezuela. They were worked by imported African slaves and their decendants, and have to the present a large Negro population. Apart from sugar, other crops produced in this way include: cocoa in Venezuela, coffee and rubber in Brazil, wine in the vineyards of Chile and Argentina, yerba mate and tea in Misiones province of Argentina. Production of a high-value crop such as grapes, tung nuts, rubber, or yerba mate made an interior location possible.

As with plantations elsewhere in the world, the use of heavy infrastructure and machinery is normal and feasible given the concentration on one product. Farming is conducted efficiently, relying on the use of fertilizers and advanced forms of pest and disease control. In the past, many such enterprises were controlled by overseas firms, as in the case of Guyana's sugar cane plantations, owned by the Booker Corporation until recent times.

Primitive agriculture

In the Andes, truly primitive systems were superseded by the pre-Columbian farming that has survived in what was called above Andean subsistence agriculture. In the temperate lands, Amerindian populations have been largely exterminated, and in any case were more hunters than farmers. In the tropical forest areas, however, primitive agriculture continues amongst tribal groups. An example cited in some detail is that of the Yukpa (see the chapter on Venezuela), but we may note some general features here. A multiplicity of crops is found in any one clearing, so that no particular plant nutrient is under heavy pressure and pests are unlikely to cause great damage. A storied structure with trees, vines, bushes and ground crops serves to filter sunshine and rain and prevents erosion or rapid burning-up of the humas. The system is one of shifting agriculture, a swidden type, so that after three years or so the land is left and a new clearing made, again avoiding too long and heavy a tax of soil resources. The swidden may be used in years after cultivation ceases, in an informal manner, because the tree and bush crops, such as bananas and peach palms, continue to give good harvests up to ten years on, though the usual manioc staple can no longer be grown. Such a system provides food with little protein, but supplements are available through hunting and fishing on the rivers. Useful timber trees such as cedar (*Cedrela sp.*) are protected in the swidden, so that they form resources for later generations.

The above system is followed approximately, but in an ecologically much more dangerous way, by many cultivators in the Andes. Large areas of the mountain slopes are inaccessible by road and are owned by private individuals who do not use them, or the areas remain public lands. These lands are occupied, usually illegally, by squatter farmers who grow a few crops and then move on. Their job is made easier by the fact that only secondary forest, or even low scrub, is the vegetation cover instead of forest. This means that the soil does not have time to recover between cultivation periods, perhaps only five years instead of the fifty years, optimal period. As population pressure increases, the erosion problem and marginality of such farmers increase.

STRUCTURAL PROBLEMS AND THEIR SOLUTION

The agrarian problem has long been central throughout Latin American. The Mexican Revolution of 1910–17 took as a major slogan the reform of agriculture, as did the Bolivian 1952 Revolution, the Cuban Revolution under Fidel Castro in 1959, and the 1968 military revolution in Peru.

What is the agrarian problem and how should it be tackled? Most writers would agree that there are two principal structural problems, which are not unrelated: the distribution of farm sizes, and the tenure of farmland. It is these problems which have been addressed by agrarian reforms. Some writers would go much further to say that the structural imbalance is much wider, one between urban areas generally and rural areas. Urban bias (Michael Lipton, 1976) operates in many ways, through the greater investment in cities' infrastructure and social services by Latin American governments, through low pricing of agricultural goods, through the concentration of decision-making in the central cities. In this chapter we will examine only the narrower agrarian problems, but return to the wider theme in the chapter on economic development.

Farm size

The table shows distribution of farm sizes for most South American countries. The point is readily made: distribution of farmlands is highly polarized between a minority of very large holdings and the great bulk of small farms, some of them too small to be ecologically or economically sound. Some of the data are far too old to be valid today (Bolivia's lack of census data is notorious) but they illustrate the pattern and the problem which confronted reformers.

In Bolivia, the pre-revolutionary 1950 pattern was that a few hundred owners had 95% of the farmlands, while nearly 70% of the farms had units of under 10 ha (25 acres). Medium-size family farms which would be recognized as of viable size in developed countries were only 22.5% of the total. The degree of concentration may have been underestimated because the data refer to farm units rather than the total holdings of any one owner. Big estate owners, usually absentee urban dwellers, might own several estates which they would run through estate managers.

It is of course unreasonable to expect all farms to be the same size. In Bolivia, as in every one of the countries, there are large areas of negative character, mountainous or with poor soils, where small farms would be inappropriate and uneconomic. It is possible to get over this problem by working out the amount of land needed in each area to support one farm worker, and adjusting farm sizes accordingly. This was done in the

FARM HOLDINGS IN SOUTH AMERICA

Country (date)	Smallest and largest size classes (ha)	Percentage of farms	Percentage of farmland
Argentina (1960)	0–5	15.2	0.1
	Over 1000	5.9	74.5
Bolivia (1950)	0–10	69.4	0.4
	Over 500	8.1	95.1
Brazil (1970)	0–10	51.4	3.1
	Over 1000	0.8	39.2
Colombia (1970)	0–5	62.5	4.5
	Over 500	0.6	40.5
Chile (1965)	0–5	48.8	0.7
	Over 1000	1.4	72.6
Ecuador (1965)	0–5	73.0	7.2
	Over 1000	2.0	27.1
Paraguay (1981)	0–20	78.6	5.5
	Over 500	1.3	81.3
Peru (1972)	0–5	72.4	4.6
	Over 500	0.5	67.6
Uruguay (1970)	0–10	29.3	0.7
	Over 1000	5.1	58.4
Venezuela (1961)	0–5	42.9	1.0
	Over 1000	1.7	67.0

Sources: Various.

1960s for various countries. Farms whose land could give work to less than two persons full-time, under the conditions of farming of that area and time, were regarded as sub-family, i.e. too small to be family farms, which latter were units giving two to four full jobs. Multi-family medium farms gave 4–12 jobs, and multi-family large farms were the biggest category.

This table shows that, for example, in Argentina, 43% of all farms were sub-family in size, but that these farms only held 3.4% of the land, and at the other end that big farms held 3.69% of the agricultural land. In the Andean countries this inequality becomes still greater. Thus, despite the moderating effect of taking land quality into account, there is a great imbalance in farm holdings.

PERCENTAGES OF LAND AND OF FARM UNITS IN DIFFERENT SIZE CATEGORIES

Country	Sub-family	Family	Multi-family medium	Multi-family large
Agentina				
% farm units	43.2	48.7	7.3	0.8
% farm area	3.4	44.7	15.0	36.9
Brazil				
% farm units	22.5	39.1	33.7	4.7
% farm area	0.5	6.0	34.0	59.5
Chile				
% farm units	36.9	40.0	16.2	6.9
% farm area	0.2	7.1	11.4	81.3
Colombia				
% farm units	64.0	30.2	4.5	1.3
% farm area	16.6	19.0	19.3	45.1
Ecuador				
% farm units	89.9	8.0	1.7	0.4
% farm area	16.6	19.0	19.3	45.1
Peru				
% farm units	88.0	8.5	2.4	1.1
% farm area	7.4	4.5	5.7	82.4

Land tenure

The second major structural problem is that of the contract under which land is held. For the developed countries the norm is either owner-occupier farms or a money rent paid by tenant farmers who are given substantial legal protection against eviction. In South America the traditional pattern was quite different. One set of tenure relations was that of the *hacienda* system. Here the home farm part of the estate was worked by labourers who each had a *minifundio* of a few hectares, the rent for which was paid as labour on the home farm. This labour might be accompanied by rent in kind, as various products of the small farm and by other services, such as sending girls to work in the estate house as domestic workers.

An example may be cited from the Ecuadorean Sierra which will add to the general description.* Three main groups of tenure existed on the haciendas here:

1. The *huasipungo*, whereby the tenant (*huasipunguero*) worked four or five days per week for the right to a plot of 2–4 ha. A somewhat similar relation was held by the *yanapero;* this was usually an Indian, living on a community adjacent to the *hacienda,* which had probably taken over the communal lands in the past for want of any individual legal rights established over them. He worked the *yanapa,* perhaps one day a week labour, for the right to the pastures, to collect firewood or merely cross the *hacienda* lands.

2. Sharecropping was a second type, whereby the *partidarios* or *medieros* worked a piece of land belonging to the hacienda in exchange for a share (a half or a third) of the harvest, plus occasionally a tiny wage. The landowner could usually stipulate the crop to be grown, and act himself as purchaser of the harvest, making still more profit.

3. Finally there were wage labourers, *peones libres,* who lived on the *hacienda,* and *empleados*, those who lived elsewhere and who might in consequence receive a somewhat higher wage in place of the board and lodging of the *peon.* The *peones* were often children or relatives of the *huasipungueros,* perhaps living with them but with no land rights.

On top of this complex workforce there were administrators who were paid a wage, and the absentee landlord who might visit the estate only twice a year.

Such a system had several faults: it concentrated all power over land and production in the hands of a few absentee owners, maintaining the powerless tenants and labourers in a state of extreme poverty. Secondly, the system did not encourage modernization or efficient production — investment in machinery was not worthwhile if 'free' labour was available. Thirdly, it did not encourage the small tenant farmers to work harder or more productively — most of their energy went directly to the owner as labour-rent, or indirectly as a part of their harvests. The combination of these negative elements meant that

*Andres Guerrero (1977) *La hacienda precapitalista y la clase terrateniente en America Latina y su inserción en el modo de producción capitalista: el caso Ecuatoriano,* Occasional Papers No. 23, Inst. of Latin American Studies, University of Glasgow.

the farming population for the most part remained in a vicious circle of poverty and powerlessness. This static situation suited landlords, who may not have received the highest returns from their land, but did not have to worry about competition from more productive farmers round about them, and whose main source of income was probably not the *hacienda* itself.

Besides these two main problem areas, there were others which need to be mentioned, because they are important to the matter of agrarian reform:

1. Access to markets. Many traditional haciendas are poorly connected to markets or indeed to any kind of road. With very low levels of production this did not matter, but if land reform takes place and intensive farming is to be brought in on the post-reform small farms, then good access is necessary, in the form of farm-to-market roads.

2. A related matter is the marketing system. From the *haciendas,* goods were taken to contacts in neighbouring towns or to the landlord's own store. Small farmers are at the mercy of intermediaries in South America because they lack the storage space and means of transport to take their goods to market, or contacts in the towns to provide information on prices, alternative markets and the like.

3. Extension services are commonly absent, and thus small farmers have no knowledge of important matters such as soil erosion and its control, the correct use of fertilizers, conservation matters such as terracing and contour ploughing. They also have had no experience of the use of credit, having worked on the hacienda in a largely moneyless economy.

LANDLESS IN SOUTH AMERICA

Country	Landless as a percentage of rural labour
Argentina	24
Bolivia	38
Brazil	40
Colombia	20
Ecuador	28
Peru	23

4. In most rural areas there are large numbers of landless or near-landless labourers. The Table gives some idea of the problem from six countries of the region. For most of these people, who constitute the core of very poor in these areas, there is little chance of solving their problems by an agrarian reform, and modern ideas are towards encouraging non-agricultural employment in the rural areas, in, for example, the small rural towns.

AGRARIAN REFORM

There are many ways in which agrarian change may be induced. Technological innovation and industrial alternative employment were useful to the developed countries, but do not present the same opportunities to poor countries. Devices such as better pricing structures, or the provision of infrastructure and credit, can be useful if directed at the small farmer, but might possibly not constitute a sufficient solution. Taxation means would be effective in developed countries where efficient tax-gathering systems operate and are hard to evade. But all fiscal devices can be evaded by big farmers in Latin America, and none of the measures suggested so far has much appeal to the politicians, who prefer measures with high public visibility.

Reform has been a major issue in Latin America since about 1960, when outside pressures, particularly from the USA, began to be felt by politicians of the areas. The example of Cuba's 1959 Revolution made it important that reform be attempted. Every country has made some gesture, though usually feeble, towards reform. The main difference is between countries which have tried to compensate owners for land taken over, and those which have expropriated the land directly. Only in the latter case has there been a powerful reform movement, though Venezuela, with its oil wealth, has managed to carry out an apparently substantial reform programme.

The critique of agrarian reform may be made on two levels. First, there are the technical matters, such as the agility with which land transfers are legalized, the provision for new infrastructure such as roads and storage facilities, bank credit, or technical training for new small farmers, the problems mentioned in the previous section. There is too much temptation for administrators to limit their action to the carving-up of previous large estates into new small farms. Secondly, at a political level, agrarian reform frequently involves too many theorists and ideologues, who are little concerned with practical help to farmers, and instead seek perhaps a return to traditional native communities, revenge on the landlord class, or an increase in national food production, rather than a means to help increase farmers' welfare. Most often, only lip service to the idea of agrarian reform has been paid, although many laws have been passed, and only a few countries have important changes in their farming patterns as a result. The most significant are Bolivia, Chile and Peru. We may discuss each of these briefly.

Chile

Reform was effectively begun here under the 1964–70 Frei government. This Christian Democrat government moved slowly in its reforms, settling only 4000 families a year during 1966–70. As has tended to be the pattern elsewhere in the continent, reform never benefited the agricultural populace at large. The radical and most equitable solution, that of giving land to the totally landless, was not tried. Nor yet was the less extreme one of using expropriation to increase farm sizes for the *minifundistas,* to make their farms of viable size. What took place was a division of the large estates amongst their permanent workers, creating new *asentamientos* which were agricultural production cooperatives, and allowing a little privately farmed land to the same permanent workers.

Compensation was paid to estate owners, but this was less valuable (90% was in the form of state bonds which soon lost their value) than the right to retain the equivalent of 40 irrigated hectares as their own land, on their own choice of the estate lands. This allowed the creation of a core of new, medium-sized commercial farms, whose owners could afford to invest in machinery. More of these farms emerged because other landowners anticipated land reform by selling off their own estates in medium-sized blocks.

The new and more radical Allende government of 1970–73 used the Frei reform laws energetically to expropriate much more land on all estates over the equivalent of 40 basic irrigated hectares (or BIH), which could be 400 hectares of poor hill land. Allende's reform work affected over five million ha, 45% of the productive capacity of the country, converting most land into *asentamientos,* but also creating a few state farms. There was, however, a constant tendency for the farms to become individual holdings, and most work was done on these. By 1973, there were 75 000 families who had benefited from reform, mostly the estate workers but also some others who had been allowed to join them in the cooperatives.

Pinochet's military government has since returned perhaps half of the lands to their original owners, but much was accomplished by the reform, and new independent small farmers were much helped by special provision of credit facilities and the use of state-backed marketing agencies to handle the products. The reform virtually abolished *latifundios,* units equivalent to over 80 irrigated ha, comprising in 1980 only 5.6% of farmland instead of 55.3% as in 1956. The number of cash tenants and *inquilinos,* labour tenants, who were 21.3% of all farmers in 1965, has been reduced to near zero.

The overall result of the 1960s and 1970s of most significance, however, has not been the rise of small farmers, but of medium-sized commercial farmers, both as a result of reform as outlined above, and because the Pinochet handback also entailed some sale of medium-sized farms when they were not returned to the owners. The group of farmers with 40–60 ha irrigated equivalent has grown from 7.1% of farm land to 19.6% in the period 1965–77. While basic food production has declined rather sharply and imports have gone up, commercial farmers producing fruit and vegetables for export markets, using intensive mechanization and standard packing acceptable to exporters, have been most successful.

Peru

As in Chile, reform here failed to provide land resources for the landless and, given the dense rural population in the Sierra, it could never have done this. A need for some solution to the problem of land was evident from the 1950s, when there were farm strikes in both coast and Sierra, followed by invasion of some large estates during 1960–63, leading to reform laws in 1963 and 1964. The military government of 1968–80 undertook a major agrarian reform, distributing 7.8 million ha or 40% of total farmland to 338 thousand families.

A highly complex reformed set of units was envisaged. On the coast, plantation-type estates were the first object of reform, and in 1969 were successfully converted into production cooperatives, which continued to operate as before, merely sharing the profits amongst permanent workers and leaving out seasonal labourers. In the Sierra, broader units of thousands of hectares, the SAIS or Agrarian Societies, were made out of both haciendas and adjacent properties, trying to set up here services such as seed and fertilizer provision. This was an effort to overcome the fact that simply splitting up the haciendas would give land to only a minority of rural dwellers, just as the production of cooperatives on the coast only gave shares to permanent workers. In areas where traditional community structure had survived, a third type of unit was to be created, the Community Cooperatives. In general, post-reform farming was to be collective rather than individual, as in Chile.

The mechanism of reform was to set limits above which land was expropriated, as in Chile. The coast had a 150 ha limit for irrigated land, and Sierra limits were between 15 and 55 ha of irrigated land or its productive equivalent. Compensation was paid, but the cash awards were often made useless by rapid inflation.

The experiment cannot be said to have failed entirely, as it did break up many large estates. But as in Chile, food production has failed to keep pace with population and the Sierra has particularly suffered. On the coast, plantation agriculture was not disturbed, and food production also increased for the growing urban markets here, compared to the poorer, stagnant Sierra.

One set of problems is to do with the appropriateness of reform. One calculation was that only 20% of Sierra estates was suited to redistribution in a physical sense. Elsewhere, poor soils and steep slopes made the large unit the only viable one. In any case, subdivision had already taken place, in the central and southern Sierra, in the sense that tenants were already farming all the hacienda land, and the home farm worked by tenant labour had disappeared. In these circumstances there was no land to be handed out to the landless or near-landless. After reform many farm labourers had to emigrate to the cities, mostly to Lima, moving their problem

4 A vineyard in Mendoza Province, Argentina. Irrigation culture is vital to the economy of many Latin American countries

from country to town. There were further problems with the introduction of communal work — this ideal of traditional native society was laudable and potentially an efficient solution, but communal farming had died out over much of the Sierra and the peasant motivation had become the market.

Peru's reform was more thoroughgoing than most — it also included local organization. Existing unions were banned and a new organization was created, the National Agrarian Confederation. The road was towards the Yugoslav model of local self-management of each rural unit, and a substantial effort was made to educate the rural population to this.

Bolivia
In this country the situation of the peasantry was perhaps worse than in most countries, with near-feudal conditions of work. One antecedent of reform was the revival of the indigenous community, recognized and guaranteed by a new constitution of 1938, after centuries of deprivation by landlords. Forced and non-salaried labour was abolished in 1945, though it went on clandestinely. A revolution took place in 1952, leading to agrarian reform in 1953. Given the degree of repression which had existed, the violence of the revolution was not surprising, including many forced takeovers of haciendas and killing of landlords.

The reform provided for some compensation in state bonds of dubious worth, but often no compensation was paid. The lands were expropriated above a size limit varying according to zone. Estates which could show they had done some modernization and made investments were allowed to continue with only a one-third reduction in size. The post-reform units were to be individual farms, or peasant unions (*sindicatos*) replacing the old communities.

In production terms the Revolution has not been unsuccessful. In the early years, there was much comment on the apparent decline in production, but this seems to have been due to legal problems over the disposal of some haciendas, and to a breakdown in the traditional marketing system, which meant reduced quantities of food were reaching the urban markets. The table at the beginning of this chapter shows a continuing growth in production, which is not due to growing farm area in the Oriente — there has been

only 3.4% increase in the arable and permanent crop area of Bolivia from 1974 to 1983.

In tenurial terms, the reform has had mixed results. In some parts, the land of the *haciendas* was already divided up among tenant farmers, leaving little as home farm which could be split up when reformed; only 27% of the land was the owner's home farm in the *haciendas* surveyed by Carter in the 1960s. Nor did Carter find that the problem of fragmentation of farm holdings had been solved. In pre-reform days, through a constant division under inheritance laws, and through conscious selection of plots in different fields, the peasants had had many different plots, up to ninety per family. The reform did not seek to combine these in a more rational fashion, nor to sort out the problems of most families holding some land in common, and some privately.

Overview of reform
The preceding descriptions have given some idea of the elements found in agrarian reform programmes. That only three examples are cited speaks for the difficulty of enacting any thoroughgoing reform laws, and these examples show that the reality of reform is far short of the ideals. In some countries, there has been a process of improving farm productivity and elimination of the old systems which has not been due to agrarian reform direct, but to the threat of it, since the criticism has always been of the underused *latifundios*. In many countries these have gone through their conversion into modern commercial farms, mechanized and with few employees. Throughout the Andean countries, the tenants have constituted a threat too, because of their claims for lands, occasional strikes and land invasions, and owners have sought to expel them altogether and replace them with machinery as a less problematic alternative. As minimum wages have been increasingly insisted on, this is an economic alternative too. This conversion to capitalist farming has had a tremendous expulsion effect, sending thousands of farm workers to the cities to look for employment.

In terms of the two major elements of the problem, farm size and tenure, the greater success has been with the latter. The old semi-feudal forms of tenure have not disappeared but have become increasingly infrequent. Farm size distribution has not become even, however, and the *minifundio* problem is aggravated by fragmentation of farms, as we have seen in the case of Bolivia. The farm size structure of Paraguay is illustrative. Some sub-division of the great ranches in the Chaco took place through inheritance and splitting, but more small farms were created in the east through colonization of the forest area. In neither case was reform involved. The overall pattern is still a *minifundio/latifundio* division.

PARAGUAYAN FARM SIZES, 1956–81

Category (ha)	1956	1981	1956	1981
	% farm units		% area	
0–20	86.1	78.6	4.1	5.5
20–50	8.7	14.4	2.0	4.4
50–500	3.8	5.7	4.6	8.8
500–1000	0.4	0.4	2.4	3.3
1000–20 000	1.0	0.8	34.5	36.5
20 000	0.1	0.1	52.5	41.5

Source: Kleinpenning, 1984.

A principal criticism of reform is that it has not solved the secondary problems mentioned earlier. In most cases, governments were ready to grant land, but were unable or unwilling to do anything about credit provision, transport and other infrastructure, marketing arrangements, or social provision such as schools or hospitals.

COLONIZATION PROJECTS

Agrarian reform is the restructuring of farming on areas already occupied, with the aims of improving the lot of the rural poor and of increasing farm production. In the eyes of some governments both aims may be met by the alternative of colonizing new farm lands, so that it is necessary to ask here whether such an alternative can be viable.

Colonization has a long history in the post-independence period of Latin America. In Argentina, thousands of South European migrants were made into colonists on the edge of the Humid Pampas in Santa Fe between 1850 and 1900. In Brazil, many settlers came into the southernmost states in the late nineteenth century, 1.4 million of them between 1887 and 1898, and many became colonist farmers. But European settlers were not easily attracted to the low tropics and twentieth century colonists of the Amazon Basin have been citizens of the various countries concerned, except for special cases as with Japanese in Paraguay, Bolivia and Brazil.

Most colonization involves poor native farmers, moving out from densely settled areas into virgin or long fallow land, often into a region of different soils and climate from what they knew, either as spontaneous colonists, i.e. colonists who move of their own accord as individuals and families, or as sponsored or directed colonists under a government programme.

We may identify three broad kinds of problem in colonization projects: the natural environment, the human material, and the organizational and technical problems of colonies. Dealing with these in turn, the physical environment problems include the enervating physiological effects of hot humid climates, which may reduce resistance to disease; the poor nutrient base of soils commented on in the first chapter; liability to flood and high water table in many regions; and tree weed invasion in natural forest lands. These physical problems are compounded by colonists' lack of experience. In the Colombian Putumayo, for example, colonists try to grow coffee though it is unsuited because of excessive moisture, lack of dry season, and poor soils; the farmers insist on it because it is a crop they are familiar with from the higher mountain slopes of their area of origin.

This leads us on to consider colonists character. Those best adapted are the spontaneous colonists, who migrate into the area because they know its potential, often have friends or relations in the area, and know about farming. These men stay longest in the frontier areas and are most successful as colonists. In contrast, former townsmen are not good colonists. In the Turen–Las Majaguas project in the Venezuelan Llanos 500 lots were set aside in the mid-1960s for slum dwellers from Caracas, as a gesture towards relief of their condition. By 1970 over 60% of these lots had been abandoned. Unrest and settler disputes have also been a problem in Las Majaguas, because the settlers were brought in from different areas with distinct cultural backgrounds, instead of making each group a homogeneous unit.*

Other disputes may occur, as for example in south-east Colombia, between spontaneous settlers who have entered the region without legal title to land, and colonists brought under government schemes. Another group conflict is between colonists and Indians, as has occured continuously in Brazil where ranchers have pushed tribal peoples off their traditional territories using the same tactics as the Wild West: threats followed by brute force.

Organizational problems are universal in settling new areas under government-directed schemes. Title to the land is not usually given at once, but made subject to conditions. In the Peruvian *montaña*, government surveyors have to survey the land before granting title, and survey costs may exceed the cost of the land. Size of holdings in planned colonies is often a difficulty. In Venezuela, a small colony at Barbacoas has been successful with only 5 ha holdings, because intensive vegetable and fruit crops could be grown and marketed in Barcelona. Further west in Barlovento, 5–10 ha holdings are farmed on a shifting basis, using a hectare or two at a time, because of tradition and the type of crops grown. In contrast 5 ha lots were too small for rice and maize farmers in Turen-Las Majaguas in the poorer soils of the western Venezuelan Llanos. Obviously considerable flexibility is required in this matter as in others. Organizational failings go much farther than farm size and title; as with land reform, it is not enough to hand out land, and lack of credit, machinery, good road access, planned settlements with services, are constant complaints.

Colonization in Bolivia's Oriente presents examples of some of the features mentioned. The areas affected are shown in the chapter on Bolivia (Chapter 9). As an alternative to agricultural development in the *altiplano*, colonization here is more justifiable than in other countries, simply because there is no more good land available in the highlands. The peasants' response has been either migration to the city, a wholly alien solution for Indian groups who may speak no Spanish, in the case of the Aymará communities, or frontier colonization in the

Oriente. There had long been a trickle of *spontaneous colonization* in the Oriente; this was amplified in 1960 by the first directed colonization. Directed colonization of the three main areas, the Alto Beni, Chimoré and Santa Cruz regions, was begun in 1960, with IDB financing from 1963. The programme was ambitious in first aiming at 1.8 million ha and including settlement, housing, land clearing, fencing, water supply and roads. Roads in the event took up over half the public budget on the programme.

Physical problems

In Santa Cruz and Chimoré, some of the lands were infertile, only suitable for cattle and not arable, others liable to flooding. Settlers coming from the highlands were unable to manage these infertile areas properly. There was no satisfactory system of combining tree and ground crops, for example, so as to protect the soil, and a monoculture of rice or maize has tended to develop on small farms. If floods are effectively combated, then soil fertility will present itself as the main problem, since the annual floods improve soil fertility with rich new silt. In the Alto Beni, the foothills of the Andes at 500–1000m, there is rainfall of 1500 mm and steep slopes, inducing erosion. Farming has evolved over 30 years towards bush fallow and abandonment. Land at Caranavi lasts in cultivation for 10–12 years.

Economic problems

The Alto Beni area, though so close to La Paz, is effectively isolated from it by high mountains of the Eastern Cordillera, and the road into the colonisation region remained unsurfaced, a mud track, until the late 1970s. Elsewhere, there are regional roads but no roads right to the farms. Access to credit and marketing facilities has been poor, the same complaint as is found among agrarian reform beneficiaries. The transport crisis is amplified by the choice of crops — rice and maize are both heavy and bulky per unit value; here it would have been advantageous to find a high value crop. The attraction of coca, which the government tries unsuccessfully to limit, is evident.

Social problems

In the Oriente, a mixture of highland Indians speaking Quechua, Aymará and Spanish, and foreigners from as far afield as Japan and

*R.C. Eidt, 'Agrarian reform and the growth of new rural settlements in Venezuela', *Erdkunde*, 29, (1975), pp.118–33

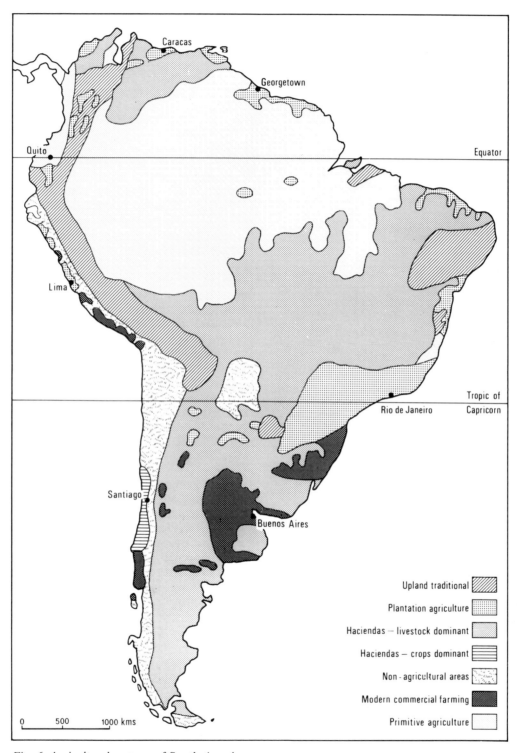

Fig. 6 Agricultural systems of South America

Taiwan, make social communication difficult, and it is not aided by the general lack of schools, meeting places and service centres. In the North American West, the highly mixed ethnic character of the frontier settlers was supposed to have had a good overall effect, making each farmer equal and democratizing society. But this was probably a long-term effect, and in the shorter term of twenty years the social problems seem to be more important.

Many of the problems are those of *directed colonization* schemes as opposed to *spontaneous colonization*. In the latter, only colonists with some appropriate skills are likely to settle, and a natural process of selection of the best lands, best access, occurs. Service centres are built up 'naturally' and a community evolves.

Other issues

A broad question remains as to the overall desirability of colonization versus agrarian reform. In the short term, colonization may be successful in allowing surplus farm population to be settled, and even in supplying an increasing amount of agricultural production. In the period 1974–83 two South American countries have been successful in incorporating large amounts of new land into farming. Paraguay is one, with a 57.3% increase, and Brazil is the other, with 23.1%. Unfortunately there are political overtones in these two cases. Brazil has long sought to expand its occupied territory, against any expansion of its neighbouring countries, by settling its frontier. In this way it has in the past been able to take land claimed by the Spanish-speaking neighbours. Brazilian expansionism may also be responsible for a large part of Paraguay's eastern settlement, where Brazilian farmers have been encouraged and allowed to settle in the forest west of the Parana.

A quite different critique is that colonization does not solve the structural problems of the countries concerned. All too frequently, large estates and irregular tenure forms are carried down, from the old settled areas into the new colonies, through such devices as monopoly of the transport and marketing of farmers' goods.

TECHNOLOGICAL SOLUTIONS

It may be argued that neither agrarian reform nor colonization offers an appropriate solution to agrarian problems. In fact, these will be solved as in the developed countries by technological breakthroughs that will improve farmer productivity and welfare without any major governmental intervention. Simplifying a little, we may describe two alternative routes, one which is ecologically based, the other based on high technology.

Agro-forestry

Ecological solutions involve many different aspects, such as the use of biogas and sugar alcohol instead of fossil fuels, the restriction of arable cultivation in tropical plains to the alluvial floodplain, leaving the uplands to low-intensity uses. In this section we concentrate on one aspect, the use of forests, not simply as sources for sawmills or paper factories, but as integral parts of rural life.

In this chapter, mention has already been made of the aboriginal people's multiple use of forest lands, such as storied canopies, mixture of trees and annual crops, and the idea of forest fallow after cultivation has ceased. There are also some special uses of trees which need to be encouraged. Over most of the Andes, firewood is the principal use of wood, and trees able to produce many shoots small enough to be cut with machetes are at a premium. Eucalyptus, with its coppicing ability, is one good contender here. Other species are needed, however, to provide charcoal, still much used in city and countryside. At high altitudes, rows of trees planted at right angles to predominant winds can protect cattle directly and allow more intensive cattle farming. In intensive farming areas, fruit trees may be planted for their crops and as partial shade; in hill lands, trees or more probably shrubs, such as the widespread agave and Spanish broom, can provide a firm terrace edge to prevent terrace collapse and gullying. Throughout farmlands, acacias provide nitrogen to the soil, being leguminous plants, and in tropical grasslands they also give much-needed shade and nourishment (from their beans) to cattle.

An example of present-day agriculture-forestry relations which demonstrates these points is from the southern Sierra of Ecuador. Here a regional development agency, realizing the value of forestry in diversifying the local economy, has been distributing plantation trees at nominal prices to all interested farmers. The

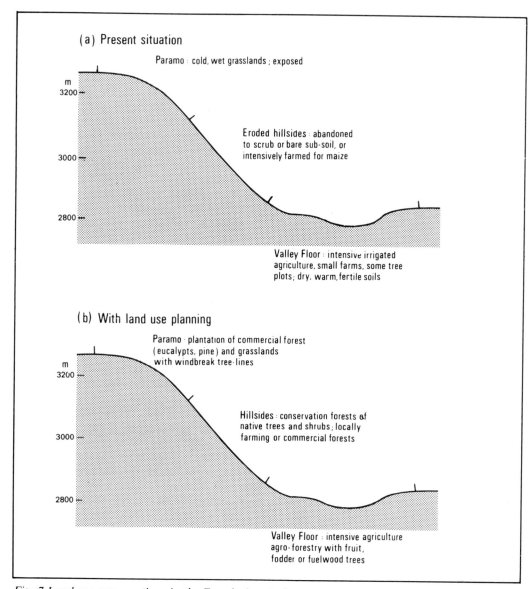

(a) Present situation

Paramo : cold, wet grasslands ; exposed

m
3200

3000

2800

Eroded hillsides : abandoned
to scrub or bare sub-soil, or
intensively farmed for maize

Valley Floor : intensive irrigated
agriculture, small farms, some tree
plots; dry, warm, fertile soils

(b) With land use planning

Paramo · plantation of commercial forest
(eucalypts, pine) and grasslands
with windbreak tree-lines

m
3200

3000

2800

Hillsides : conservation forests of
native trees and shrubs ; locally
farming or commercial forests

Valley Floor : intensive agriculture
agro-forestry with fruit,
fodder or fuelwood trees

*Fig. 7 Land use cross sections in the Ecuadorian Andes
(a) — Present Situation   (b) — With Land Use Planning*

pattern it was thus creating is shown in Figure 7(a). Larger valley farms which could afford to plant trees, or sought to reduce their labour needs, were planting trees, while the rest of the valley floors were intensively cultivated, as were the hillsides except where these were precipitously steep or heavily eroded and consequently abandoned. Above 3000 metres' altitude, the flatter *paramo* lands were in permanent grass up to the limits of vegetation.

For this environment a more ecologically balanced solution was suggested by the writer (Morris, 1985) to create plantations only on the wet *paramo* where they would not compete for water with irrigation canals or with a major HEP installation, the Paute dam opened in 1983, destined to produce 1500 megawatts, and where erosion would not be a problem. The plantation trees, pines and eucalypts, were seen to have little soil protection value because of their toxic leaf fall which inhibits the growth of a protective undergrowth. On the lower steep valley sides protection measures such as terracing, leguminous crops, shrub planting and conservation areas were advisable; while on the valley floors, only immediately useful trees should be planted such as firewood trees and fruit trees. This pattern is indicated in Fig. 7(b).

The Green Revolution

The previous section concerns low-technology solutions which conserve limited resources. A relatively high-technology solution has been tried in some areas, based on plant breeding to find more productive varieties of basic foods for production in Third World countries.

This Green Revolution began in Mexico in 1943 under a programme financed by the Rockefeller Foundation. Initial attention was given to wheat and maize, and as wheat did well, this was concentrated on for the next twenty years. In Latin America, only a limited success has been had with these wonder crops. Wheat has been successfully introduced, replacing traditional varieties in Colombia, and rice is being improved throughout the northern Andean countries. There has been no breakthrough with maize, or manioc, or potatoes, which illustrates some important limitations of the approach.

Rice and often wheat are grown by commercial farmers, who produce using machinery and are ready to make investments in fertilizer, pesticides and irrigation equipment. For the Green Revolution crops, a high level of these inputs is required if output is to be satisfactory. Maize, and still more potatoes in the Andes, are subsistence crops, just as is manioc in the tropical lowlands. In the case of both maize and potatoes, a great number of varieties are already in use, adapted to different ecological niches, levels of soil fertility, water provision, etc. It is possible to produce higher-yielding varieties, but not ones which will be able to grow under the conditions which the present varieties have to endure.

In general, we may summarize this section by saying that technological advances may be useful, even necessary, as an aid to improvement in farm production in South America. But they cannot be a total answer, because the structural problems which are responsible for rural poverty are not solved by them. A desirable solution would thus be a programme of agrarian reform, accompanied by the introduction of new techniques and land use planning, so that the new beneficiaries of reform would be able to increase production rapidly and ensure a successful enterprise, not one which they might have to abandon to the big farmers because of erosion or falling yields or lack of access to markets.

As regards colonization and agrarian reform, the first may be dismissed quickly as only a palliative to the problem, though it possibly constitutes a long-term national source of important tropical products in countries like Bolivia which had only a slight use of its tropical lands before. As to agrarian reform, it has been widely criticized on many counts. Some of the criticisms are internal to the mechanisms of reform, regarding the way in which lands were divided up, compensation paid, or aid given to post-reform farmers. Often enough, the process of reform went on for too short a time, before it was modified or totally stopped by a change of government, so that such imperfections are inevitable.

More important is a critique of the whole idea of "reformism". One political view of it is that it is within, and a product of, the capitalist system, and is a way in which the system is legitimized, made acceptable to the electorate. The implication of such a critique is that only a more radical reform, perhaps along the Cuban lines, which nationalized much of the agricultural sector, would be acceptable.

4. Industrial Infrastructure and Manufacturing

Latin America is not generally thought of as a major manufacturing region, but as provider of minerals and other raw materials, as well as farm products, to the world. Two world wars, however, and the trade restrictions and tariff barriers they engendered in order to protect home industries, have made for the emergence of new industrial centres of some importance, on a domestic and even a world scale. In the present chapter a review is made of these industries and of the transport, mineral and power infrastructure which they require. Agricultural resources which are used in industry are discussed separately in the chapter on agriculture.

MINERAL INDUSTRIES

Manufacturing industries rely on a variety of raw materials, fuel and power resources, for the most part highly localized and costly to make available at the sites of consumption. In South America, many minerals are mined primarily for export markets, so that locations for mining near the coast have been at a premium, and the interior regions are still little developed. Thus, of the two major regions with metalliferous ores — the Andes and the Brazilian Shield mass — the second has been tapped only to a slight extent, for it occupies a largely interior position. The intervening plains of sedimentation have no major metal ore deposits to speak of, so that

Argentina, Paraguay and Uruguay, dominantly plains countries, have unimportant metal mining industries compared to the wealth of Peru, Chile or Brazil.

The manner of mineral extraction varies greatly in the continent, even within one country, for the great modern mining companies have not displaced traditional small-scale producers. Often giant mines owned by foreign capital and producing efficiently can be seen alongside one-man enterprises using pick and shovel to scratch a meagre existence from the subsoil. The great companies have their own concentration plants for processing ore, their own transport arrangements for exporting it, their own power, water and fuel supplies, sometimes their own housing for employees. Thus the company forms an enclave of the world economy within a peasant landscape, a state within a state in extreme examples, where education, wages, health and welfare are attended to at a different level from the rest of the country, and it is natural that such a situation should arouse the antipathy of governments and people, forming an easy target for nationalistic outbursts and calls for expropriation.

In effect there arises a dual economy, in minerals as in agriculture, one sector well supplied with capital and modern, the other, composed of the poor single miners, completely without capital and relying on the only factor available, personal labour. Poor miners are the products of the local economy, where a whole set of different costs for factors is to be found, and where the cost of labour and capital must be compared, not with costs in other producing countries as in the case of the large mining company, but with labour and capital costs in agriculture and industry within the country.

An example: Chilean copper

The Chilean copper industry before the expropriations of 1972 is illustrative of the situation. Here, at the large mines owned by North American interests, was produced 90% of all Chilean copper, yielding substantial excise tax income to the state and employing 15 000 workers. In addition, there were 400 medium-sized companies with modern capital structure and thousands of one-man or very small operations. Medium and small mining employed about 40 000 persons, but produced only 10% of the copper. The dilemma faced by Chile, and in different form by all countries in Latin America, was whether to allow foreign companies to continue and maximize short-term revenues, or to nationalize and have full control of the mines.

The aims of expropriation would be to help employment by using more local manpower, to help training of local engineers and administrators (the upper professional element in the big companies was normally foreign), and to direct all the profits into the national economy instead of having them siphoned off to the foreign headquarters of the company. It was also thought in the Chilean case that the level of production could be controlled, to meet national economic needs rather than the ups and downs of the international markets.

A national company, CODELCO, has been created to manage the four largest mines: Chuquicamata, El Teniente, El Salvador and Andina, which is a typical move in Latin America, from a multinational to a state-owned enterprise. It does not solve the problem of small mines.

Some major ores

COPPER

Copper is the most important of the region's metal ores, produced very largely to feed international markets. Chile, for example, exports all but 3% of her copper to other countries. Concentrations of copper associated with great

magmas are to be found throughout the Southern and Central Andes, and now Chile is being challenged in copper production by Peru, which in 1955 had only 1% of world production, but in 1974 nearly 3%, a result of foreign investment on a massive scale, opening up three major mines in the south of the country with reasonable access to the coast.

Massive investment is in fact the key to copper developments, because copper occurs largely as a 1 per cent or even smaller element mixed into a ground mass from which it can only be separated using modern large-scale methods. The mining of large volumes of ore also requires heavy investment in machinery. Thus copper mining has not yet come to Argentina and Bolivia, on a large scale, for want of permits to the international companies, or because of political uncertainties in the country which deter investors. Both these countries have known reserves of disseminated copper capable of supporting a major industry, and in the case of Argentina there are plans for a long-term development of the resource by the raising of internal capital.

TIN

Bolivia is the only large tin producer in the continent, and tin still dominates the Bolivian economy, providing the greatest single contribution towards the country's foreign exchange. Like Chile or Venezuela, Bolivia has had a one-product economy with the resultant crises and booms that this engenders. In the late nineteenth century the industry was developed here when there were no other world producers, and the difficulties of transport to the exterior were overcome, with rail lines to the Pacific to take out this vital ore. Tin came at a useful moment in time, when the decline of silver mining, because of a gradual disappearance of bimetallism and acceptance of the gold standard, was causing gloom and crisis in the local mining industry — an earlier example of the effects of a one-product economy.

Large investments soon became necessary in Bolivia because of the depth of deposits and low grade of ores, so that three large companies, dominated by three leaders, Patiño, Hochschild and Aramayo, made the tin-mining oligopoly, and comparison with other countries became more direct over the years as these three companies came under foreign ownership. Small miners were never excluded, but their production was small and their control of the industry nil.

In recent decades the inefficiencies of the enormous industry compared with its world competitor, Malaya, which works accessible alluvial ores, have made for a modern situation of economic crisis. The industry, representing U.S., Chilean, British and Swiss interests, was taken over in 1952 after the revolution, but the basic physical problem of high extraction costs from deep mines and poor ores could not be by-passed or overcome.

In recent years a major effort at diversification and emphasis on the ores which are associated with tin — notably wolfram, bismuth, lead, zinc and silver — has had some effect in solving this problem. The share of tin in exports has decreased from 70% in 1963–5 to 50% in 1971 and 38% in 1983. Petroleum and natural gas are helping this movement, and cotton from the agricultural sector.

IRON

Both production and markets in the case of iron are somewhat different from tin or copper: there are many producing countries all round the world; the mineral is not stockpiled in the same way as tin or copper; and there are substantial markets growing up in Latin America itself. All these are conditions leading to somewhat more secure and steady mining, though exports to industrial countries still account for a large share of production. As late as 1970, Chile, Brazil, Peru and Venezuela were all exporting 90% of their ore despite large domestic industries. Thus coastal sites and the involvement of international companies have been normal.

Another factor influencing iron ore development has been that of national security. In Argentina, for example, low-grade ore from Sierra Grande (fig. 28) in Patagonia is used to supply the national steel industry though total delivered costs can never match those of Brazilian ores. For the most part, South American ores are of high grade, reaching over 65% iron content in the major Brazilian, Chilean and Peruvian deposits, which fits them well for the international markets. The Brazilian deposits benefit from the fact that they are associated with manganese, the most important of the ferro-alloys.

Only one major iron ore deposit of the interior is likely to be developed in the near future, the Mutún deposit of southeast Bolivia. This remote ore has no markets in Bolivia or nearby Brazil which has more than adequate domestic supplies, but it is close to the river Paraguay, and experimental shipments by barge down to the San Nicolás steel mills of Argentina are being made. For most other interior iron ores which may be discovered, the transport costs are likely to prevent development.

Where other conditions are favourable, the use of an iron ore below 50% iron may be warranted; the Colombian industry provides us with an example in the works at Paz del Río, built up at a site with ready access to coking coal, limestone and water all within the Chicamocha valley, and with fair access to the principal market of the country, Bogotá, for the steel produced.

BAUXITE

World aluminium production is mostly in the hands of a few great multinational firms, which extract bauxite in the tropics to convert it into alumina in the rich countries, and then process it further into aluminium and products. Discovery and development of low-cost energy sources, growing markets within Latin America, and governmental pressures, have combined to change the scene and produce a more complete industry in the region.

Bauxite is a product of long weathering of tropical soils. Silicate rocks in tropical wet-dry climates have alkalis and silica washed out of them, leaving iron and aluminium sesquioxides. These accumulate as thick layers at or near the soil surface, and these layers can readily be mined. They are widely distributed in Latin America and have not been well surveyed because they far exceed present needs, but seem to be most prominent on ancient planation surfaces from the Tertiary geological period, cut into the Guyana Shield north of the Amazon. Surinam and Guyana are major producers in S. America, and have developed under the aegis of international investment. Now Venezuela has decided to develop major bauxite ores located on the edge of her section of the Guyana shield, to be processed at Ciudad Guyana. Brazil is also developing bauxite extraction in connection with its Amazonia policy, near the Carajas iron ore

PRODUCTION OF SOME LEADING MINERALS, 1982

| Country | METALS | | | Bauxite | Coal | FUELS | |
	Tin*	Iron ore*	Copper ore			Crude oil	Natural gas†
Argentina	0.3	389	–	–	515	36 635	13 403
Bolivia	26.8	5	2.3	–	–	1 649	3 123
Brazil	(8.3)	81 559	19.2	4 186	4 574	18 879	1 809
Chile	–	3 874	1 255.1	–	994	2 912	1 177
Colombia	–	205	–	–	5 550	10 651	5 933
Ecuador	–	–	0.8	–	–	15 625	121
Guyana	–	–	–	(953)	–	–	–
Paraguay	–	–	–	–	–	–	–
Peru	(1.7)	3 403	369.5	–	100	13 989	1 494
Surinam	–	–	–	3 060	–	–	–
Uruguay	–	(3)	–	–	–	–	–
Venezuela	–	(7 258)	–	–	47	145 969	23 337

* Metal content of ore, ( ) Estimated.
Fuels are recorded in thousand metric tons coal equivalent. Other figures are in thousand metric tons.
†Natural gas figures exclude gas flared and vented at well head, and gas reinjected to maintain oil pressure. These categories account for much Venezuelan gas.
Source: United Nations Statistical Yearbook, 1982

and Tucurui power developments. Intermediate processing of the ore to alumina is also done in Surinam and Venezuela, which latter country has built up a state aluminium industry and is beginning to produce finished aluminium as well, as is Brazil.

OTHER METALS
Associated with the major ores in the ore mix, or associated regionally because of the type of geological structures obtaining, are a variety of minor ores. The bismuth, wolfram, antimony and lead of Bolivia have been noted. In the case of Chilean copper, as in North American copper, there is an important associated production of molybdenum, and Chile, with 15 000 tonnes out of the world's total of 62 500 tonnes molybdenum content in 1983, is second only to the United States in the free world. Brazil holds a similarly important position with respect to manganese, in 1983 producing 1.40 million tonnes manganese ore out of a world total of 22 million tonnes. Finally, Peru is still a world leader in silver production, with 1739 tonnes out of a world total of 13 569 tonnes in 1983. It should be noted that none of these minor ores weighs heavily in the overall national production structure. Peru, for example, only earns about

7% of GNP from mining, and this is spread over a number of minerals, from important and large mines of iron through copper, lead and zinc to silver and many minor products. Minerals, for nearly all countries of the region, are important because of the export trade and foreign currency earnings they provide.

FUEL AND ENERGY RESOURCES

Among fuel sources, as the above table demonstrates, petroleum has an overwhelming dominance in South America. Coals are produced by Brazil, Chile and Colombia on a moderate scale, but even in these countries the role of coal as a fuel is very much subordinate to that of oil and gas. In most cases the coals are relatively low-grade sub-bituminous types and not suited to the production of metallurgical coke, so that there has been little spur to their exploitation. Many small Tertiary basins with low-grade coal in the Andean countries lie unused for want of effective demand.

It is fortunate considering this reliance on petroleum that supplies are reasonably abundant. Until recent years production was heavily concentrated in the hands of Venezuela, and this country still has the lion's share of reserves and production. Some countries, like Paraguay, the Guianas and Uruguay, which have not yet found oil, and Ecuador, which only found significant quantities recently in dramatic discoveries in the Oriente following decades of drilling dry holes, have seen their twentieth-century economies suffer for want of ready fuel and power in comparison with the oil producers. In the long term, countries such as Argentina and Bolivia, owning large sections of sedimentary geological basins between the Andes and the Shield where oil is likely, may produce considerable amounts and be able to become major exporters. Brazil has high hopes too, based on recent offshore finds reported in the northeast and near Rio, but Petrobras, the state oil firm, only produces a quarter of national requirements at present.

Oil and Venezuela

This country is the closest approach to a Middle Eastern 'oilarchy', with one product providing 90% of exports, though even in this extreme situation the mining sector of the country only contributes in direct form about 8% of GNP (1979). Overdependence on a single product has become a matter for concern as the oil wells produce increasingly heavy oil, as international firms have been excluded from production, and as the search for an alternative to oil for governmental revenue continues to bring up no real answers. Over time, too, Venezuela's economic strength relative to its neighbours is being eroded because of the stagnation in production since 1960. Whereas in 1960 Venezuela contributed 32.7% of all LAFTA exports, in 1969 it was 22.6%, symptomatic of a general economic decline prior to the rapid increase in oil prices of 1974. Venezuela is now only gradually shifting her economy away from oil because of the OPEC price rises; diversification of exports has been a minor feature and industrialization has been advanced by using oil in petrochemical industries, on lake Maracaibo and the Caribbean coast.

In Peru, expropriation of oil firms held back the development of rich country in the Oriente for a while, though the selvas is now being developed and foreign firms are working under contract to Petroperu, the state oil firm, an Argentine firm for example helping to build an oil pipeline from the selvas out to the Pacific at Bayovar. In Bolivia, expropriation came after a period of oil development, and recuperation of production under national control has been possible. For Argentina, there has been an alternation of permissive attitudes towards foreign participation and harsh controls or expulsion. This has done nothing to encourage new foreign investment though it has made the state company YPF an experienced oil producer and marketer.

In Ecuador, political thinking at present is towards increasing national control of an industry which has recently become prominent, and Venezuela has taken complete control of her production, refining and petrochemicals industries. Harsher attitudes towards foreign investment are of course part of a world pattern emanating from the Middle East, which Latin America is able to follow with difficulty because her industries are younger and less experienced. Only Venezuela and Argentina with strong and mature national oil companies, can afford to exclude foreign finance and technology from the industry.

Other oil resources

There are major oil reserves which are currently untapped because of various difficulties in their exploitation. The two most important types are submarine oil deposits and heavy oils. The existence of offshore oil is now known in many areas, and the oil is of course exploited in Lake Maracaibo by Venezuela. There is in addition much gas associated with this oil; the gas is only partially used, half of it being flared off at wellheads. Further north oil is thought to be abundant in the Gulf of Venezuela and the southern Caribbean geological basins off Venezuela's north coast. Brazil has begun to discover offshore oil near to Rio, in comparatively deep water, which will slow down exploitation.

Oil shales are significant in Rio Grande do Sul in Brazil, as yet unused, and there are oil sands in the strip of country just north of the Orinoco in Venezuela, where there is some experimental production.

New alternatives to oil

Most non-oil energy produced in the area is hydroelectric, with many massive schemes that are mentioned in the regional chapters of this book. There is still scope for much more hydroelectric power to be developed, though it becomes increasingly expensive as the most economic sites are used up. The search for alternatives is on in earnest.

Hydroelectric power (HEP) is ecologically acceptable, as it runs on a readily renewed form of solar power, rather than on fossil stores of this power. It can, however, create ecological hazards (see Chapter 1, section on ecology and conservation) if it is not handled with care. Another major energy source in the Amazon Basin ought to be wood. Waste wood products such as sawdust may be used to fire steam engines, as is done in some sawmilling operations in Brazil, using ancient engines brought north from the Parana pine forests as these became exhausted.

Atomic power is an alternative to conventional sources and has long-term potential. Argentina has long had a working reactor at Cordoba and is now entering a state of nuclear self-sufficiency, from provision of uranium from Mendoza, to heavy water manufacture and to the design and construction of generators. She is now aiding Peru in the latter's first attempts to generate nuclear power. Brazil is next in line after Argentina, having a major nuclear energy programme but one which has suffered many delays. In 1975 Brazil signed a contract with West German companies for a complete integrated set of plants, the first at Angra dos Reis near Rio. Brazil has large uranium reserves, and an urgent need to substitute alternative power sources for her oil imports.

A non-conventional source of power is gasohol or vegetable alcohol (methanol) which has been developed in Brazil. Surplus cane sugar is mixed in large tanks with yeasts which convert it into alcohol, then the product is run off. This product is already being improved by continuous production methods to replace the batch method, and by use of more alcohol-productive strains of yeast. In February 1986, however, the Brazilian government withdrew, at least temporarily, its support for the cane alcohol programme, when 2.4 million of the 8.2 million cars on the roads had alcohol engines. Without subsidy, the alcohol is more expensive than petrol, and a promising trend may have been seriously checked.

Another large energy source is wood waste from timber mills, especially around the Amazon Basin. Guyana is using this waste in a thermal electricity generator, solving simultaneously problems of waste disposal and producing ash which is a good mineral fertilizer. There is also plant used for reducing wood chips to gas in a gasifier for local consumption in forestry areas that are remote from alternative supplies of fuel. Sugar cane mills are notoriously poor users of their waste, which could be used to produce energy. The bagasse, which is the residue from crushing, is either unused or partially burnt inefficiently for the mill's own supplies. It could form a major energy supply in cane-producing regions.

Small-scale energy sources that can be used without the need for expensive long-distance transmission lines are at a premium in rural areas. Throughout tropical S. America insolation levels are high enough to justify the use of solar power, which could be used directly, without electric power generators, for drying grain, desalination of water, heating of houses and cooking. In some frontier areas, the availability of large amounts of vegetation from forest clearance makes biogas a viable alternative for domestic use.

In the poorer countries a most important present-day energy source is firewood, providing 90% of the energy used in some rural parts of Brazil and Ecuador. Here the low-technology solution is not to change this pattern, but to provide more and better firewood sources rather than attempt electrification. In Andean countries the land around towns has been denuded of trees for many kilometres, and wood-sellers have to travel up to sixty kilometres to collect useful supplies. Small plantations of rapid-growing species, with the ability to coppice and form new shoots when cut at waist height, could well be introduced, though the usual tendency is for plantation to be only for commercial use in paper pulp mills.

Electric power

Provision of electric power is an important element of the manufacturing infrastructure, and the existence of a power grid is especially useful for small manufacturers who may use it as an external economy. This factor is often overlooked by observers familiar with the industrialized countries, where a grid is universally available, but the alternative, private small generating sets, often very inefficient, has to be accepted in many parts of Latin America. Reliable systems are by no means universal, and irregular supply or blackouts are frequent occurrences in all

ELECTRIC ENERGY : INSTALLED CAPACITY

Country	Year	Total	Thermal (megawatts)	HEP
Argentina	1970	6 691	6 082	609
	1982	13 480*	8 464	4 646
Bolivia	1970	267	95	172
	1982	508	225	283
Brazil	1970	11 233	2 405	8 828
	1982	38 904	6 012	32 892
Chile	1970	2 143	1 076	1 067
	1982	3 358	1 586	1 772
Colombia	1970	2 427	892	1 535
	1982	5 820	1 795	4 025
Ecuador	1970	304	198	106
	1982	1 315	1 072	243
Guyana	1970	160	160	–
	1982	165	163	2
Paraguay	1970	155	65	90
	1982	370	170	200
Peru	1970	1 677	754	923
	1982	3 237	1 320	1 917
Surinam	1970	260	80	180
	1982	400	200	200
Uruguay	1970	560	324	236
	1982	1 364	483	881
Venezuela	1970	3 172	2 264	908
	1982	9 312	6 312	3 000

Source: United Nations Statistical Yearbook, 1982.
* Argentina also has 370 megawatts of nuclear power capacity, the only country in this category in 1982.

countries of the South American continent. In addition, most countries do not operate their electric power systems under a single controlling body, but have a motley combination of federal, provincial, municipal and private concerns generating and transmitting electricity to the public.

THE EMERGENCE OF NATIONAL GRIDS
No really national networks of power lines are yet in existence, but there are several countries with grids on a macro-regional scale. In Argen-tina, high voltage lines connect the Pampas cities, Buenos Aires, Córdoba, Rosario and Santa Fé, to one another and to power sources on the Rio Negro and in Mendoza.

In Brazil, a network has also emerged in the industrial core, the Belo Horizonte–Rio–Sao Paulo triangle, fed by thermal and hydro plants in the core and also by the Ilha Solteira–Jupiá plants on the Paraná. Some planning has been done to integrate the network, a particularly desirable process in south east Brazil where many companies operate. In Minas Gerais, for example, 359 companies were in operation in 1950, most of which have now disappeared or amalgamated.

Colombia provides another example of regional integration, in the industrial triangle of Cali-Medellín-Bogotá, also linked to Barran-cabermeja on the Magdalena, but with no links to the northern thermal-based electricity of the Caribbean cities. Integration of a national scale here and elsewhere is necessary to balance and share loads so that one region can make up deficiencies elsewhere, or take up slack in demand.

A considerable amount of the electrical energy (as opposed to total energy) comes from HEP installations, much more than is common in the major industrial countries of the Northern Hemisphere. The table shows the dominance of hydroelectricity in the Brazilian, Uruguayan, Colombian, Peruvian and Bolivian economies. It also shows the spectacular growth of Brazil, while Venezuela also stands out in the way in which it has increased the participation of HEP in its installed capacity despite huge petroleum reserves, with the harnessing of the Caroní river. In the long term, the concentration of power from rivers is likely to be in two major regions, the middle Paraná valley, where the gorge section of the river produces excellent heads of water and basin shapes for retaining water, and where there is ample flow; and on the Sao Francisco river, notably at the Paulo Afonso Falls, where similar conditions obtain. In addi-tion there are thousands of individual sites in the Andes south of 35°S and north of 10°S, between which parallels the mountains are too dry for very large rivers. Sites on the middle Paraná, which are shared by Paraguay with her two large neighbours, Brazil and Argentina, are likely to convert this country into a major exporter of power within a few years.

5 At the Paulo Afonso Falls the river Sao Francisco leaves the Brazilian plateau, producing a highly concentrated hydro-electric potential which has been gradually harnessed since the 1950s

FOREST RESOURCES

On world vegetation maps South America is usually depicted as mainly forested, which is accurate enough in botanic terms, but must not be taken to imply a wealth of timber or other products merely awaiting the logger and sawmill. Over many parts collection of wild forest products is still the only way of utilizing the forest. In Brazil, *yerba mate*, from a member of the holly family which inhabits the Paraná Plateau region, carnauba wax from a palm growing in the northeast, Brazil nuts from the Amazon valley, are all still collected from wild trees. Not long ago, wild rubber from the Amazon was responsible for a brief but spectacular boom in the northern interior of Brazil, halted only by competition from plantations in the Old World.

Much forest has poor timber value as it is today, being composed of secondary growth following slash-and-burn farming for a few years by migratory subsistence farmers. Where cutting

has taken place, it has been destructive, with no replacement, and no concern for conservation. Farmers and ranchers seeking new pastures have set great fires on the forest frontiers of the continent, eliminating major tracts of virgin forest. Some attempts at conservation are being made now — in Argentina, with poor resources of timber, planted eucalyptus, willow and pine are replacing natural forests in the delta of the Paraná and in Misiones province in the northeast. In Chile, on the southern fringe of the central Mediterranean belt, there are increasing plantations of Monterrey pine (*Pinus radiata*) to serve the needs of pulp and paper mills. In Colombia, substantial plans exist to convert the central Magdalena valley into a great timber producer for sawmills and paper mills in Barrancabermeja. In this country, as in others, tree planting could well be incorporated into general plans for river basin management, to conserve soils and help control flooding and silting of the rivers, but organizational problems have prevented the emergence of this type of thinking in the continent.

A problem in forest use held in common with other tropical regions is that of species mix; much forest is selvas with enormous abundance of species, so that the exploitation of any one is quite difficult. This is part of the reason for concentration of forest utilization on two regions, southern Chile and the Paraná Plateau of southern Brazil. In the former, pine-laurel forests, with good stands of single species, are available, and make Chile an exporter of timber to other countries. In the latter, *Araucaria* forests produce wood suitable for either paper or construction; in foreign markets the wood is known as Paraná pine. Even in these major forest industries, there are problems of management.

Despite the large natural resource, much of the commercial production of timber, especially that of softwoods used for paper production and cheap constructional timbers, comes from plantations. In this context Chile is the outstanding contributor. Taking roundwood (unsawn) timber exports as an example, Chile started from a base of zero exports in 1974, to reach 17.67 million dollars' worth in 1981, the largest in all Latin America, and mostly from her Monterrey pine plantations of the Little South. Chile also exports some sawnwood and wood pulp, though for this and most items Brazil is expectably the most important provider. Brazil and Peru also produce about 150 000 tonnes each of pulp from bagasse.

TRANSPORTATION

The peripheral pattern

Although the continent is apparently entered quite easily along the major rivers, to judge superficially from the map, trade and population have always kept close to the coast so that most long-distance movement has been by sea. Important physical reasons exist for the coastal orientation of transport — the rivers are in fact not readily navigable by large vessels, in the case of the Amazon because of many rapids both on the main stream in its upper course and on all the principal tributaries. On the Paraná-Paraguay system, it is the silt load that deters river traffic, and makes the river fit only for shallow draft steamers and barges or rafts of timber. The line

of the Andes has also helped to orient countries outwards, to either the Pacific or the Atlantic ocean, and links across the mountains have always been difficult.

The other factors in peripherality of transport are economic ones; trade orientation has always been with overseas countries, predominantly those of North America or Europe, and transport has been improved mainly to serve this trade. The Spanish policy of divide and conquer meant in effect very little trade between her subject colonies, each of which required roads only to the ports leading to Iberia.

Railways

In colonial time, oxcarts and mule trains — or in difficult country human carriers—sufficed for transport. During the nineteenth century, the steamer, operating on the rivers, made some impact in changing and improving movement, but it was the railways, superseding river travel and taking new overland routes, that really

6 Peasants in a landscape — a scene on the middle São Francisco river. This river is still the principal means of transportation in the region, as well as a food and water resource to the local populace

changed the pattern. Rail development was made, however, during the period of maximum dependence on the transport of goods to and from South America, rather than among the member countries of the continent. Rails served more often as dividers of regions than connectors, for, while agricultural interiors might be linked to port cities, the ports remained separate and isolated from one another, as did the interior regions.

Railway expansion went through the stages of main line construction to ports, followed by feeder extensions to either side, but failed to complete a final stage of filling out a complete net with multiple-direction main through lines. Under nineteenth-century conditions there was no need for such filling out, given the export orientation of transport. In any case, construction was never unified under a national plan, but entrusted by provinces or governments to private, foreign firms whose responsibility was only for individual lines.

After the private construction stage, governments attempted to fill in the gaps by building 'developmental lines', but these were doomed to unprofitability as they were built quite generally with more political and strategic motivation than economic. Such developmental lines were built in the Argentine Chaco and the northwest, and in Patagonia to the south. Strategic interest accounts in part for the construction of the north Chilean line, which helped to link the nitrates region won in the War of the Pacific to the centre at Santiago. Similar interests were uppermost in the building of a railway through Brazil's far south in Rio Grande do Sul.

The end of the railway era

Figure 8 shows the cycle of railway development, starting in 1850, rising to a peak around 1930, and declining thereafter. In most countries it was almost inevitable that railways should lose importance, for they were composed, for example in Venezuela, of single-purpose lines linking mines with ports and dependent on a single type of trade. Construction was usually lightweight, often of a type which would not permit the later adoption of heavy diesel locomotives or of high running speeds. Rail gauges were varied, and some of them were even abandoned in the countries of manufacture so that new rolling stock could never be acquired easily, and transfers

from one gauge to another were another obstacle to development of a network.

After the Second World War, most railways were expropriated by local governments, which meant a further run-down of the equipment: worn-out track, ancient locomotives and rolling stock, inefficient and excessive manning of the railways. All these mean that the rail systems are great loss makers for their countries and have been losing traffic to roads. But is the railway age over?

In some cases, apparently not. In Brazil, where at present only the iron ore line down the Rio Doce valley is profitable, a 890 kilometre line has been built from the Serra dos Carajas iron ore body, discovered in 1967, near the Transamazon Highway, out to Itaqui near Sao Luís in the northeast, and the government has a five-year plan involving 3800 kilometres of new line, gauge widening of 3200 km, and electrification of 1439 km. Further north, Venezuela has plans for a railway system, with 3000 km of track, linking San Cristóbal in the west to Ciudad Guayana in the east, and connecting with the short line linking Barquisimeto to the coast at Puerto Cabello. Bolivia too is expanding her rail lines into the flat Oriente, linking to Argentine and to Brazilian lines, and so forming a transcontinental line across the wide tropical section of the continent, as well as giving Bolivia an outlet to both oceans.

An overall trend towards road and away from rail transport is, however, present. Rail's main area of advantage in S. America, given the poor state of the lines and low speeds attainable, should be freight. But the table shows that this trade has moved away too, in countries which are typical of the overall movement.

PERCENTAGE OF RAIL IN ALL FREIGHT MOVEMENT

Country	1950	1975
Argentina	51.1	10.6
Brazil	28.6	18.1
Colombia	21.2	7.7

Source: Interamerican Development Bank — INTAL, La industria ferroviaria latinoamericana, Buenos Aires, 1980, p.46.

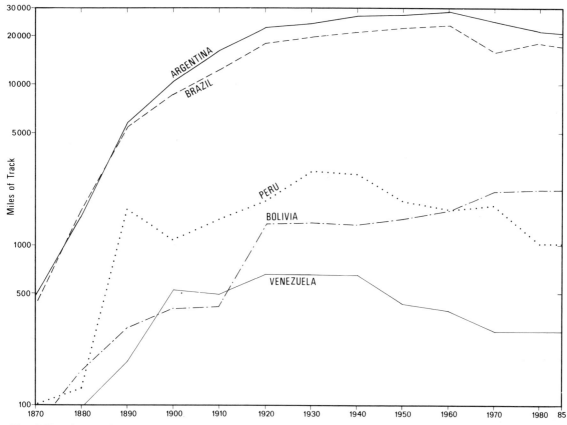

Fig. 8 Trends in railway development in South America

Roads

In the countries whose standard of living does not demand a massive road-building programme, and where national planning can direct infrastructure and manufacturing, the railways may yet present a viable, perhaps even optimal, solution to the transport problem. But roads and lorry traffic have seen the greater development over the last thirty years, and for the extension of farming areas into the interior as well as for the development of intra-continental trade, roads would seem to have an advantage. Brazilian road-building has been the most rapid and far-reaching in the continent, and has had the advantage of no competition from rail or water since neither achieved a real penetration of the deep interior.

Roads and economic development

An important question is whether there can be a genuine fostering of development by road construction alone, or more generally by improvement of the economic infrastructure in any way. There are two quite different types of situation which may be considered: first, that of the farming frontier, where new lands, usually tropical lowlands, are being opened up by small farmers; secondly, there is the case of an already densely peopled region making investments in roads or transport of some form.

In the first of these cases, provision of a road has value as giving an outlet for lowland produce. Plenty of examples, such as the road to the Bolivian Yungas from the capital La Paz, may be cited, showing the direct benefits of the road, without which the citrus fruits, bananas or coffee could not be marketed. Here the road has an absolute value, and in its absence a semi-subsistence economy would prevail. On the other hand, success of the peasants in this frontier situation is not assured merely by having good transport. Marketing problems and the action of

7 *The Transamazon Highway. Much vaunted in 1970, it has attracted little planned settlement and has high costs in terms of construction, environmental and cultural effects*

middlemen in marketing, insecure land tenure and the breakup of farms into *minifundios* may all constitute barriers to economic progress.

In the second case, that of densely peopled areas such as the Nordeste of Brazil, roads intended to help the movement of farm products and industrialization have led instead to a migration out of the region to Rio and São Paulo. Improvement in transport and communications has led to rising expectations and information about better-off regions, in advance of local improvements in employment or social services. There is perhaps a case here for the bettering of social services and the building of farm-to-market roads before the construction of giant inter-regional highways, so that local levels of living can be raised before the raising of information levels concerning opportunities in other regions and increased ease of travel to them.

Stated aims of the Brazilian government have been to bring settlement to new zones via the Transamazon and Belém—Brasília roads and

their like, and also the reduction of inter-regional differences in standards of living. The priority given to motorway construction and to roads in isolated peripheries with tiny populations may however remind us more of the *autobahn* plans of prewar Germany with their strategic implications, than of any plan for economic and social development.

The Carretera Marginal de las Selvas
This is one example of the dramatic roadbuilding projects in the western selvas (fig. 9). Under the inspiration of Peru's President Belaúnde, Peru, Bolivia, Ecuador and Colombia agreed to make the Selvas Flanking Highway, a road providing international links north—south and connecting to the highlands and west coast. This road was expected to lead to the opening up of much new farmland and to add, according to estimates, 5-12 per cent to national totals of cultivated land, as well as allowing nearly a million farmers into

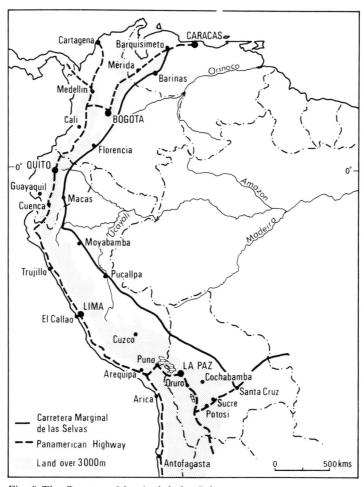

Fig. 9 The Carretera Marginal de las Selvas

the region. In fact only a quarter of the 5500 km road has been built, and it is pertinent to ask why enthusiasm waned. According to one ethusiastic proponent of the scheme:

> The role of the Carretera Marginal de las Selvas is both permissive, in that it makes possible the elimination of regional differentials, and compulsive, in that it forces a realignment of the use of resources.

C.J. Stokes, Transportation and Economic Development in Latin America (*Praeger, 1968*), p. 127

The road would in fact only permit elimination of differentials if other improvements were made, in the fields of education, social services, the creation of town centres and perhaps the introduction of industries. These phenomena cannot be expected to accrue naturally to a new road in the wilderness. There are technical and broad economic difficulties in achieving the results hoped for from the road; the physical potential of much of the land is suspect, or even known to be low, with highly infertile soils in some regions. The road runs in a north—south direction which does not meet the needs of the majority of farmers, who would wish for links to the highlands, rather than links to their neighbour tropical zones, with which there can never be much agricultural trade. Most importantly, the whole scale of the project, and others like it such as the Brazilian Amazon roads, seems wrong. Rather than inter-regional major roads, there seems to be a need for farm-to-market roads, to make the first move away from sub-sistence farming towards commercial farming. The issue seemed to have been resolved by a lack of general interest and the replacement of President Belaúnde by a military government. With his return to office in 1980, the project has returned, associated with a massive drive to colonize and exploit the Oriente.

MANUFACTURING

Industrial location
A problem long familiar to geographers in developed countries is to explain the choice of location by given industries. In S. America many of the factors are the common ones, and we may start with the standard Weberian location theory, which places industries at or near least-cost sites, i.e. where labour, material and transport costs are lowest. What has to be explained is a pattern of industry where one large city contains most of the nation's industry — Buenos Aires with three-quarters of Argentina's manufacturing, or Santiago with a similar proportion of Chile's.

LABOUR COSTS
Labour costs are at first sight difficult to explain. One writer (Gwynne, 1985) has shown that, because labour costs in Chile are higher in the peripheral provinces, manufacturing in the centre has the advantage of lower wage costs. But this is probably not typical; in Chile there are some large multinational firms operating in the periphery which push up the wage rates, and taking out their effect would eliminate the differences. In Brazil, more characteristically, industrial wage rates in 1969 were almost four times as high in São Paulo, as they were in Piaui in the northeast, though, as Boisier shows here, this was partly due to the reverse effect — large firms in modern industries are concentrated in São Paulo, in the centre (Boisier et al, 1973).* Perhaps wage costs may be seen as a resultant more than as a cause.

MATERIAL COSTS
Material costs are lower in the large cities, especially when these are ports or near to ports. Assembly of imported goods is best accomplished at these points, and industrialization begins in many countries with import substitu-

tion industries which are really the assembly of imported components. The transport system centring on the metropolitan city means that any other place must have higher costs.

PRODUCT TRANSPORT COSTS
Transport costs favour a central location in most cases too. Peripheral regions have poor communications and transport, and the shipping of goods from any non-central place entails serious penalties in moving them through the centre and out.

AGGLOMERATION FACTORS
Agglomeration factors work the same way. In the large city such services as financial advice, legal and business services, as well as physical infrastructure such as water and electric power, are available. In advanced countries these may have limited availability in other regions. In South America they are likely to be totally absent elsewhere.

BEHAVIOURAL FACTORS
Whether because of limited information or a distorted perception of that information, an industrialist may not choose what might be found to be a least-cost or highest-profit location. Executives working for multinationals, for example, may be unwilling to work in any city other than the largest, which they perceive as the most desirable. The industrialist too, may have little or no information about alternative locations, and thus have no real choice at all. One kind of factor which is mostly behavioural is the matter of capital city location to be close to government offices and agencies. Both domestic and foreign firms will select this location in order to be able to speak readily to influential decision-makers. "Knowing people" and making contacts is extremely important, and more so in the Latin world than in Anglo-Saxon societies.

STRUCTURAL FACTORS
This includes such matters as the organization of firms and of controlling institutions, governments and trade unions. Multinationals have already been mentioned; their decisions are distinctive because such companies can be mobile,

*Boisier, S., M.O. Smolka, and A. de Barros, *Desenvolvimento Regional e Urbano,* Rio de Janeiro, IPEA/INPES (1973), pp. 66-70.

move in or out of countries to make use of grants, wage-rate differences, or overcome tariff barriers. They are sometimes footloose, and sometimes they work together with local governments. In South America, a substantial amount of intervention by governments does affect some industries, but the major effect has to bring them in to the centre, because the main policies have been tariff barriers to protect infant industries. Only occasionally, as with the CVG, which set up an industrial pole in a distant region of Venezuela, does a government agency manage to change the pattern.

Stages of industrial growth

We can describe modern industrial development fairly simply in terms of a three-stage model, which has spatial and sectoral connotations. These stages are primary processing, import substitution, and general industrialization. As will become evident, they can also be viewed as types of industrialization, and the stages do not follow one another with any precision. The premodern period may be skipped over quickly, as the previous chapter has shown that manufacturing was effectively suppressed by the mercantilist policies of Spain and Portugal, and the towns were administrative centres with little industrial tradition.

PRIMARY PROCESSING

Primary processing is the name that may be given to a first stage, in which raw materials moving out to Europe were first subject to some processing. Thus from 1880 to 1930 Buenos Aires and Montevideo built up their *frigoríficos* or meat packing houses to process the cattle moving out from the Pampas. There were linked industries for canning and preserving meats, leather manufactures and meat extracts.

Other similar industries are the grain silos and flour mills of these ports, and in other environments, fishmeal processing plants, iron ore concentration plant, cocoa, palm oil, banana packing and the like, developed at Rio, Santos, El Callao and Valparaiso. This type of industrialization is not finished — at Vitoria the iron ore moving down the Rio Doce is processed into concentrate before being exported. Wool, which was sent raw from Buenos Aires or Montevideo,

is now more frequently converted into thread or cloth before export. The spatial pattern of this development is one of a few dispersed ports.

IMPORT SUBSTITUTION

A second stage is import substitution. During the First World War and again during the 1930s and the Second World War, South America was virtually isolated from the warring countries and forced to develop its own industries. Given the low level of technology available, most new industries were simple — textile industries have for example been commonly introduced in virtually all countries. Another factor was the high tariffs raised as barriers to imported goods of the same type, and as these tariffs were most easily placed on consumer items, it was this kind of industry that emerged. Industry became heavily concentrated in a few cities, though now not solely the major ports. Big cities were closest to the markets for the consumer goods being produced, and had other advantages of industrial infrastructure.

GENERAL INDUSTRIALIZATION

A third stage is of general industrialization. In the countries with largest markets, Brazil, Argentina, and to some extent in those countries with a good natural resource base, there is a tendency to move beyond import substitution. A first way in which this happens is through multinationals developing an extraction industry for export, which then leads on to manufacture, and possibly to takeover of the firm by the national government, as in the case of Venezuelan iron or petroleum. Another approach is the strategic one, where investment in heavy industry is as a measure to ensure national security (military supplies). Argentina's first iron and steel plant in Jujuy, near the Bolivian border, is an example, as to some extent are all the continent's steel mills.

Some writers prefer to think of recent industrial growth as related to a new philosophy, manufacturing for export. This is partially true for one or two cases, notably Brazil, though even here the main force has been domestic demand and not exports. In Brazil, manufactured exports (including semi-manufactures), have increased to nearly 60% of the total, and the old reliance on manufactures of local raw materials has gone.

Fig. 10 Integrated steel mills, coal fields and iron ore deposits

The car-manufacturing industry has been a key industry, especially because of its links to other industries. But South American manufacturing exports are not comparable to those of Korea, Taiwan, or Hong Kong, with their low material content and heavy use of cheap labour. The labour/material ratio in S. America is quite different and the products and markets must thus also differ.

Spatially, this third phase of industrialization leads to some deconcentration, as capital goods and materials-based industries like aluminium or petroleum refining and petrochemicals grow up in regions near raw materials sites.

PUBLISHING

This industry illustrates several facets of the 'big city' type of industry; its emergence is partially as an import substitution industry, replacing book imports from Spain or Portugal with local products. It grows partly as an industry feeding the local region, since the remainder of the country is unimportant as a market. And in addition it has some of the variable character seen in industry, with formal industries established in the usual way competing with 'informal' firms, using irregular or family labour, combining printing and bookselling, and the like.

The import substitution character is of course applicable primarily to book publishing, rather than to papers and periodicals. Many books are still imported from Europe, but several big centres have grown in Latin America, Buenos Aires, Rio, Caracas and Mexico City. Buenos Aires became a leading centre during the Spanish Civil War, when émigrés from the war left and set up three major houses, Losada, Emece and Sud-Americana, there in 1938–40. In more recent years, military and Peronist governments with severe censorship and controls have relegated Buenos Aires to second place after Mexico City among the Spanish-speaking countries of the continent. All the big publishers still act as book importers and distributors, so that the European link remains strong.

The industry is highly concentrated in a few cities. In Argentina, 85% of the books come from Buenos Aires. In many countries there is only a tiny industry, reflecting low levels of literacy. In Bolivia, for example, there is (1980) only 63% literacy, and there are virtually no books for the large Quechua and Aymara speaking population. In Brazil, the concentration is in the two largest cities, São Paulo and Rio, which handle respectively 30% and 40% of the local book titles. Rio, with its greater cultural background, handles 75% of the translations of foreign works.

The third element, variable character, is seen by examining a smaller country, Ecuador, where the only large book publisher is the one producing school textbooks. There are half a dozen smaller ones in Quito, but they only survive by combining a book shop, a tiny printing works and a publishing operation that consists of little more than editing the works and placing them for sale in the shop. This kind of industry did exist in such countries as Argentina in a previous stage, during the nineteenth century (Lagarde, 1980).

A KEY INDUSTRY: STEEL (fig. 10)

For steel the twin factors of national security and prestige have been important. A steel industry has been regarded as a badge of the developed country and has been developed in part because of this, and also because of a desire by governments to establish independence of other coun-tries in steel manufacture, a strategic industry. This helps explain the steel industries of Argentina, Venezuela, Colombia, Chile and Peru, which have state backing despite many negative economic features such as high material costs and small markets.

The Chilean and Venezuelan cases have curious similarities; in Chile there are good ores in the north, coal and limestone in the far south. Despite great distances, sea transport makes total assembly cost reasonably low, and the tiny market which in 1945 could not absorb a large mill's output, has grown to economic size since then. In Venezuela, ore and HEP were found together on the Caroní river, together with coal from the coast; transport by sea for coal and finished steel was possible and a market restric-ted largely to pipelines for oil has broadened to take all kinds of steel products. The venture has also allowed some regional development of the Guyana region in the southeast.

Markets and Politics

In Brazil the large integrated iron and steel in-dustries are state-owned or partly-owned. In-evitably then, a decision on steel-mill locations is partially a political one, though a successful large industry could scarcely have grown up without the demand emanating from a large and growing industrial market in Brazil. The very building of the first large integrated mill at Volta Redonda (see also Ch. 17) was due to the dynamic per-sonality of President Vargas, added to a Latin American penchant for building great monu-ments to political figures. Volta Redonda was built in the early 1940s, in a market position halfway between São Paulo and Rio in the Paraiba valley, bringing iron ore and limestone from Minas state by rail, and coking coal from abroad or from Santa Catarina state. But the mill was located in the state of Rio, and the other two major industrial and political states, Minas and São Paulo, sought their own rewards. Thus a big new mill was built for São Paulo in the 1950s, at Santos, and another for Minas at Ipatinga in the Rio Doce valley. The end result divides honours equally, though remaining located in a general market location.

The industry has become differentiated too however, as in addition to the integrated mills there are over 40 blast furnaces on their own in Minas, using local ore and the charcoal made from large plantations of eucalyptus. In the São Paulo metropolitan district there are also some ten small steel works and rolling mills and a few more in Rio. These produce special steels and are linked to the engineering works of these cities. Steel was to be one spearhead of Brazil's Economic Miracle in the 1970s, with massive production for export in raw or manufactured form, requiring great new works at the outlet from the main mining areas for Brazilian ore, Minas and Carajas in the north. This plan has been cut back, and Brazilian production has even declined, from a peak of 15 million tons to under 13 million.

At the other end of the market scale, small countries such as Bolivia, Paraguay, Guyana or Uruguay cannot contemplate steel industries, unless export demand supplements that of the home market, which does not approach the output of a modern mill.

Colombia, with its excellent combination of resources for steel in the Chicamocha valley, has not been able to expand its industry, despite the continent's lowest assembly costs, for want of markets. Peru's small industry is similarly confined.

Obviously future steel developments will depend on international rather than internal markets, and it is likely that only a few steel centres will emerge, the question being whether these will all be market centres, or sites where material assembly costs are low, such as Colombia or Venezuela. Market sites are now in the ascendant, and must maintain an advantage as long as free movement of goods is promoted.

OVERALL VIEW AND OUTLOOK

Manufacturing has come to the region only recently, but its impact is already considerable, providing as much as 35 per cent of GNP in Argentina, and 13 per cent even in Bolivia. This impact is not apparent to the outside world, for most industries cater solely to domestic markets, but it is nevertheless real.

One observable feature has been the geographical concentration of industry, which is explicable in historical and economic terms. What is now needed, for the benefit of the countries concerned, is perhaps a more vigorous policy of regional deconcentration — moving industries out to growth poles outside the metropolitan cities. Given that industry must be the major future revenue earner for the region, it is important that its inevitable growth and dynamism be guided to the best effect, both in terms of industrial type or sector, and in terms of location.

Another feature which has earned comment is foreign ownership and influence. Simple expropriation is not an answer to this problem, especially in a world where trade between countries is continually increasing and international connections are made ever closer at the commercial level. In any case, administrators and entrepreneurs will not grow up overnight to replace those expelled in revolutionary movements. What seems to be needed is an arrangement between foreign investor and home government, whereby nationals of the country are brought into high executive position or trained as technologists, as well as profit-sharing policies which earn the home government some revenue from the industry. Instead of such an arrangement, the usual and depressing story is of little profit or skill sharing, until a moment of revolutionary takeover, and subsequent decline of the industry in question. Such problems must slow down and undermine the stability of Latin American manufacturing industry.

5. Population Patterns

Population in Latin America is mostly distributed in the vicinity of the coasts, and the far interior of the continent still has very few inhabitants. Reasons for this concentration are not far to seek. Physically, the interior presents difficulties for agriculturalists, especially in the Amazon selvas and, to the south, drought in the Chaco and poor soils are long-term problems. Historically, the status of economic and political dependence on Europe has enforced concentration of all activity at or near the coast, accessible to Spain and Portugal. Aboriginal settlement too, at least at the time of the Conquest, did not penetrate much into the interior, though evidence of Indian fields from the pre-Hispanic era in the Oriente of Bolivia and Llanos of Venezuela—Colombia suggests that savanna lands with reasonable fertility may have had permanent occupation by organized groups.

The potential of these interior lands assumes a growing importance for modern nations, since today the most obvious thing about Latin American population is its rate of increase, though even within South America there are contrasts in demographic trends, so that some countries are presented with immediate food supply problems, while others stand in need of more people to occupy their peripheral regions.

RACIAL AND ETHNIC PATTERNS

Before the Conquest, the racial makeup of the Americas was simple, for the continent was populated in archaeologically recent times, and by only one major group, the 'Indians', who migrated out of East Asia and occupied the whole continent. This human group has been substantially modified by European contact and miscegenation. Only in one area, the highlands of Bolivia—Peru—Ecuador, has there remained a dense population of reasonably pure Indian blood. In Bolivia it is estimated that 50% of the population is pure Indian, against 40% in Ecuador and 45% in Peru; these figures must always be estimates in view of the impossibility of checking everybody's pedigree, but they give an idea of the mix. Apart from this highland group, there are tribal Indians living in the Amazon basin, often without any permanent contacts with civilization, but these only number a few thousand and their domain is rapidly diminishing in the face of modern ranchers and farmers, who have been responsible for real atrocities in removing Indians from their lands — in some documented Brazilian cases hunting and shooting them like wild animals.

Spaniards and Portuguese came as minorities into the New World, nowhere forming a dense rural mass as in North America. They and their descendants, however, formed a sizeable part of the urban populations. In contrast, the Negroes brought in from West Africa were, and remained, largely rural, forming the bulk of the population in two areas, the Nordeste of Brazil, where they were the work force for the sugar plantations, and the Pacific coastal regions of Colombia, where they formed the mine labour force.

European settlement restrictions

Iberian policy did not permit foreigners to settle in their possessions, so that Europeans in South America are mostly Spanish or Portuguese in origin. Only in the temperate countries, Argentina, Chile, Uruguay and southern Brazil, and only after 1800, has there been any settlement by north Europeans, and even here this group is outweighed by south Europeans, Italians and Iberians, who formed a very distinctive group as they came into the Pampas and Southern Chile, into regions from which the Indian had been totally eradicated, so that racial mixture could not take place.

Race and class

Elsewhere, Spanish and Portuguese have mixed with the Indians to a considerable degree, the result being a blurred colour distinction and the claim by Latin Americans that colour bars are not to be found. This is true in a formal sense, but because of historical distinctions between white masters and black or coloured serfs and slaves, there remain very decided differences between the prospects for coloured and white persons. In the colonial period, only first-generation Spaniards were allowed to hold major offices, a source of resentment which was one cause of the independence moves of the nineteenth century led by the *criollos*, American-born people of pure Spanish blood.

At the other end of the social scale, the Negroes were almost entirely used as slaves until the mid-nineteenth century, and, only slightly higher up the ladder, the altiplano Indians were held as serfs, working for the Spanish at least as hard as for the Incas in olden times. In the twentieth century the results of these old limitations are to be seen in the fact that Negroes, mulattos, Indians, mestizos and other mixed groups occupy socio-economic niches much lower than those of Europeans, in part because of the poor regions where they live, in part because of continuing discrimination against them.

The Guianas, with their complicated colonial history, have different patterns and the reader is referred to the discussion in Chapter 16 for details.

Guamote

To give some idea of the divisions and their spatial impact, we may refer to a study of a rural community in the Ecuadorian Sierra near Riobamba.* Guamote is a canton with three parishes, lying at about 3000 m altitude. It has a small town, several hamlets and a dispersed rural population. This population is *mestizo* and Indian, the Indian majority being very much the rural, peripheral, backward group, while the *mestizos* have retained power and urban wealth. Employment data in the table suggest this, with the *mestizos* occupying nearly 90% of service sector employment and 70% of the secondary sector.

Economic sector	Total employment (%)	Mestizos (%)	Indians (%)
Primary	88.2	1.9	98.1
Secondary	6.0	69.5	30.5
Tertiary	5.8	88.5	11.5

Another index is in the urban-rural residence of the Indians and *mestizos*. Here the dominance of *mestizos* in the urban areas is readily seen in the table. Although they do not live in the countryside, they also dominate it through ownership of the land, and ownership of the trucks and shops which form the marketing system for farm products.

DEMOGRAPHIC CHARACTERISTICS

The most significant Latin American population statistic is the growth rate, which for the LAFTA countries generally is 2.9 per cent per annum, a figure higher than that of any other continental size unit, and one which calls forth numerous demands for regional and national population control policies. The Catholic Church's opposition to most forms of birth control is often adduced as the reason for such high figures. On inspection, however, the relationship of high birth rates to Catholicism seems slight. Uruguay

*Iturralde, Diego A. (1980) *Guamote: campesinos y comunas*, Instituto Otavaleno de Antropologia, Otavalo, Ecuador.

and Argentina are, like all Latin countries, nominally Catholic, yet their birth rates, currently about 2.1% per annum, stand well below the average and a long way behind Brazil, with 4%, Venezuela with 3.6%, or Bolivia with 4.4%. A host of factors is related to the level of births and deaths, including the provision of health services, social attitudes towards family size, and the degree of emphasis put on material wealth as opposed to production of the next generation and enjoyment of a family. Evidently, population changes occur as a part of the general process of modernization and socio-economic change towards western standards. In any case, the influence of the Church is difficult to guage because most people are only Catholic by baptism. There is little Church influence among either the anticlerical Italian nineteenth-century migrants to Argentina, or the peasants of the Andes where Christianity was never much more than a veneer over older faiths.

Death rates are seen to be at or even below European levels, at first glance a surprise but in fact to be expected, for the large proportion of young people in a growing population means an artificial lowering of the death rate until these people age. In Colombia, Chile and Brazil, over 40% of the population is under 15 years old, because of continuing high birth rates, which are

showing slight tendencies to decline; from what is known of the 'demographic transition' (the change from high birth and death rates to low rates as socio-economic development takes place), birth rates will take another twenty years to fall to stable levels, accelerating in urban areas where new ideals about family life and economic opportunity are accepted, slow in conservative rural areas.

RURAL–RURAL MIGRATION

Most modern migrations are citywards, and rural colonization faces great problems of isolation and limited opportunities. Despite official support for colonization programmes in the eastern lowlands of Bolivia, Peru, Ecuador and Colombia, achievement has been slight and limited to the Andean fringe. Brazil has had perhaps the most successful colonization programme, supported by active roadbuilding, and regional figures indicate in part the process, though they are also an index of high rural fertility rates. Only the industrial and urban Sudeste has suffered rural decline in the face of massive migration to towns.

Little research has been done on the nature of the migrants to new farm lands, as compared to that done on migrants to the urban frontier, but

BIRTH AND DEATH RATES PER THOUSAND, 1960-5 & 1970-5

Country	Crude birth rate		Crude death rate		Infant mortality	
	(60-65)	(70-75)	(60-65)	(70-75)	(60-65)	(70-75)
Argentina	22.5	22.9*	8.5	9.4	59.1	59.0
Bolivia	44.0	44.0	21	19.1	73.3	77.3
Brazil	42.0	37.1	11	8.8	n.a.	n.a.
Chile	35.3	26.0*	11.5	8.7	91.6	77.8
Colombia	42.5	40.6	13	8.8	89.6	62.8
Ecuador	48.5	41.8	14	9.5	48.5	70.2
Guyana	39.7	33.4*	9.5	7.2	48.1	42.3
Paraguay	43.5	39.8	13	8.9	44.3	38.6
Peru	44.5	41.0	13	11.9	93.2	65.1
Uruguay	24.5	20.9*	9	9.6	41.6	45.4
Venezuela	47.0	36.1	9.5	7.0	52.9	46.0
Mexico	44.5	42.0	10.5	8.6	60.7	52.0
United Kingdom	18.3	13.3	11.5	11.9	19.6	16.3

*One year only

Source: United Nations Demographic Yearbook, *various years*

it appears that the rural-to-rural migrants differ substantially from rural–urban migrants. They seem to be older, often with families, less well educated than those who migrate to towns. One implication of this is that agricultural extension services, the provision of technical and general education to the settlers, is essential to maintain their impetus in colonization, if in fact colonization is a desired feature.

URBAN MIGRATION AND METROPOLITAN GROWTH

Large-scale migration from rural to urban areas is causing major changes in the overall distribution of population, so that dense settlement is accumulating in a few relatively small zones, such as the Plate estuary, the São Paulo–Rio–Belo Horizonte triangle, and the Lima–Callao conurbation. Until this century, most people could be classified as rural in the strict sense of living in small settlements or isolated houses and working the land. Now large cities are growing up rapidly because of migration, leaving a stagnant ageing population in the rural areas. In Brazil, as late as 1940 the population was 70 per cent rural, but by 1975 it was only 38.6 per cent. In Colombia, the rural population percentage declined from 71 per cent to 36 per cent in the period 1938–74. Yet the natural rates of increase are universally lower in cities, so that migration on a massive scale is taking place.

In the countryside, many regions maintain rural growth, as the table shows for Brazil, but in the south-east region outmigration to towns means an absolute decline in rural numbers. In another country, Colombia, rural depopulation is reported on a massive scale (Griffin and Williams, 1980). Contrary to the traditional view, that migrants going to the city merely 'took away' a surplus and left rural areas still growing, regions close to the big cities of Bogotà and Medellin were recorded as losing population since the 1950s. Many localities lost over 10% of their population in 1964–73.

Models of migration

Many studies have been made concerning the movement to the cities, some highlighting the factors determining migration, others looking

8 *A shanty home on the outskirts of Popayán. Rural-urban migration affects even the sleepy colonial towns of the Andes and, in the absence of either sufficient income or public housing, leads to shanty construction*

for patterns. From the pattern studies, it is agreed that Latin American urban migration differs from African and Southeast Asian in being composed often initially of young women rather than men, with girls moving to work as domestic servants in the houses of the urban rich. The pattern is also one of progression, a step migration, along the urban hierarchy, with people moving first to small towns and then to larger cities and so to the metropolis. This series of steps may be accomplished by one individual or it may occur over several generations. As in Africa and Asia, return migration is important, up to 20% for example in Colombia, the migrants going home to the rural areas because they find no job or cannot adjust to city life (Cardona and Simmons, 1975).

A feature noted worldwide is that migration is selective, taking the younger, better-trained, more ambitious and energetic individuals from rural society, a very detrimental process for the source regions. From a variety of sources, Cardona and Simmons conclude that, while in the early stages of migration for any country it is selective, as time goes on it becomes less so, as whole populations seem to be affected by the wish to migrate, and the stepwise progression changes into a direct surge into the big cities.

There are some interesting variations in the pattern. In the vicinity of some cities such as Quito, or even the smaller (150 000) Cuenca, both in Ecuador, there are many villages and small towns. People commute daily from these to the city in large numbers, over 5000 into Cuenca, using the frequent buses. Others, from over 50 km distance, come in to work during the week, taking lodgings, or for a few weeks, before returning to visit family and friends. This journeying allows the transition to urban life to be made with less social trauma and may avoid some of the shanty growth typical of big cities. Commuting in the Western sense, using private cars or fast suburban railways, is less frequent in S. America, being observable only in cities like Buenos Aires and Caracas which have a sizeable élite.

On a grander scale, much migration is international. In the nineteenth century this was Europe–Latin America; today it is largely between the Latin American countries, in a clear pattern focusing on a few great foci (the pattern is mapped in A.S. Morris, 1981, p. 128). Argen-

tina is the target for many migrants, especially from Paraguay and Bolivia; some are temporary farm workers in the north, others political refugees or educated people looking for jobs that can use their skills. In the north, Caracas is the target, receiving primarily Colombians. These flows are to some extent illegal, so that the numbers are poorly known. The Colombian flows in Venezuela are along the *caminos verdes,* the paths through the forests which avoid frontier posts, and domestic servants or farm workers may reside many years in their host country without acquiring identity documents.

As to the reasons for migration, some writers argue in terms of family linkages; a first migrant writes or visits home and encourages others to go, or provides lodgings for the next arrival and help to find jobs. This information chain will obviously be useful in the poorer countries where radios, newspapers and the like are less in use. Economic factors have commonly been sought for the migration, and the differences in wage levels between cities and rural areas are very great, though many migrants cannot gain access to regular well-paid employment until years after they arrive. It is therefore necessary to see their migration as a move towards the long-term possibility of a good job, rather than a direct move into such work. For the first years, a more probable situation is one of temporary jobs in the informal sector, outside the ordinary company structure.

BRAZIL: RURAL POPULATION 1940–1980

Region	1940	1970	1980 (estimate)
Norte	1 057	1 977	2 466
Nordeste	11 053	16 359	19 054
Sudeste	11 114	10 889	8 346
Sul	4 145	9 193	11 464
Centro-Oeste	988	2 636	3 548

Source: Anuario Estatístico do Brasil, *various issues.*

Rates of growth: the hierarchy balance

Urban geographers have long established a hierarchical structure of cities, following such descriptive models as the rank—size rule, or Christaller's more analytic approach through hinterland demarcation. The findings of such models, based on the interweaving of a large number of economic and social factors, are that a pyramid grouping of cities occurs, with one or two very large cities at the top, followed by a larger number in the next lower size group, and a regular progression of larger numbers of towns in each lower size class.

In Latin America, some commentators have remarked on the unbalanced, top-heavy nature of this pyramid, with one 'primate city', followed at a great distance by the smaller settlements. An index of this primacy, the degree to which one city dominates, may readily be constructed from the ratio of the largest city's population to those following: the table shows some results for South America using as the index the 1970 population of the largest city divided by the next three cities' population.

Index of Primacy

Country	Index	Date	Country	Index	Date
Argentina	4.503	1975	Peru	4.927	1972
Brazil	0.939	1975	Venezuela	1.551	1976
Chile	2.095	1978	Bolivia	1.179	1976
Colombia	1.005	1973			

Source: United Nations *Demographic Yearbook 1978*, Table 8, pp.214–217.
Note: Valparaiso is included with Viña del Mar as the second city in Chile, and Concepción with Talcahuano as the third. Lima is counted with El Callao as the largest city of Peru. In every case where they are given figures for the whole urbanized area, rather than the political city, are used for the city size.

An example of the uneven structure is the comparison in the table, of the sizes of cities in Ecuador estimated for 1980, and the sizes that would obtain if they followed the rank-size rule, the nth town having a population of A/n where A is the population of the largest city, Guayaquil. Quito, the capital, is evidently a second metropolis, but the others are far smaller than this model predicts.

There are many reasons for this structure. In part it is a historical legacy from the colonial past when a few towns were made centres of political power and trade, and others neglected. But to ascribe metropolitan dominance to history is insufficient. Current growth is based on political centralization, but also on economic power, and the main cities are the foci of industrial growth, which itself is highly centralized because it is mostly market-oriented, and the market is in the urban centre. In part the locational decision

CITIES IN ECUADOR

Rank number	City	Population 1980	Rank/size population
1	Guayaquil	1 116 280	1 116 280
2	Quito	807 665	558 140
3	Cuenca	139 209	371 093
4	Ambato	100 046	279 070
5	Manta	89 468	223 256
6	Esmeraldas	87 464	186 046
7	Portoviejo	84 574	159 468
8	Riobamba	71 104	139 535
9	Loja	61 610	124 031
10	Ibarra	54 116	111 628
11	Santo Domingo	51 377	101 480

makers may be blamed — professionals such as doctors, and industrialists, will not seek locations where infrastructure and social provision are poor. In poor regions even the larger towns that exist have a limited function and that function shows imbalance between them and their region. Portoviejo in the Ecuadorean list, for example, has many doctors, dentists, and markets, bazaars and shops providing essentials such as sugar and rice, all for the surrounding region, because these commodities and services are not available at all in smaller towns. Country folk here will make a weekly or monthly trip to town to find all their needs.

In this way the vicious circles of international imbalance are repeated at various scales, national and regional. Mobile (i.e. urban) functions are concentrated at central points and help bolster their wealth, peripheral areas are poorly provided, and because of the initial advantage of the centre there is no tendency to even out disparities.

SOCIO-DEMOGRAPHIC CHARACTERISTICS

Economic differences between urban and rural areas are apparent over the whole continent, for higher standards of living are generally observable in towns, though urban poverty makes the cities areas both of great wealth and great poverty, often in close proximity. The expression of poverty is varied, and a fascinating set of symptoms is that of various diseases. The map (fig. 11) shows as an example some aspects of

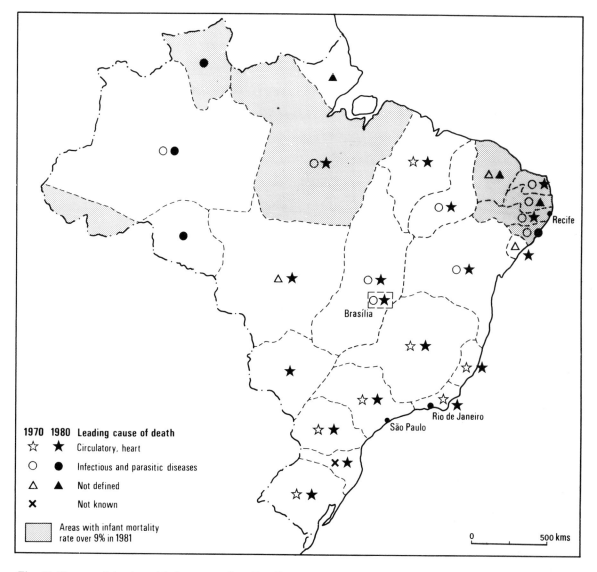

Fig. 11 Causes of death and infant mortality, Brazil

Brazilian medical geography. Two kinds of region emerge, central and peripheral. Circulatory diseases, including strokes, heart and circulation system diseases, are the leading cause of death in the centre, appropriately enough for a region of relatively good diet, resistance to infection, and sanitation, but high living stress and a larger percentage of old people. In the peripheral regions, gastro-enteritis, dysentery, tuberculosis, and other infectious diseases are dominant as killers. Another index of regional difference which is shown is the infant mortality rate, again high in the periphery, all regions, that is, outside the south and southeast.

Apart from disease, the urban areas are characterized by the relative youth of their populace, higher levels of education, and often by social instability, shown in crime, delinquency, prostitution and other social deviations. All these features distinguish them from the countryside. To understand these characteristics, it is necessary to revert to the migration process.

Migration attracts younger people, because of better job opportunities, better use of qualifications, and fewer ties to family, house and other commitments. This leaves the countryside with an older group, a stable society where little is changed by migrants coming in with new ideas, while towns open up new horizons and at the same time make social abnormalities much more likely, for the checks of the rural hierarchy are gone, unreplaced or poorly replaced by public authorities in the city.

SETTLEMENTS

Population patterns over the countryside are a reflection of economic structure and social groupings, physical environment and sometimes administrative fiat. In South America rural settlements include a good number of pre-Columbian towns, especially in the civilized parts of the Inca empire, but for the continent as a whole, settlements mostly date from the colonial period. A limited number of settlements postdate the Independence movements of the nineteenth century.

Old Indian settlements have been most frequently maintained in use in the dry Andes, where water is at a premium and most settlements must seek riversides. Here the Spanish took over the old towns, partly because this allowed them to control the surrounding rural population and make the hinterland produce for its new masters. Thus the Inca settlements, Cuzco and Quito, were made Spanish centres, as were Bogotá and Tunja in the Chibcha area of Colombia, although little is usually to be found of the Indian settlement form.

9 Peasants transporting canes for thatching and craftwork at Capachica, on the shores of lake Titicaca. Concentration of settlement into villages was brought about largely by Spanish administrators

Apart from taking over intensive Indian agricultural areas, the Iberian newcomers brought in new domestic animals, sheep and cattle, which required a new settlement form, the *hacienda* (Portuguese *fazenda*), an isolated and specialized form of settlement, with ranch and outhouses for peons; the horse was another animal which allowed such dispersed settlement to come in despite the great distances which had to be covered. In some areas, notably in Peru, royal and viceregal ordinances caused concentration of settlement, bringing Indians together in new villages for better control (plate 9); the Jesuits and other fathers practised a similar concentration in their *reducciones*, villages where they taught the Indians and protected them from slavers.

Most of the colonization and settlement described above was into land occupied to some extent by Indians. In the nineteenth century a new move began, into land devoid of settlement or nearly so. This was the movement into the Pampas grasslands, involving a usually dispersed settlement pattern but occasionally European-style villages (fig. 12). From the late nineteenth century a further plunge has taken place, into the selvas, starting from the Brazilian side and now vigorously pressed on all fronts, usually following linear forms along the roads of penetration into the forest.

It is hard to reconcile this linear pattern of settlement with the standard geographers' model for settlement, that of 'central place theory', in which complete areas are occupied with no gaps,

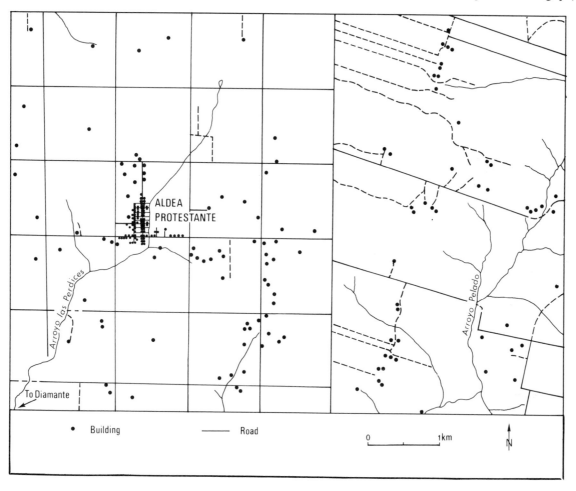

Fig. 12 Rural settlement in a part of Entre Rios, Argentina

by a regular lattice of hexagonal hinterlands or trade areas. In colonization areas the settlements are farms necessarily strung out along or near the roads which lead to the small towns providing services and essential goods, and the merchants who buy and sell farm products. It is perhaps desirable to refer to another kind of settlement model in which the role of the merchants and of the long-distance trade that they dominate is made explicit, allowing that large areas are not incorporated into the market network at all during the colonization phase.

URBAN GROWTH MODELS

A number of models have been used to describe urban growth in advanced industrial cities. With some modification they may also be applied in South America. The most frequently used has been the sectoral model first employed by Homer Hoyt in North America. As adapted to South America (Amato, 1970; Morris, 1978) the model is one of expansion very largely determined by the search for residential space of a small upper class or élite. A small social group can dominate the market and the physical expansion of a town because it uses a lot of land — in half acre or acre plots — compared to its population size. This model starts with a compact town in a chessboard grid layout, such as was typical of all Latin American towns and was enshrined by the Laws of the Indies. From this base an initial expansion may have been in several directions, guided by the first horse-drawn trams in the nineteenth century.

In the twentieth century, major expansion has been along a single sector (Fig. 13), that chosen by the élite group, in successive waves. This group searches out the most desirable directions for expansion; upwind of the city (as in Caracas), above the level of city pollution and to sites with views from hillsides (Santiago), onto good flat land for building (Quito), or into areas already established as desirable by previous setting-up of summer/weekend villas (the Parana delta for Buenos Aires, Miraflores in Lima, Sabana Grande at Caracas).

The main alternative to this kind of model is that which combines the sectoral expansion with concentric rings of expansion, producing a rounded city structure. Starting with the same

10 This barrio, a shanty town in Baruta, Caracas, is located adjacent to an old village centre. It is accessible only by steps or narrow lanes, and shoppers or vendors must go on foot

chessboard pattern, expansion takes two forms — sectoral growth along a wedge as with the Hoyt model, with a spine which is simply the commercial expansion of the CBD (central business district) along a main road; and ring growth, covering most of the city in the diagram of the model and in the examples used by the authors (Griffin and Ford, 1980). The inner ring is the zone of maturity, of solid and conventional buildings; it is surrounded by a zone of accretion, where the shanty towns are being converted into permanent dwellings, and around the edge is a third ring of squatter settlements where roads and services may be absent and construction may be of waste materials such as scrap timber and oil drums.

Over time, as the city expands, the peripheral squatter zone is transformed into a new zone of accretion, as electricity, roads, gas and water are brought in, and oildrums are replaced with bricks. At the same time, the previous zone of accretion becomes one of maturity by the addition of second floors, roofing with tiles in place of corrugated iron, and completion of the services infrastructure, such as proper surfacing of roads, with sewage lines and storm drains beneath them.

Which model is correct? The answer is that either may have applicability in particular cities, and both use the concept of an élite sector and stress the dominant influence of residential growth, appropriate because industrial and commercial uses occupy only a small part of the urban space. The concentric ring model is, however, most applicable to cities of very rapid growth, where the poor population cannot be contained in existing housing or through building standard new houses which cost too much, and it must rely on illegal (squatter) occupation of large tracts of land which can only be found on the city margins. In such cities, the "filtering" process of Western cities, whereby old residential high-quality areas are gradually passed on from the more to the less wealthy as rich people move to new homes, cannot operate. The model will work for Bogotá, with its rapid expansion of population; for La Paz, where the periphery tends to be the squatter area because of the lack of water on the high sides of the basin in which the city sits, and where the basin shape dictates a circular growth; and at Guayaquil, where the squatter growth has been notable onto the marsh lands of the estuary and where filling-in of land takes place thereafter. Elsewhere the sectoral model seems more appropriate; for most cities, the shanties occupy only a small part of the urban fabric at any one time — they occur for example in Caracas (see Chapter 21) along the stream lines where legal housing was forbidden, on hills in the city of Rio de Janeiro, supposedly too steep for construction, everywhere as a filling-in element.

Neither model seems very representative for the intermediate-size cities, which tend to grow more slowly and by more standard means. In Georgetown, Guyana, much growth in recent decades has been simply filling-in and densification of the existing urban fabric, with standard housing on smaller plots, without the need for large squatter developments or an élite sector. In Mendoza, Argentina, the expansion has been

that of the middle class rather than upper or lower, in a set of estates around the urban fringe. For the southern cone countries with their substantial middle classes, this must be an increasingly important element in urban expansion.

Migration and urban growth

Some variants of the models above have stressed the nature of the migration process which accompanies and in part causes urban growth. This certainly distinctive; migrants from the countryside, or from intermediate-sized settlements, move into the metropolitan city in search of employment, young women often first, as they can find domestic servant employment in the élite areas. Men and families, however, tend to concentrate

11 *Rural housing at El Quibor, a small town in Venezuela. This typical building in* bahareque, *sun-dried daub and wattle, with no improvements, is unhealthy for many reasons. One is that it allows carrier insects of a form of sleeping sickness,* mal de chagas, *to live in the cracks in the mud walls*

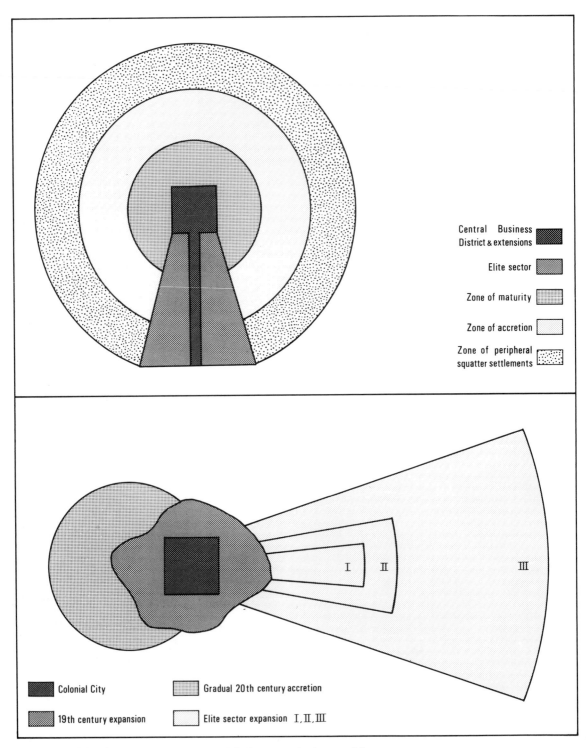

Fig. 13 Models of urban growth (a) a modified concentric ring model
(b) a sectoral growth model

in the central areas, where cheap private rental housing is found. From this central area they form associations which collectively organize the occupation of new squatter settlements, wherever these are to be located — obviously they are not chosen on the basis of desirability of environment or accessibility, and more important is simply the availability of land and ease of initial occupation with least chance of being thrown out as illegal squatters.

The migration of the élite is less complex. They lived traditionally in the city centre, since the colonial laws also designated central sites, to be occupied by the most important city residents, and proximity to the central *plaza* gave prestige to the house owner. In recent decades, assuming more of the standards and values of industrial society, they have sought suburban sites with gardens and thus moved out to become commuters, clustering in the chosen sector of high amenity and access value. The relative importance of this élite movement, and of the mass migration into peripheral shanties, will help to determine the relevance of the sectoral versus the ring model of urban growth.

THE POPULATION AHEAD

Within Latin America itself, population problems are not generally seen to have the same urgency that is claimed by the outside world. It is felt by many of the nations concerned that they have no problem of feeding their populations because vast reserves of unused land are available. Birth control programmes initiated from abroad are looked at somewhat askance, for they are often seen as instruments of the major powers, who would seek to maintain their numerical superiority and thus their power. By some, birth control is seen as an agent leading to immorality and breaking up the family bonds which centre on the children.

Looking at the purely demographic facts, and at some of the sociological phenomena behind them, there is no cause for optimism in the continent. For the remainder of this century, it is likely that the present areas of high mortality, especially infant mortality, that is, most of the rural tropical areas where poverty, disease and lack of public services are most apparent, will see a decline in these death rates, through improving

medical services, so that population increase will continue as at present, through the imbalance of births and deaths, doubling the population every 25 years, the highest rate for any area of this size in the world.

A very large question-mark must be placed over birth rates. Most of the continent is nominally Catholic and, despite a deep-rooted anti-clericalism, is likely to be slow to adopt birth control unless a change in the Church's attitude is also made. Real moves towards birth control are limited to some urban areas, where high rates of illegal abortion are found (estimated in Chile at 40 per thousand), because of the lack of alternative controls and the inconvenience of large families to these city people. Public programmes for birth control, apart from clinics to avoid the unhealthy practices of illegal abortion, are absent from the continent except in Colombia, and of little effect so far in that country.

The present coastal pattern of population may be expected to remain. Pressure by farmer colonists on the Amazon Basin may provide that land with a moderate scatter of settlements, but the superior physical infrastructure of transport, irrigation works, power and better soils must always remain an attraction near the coast. Soil erosion and soil depletion limit the viability of settling the Amazon, compared with the use of more productive lands outside it.

> The problem, how to obtain a labouring class for a new and tropical country, without slavery, has to be solved before this glorious region can become what its delightful climate and exuberant fertility fit it for — the abode of a numerous civilized and happy people.
>
> *Henry Walter Bates,* The Naturalist on the River Amazon *(London, 1863), p. 178*

This quotation from the nineteenth-century English naturalist shows the old optimism of early visitors to the deserted heart of the continent, an optimism unjustified by physical potential. The encouragement of immigration to the region is indeed difficult, but for good reasons.

Development of industrial zones and urbanization in general also favour the continuation of a coastal concentration of population, for nearly all metropolitan growth is near the coast, focussing on ports and administrative—industrial centres. Despite energetic programmes to populate the interior, such as the foundation of Brasília as an interior capital (similar proposals have been made for the capitals of Argentina and Venezuela), and the extension of roads and railways into the wilderness, economic and social forces pull out to the coast. Trade linkages to Spain and Portugal have been replaced, but by other links to the exterior, not links between the countries of the continent. The difficulty seen in building up intra-continental trade within LAFTA and similar economic groupings of countries reflects the long-established orientation of each country to the exterior, not to its neighbour.

It may be confidently predicted that a major problem area for at least the next fifteen years will be growth of the big cities. There were at least fifteen cities of over a million people in 1984. These are now distinctive not only in their scale but also in the *kinds* of problems encountered. For example, growing problems of waste disposal, air, water, noise and visual pollution call for solutions such as water transfers, recycling, ecological strips and limitation of car use. We may already speak of 'megalopolis' — a term used to describe N. America's Great Atlantic Seaboard line of cities. Caracas — La Guaira (with 3.5 million people in a region of Northern Venezuela), Lima — El Callao (4.6 millions) and Santiago — Valparaiso (4.7 millions) are all acquiring this character. All are in dry regions where a continuous supply of fresh water is difficult to maintain. Hemmed in by steep mountain walls, efficient transport and communications flow are made difficult in the urban region. In sub-tropic latitudes, comparatively still air for much of the year and basin-shape valleys mean frequent heavy air pollution. Buenos Aires (10.0 millions) and the River Plate towns and Sao Paulo — Santos (12.6 millions) are relatively favoured in their sites.

Beyond the physical aspects, the socio-economic problems of these great cities are equally daunting. There is not the manufacturing base found in many big cities of richer countries. Tertiary employment dominates. In real terms, there is only a very limited economic base, because much of the tertiary employment is in the informal sector. Part-time jobs such as market or street selling give only subsistence returns.

6. Politics and Territory

This section concerns territorial issues which are broader than those commonly treated by political geographers. The most newsworthy of these are the international disputes over boundary lines and their location. Many such problems date back to the colonial period and the Wars of Independence, 1810-25, when new republics were created in a structure uncontemplated by imperial Spain. At best, the limits inherited were interprovincial boundaries that had little significance for the local populations. Most ran through public lands that had not been settled by man, in desert country or high mountains, and as a consequence they had not been surveyed or precisely described. It seems that the Spaniards were particularly weak in definition of water boundaries, such as the Argentine-Uruguayan frontier along the Uruguay river, with its many mid-river islands claimed by both sides. Similar conflicts occurred along the Pilcomayo bordering Argentina and Paraguay. Another kind of problem occurred through the expansionist nature of some states, notably Brazil. A secular process of *de facto* settlement in frontier zones has traditionally been followed by territorial claims and minor skirmishes on the frontier, then a settlement which has commonly favoured the occupying power. The third issue examined is that of regionalism, local political feeling which occasionally builds up to arguments for separation from the nation.

BOUNDARY DISPUTES

Argentina — Chile boundaries

One of the best-known demarcation disputes was that over the Southern Andes, between Argentina and Chile in lat. 40-52°S. In colonial time the effective Chilean-Argentine boundary was the 'Sierra Nevada' of the Andes, which needed no precise definition, as it was such an obvious barrier. In the nineteenth century it was realized that this was insufficient and a treaty of 1881 established the line as that of 'the highest peaks which divide waters', i.e. the combination of the drainage and topographic divide. Unfortunately these two do not coincide, because the Pleistocene glaciers left their terminal moraines well to the east of the mountains and diverted rivers flowing east, back through transverse fractures in the mountains and towards the Pacific. Thus the Atlantic/Pacific divide lies up to 150 kilometres east of the line of peaks. The solution given to this problem in 1902 was a compromise dividing the disputed area in two between the litigants, but failing to please either of them.

A more recent dispute which has almost led to war between Chile and Argentina is the Beagle Channel dispute. At the outlet of this sea channel running east-west on the south side of Tierra del Fuego lie three small islands, Lennox, Nueva and Picton. These isles have no importance in themselves, but are the basis for Antarctic claims, since recognition of them as Chilean extends Chilean territory sixty kilometres eastwards. This is significant because both Chile and Argentina claim that part of Antarctica which lies pole-wards of their continental lands. Chile has in fact been granted the islands and a three-mile zone around them in a November 1984 settlement, following papal mediation from 1979. But the settlement specifically excludes any Antarctic claims, and both countries still take as the marker a line drawn south from Cape Horn.

Falklands–Malvinas

In 1982 an armed conflict took place between Argentina and Britain over a territory of 12 000 square kilometres with a population of 1800 persons. The Falklands question cannot be classified as a border dispute nor as geopolitics, though it contains elements of both. Again, a new republic had uncertain claims to a border area, in this case islands, which had seen more occupation by French and British in the eighteenth century than by the Spanish. At independence time there were no occupants, nor did Spain make any specific delegation of rights to Argentina or other powers. Britain's occupation in 1833 followed her eighteenth-century claim, but was opposed by Argentina up to the present. Geopolitics entered early, for Britain used the islands, especially prior to construction of the Panama Canal, as a relay point and coaling station on the route to the Pacific, for naval and merchant shipping. For Argentina, the Falklands must be seen as an extension of the aggressive expansion which moved from the River Plate in the late eighteenth century to finish with Patagonia in a campaign called 'The Conquest of the Desert' in 1883. It also serves as the basis, together with S. Georgia and the S. Sandwich Isles, for claims to all of Antarctica between 25°W and 74°W, a claim that overlaps with that of Britain.

There were other issues. The immediate cause of the conflict was the military government's need to resolve its internal crisis of confidence by a well-known tactic: turning public attention to the exterior through military occupation of land long claimed. The conflict could also be presented to the public as a final defeat of imperial powers, since the Falklands are a colony and the land worked as what Argentines would easily recognize as a series of great *estancias,* with little

access to land for small farmers. On the other side, Britain claimed the need to uphold the principle, established after the First World War, of the self-determination of nations, i.e. the right to local choice of which state to belong to, though this was perhaps less applicable here, given the small size of the community. Behind this argument observers saw a fight over resources, especially the marine resource including a giant protein resource of krill, a shrimp species found particularly off S. Georgia, and oil possibilities in the continental shelf which here extends out to the Falklands from the mainland. Surveys done by the British government have seen little by way of land resources in the Falklands; although the wool industry of the islands leaves many sheep carcasses unused, there are considerable difficulties in setting up a meat-processing industry to feed distant markets which are already well supplied.

The aftermath of the Falklands dispute is of interest. On the British side there has been considerable investment, mostly military, in the airport and defences, but also a little in the local economy. For Argentina there is a continued interest in settling the score, which has been combined with the need to assert finally Argentina's claim to Patagonia (Chile has had a claim here since colonial time), and to encourage regional development, through a new proposal to set up a national capital in Patagonia, replacing Buenos Aires and its big-city problems with Viedma, a tiny town on the mouth of the Rio Negro. Viedma lies at 41°S rather than 52°S, as is the case with the Falklands, but it must in part represent a new focussing of attention on Patagonia and the Malvinas, following the example of Brazil in moving her capital on political rather than economic grounds.

Venezuela

Venezuela has two important contemporary border issues: the first concerns the Colombian frontier in its northernmost section, where it passes through the Guajira peninsula within 10 km of the Gulf of Venezuela, emerging at Castilletes. The main question concerns the line taken out to sea through the Gulf, which Venezuela considers should follow northeast as on land, but which Colombia, believes should extend out at right angles to the coastline. The interest resides in the large oil resources known to exist under the Gulf, as yet untapped, since they lie in deeper and more exposed waters than those of L. Maracaibo.

On the eastern flank, Venezuela has other quarrels with Guyana, claiming up to the Essequibo River, i.e. most of present-day Guyana. This dispute shows little sign of an early termination. Ecuador too has kept alight her quarrel with Peru, over eastern plains territory lost as recently as 1941 in a short war. Ecuadorean documents, even school notebooks, state that the country is an Amazonian country, emphasizing that the land lost to Peru was that reaching down to the Marañon and thus to the Amazon. There are skirmishes in the border country between these two countries virtually every year.

GEOPOLITICS

Brazil

A feature of S. America is that politics *is* a geographical subject. In several countries, and notably in Brazil, governments have paid close attention to the study of geopolitics, viewing the state as an institution with a strong relationship to specific territories. Brazil has a history of constant expansion to the west, which has been very successful because each claim was backed by real settlement. Settlement within the Andean colonies was in the mountains, and few farmers ever wished to settle in the lowland jungles, with their unkown diseases, isolation from the core areas, and need to learn new ways to survive and produce food. By contrast, the Brazilian *caboclo*, starting near the tropical coasts whose climate and other conditions were not too different to those of the interior, saw fewer disadvantages to a life on the frontier and was better adapted to it. Brazil thus spread far to the west, far beyond the area allotted to her under the Treaty of Tordesillas, with effective occupation that was much more important than diplomatic claims.

In the 1930s, the populist Vargas government established a catch-phrase, *Marcha para Oeste,* the March to the West, which was a symbol of the colonizing spirit, and seems to have been an effective slogan for one of the government's aims. In the 1930s too, there first arose interest in geopolitics, with notice being taken of Germany using geopolitical arguments to justify her expansion. The theory could be applied in two ways in Brazil, internally and externally.

Internal expansion was most desired into the Centre-West region of Mato Grosso and Rondonia, and into Amazonia in the north, two regions of very slight population density. A specific danger was noted, that of Argentina, a state with a more sophisticated economy than that of Brazil at the time, which through her rail network had already extended links into Bolivia and was thus outflanking Brazil along the line of the Andes. A way of combating this danger was through expansion of effective settlement and economic power, including good transport links, first between the central region around Rio and São Paulo, and the Northeast region, followed by an expansion into the Centre-West, to the strategically dominant central Brazilian plateau, at the headwaters of the three main river systems, Paraná, Amazon and São Francisco. The move of the capital from Rio to Brasilia both symbolizes and is a part of this move. A final stage is of colonization down the interfluves between the great river valleys, into Amazonia, the last frontier.

This last phase, supported by state colonization schemes and by the Transamazonia road scheme, has aroused considerable controversy. While Amazon roads, mineral development and farmer colonization have been presented to the outside world as a solution to land problems in the Nordeste, as a programme for national integration and a way to increase national food and materials production, they are criticized not only by ecologists as destroying the last major rain forest, but by those who regard the whole plan as one of expansionism.

Expansionism is also seen in Brazil's external manoeuvres. Paraguay is increasingly dominated by Brazil, which provides her with free port facilities at Paranagua, has financed her part of the costs of construction of Itaipu, and buys at a (low) contracted rate Paraguay's share of the power this huge dam on the Parana is producing. Paraguay is also the target area for many thousands of Brazilian farmers who have pushed the farm frontier westwards continuously through Parana state and now into Paraguay.

Bolivia

Bolivia is also a target for Brazil's expansionism. Since several 'bites' of land have been taken from Bolivia in the last century, Brazil's geopolitical writers have seen the reduced Bolivian territory as an important hinge zone, a heartland for S. America. The area of southern Bolivia is a watershed zone, between Parana and Amazon to north and south, and between Atlantic and Pacific drainage. Various moves have been made to integrate this country into Brazilian economic life, including offers to use its iron ore in exchange for construction of a steel plant, or to help with a railway linking it to the Andean lands and thus the Pacific.

The other side of the coin of Brazilian expansionism is the case of the small state which is dependent on its neighbour, has suffered territorial or economic loss at its hands and seeks some redress of grievances. In Bolivia this situation surfaces as irredentism, the drive to recover lost territory. Some details are available in the chapter on Bolivia, but it may be mentioned here as an interesting political issue. A major grievance is the loss of access to the Pacific as a result of defeat in the War of the Pacific, when a Bolivian corridor to the ocean was taken by Chile. A 1978 proposal to cut Bolivia a corridor through the northernmost fringe of Chile was rejected by Peru, and tension continues. Peru's argument is that the corridor would run through the land which Chile won from her (Peru) in the War of the Pacific and which she still claims is rightfully her own, and the corridor should thus go further south, in the original Bolivian territory.

REGIONALISM

Compared with Europe, the issue of regionalism in S. America seems relatively unimportant. There is nothing to parallel the old separate cultures of Europe, such as Wales in Britain, Brittany in France, or Catalonia in Spain. There are deep historical reasons for the lack of such cultural divisions — the Iberian conquerors destroyed most of the native high cultures in the Andes, and did not settle in large enough numbers to create their own culture, as happened in N. America. Through the colonial time and into modern days too, there has been in S. American countries a strongly centralist type of government, with vertical links of patronage to lower levels of the administrative hierarchy, supported by strong military and clerical hierarchies. Only now is there emerging some realization of folk cultures in those areas with a surviving Indian

tradition, a new interest in, for example, the use of native languages including the publication of books and school instruction, particularly in the Central Andes.

Argentina
Regional culture and economy did however find some expression in the nineteenth century, and this might come to surface again in the future. In Argentina, a long-standing difference in orientation between the Humid Pampas, basically Buenos Aires' province, and the interior provinces, came to a head in the search for a new political structure after Independence. On the one hand the Buenos Aires Unitarians supported free trade, on which their wealth rested, and tried to form a centralized type of government which they would head. The interior had during colonial time built up local economies based on production for home markets, grain, wine, sugar, textiles and craft works. Here the argument was for a federal government which would reduce the omnipotence of Buenos Aires, seeking some protection for the local, regional industries of each province.

Behind economic differences lay long-term differences in treatment under Spain, whereby Buenos Aires, but not the remote interior, had been opened to external influences. Domingo Sarmiento, the Argentine statesman, characterized the difference as one between barbarity and civilization, an exaggeration but enough to allow a clash. The civil war was not finished until the 1860s, when Buenos Aires established a fully centralized control over the whole country, despite a constitution which resembles that of the United States.

Venezuela and Brazil
In a more fluid situation, this economically-based regionalism was solved in Venezuela and in Brazil in comparable ways. In Venezuela, Romulo Gallegos, the president and noted writer of the 1940s, described the nineteenth-century divisions as those between barbarism and civilization like Sarmiento; the Llanos of the south was a wild country where there was a constant danger of its lapsing into anarchy through the rule of local strong men; Caracas was the centre, with links to Europe and N. America, and with some flowering of culture through these influences. Here the regionalism of the Andean

region, the strongest in the nineteenth century through its development of coffee for export, was resolved by the Andean politicians taking over the central government in Caracas itself, from 1908. In Brazil too, regional consciousness was a limited aspect of nineteenth-century life and was mostly based on economic considerations. It has been argued that Brazil held together as a unit after Independence because there was only one focus of economic power, changing from brazil wood on the coast, to sugar in the northeast, to gold and then coffee in the nineteenth century.

The time of greatest potential for separation or division of Brazil was in the late nineteenth century, and the Republic then formed (1889 up to 1930) was relatively decentralized and regionalist in character. But very few people were politically aware; the political issues of the day — slavery, which was opposed by Rio Grande do Sul; the African heritage, sought in Pernambuco in the northeast — these were understood only by the educated minority.

Ecuador and Peru

There is some expression of regional feeling in the Andean states. One such is in Ecuador (Kasza, 1981). Here the main division has always been between Costa and Sierra. The conflict is perhaps stronger than elsewhere because there are only two important regions, each of comparable size and each with a sizeable metropolitan centre: Guayaquil on the coast, Quito in the Sierra. Quito's interest has generally been far more inward-looking, connected to the Church (which held much land here), to traditional semi-feudal agriculture, and life has focused on regional trade, plus the central government offices sited here with related civil service and agency offices. There have been cultural differences, but they did not form a basis for political movements. On the coast, plantation agriculture led to a predominance of Negro slaves, and Negro mixtures still dominate, whereas the Sierra has either *mestizo* groups or even pure Indian blood in some highland basins. The *montubio* of the coast is usually depicted as an independent, restless type, contrasting with the Indian *longo* of the Sierra, a stoic, passive, immobile and long-suffering type. The Spanish language spoken in the Sierra is more correct and less fluid than that on the Coast. In the event,

quarrels between the two regions have not been about culture but economic differences, because of the very different economic orientation of the two, and because of the perceived bias on the part of the central government, favouring the Sierra region in its investments.

In Peru, a far more serious movement with regionalist origins is the Sendero Luminoso movement, based on Maoist communism mixed with indigenous ideas. The southern Sierra has a long history of peasant rebellion reaching back to colonial time, when the most important movement had been that of Tupac Amaru in 1780–1, started in Cuzco as a revolt against abuses of colonial power and eventually calling for an Indian–*mestizo* republic to be set up. Apart from ethnic exploitation, there were bases for regional separatism in the fact that the south was administratively marginal, between the viceroyalties of Lima and the River Plate, and was indeed placed in the latter on its creation by Spain in the eighteenth century.

Sendero began in 1970 as a university movement in the impoverished southern Sierra, the poorest region of Peru, based on Mao's analysis of capitalism as an urban-industrial-based force, which would need to be combated from the countryside by the opposing force of the traditional peasant economy and society. It would reject modern technology and start rebellion among the peasants who were least drawn into the modern market economy. Since 1980 a terrorist campaign has been conducted by Sendero, with violent reprisals by the government forces which have failed to quell the movement — in 1985, Lima was without electric power for days as a result of Sendero dynamite attacks on power stations.

We may summarize some of the foregoing points on regionalism with some generalizations.

1. Regional identity was nearly completely crushed by the colonial experience and that of nineteenth-century neo-colonialism;

2. In some countries, as a result, little cultural regionalism may be seen, and the only type is economic, based on a lack of full central control and on the varied interests of provincial élites. This was the case in nineteenth-century Brazil and Argentina. Even in those countries with some evidence of regional feeling, like Peru, only certain regions, like the southern Sierra, are

affected, while others, like much of the Costa, have little identity.

3. There is a model of national growth, wherein localist or regionalist feelings are suppressed or lost as the central power extends itself to all areas and imposes its ideas, aided by expansion of transport and communications. Regionalism might recur at a later stage, when peripheral regions experience a fuller realization of their dependent status through the spread of education. For S. America, the early stage of modernization and unification is still in progress; despite 160 years of independence, full integration of society is still taking place as national school systems are created, roads built, and particularly as many rural people are brought into contact with the national culture through visits to the big cities or permanent migration to them in search of work.

7. Patterns and Policies for Development

Using standard indices of economic development, South American countries are classified within the Third World, though their standing within that group is relatively high, higher than the countries of Africa or Southeast Asia. In measuring economic development, a common indicator is per capita GNP (Gross National Product). The World Bank makes a division at 400 dollars per capita GNP. Countries below this level are regarded as the low-income group.* No S. American country comes into this category — all are lower-middle or upper-middle income countries. It is also now accepted that there are important social and demographic aspects of development which an index should incorporate. A simple representation of the two major dimensions is provided in the graph (Fig. 14), which for S. America shows a general correspondence between the two dimensions, but also some deviations.

One such deviation is seen in Venezuela. This country has achieved very high income levels from its oil revenues, comparable to European countries, but has not been able or willing to distribute this wealth in social services. The problem arises partly because income is generated in one major industry, the oil industry, which employs less than 1% of the labour force. This industry has few linkages to the rural population, or even to most of the urban population; the government owns the industry and has long sought to 'sow the oil', but has had little success in doing this. This sectoral lack of linkages is matched by a spatial lack of integration, which has created problems of regional inequality.

DEVELOPMENT TRENDS

Economic development is proceeding in most parts of the continent. The figures in the table, for 1960–80, show a very varied pattern of change, dependent on political controls and international markets more than on internal processes of any one country. The 1984 figures are appended, showing the varied effects of world recession. It is tempting to ascribe Argentina's poor performance, or that of Chile, to political turmoil in the 1970s and frequent changes in the management of development, except that Uruguay, with little political change, has the same history. What seems to have happened is a fading of earlier growth based on import substitution industrialization, and a failure to find new ways forward. Argentina seems to have been most hurt by monetarism, while Chile and Uruguay have been more damaged by the decline in prices for the exports of raw materials.

Among the poor countries, Bolivia, still very reliant on tin mining and related processing, and Guyana, reliant on sugar cane, made limited progress. However, Ecuador moved ahead rapidly, aided by oil discoveries, and so did Paraguay, with her economy boosted by agricultural colonization and hydroelectric development, both of these linked to Brazilian participation. Brazil was indeed the dynamo of growth within the continent, able to survive the oil crisis by a variety

*World Bank (1985) *World Development Report 1985*, Oxford University Press, Table 10, pp 192-193

GDP PER CAPITA *(1982 dollars)*

Country	1960	1970	1980	% growth 1960–80	1984
Argentina	1586	2065	2240	41.2	1929
Bolivia	441	550	655	48.5	475
Brazil	761	1078	1924	152.8	1626
Chile	1413	1735	1878	32.9	1674
Colombia	656	764	1059	61.4	1045
Ecuador	582	697	1216	108.9	1124
Guyana	721	851	905	25.5	665
Paraguay	613	743	1336	117.9	1633
Peru	814	1051	1135	39.4	978
Surinam	n.a.	n.a.	2615	–	2516
Uruguay	1710	1887	2427	41.9	2024
Venezuela	2054	2649	3064	49.2	2340

Source: IDB Annual Report, 1984, Washington D.C.

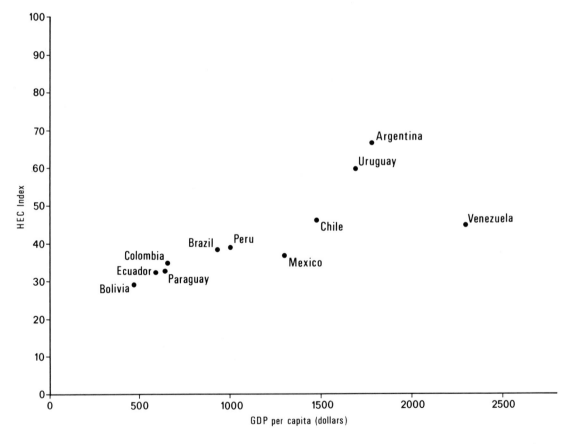

Fig. 14 The relations of income and development (HEC = Health, Education and Communications Index 1940–1970, based on data from the Statistical Abstract of Latin America, *vol. 23, p.16)*

of growth strategies, promoting export of soya-beans in place of coffee, and manufactured goods in place of raw materials. Overall, the trend of the last twenty years has been positive, despite the negative effects of world markets, and certainly has been much better than the achievement of many African and Asian countries.

STRATEGIES FOR DEVELOPMENT

Historically, development depended on relations with the mother country and trade with it. Trade was dominated by Spain and Portugal, or rather, by the countries of Northwest Europe through the intermediary of the Iberian countries. The colonies sent primary products (wheat, cocoa, sugar, or silver) to the mother country, which in turn used the silver to pay for imported manufactures from northern Europe. This colonial pattern was maintained during the nineteenth century, the time of neo-colonialism or economic colonialism, which implies a position of dependency through trade and investment without any need for the overseas power to own colonies. Britain and later the United States of America were the dominant partners in this relationship, which for some countries lasted until the recent past.

Import substitution

The primary-product export period was succeeded in many countries, during the twentieth century, by moves towards domestic manufacturing. This had been discouraged, even prohibited, during colonial and neo-colonial times, but during the First World War and again in the 1930s and the Second World War overseas supplies of some manufactures were cut off and an effort was made to replace them, notably in the more advanced countries where markets were strong — in the countries of the southern cone. This overall policy may be classified as one of import substitution, i.e. the replacement of imported goods by domestic equivalents. Replacement was never complete; it depended partially on the raising of tariff barriers, and these for a number of reasons tended to be greatest on finished products. As a result, the industries which were set up themselves tended to be consumer industries, making clothes, furniture, cigarettes, or assembling cars from knocked-down kits.

In the 1950s and 1960s this kind of policy was given official endorsement, as writers such as Raul Prebisch of the United Nations Economic Commission for Latin America called attention to the deterioration in the terms of trade between raw materials and manufactured goods, the latter's price rises affecting badly the economy of countries which had to export materials at stagnating or even declining prices. It was also noted that the demand for manufactured goods is always expanding and more products are constantly coming onto the market, which does not happen with raw materials producers.

Import substitution had its own limitations, as countries were quick to find out in the 1960s. The new industries were technologically limited — advanced technology was difficult and expensive to bring in, if it could be acquired at all. Production was often excessively expensive, because the infant industries, behind the protection of the high tariff barriers, did not have to be highly efficient and produce at internationally competitive prices. Nor did the industries reach a size where maximum economies of scale were achieved; even today, the continent's steel industries, such as that of Chile with an annual output of two million tonnes, are far short of the optimum size of perhaps 10 million tonnes for one plant. In addition, many of the new factories set up on industrial estates in Brazil, Venezuela, or Argentina, to name those three which attracted the heaviest foreign investment, were branch plants of major multinational firms and placed the host country in a position of dependency, unable to plan its own development.

Manufactured exports

One way forward from the impasse of small size markets was to increase manufactured production for export. The table shows the structure of South American exports for 1965 and 1982. Brazil has had the greatest success, her manufactured exports building up from 9% in 1965 to 39% in 1982. Much of this consists of processed foodstuffs such as soyabean oil and cottonseed oil, but cars are an increasing element, as are iron and steel, textiles and leather goods. No S. American country can match the Asian NICs (Newly Industrialized Countries), of which South Korea is given as an example. And there are other differences — most countries have not emulated that Asian concentration on textiles, though these are important in Colombia and

Uruguay. Capital goods exports are a distinctive feature, forming about 20% of the total in Argentina and Brazil. Nor are the markets the same as for the NICs; much of the market for Argentine manufactures is found in neighbouring countries.

Argentina, Brazil, Uruguay and Venezuela have made the further step, into direct investment in foreign countries, either through their great state monopolies such as petroleum, or through large private firms. Argentina, for example, has a long history of foreign investment. Her state petroleum industry has been active in recent years, building pipelines in Peru and exploring for oil in the Andean countries, and Peru has also received Argentine aid in her atomic energy industry. Among the private firms, Siam di Tella, Alpargatas and Bunge and Born can all be regarded as multinationals, with many subsidiaries. They have been engaged in many activities since before the Second World War.*

REGIONAL ASSOCIATIONS

There were other ways in which countries could react to the lack of progress resulting from import substitution. One was to rely again on primary exports, as has been done to some extent by Chile, Bolivia and Peru. Another way was to

PERCENTAGE SHARE OF MERCHANDISE EXPORTS

Country	Textiles & clothing 1965	1982	Machinery & transport 1965	1982	Other manu- facturing 1965	1982
Argentina	–	1	1	7	4	16
Bolivia	–	–	–	–	4	–
Brazil	1	3	2	17	6	19
Chile	–	–	1	3	4	5
Colombia	2	7	–	3	4	15
Ecuador	1	–	–	1	2	2
Paraguay	–	–	–	–	8	–
Peru	–	8	–	1	1	5
Uruguay	2	13	–	1	3	18
Venezuela	–	–	–	1	2	2
S. Korea	27	21	3	28	29	43

Source: World Bank (1985), World Development Report 1985, Oxford University Press, Table 10, pp192–3.

*UNIDO, United Nations Industrial Development Organization (1983) *Technology Exports from Developing Countries (1): Argentina and Portugal,* U.N., New York

overcome the market size problem by forming regional alliances which together would form an enlarged market, a common market.

LAFTA and LAIA
The Latin American Free Trade Association, LAFTA, was created in 1960, a first attempt at integration and embracing all of South America except the Guianas, with the addition of Mexico. As a functioning unit it had limited success. No common external tariff levels were agreed, and member countries found it difficult to agree internal tariff levels, especially as each item was to be negotiated separately. There were also problems because of the differences in development level between the richer and poorer countries of the group.

LAFTA negotiation had reached a standstill by 1969, when the Andean Pact was made. Intrazonal trade has continued to grow up to the present, but the share of trade subject to LAFTA agreements has declined from a peak in 1966. Countries like Paraguay and latterly Bolivia have a strong intra-regional trade, but most look outside the continent for trading partners.

A reshaping of the framework was carried out in 1980, forming LAIA, the Latin American Integration Association. The aims here were far-reaching, but started from a looser and smaller base than LAFTA, relying on bilateral tariff reductions for any pair of countries, to which others might be added later, plus tariff reductions by individual members with respect to all others. It remains to be seen what progress will be achieved under this arrangement.

INTRAREGIONAL EXPORTS AS A PERCENTAGE OF TOTAL EXPORTS

Country	1962	1970	Most Recent Yr.
Argentina	13.0	21.0	20.3 a
Bolivia	4.1	8.5	31.5 d
Brazil	6.4	11.6	15.0 a
Chile	8.5	11.2	24.7 c
Colombia	5.5	13.5	20.7 a
Ecuador	6.0	11.1	24.1 d
Mexico	5.0	10.4	6.7 d
Peru	9.6	6.4	15.6 a
Paraguay	32.6	38.5	34.4 d
Uruguay	n.a.	12.6	28.7 b
Venezuela	10.1	12.5	16.9 b

Source: Inter-American Development Bank (1984) Economic and Social Progress in Latin America, p.101.   a–1982; b–1981; c–1980; d–1979.

The Andean Pact

Dissatisfaction with LAFTA over the rate of progress, and poorer members' fears for their own position as those whose markets might be monopolized by the bigger countries, lay behind the decision to form a group within LAFTA, the Andean Group, in 1969. The countries involved were Bolivia, Colombia, Chile, Ecuador and Peru, joined by Venezuela in 1973. In addition to a free-trade zone among members, the group aspires to a common external tariff, though this has not yet been agreed and is still a bone of contention among members. Bolivia and Ecuador are given special treatment as poorer countries in the group, but this is a lesser problem than for LAFTA.

One distinctive feature of the Group is the idea of international agreements on the location of industries, so as to achieve maximum economies for the whole group. Initially eight proposals were made for sectoral industrial development of new industries; petrochemicals, metalworking, automotive, steel, electronics, chemicals, pharmaceuticals and fertilizers. Only the first four were agreed to and only three, petrochemicals, metalworking, and automotive, have been worked on. In every case, however, agreement has been reached with enormous difficulties and continuous adjustments up to the present, the problem being that each country wishes to maximize its share of any given industry. One measure that caused problems and led to the resignation of Chile from the Pact in 1976 was the limitation of foreign firms' activity and particularly the restriction on remission of profits to home countries. Chile sought a much more open foreign policy and did not wish to discourage new investors from overseas.

The River Plate Basin and the Amazon Pact

As distinct from these trading associations, there are physical groupings of the two major river basin countries, Amazon and River Plate. For the River Plate group, set up in 1969, the countries are Brazil and Argentina, with Bolivia, Paraguay and Uruguay. The agreement is simply to co-operate in schemes for physical development, such as the setting-up of electric power distribution networks, which now frequently do cross international boundaries, and especially the development of river resources. Up to the present little has actually been done under the provisions of the group, and the balance of power within it is most uneven.

Parallelling the Plate treaty, a treaty between the Amazonian countries was signed in 1978. The Treaty for Amazonian Cooperation (Amazon Pact) involves the countries with Amazon drainage, Venezuela, Colombia, Ecuador, Peru, Bolivia, plus marginal countries, Guyana and Surinam. It may be regarded as another vehicle for multinational development, though in fact the impetus for it came entirely from Brazil (Medina, 1980), and it has no agency or established machinery for building links. Like the River Plate Treaty it seeks primarily to control physical planning in the area, having articles referring to economic development, but most refer to water resources, navigation, transport and communications, scientific research and similiar themes. It may be seen as another extension of Brazil's geopolitical stance with respect to the Amazon, and Brazil is likely to be the main beneficiary of improvements, because of her central position in the Basin, her great economic and strategic strength, and her aim to have access to the Pacific.

The Guianas

Because of differences in history and culture the three Guianas have not been involved in the Latin American groupings. Guyana has since 1968 been a member of CARIFTA, the Caribbean Free Trade Association, superseded in 1973 by CARICOM, a common market arrangement. This gives it some advantages as a relatively resource-rich member of an island grouping, but isolates it from its Latin neighbours. Surinam has not seen the need for regional groupings, as it has had special access to the Common Market of Europe through its association with Holland, as has French Guiana, given its status as an overseas *département* of France.

Overall view

None of the regional associations has been as successful as might have been hoped. Perhaps we should not be too critical, for the starting position was one which saw no real cooperation or agreement at all between the different states, rather a state of general hostility. Also, there was virtually no trade, resulting from the lack of complementarity in production and high tariffs (over 100% tax in some cases) on imports from neighbouring countries. Given this situation in 1960, the present position is quite creditable.

A regional grouping of states is not wholly beneficial for each of its members. Development of manufacturing is likely to be monopolized by the stronger firms with experience of working abroad. Beyond the economic issues, there is a geopolitical element in the river basin treaties which have been signed. The River Plate Basin treaty concerns a major river whose outlet to the sea is controlled by Argentina, while much of the flow originates in Brazil. Development of this river is one aspect of a peaceful power struggle between Argentina and Brazil in which Paraguay and Bolivia are pawns used by both sides. The Amazon Treaty is still more one-sided, with Brazil as the dominant power.

FOREIGN AID AND INVESTMENT

Even with the regional association, there has been insufficient capital available for building up large industries or improving infrastructure through, for example, major roadbuilding or electric power projects. Countries have had to use foreign aid or international loans to make these investments, and this has itself caused major problems in recent years. The debt crisis of the early 1980s has grown out of a change in the volume and nature of foreign investment. Between 1978 and 1982, external debt was doubled in Brazil, Chile and Colombia, tripled in Argentina. Also, much of it was debt with variable interest rates, so that as interest rates rose over the period, debt servicing became increasingly onerous.

In the past, inter-governmental loans or loans through the major agencies — The World Bank, the Interamerican Development Bank — were the norm. Today, a larger proportion of private bank finance is found. This change started with the 1973 oil crisis, which generated large amounts of new cash from oil-rich countries without any immediate outlets for investment. Much of this petrodollar money returned to the West as investment in banks, which in turn sought investment outlets and turned to Latin America. The Latin countries used the money correctly enough, but because of the economic downturn of the 1980s, and the high interests they were asked to pay, ran heavily into debt, especially Argentina, Mexico and Brazil. For these countries, dependency had moved from physical trade, through that of multinational ownership and new technology, to that of finance. Among the lessons to be learnt from this episode is the need for more powerful financial institutions within Latin America, and for more control over the type of loan responsibility assumed by any one country.

REGIONAL DEVELOPMENT

Various chapters in this book have already examined the problems of individual countries in their internal development. In general there is the pattern of a core region for each major country which attracts capital investment, the best-trained and most valuable elements among the workforce, and which becomes the site for all new industries as they develop. This situation seems to come about as a concomitant of national economic development. As development proceeds, the differences between regions seem to grow to a maximum, because the first spurt is made at just one centre, which leaves the rest behind, until at a later stage the development impulse spreads out to the other regions. What may be noted in South America is that the spread process is notoriously slow in occurring.

The differences in income per capita between regions in Argentina, for example, perhaps the most advanced country in this respect, were in a ratio of nearly 10 to 1 between the poorest provinces of the Northwest and the province of Buenos Aires. This level of interprovincial difference is seen elsewhere, in for example, Brazil, Venezuela or Bolivia (Gilbert, 1978). What is worse, the differences within regions, between different social groups, seem to be ever stronger and less amenable to change. Thus while Brazil has been broadly successful in reducing her inter-regional differences over the years, the *intra*-regional differences between the top-paid group of society and the poorest seem to have widened over the 1970s (see Chapter 15, table on income).

Regional policies are apparently only of marginal utility in solving the core-periphery problem. While programmes have been widely publicized as giving aid to this or that region, the investment is typically under 1% of the national budget. Thus Colombia's well known CVC river basin agency is only one of nine such agencies, but between them they receive under 1% of the national budget, and 80% of this goes to the CVC alone. The CVC (see chapter on Colombia) has itself been restricted in its activities so as to deal only with water management problems, dam building and electric power generation. In Ecuador, while the agency CREA has wide-ranging roles, it has little cash and has used it for such basic matters as establishing proper local government in some rural areas where there has been no sound local administration.

Rather than the regional agencies, sectoral programmes have been significant in several countries for guiding regional change. Agrarian reform and colonization, for example, have a potentially powerful role in redistributing growth to rural regions; to date they have had a limited role in reality, because of the political and administrative difficulties in application of any reform, and the failure to back up legislation with major investments in infrastructure such as roads, marketing systems, farmer credit and farmer training. Industrial planning has been similarly unsuccessful so far, but has at least aided the development of some towns outside the national metropolises. In Argentina, Cordoba received industrial estates and attracted new industries, though the rural region around it felt little impact. In Peru, Arequipa had similar investment in industries during the 1960s during a programme of industrial deconcentration, but most were guided from Lima and had few links to the rural hinterland. In Chile, CORFO helped the expansion of the Little South region around Concepcion with its steel industries, textiles and ceramics. And in Venezuela industry was attracted to the Valencia–Maracay–Caracas transport corridor outside the federal district itself.

Overall the problem of regional development may be said to parallel that of national development — there is the choice between externally-oriented development, which involves a degree of dependency on the outside, specifically on the national metropolis, and locally based development. The latter would be achieved through some partial closure of the local economy comparable to that at national level achieved by erecting tariff barriers against imports, in order to protect local development.

This 'development from below', according to its proponents (Stohr and Taylor, 1980), would use local raw materials, produce with locally-available technology, and link local towns with their rural hinterlands. The towns would process resources from the countryside and provide services to it. Maximum local participation in development schemes would be sought, so that success would be ensured by the degree of commitment of local residents. Diversification of production would be sought, to make the region less dependent on any single product.

Elements of this kind of development have been adopted here and there on a small scale throughout the continent, but there are obvious practical difficulties in achieving any local regional closure unless the region is naturally isolated from the centre of the nation, and has a history of independent enterprise, as has been the case in Arequipa in Peru, or at Medellin in the Antioquia region of Colombia (Morris, 1981). There are also political difficulties involved — very few regions now have any strong sense of regionalism, even at the level of a separate regional culture, let alone any regional institutions or organizations which might bring about an autonomous development process. The old pre-colonial Indian cultures are still represented by languages and individual customs, but they are remnants which need much reviving. The nineteenth-century economic regionalisms seem to have little weight in a centralist twentieth century.

Reformist governments such as the 1970s Peruvian military have sought to incorporate some elements of the old community structure of pre-European origins in their agrarian and industrial reforms, by creating or regenerating communities and cooperatives to run different land areas or industries; cooperatives have been widely sponsored in Chile and Ecuador too. But in none of these cases has there been great success, one of the principal difficulties being that the communities have to survive within a general capitalist economic structure, where it is difficult for them to compete.

Over the long term, regionalism may come to life again as a force and help along the peripheral regions of today. In the meantime, however, the balance seems to be estalished between regions by a process of massive migration from rural areas to the cities, with migrants abandoning the poorer regions and seeking the better-paid urban jobs. Instead of moving jobs and capital investment to the regions, the people are moving to the jobs. This has tremendous social costs in the breaking-up of traditional societies and their replacement by the social anarchy of the big Latin American cities.

THE HIGHLAND CORE

8. Peru — the Heartland

Peru with Bolivia, or Alto Peru as the latter was known, was the cultural and economic heartland of South America from pre-Conquest times till the nineteenth century, centre of an empire and home to the highest civilization on the continent. There is no longer any economic or political centrality to the country, but it is still a heartland in another sense, in displaying all that is most typical, most quintessentially the continent's problems in internal relations, between Indian, mestizo and white man, and in external relations, between foreign companies and states seeking its riches, and the home needs of a poor nation. In the forms and purposes of exploitation of man by man, region by region, country by country, it is typically Latin American, and seems destined to remain so despite drastic measures towards nationalization in recent years.

ECONOMIC AND SOCIAL HISTORY

The early civilizations have been mentioned already, but here their forms of social and economic conduct may be outlined. The pre-Inca highland economy, to judge by its remains among the Aymará, the dominant Indian cultural group apart from the Quechua-speaking Incas, was communal; the term *ayllu*, still in current use, signifies a community with close social ties, where land was held in usufruct by the village members, ownership being held by the whole community. The land area of the *ayllu* was the *marca*, a word which still occurs in the place

names such as Cajamarca. Cooperation in village life was typical and some forms of it, especially in crop harvesting or road and bridge building and maintenance, have survived to the present, despite later governments' insistence on private property as the only legal possibility. This communalism was scarcely communism as modern writers have sometimes insisted, but a forced cooperation for survival, to farm a difficult land. Later, under the Incas and perhaps for some centuries earlier, it was organized still further but not in communal form, rather in a despotic way in order to build the great palaces and temples of kings, to construct irrigation systems and level terraces. It may have been, as Karl Wittfogel suggested, that there is a strong causal relationship between the rise of civilizations needing massive hydraulic engineering feats, and despotic, intensely hierarchical political systems, where the king or leader is elevated to the position of a god.

The Incas

Chief of the pre-Columbian Peruvian state was a god-king, the Inca, surrounded by a large court, military leaders and a bureaucracy of priests. This strongly structured administrative order probably kept most of society in great poverty, because all cultivated village land was divided into three parts, one designated as lands of the Inca, and used for his purposes, another as lands of the Sun, feeding the priesthood, and the third for the *ayllu*. This third part was adjusted so as to suffice for the *ayllu* population, but poverty was the norm for all but the upper classes, a poverty derived in part from the unbalanced and limited diet. Protein foods from animals were generally scarce, and there were few wild animals to make up for the lack of domesticates. Potatoes and maize seem to have been twin staffs of life, and a variety of plants unknown outside the altiplano were also minor food sources: quinua, a useful grain because of its high protein content, oca, olluco, añu (tuberose plants), mashua, lupins and cañihua, all of which could be grown on the difficult lands at over 4000 m altitude.

Inca engineering feats are well known, especially their ability at drystone wall construction using great irregular-faced rocks. In Cuzco and elsewhere these have proved earthquake- and decay-proof over the centuries, more so than Spanish buildings built above them. They were skilled in irrigation works, terraces, drainage and irrigation canals passing long distances across irregular ground. Inca knowledge must have been largely an inheritance, for the builders of Tiahuanaco and other military—ceremonial cities before the Incas had used similar techniques and massive labour organization to build their monuments. The ultimate origins of altiplano civilization are uncertain; old civili-

zations are found on the coast but this is partly due to better preservation than on the uplands. The oldest Tiahuanaco architecture has stone designs based on timber design principles. Timber was in short supply both on the deserts of the coast and in the sierras, which leaves the Amazon region, rich in timber, a mysterious possible source for later high cultures. More immediately the heritage is from the Moche—Chimu state of the northern coastlands in the Moche valley, a hierarchically organized state with its centre at Chan-Chan near modern Trujillo, where 23 sq km are covered in adobe remains.

There may have been an alternation of power between the Andean centre around Titicaca (Tiahuanaco and Inca cultures) and the north coast (Moche and Chimu states). The Moche origins are in an old-established coastal civilization which has been traced back to Neolithic origins (Moseley and Day, 1982). From 3500 BC to 1800 BC there were only fishing villages living off the rich marine resource here. Later, this resource was presumably insufficient and an incipient agriculture to produce cotton and gourds became dominant as a means of subsistence, through a move from the coast to the inner edge of the coastal plain. This period lasted from

12 Machu Picchu and llamas. This isolated mountain-edge site was probably only an occasional royal residence, at the subtropical margin of the empire

1800 BC to 1500 BC. From 1500 BC to 500 BC, irrigation agriculture extended downstream towards the coast, allowing an increasing population and more complex culture to develop. At its height, the area of the Moche Valley irrigation system was 30% larger than that of the present, bringing water 80 km from the Chicama valley to the north. The Chimu state, organized as successor to the Moche, lasted till it was overthrown by the Incas in 1470, but many features of its organization were passed on to the Incas, such as a split inheritance: one ruler taking the existing royal wealth, the other assuming leadership of the state but needing to create his own wealth through new lands conquered or taxes raised. This device must have been a powerful motor for agressive expansion of the state.

Conquest and resistance
Spanish conquest was rapid and crushing, but not entirely complete despite a great superiority in arms. From Pizarro's 1533 entry into Cuzco up to 1572, there was continuous resistance by the last of the Incas and their followers. This rearguard action concentrated in the Incas' Anti-Suyo (the name which gave the Spaniards their Andes) or Eastern Empire, located in the mountains north of Cuzco which border the montaña, and in the montaña itself. Here a guerrilla war was possible because of the impossibility of access on horseback to parts of the rugged region, so that a few thousand Indians could hide from Spanish arms and make occasional sorties. A remnant state of Vilcabamba was beginning to emerge, and might with more diplomacy have remained as a native state, but it was destroyed in 1572 by a Spanish war party. The subsequent search for a mysterious lost city of Vilcabamba, home of the last Incas, led to explorations from the mid-nineteenth century on, and to the discovery of the famous and spectacular ruins of Machu Picchu (plate 12) above the Rio Urubamba northwest of Cuzco. Hiram Bingham, who found Machu Picchu, thought it must be Vilcabamba, but it now appears likely that it was a royal Inca residence, on the edge of the subtropical montaña and perhaps producing coca, a royal monopoly, from surrounding plantations. The true lost city was further to the northwest, lying at 1100 m altitude right out of the upland core, at a place called Espiritu

Pampa, the Plain of the Spirits, an appropriate name for the resting place of a civilization.

Colonial economy and society
Inca hierarchy was rapidly replaced by Spanish hierarchies; the Lands of the Inca were given out to the conquistadores in distributions *(repartimientos)*, while *encomiendas*, entrustments of native people, became effective land grants despite royal edicts from Spanish monarchs and the efforts of Viceroy Toledo in the sixteenth century. Peasants were collected into hundreds of new villages *(reducciones)* to make them more accessible for control and tax payments than in their former hamlets and farms. Such shifts in settlement caused further loss of land, *ayllu* land which slipped into Spanish hands. In any case control over land was difficult for Indians whose population was almost literally decimated, the decline in numbers being very severe on the coast where old irrigation canals fell into disrepair and the economy consequently collapsed. The Inca system of forced labour, the *mita*, and European diseases such as scarlet fever and smallpox helped in the decline of population from 20 million to 8 million in 1548. Although Lima gained in importance continuously as capital of the Viceroyalty and the trade centre, the rest of the land suffered.

Huancavelica
Mining was another drain on rural resources, especially of men. At Huancavelica between Lima and Cuzco a mercury deposit was found in 1563 which, following the 1570 introduction of the amalgamation process for silver refining into Peru from Mexico, led to what Viceroy Toledo, its introducer, called 'the most important marriage in the world, that between Potosí and Huancavelica'. Huancavelica's importance was as the only source of mercury in America, and thus a controlling factor over silver production. Other mercury mines were closed and Huancavelica made a royal monopoly, so that it could be carefully controlled. Taxes were raised on production by concessionaires, royal profits were made on sales of mercury from the mines to the silver refiners at Potosí, and taxes on silver could be checked against the amount of mercury used rather than on silver mined so as to prevent any cheating on claimed production. A *mita* was

established to work the mine and was fed by Indians from nearby provinces. Abuse of this labour, mercury poisoning, tuberculosis and other pulmonary diseases from the exposure of miners to cold altiplano air after hours in an overheated mine, and deaths from poison gases in the mine, all accounted for many thousands of labourers. The provinces around the mine were depopulated by natives fleeing the dreaded *mita*, and it was only possible to maintain it under technically crude conditions because of its monopoly position in the continent, and the vital financial role it had.

Post-colonial history

After Independence in 1825, a population of 1.3 million had little importance in the new continent. Land redistribution was planned but never enacted, the growth of latifundia continuing into the present century. No immigrants came to alter what was still a strongly Indian country, and only on the coast were there changes in outlook. Short booms from guano exports and from mineral nitrates caused momentary prosperity and financed railway construction in Peru, but the slump following Peru's loss of her nitrates in the War of the Pacific brought back national poverty.

PHYSICAL REGIONS

Peruvian geography is one of great regional contrasts, between Costa, Sierra and Selvas, and even within these divisions; the division is not precise nor always the determinant for other geographical facts but it is a real and convenient division.

The costa

This is a narrow belt of desert some 45 km wide, opening out to 160 km in the north, reduced to a few kilometres where the Andes approach the coast. It is in no sense to be thought of as a coastal plain, but as a series of terraces in an enormous staircase up to the steep wall of the mountains, at 2000 m. Through the terraces forty rivers have cut their way, in deep alluvial-floored valleys; between the valleys the Costa has a completely desert aspect, though, despite low rainfall and a tropical location, temperatures are kept low through the year by the cold water of the Humboldt current, often producing seafogs which drift in and keep out the sun for days at a time. These fogs, known as *garua*, are common in winter and may, like their equivalents in Southern California, cause smog conditions in enclosed basins along the coast.

13 The cold dry southern altiplano area at 3500 m, north of lake Titicaca, with ichu vegetation, near the port of Puno

The sierra

This lies largely at inhabitable levels between 2000 and 4000 m. At 3600–5000 m the vegetation is mostly an open grass-shrub combination. From 5000 m to 5250 m there is a frost desert, between the vegetation limit and the snowline, and above about 5250 m permanent snow. Sierran topography is comprised of two elements, a gigantic dissected tableland, and irregular volcanic or fold mountain systems rising above it to peaks at 6000 m on both flanks.

A fair idea of physiography and climate is given to any traveller taking the train from Lima up to Huancayo (fig. 17). This, the highest standard-gauge line in the world (4900 m at the summit), was built by the North American engineer Henry Meiggs. It was begun in the guano boom time of the 1870s, and later helped to plunge Peru into debt as the cost of building under extreme difficulties had its effect. The line runs up the Rimac valley, which at first is irrigated and green, then above Chosica, 80 km inland, where the landscape is increasingly arid, steep-sided and rocky. The arid upper valley was only negotiable using a zig-zag system, over sixty tunnels and sixty bridges, and then only with powerful locomotives. The line reaches the snowline, passes through a long tunnel, then starts descending through the cold wet puna into the fertile Mantaro valley at 3500 m.

The sierran landscape is mild and relatively inviting in the north, where altitudes are lower, where heavier rains allow a cover of trees and good grassland, and a more rolling topography is common. Further south a more hostile environment emerges, higher, colder and drier, with only *ichu* bunch grass and low *tola* bushes on the interfluves (plate 13). Nearly all drainage is eastwards into the Amazon system, the upper rivers cutting canyons into the sierra; such is the upper Apurimac, flowing in a gorge which formed a major military barrier when its rope bridges, made by the Indians out of local materials, were cut or burnt. The Titicaca Basin of the far south is a land of internal drainage, where in consequence there is no rapid down-cutting of river gorges into the plateau, and it presents an unbroken windswept surface. Lake Titicaca, a lake of tectonic origin, with a constant surface temperature of 10–12°C, acts as climatic moderator and thus helps the farmer. It is fed by rivers and remains fresh, draining out to salt lakes in Bolivia through the river Desaguadero.

The Andes, in geological terms, are recent mountains in their present form, having been uplifted in epeirogenesis to raise coastal sections rapidly up to 2000 m and more, as shown in well-formed pebble beaches and terraces at that height. Pleistocene glaciation reaches down to 3500 m in the north and 3000 m in the south; on the slopes at 2500–3200 m there are thick masses of loose periglacial material which are subject to continuous danger of mudflows, as well as landslides and avalanches. These mass movements are most dangerous and frequent on the steep slopes of the western cordilleras, as in Ancash in the Callejón de Huaylas between the Cordillera Negra and Cordillera Blanca, because of oversteepening through river downcutting and heavy precipitation on these western mountains. The 1970 mudflow into the Callejón, due to an earthquake activating the material, which caused several thousand deaths, was a recent example of the type of devastation possible.

Montaña and selvas

East of the Sierra lies a zone of intense river dissection and spectacular scenery, which the Spanish called the *montaña*. The name signified both the wooded character and broken topography of the mountains, in contrast to the bare sierra. Along the *montaña* front, with high continuous rainfall over 1000 mm except in intermontane situations, and moderate temperatures, there are luxuriant rainforests. In the intermontane cases the natural cover is dry, thin tropical forest. As the *montaña* is an altitude level rather than an area, it is found in long fingers of country along the main rivers between ribs of the Sierra. Along the valleys there are narrow, fertile floodplains, above them several erosional terraces. Far out to the east narrow outliers of the Andes form a limit to the *montaña* beyond which is the true rainforest or *selvas*. Where the rivers cross the outliers rapids develop, forming the heads of steamer navigation. One famous rapids section is the 12-kilometre canyon of the Pongo de Manseriche, on the river Marañon, just navigable to powerful and light craft with favourable conditions on the river.

The *selvas* (sometimes the term is applied to the whole of *montaña* and *selva*), lying below 200 m altitude, comprises a huge stretch of country — half of Peru — mostly in the northeast. The *selva alta*, upper selva, is distinguished by better drainage and more slope land, while the *selva baja*, low selva, is mostly floodplain, poorly drained and all flooded except for some low terraces which form the only inhabitable land. Iquitos, centre of the Peruvian *selva baja*, lies on such a terrace formed out of old lake deposits standing 15 m above high water on the Amazon. Not all of the *selvas* is forested: on the upper Ucayali on the left bank above Pucallpa, is a region of savanna, the Gran Pajonal, occupying the ridgetops of hills which are forested below. This land is occupied by the Campa Indians, a primitive tribe with a mixed economy that places its settlements on the grassy ridges and keeps back the forest by fires.*

MODERN SOCIO-ECONOMIC STRUCTURE

The physical division between Costa and Sierra is matched in social and economic terms. Figure 15

* This large savanna on well-drained slopes is unusual in the tropics. Human factors in its development are stressed by W. Denevan and S. Chrostowski, *The Biogeography of a Savanna Landscape: the Gran Pajonal of Eastern Peru,* Savanna Research Series No. 16, McGill University, Montreal, 1970.

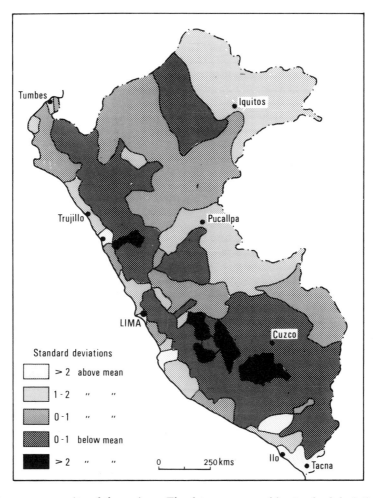

Fig. 15 Peru: income per capita of the regions. The data are mapped in standard deviation units away from the mean (adapted from a map by John Cole, University of Nottingham)

is based on a combination of eight variables including total and urban population, population change and sex ratio, hospital and bank use, and size of municipal budget. These were combined into one weighted index which is an overall expression of developmental level. It highlights the poor southern Sierra south of Huancayo, long known as the *mancha india,* or Indian patch, where Amerindian blood is strongest and least modernization has occurred. Further north, the Huaylas valley inland from Santa is also very poor, and to some extent the whole Sierra. Coastal provinces are mostly above average on the index, and the major cities are well above. Selvas provinces appear high as a result of their oil, timber and plantation-related activities, though this does not indicate the deep poverty of many subsistence farmers in the east. At another level, Lima can be contrasted with all other parts of Peru, since it has most of the manufacturing industry and a large proportion of the formal service sector industry of Peru, and concentrates nearly a third (4.6 million) of its 17 million population (1981).

PRIMARY PRODUCTION

The Costa
Costa agriculture is of a dual nature, commercial cash-crop production on one side and small-farmer diversified farming on the other. This is the only region where farm production is oriented to international markets and where subsistence farming is subsidiary.

SUGAR
This crop is highly concentrated, notably in the Chicama river valley north of Trujillo, with 45 per cent of national production, and most of the rest in neighbouring valleys. Prior to the 1969 agrarian reforms there were great foreign-owned estates here in Chicama, four of them holding almost 90 per cent of the sugar land in the valley. Plantation-type production with the usual economies of scale in production and processing, and even in this case a specialized port, Puerto Chicama, helped a profitable operation. The largest estate owned, in addition to sugar land, 420 000 ha of land in the Sierra of Cajamarca, thereby controlling its own supply of labour from the overpopulated hinterland. Men were brought in for the harvest by the *enganche,* an advance of money or goods made to entice penniless Indians to the coast where they worked to pay off debts and, if they cleared them, returned penniless home. Growth of large holdings on the Costa was aided by the traditional water law which gave pre-emptive rights to upstream farmers, and allowed water rights to be held separately from land, so that downstream farmers, or farmers without water rights, could be subjected to pressure and eventually taken over by their upstream neighbours. Since 1969 the sugar lands have been expropriated and formed into production cooperatives, while a second-level cooperative, a cooperative of cooperatives, has been formed to market the products and supply inputs such as machines and fertilizer.

COTTON
This crop is admirably suited to the desert climate and to irrigation, producing fine long-staple cotton of high quality; its cultivation goes back to prehistoric times, as is demonstrated from archaeological finds in the desert. Production is wider spread than in the case of sugar, over the northern and central Costa, and the crop expanded greatly during 1900–50, thereafter falling somewhat and occupying 147 000 ha (average 1973–5) compared to 54 000 ha of sugar cane in the same period. Like sugar it tends to become a monoculture with the attendant evils of soil destruction and susceptibility to market irregularities. There are many small farmers producing cotton, but there were also some large pre-reform estates with hired labour. As in the case of sugar, the government has set up and supported the growth of cooperatives to manage post-reform estates, and for both crops it will be interesting to see whether diversification is possible under the new structure of ownership, and whether the producing area will expand to include other small farmers who may benefit from cooperative membership. Most of the cotton crop is exported, providing an important contribution to foreign exchange earnings.

RICE
A third commercial crop is also grown as a monoculture on estates but also locally as a peasant subsistence crop. Rice is produced mostly on the north coast from Piura to

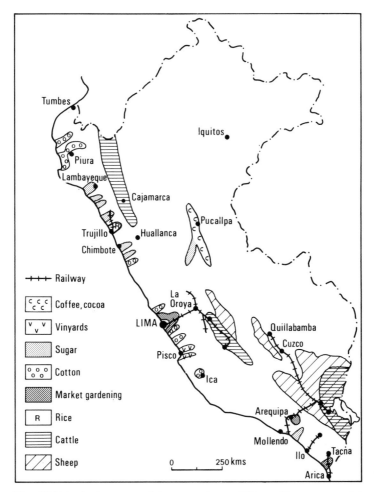

Fig. 16 Principal commercial crop regions of Peru. Non-commercial subsistence crops like maize and beans are grown widely, especially in the Sierra.

Pacasmayo (fig. 16) and it is sent largely to nearby cities, for rice and fish are basic elements of the costeño diet. Rice cultivation follows standard forms, using large amounts of irrigation water, despite a desert climate, and in view of its water requirements it may have to give way in future years to other less thirsty crops which can make better use of limited water sources. Rapid expansion of the rice area from 51.5 thousand ha in 1951 to 72.8 in 1963, and to 122 thousand ha in 1979, has made this crop the major competitor with cotton for land, and as long as near-subsistence farming is practised the area is unlikely to drop, especially when population is rapidly increasing.

PEASANT FARMING

The second sector of Costa agriculture is that of the small farmer, dominant in the south and near cities, often using irregular or poor water supplies, producing mixed crops of beans, vegetables, maize, potatoes, and fruits. Most production is for home or very local consumption, but those farmers with more land and luck can send food to the urban markets. Many of these small diversified farms are in the suburban areas and can be classified as market gardens, though they lack the technology and capital that term implies in the West.

Throughout the twentieth century, laws have been necessary to protect this small-farmer sector from the encroachments of cotton and sugar estates, but they now stand on firmer ground with the protection of agrarian reform laws. One noted area for small-farmer production was always the lower Rimac valley and nearby valleys, but because of urban expansion this area has been shifted out of farm production in large measure, and now supplies to Lima must come from areas many kilometres away, brought by truck along the coast road.

WATER SUPPLIES

All Costa crops depend on the river floods from January to April, when the snowmelt occurs in the mountains. In 1978, 1.18 million ha were irrigated, making Peru third after Argentina and Chile in irrigated area, within South America. Improvement of the irregular supplies is however difficult, because each river is short and independent of the next, so that many small schemes rather than a few giant ones must be the format for development. The need for improvement is clear, for many irrigation systems are old and achieve only flood-farming, using rough structures to divert water without any attempt at storage. There is evidence which suggests that much more could be watered, in the old pre-Columbian systems which are now lying derelict, such as those near the city of Trujillo.* The northern plain has most of the land suited to expansion of irrigation, and in the rest of the Costa, alluvial flats are too narrow, while larger flat surfaces, the high terraces, are above the reach of river water. Underground water could be supplied but its costs are still high compared to river water.

Several major projects are in hand, one on the Majes valley in the south, another in Lambayeque in the north, begun as long ago as 1926 with a dam on the Chancay river, and now being extended by diverting the unused eastward-flowing Chotano into the Lambayeque plain north of Chiclayo, a land of slight slopes ideal for canal construction. This scheme, known as the Olmos project (see also below, p. 109), is to provide water for 110000 ha more irrigated land in the area. Additional work is in hand to build a reservoir at Tinajones to control water flow and irrigate another 60000 ha of land. Lambayeque lies on the south edge of the Sechura desert. On the north side the Chira has been dammed and partially diverted since 1975 into the Piura, increasing supplies to 60 000 ha in that valley, and 40 000 ha of new irrigation land in the Chira valley.

The sea's resources

GUANO BOOM

An important adjunct of *costeño* agriculture has long been guano, which is still brought in from a number of islets lying within a few kilometres of the shore and used by cormorant-like birds for nesting while they prey on the enormous fish resource of the sea. Guano was important to the pre-Inca Moche–Chimu state, for many objects belonging to that culture have been found in the deposits, up to 47 m thick, which covered the islands before the nineteenth century. Guano was also used in farming by the Incas, who had punishments, including even the death sentence, for anyone found guilty of killing seabirds going out to nest on the island! The Spanish abandoned guano exploitation and it was only 'rediscovered' in the early nineteenth century, when the markets became largely European, especially Britain. In the third quarter of the century there was a guano boom in Peru, a boom which served to bring temporary wealth to the state and to bring North American railroad constructors to lay Peru's first railways, through the difficult Andean passes into the Sierra. Like all classical booms it turned to bust as suddenly as it had grown, through the rise of a competitor, mineral nitrates from the Antofagasta and Tarapacá deserts. The Peruvian nitrate boom was also of short duration, for it ended with the War of the Pacific in 1883, when Chile took control of the main producing areas.

THE FISHMEAL BOOM

Guano is an inefficient way of using a vital protein source, and more direct ways were practised by the Incas, though they were not great fishermen. Besides eating the fish themselves, they planted a fish head or two beside each grain of maize in the fields. In the 1950s, agriculturalists and others, pushed by rising world prices for fertilizers, finally took effective notice of the fact

---

* Gonzalo de Reparaz, in an article entitled 'La Zone Aride du Pérou', describes and maps these systems at Trujillo; *Geografiska Annaler* (1958), pp. 1-61.

that less than a tenth of the fertilizer value of fish is available through guano; to meet growing world demand for fertilizers, a thriving fishing industry grew up, based mostly on the little anchoveta, an oilrich fish which was made into fishmeal in small factories along the coast. In the 1960s, this industry experienced another boom like that of the guano industry before it. The fish catch expanded from a negligible figure in 1950 to a record 12.3 million tonnes in 1970, under the impulse of investment by small fishermen, foreign firms which soon came into the business, and the state which gave credits to stimulate fishing.

Technically the industry was backward, with small boats and factories and an unwieldy marketing structure, but rapid building of large boats of over 50 tonnes allowed longer trips and tapping of the whole Humboldt current reserve out to 80 km or more. Employment expanded to around 30 000 and beginnings were made in fish-oil production, replacing expensive imports of vegetable oils, and canning and freezing. The most important port for landings was Chimbote

in the north. In 1973 the government took over the fishmeal industry and began construction of large fish terminals and factories at Paita, El Callao and Pisco, with room to accommodate wholesalers who traded directly with the fishermen instead of through middlemen as before. In 1973, the fishing fleet was also taken over by the state.

Boom led rapidly to bust. In 1973 the government was forced to ban fishing except in March and April because of poor stocks, and only 1.7 million tonnes were caught, in 1974 five months fishing produced 3.6 million tonnes, and in 1979 3.6 million tonnes. In this year the fishing fleet was returned to private ownership, and many anchoveta boats have been converted under a government-sponsored programme to trawl for food fishes such as hake, tunny and *corvina*, in an attempt to diversify the industry and reduce a food shortage in Peru. Fishing remains very important within the Peruvian economy. Fish provide 45% of the protein consumed, and jobs for over 150 000 fishermen. Onshore there are further related jobs in some one hundred canneries

14 Traditional technology in the Sierra, Puno Province. Work here is done communally with the hand-foot plough, chakitaella

for mackerel and sardines, and boat-building and repair for the small-scale fishing which has survived along the coast.

Physical reasons for the decline, apart from overfishing, were the southern penetration of the current which opposes the Humboldt, the Niño or Child, so called because most often seen at Christmas time, time of the Christ Child. This current is low in oxygen and nutrients, and is lethal to the ocean fish life, and restriction is evidently still necessary, for yields have not recovered to their peaks and the sustained yield level now seems to be well below the 10 million tonne mark. Southern ports, such as Ilo, have in fact been able to maintain more of the traditional anchoveta industry, simply because they are further south and thus less subject to the Niño.

The Niño is a catastrophe of the first order, involving agriculture as well as fishing and trade. The Inter-Tropical Convergence zone moves south with the current and brings floods to northern Peru, which are devastating because in the desert there is no vegetation to restrain erosion. In Tumbes and Piura on the north coast, 1930 mm and 2083 mm of rain respectively were recorded in the first five months of 1983, causing 230 deaths, flooding of crops, landslides at mine sites, and disrupting oil production at Talara.

Sierra agriculture

AGRICULTURAL SOCIETY

Visually the Sierra is an attractive land, a landscape of villages and small towns of adobe houses, with Spanish tiles or reed thatch in more rural areas, the fields carefully enclosed by stone walls, by hedges of broom, or by terrace walls where the earth is held in by deep-rooted aloes. Most towns have a standard Spanish chessboard layout, with everywhere eucalyptus trees for shade in the plazas. Outdoor markets, either daily or periodic, provide scenes of colour and bustle, selling goods for the peasant population,

15 Making adobe bricks in the Peruvian Sierra

food, farm goods, sometimes secondhand, clothing from factories or from craft industries.

The pace of life is not fast, but life has not been easy either. A report from distant colonial time, on Jauja, in the productive Mantaro valley east of Lima, stated that:

In the valley there are no pastures: it is of a dry disposition, but suffers of rheumatism; that in many years the frost takes the food and the sown land before the winter comes.

> *Justicia Mayor de Jauja, cited in A.M. Quesada,* Costa, Sierra y Montaña *(Lima, 1969), p. 162*

Poverty remains a problem, to the point of engendering serious malnutrition diseases, partly from lack of food, partly because the food base includes very little animal or vegetable protein.

In the Sierra there was the classic rural polarization, between great *haciendas* on the one hand, and traditional Indian communities of small farmers on the other, a *latifundio-minifundio* division exacerbated by the *haciendas'* control of most good land, leaving steep slopes and isolated areas to the communities. With this structure it is no wonder that the Sierra produces only 25% of Peru's food, and 10% of its farm exports. Indian communities have preserved some collective ownership, usually of pasture lands, and some work-sharing in the *minga*, for example in harvesting and housebuilding. These groups must supplement their income from tiny farms with work on the *hacienda*, which also employs permanent labourers and sharecroppers.

AGRARIAN REFORM

The military regime ruling from 1968–79 introduced a comprehensive agrarian reform in 1969, first in the Costa, where the plantations saw a relatively rapid and complete transfer of power from capitalist firms to large cooperatives with indirect State control, leaving however many landless workers and small private farms without

16 Pitumarca, near Cuzco. Some common elements of the rural Peruvian landscape are present: the ox with primitive scratch plough, walls of stone and adobe, roofed in tile or straw thatch. Behind the settlement are eucalyptus trees, and in the middle distance terraced hillsides

any benefits. In the Sierra, the expropriation of *haciendas*, their combination into larger units, and reallocation to cooperatives formed mostly of the permanent workers on the estate, was more difficult because of legal complexities, such as the existence of several different claimants to a piece of land, or the lack of any proper survey of the *hacienda*. The *hacendados* were also often well connected in local society and able to influence adjudications.

By 1976, only 23% of some 960 000 Sierran farm families had received land in the 7 million ha transfer, and the remainder, mostly labourers and communities, were unaffected. An extension of reform from 1973 introduced Integrated Rural Settlements (PIAR) on the Costa, covering several thousand hectares of irrigated land each, and including both cooperative members and landless labourers and communities. On the Sierra, Social Agricultural Societies (SAIS) were set up with indirect State control and finance, to bring in the groups who had not received benefits. In both areas, these huge new land units and organizations, covering several thousand farmers and areas up to half a million hectares, have proved unwieldy so that integration has been slow.

SIERRA CROPS

A wide variety of domesticated plants are known and were perhaps first domesticated here: potatoes, beans, quinua and maize are important, among native crops, and wheat and barley have made some impact as introductions. Many different varieties of potatoes are known, some of them extremely hardy and capable of surviving on the highest levels of cultivation above 4200 m, where the poor soils will support only one crop in five or ten years. Potatoes are particularly important in the cool moist area around lake Titicaca, but are a major element of diet throughout the Sierra, a standby in time of need, as *chuño*, dried and frozen potato. *Quinoa* and *cañihua* are grain grown in the same regions as the potato. Maize is more common in the hotter and more fertile lands of the montaña edge, and cannot tolerate the altiplano climate.

Sierran farmers, unlike *costeños*, have animals as well as crops. Sheep are the best suited of the European livestock to the dry cold climates and poor pastures, and are concentrated in the high lands of the south. Some cattle are raised too, to

be fattened on the irrigated valleys near the western city markets. The whole livestock industry remains poor and backward, because most stock are in the hands of peasant farmers, with no access to good pastures, and making no use of breed improvement techniques. Animal dung is not used on the fields nor are the cattle fed with grain, so that there is little of the Western mixed cattle–arable farming with its mutually advantageous results. Cattle dung is in fact still collected on the dry treeless highlands for fuel to feed house fires.

Three species of auquenid animals are found, llamas, alpacas and vicuñas. Of these the llama is the most domesticated and is primarily a beast of burden for the peasant. The alpaca provides a superb wool; it is somewhat wilder than the llama and is reared by shepherds rather than peasant farmers, for its pasture zone is in the high slopes above 4000 m where no other animals can prosper. The vicuña lives in the same Alpine zone near the snowlimit, but it is wild and has a coat intermediate between fur and wool which is highly prized. It survives continual hunting less by the laws enacted to forbid hunting than by a rabbit-like fertility and the natural defence of its mountain habitat.

Montaña and selvas

In the upper *montaña*, in parts most accessible by unmetalled roads out of the Sierra, subtropical crops are grown both by small farmers, many of them colonists on the farming frontier, and on large *haciendas*. Coffee, maize, sugar, rice, bananas and plantains, yucca, mangoes and citrus fruits are common. Since the 1960s, coca cultivation has become the leading commercial activity in many parts of the upper *montana*, notably in the Huallaga valley around Tingo Maria, but also further south in the country east of Huancayo. Peru produces up to 50% of world coca, which is made into paste locally, then flown out to Colombia to be made into cocaine powder for Northern Hemisphere markets, or traded in Lima to a variety of markets.

As colonists move in, seeking land and cash income, there is an increase in commercial crops such as tea, oil palms and coffee, in the lands between 800 and 1800 m. While tea is a minor crop, coffee covers some 150000 ha, reaching into zones where there are no roads and the coffee must be brought to roadheads on the backs of farmers. Some colonization has been under government supervision, but most is from individual initiative.

Lower *montaña* farmers also produce sugar in a few localities, not generally in competition with the Costa but for alcohol and traditionally for *chancaca,* the coarse sugar-cake formerly used as food in rural areas. There remains an atmosphere of the frontier about sugar production here, because of the tax on alcohol and attempts to evade it by hidden stills and plantations far into the *selvas.*

The *selvas* still have a sizeable population (100 000 in 1961 according to the census) of pure Indian stock living in primitive tribal conditions, little modified by contact with white man. Most live in fairly settled conditions, building wooden huts with hardwood frames and palm leaf covers, and have a mixed economy based on tiny cultivated plots, hunting with bow and lance and fish trapping. They live near water, dependent on fish for protein food and the rivers for canoe movement. The mestizo and white population also lives near rivers, either in tiny self-sufficient hamlets growing rice, plantains and sugar, or around the few steamer ports, of which Iquitos is

the most important (plate 17). The continuing isolation of the whole region is indicated in such items as a 1974 newspaper report that natives of the southern selvas were found being exploited in conditions of virtual slavery for the panning of gold along a remote river.

MINERAL INDUSTRIES (fig. 17)

In Peru, as in other Andean countries, the mineral industries have long been a world apart, controlled by foreign capital and enterprise, and respondent not to local needs but to those of world markets. There is a curious continuity in the mining industry, controlled first from Spain, then from Europe and the United States, now also from Japan, but always a key to the economic health of the nation and always under foreign control until 1974 when the Cerro de Pasco Corporation, a wholly-owned subsidiary of the Cerro Corporation of the U.S.A., was expropriated with payment of some compensation money. This is a giant firm with six mines and smelters and refinery in the central Sierra, and it commits the Peruvian state to a definite involvement in mining. Before this, foreign interests

17 Pucallpa, river port of the southern Peruvian selvas. Shanty construction here uses the abundant timber and cane supply

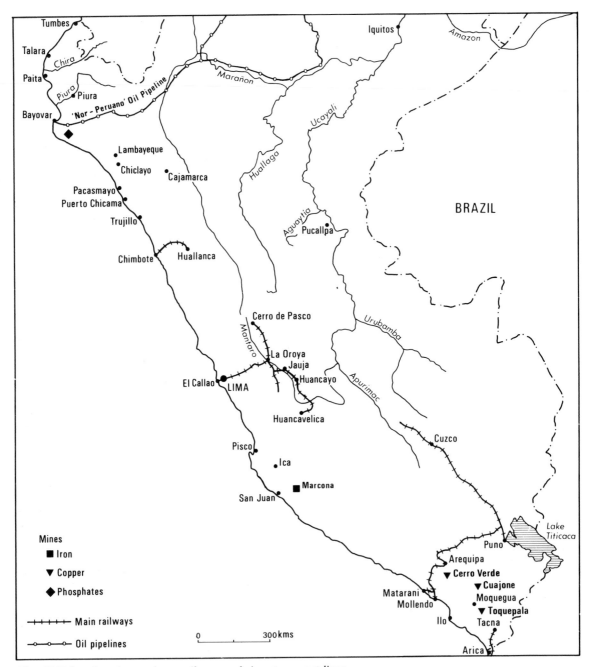

Fig. 17 Urban locations, mines, railways and river transport lines

were dominant in silver and mercury mines, important in guano and nitrates, then in copper.

Because of the isolated and remote location of much mining, foreign companies could dominate the economy and society of their region, forming local enclaves. This was the case with the colonial *mita* and still more in the present century with copper and iron mining. Copper first became important in the central Sierra with many mines in the late nineteenth century around Cerro de Pasco, which came under North American control about 1906, and led to copper concentrating and smelting at Cerro de Pasco and La Oroya. One key to this growth had been the Central Railway, built on guano and nitrate revenues in the 1870s and connecting the Sierra to Lima.

The central Sierra has been overtaken by the South since 1950, with the development on a massive scale, calling for heavy international investment, of disseminated copper deposits. Toquepala is one of these, connected by rail to the port of Ilo where there is a smelter and refinery in operation since 1975, using hydroelectricity. This mine and another at Cuajone, recently opened, are owned by the Southern Peruvian Copper Corporation (SPCC), United States owned. Cerro Verde and Santa Rosa are other giant deposits in this area, controlled by Mineroperu, the state mining corporation. Copper is usually found in association with lead, zinc and silver which are subsidiary resources.

Iron-ore production is substantial, mostly going to export markets, though increasing amounts are absorbed by domestic steel plants at Chimbote. The ore comes from Marcona in the south, and production is also under Mineroperu following a state takeover of the North American Marcona Company's operation in 1975. Peru does not have large coal supplies and coal production has been declining, in 1972–4 averaging only 85 000 tonnes. One field, that of the Alto Chicama valley in the north, is to be developed for thermal electric power.

Apart from coal there are significant petroleum and hydro power supplies in the country. Electric energy is increasingly from hydro sources (63% in 1963, 74% in 1974), largely because of efforts by the state. Before 1960, most electricity was produced, not by public services but by mining and other private firms producing for their own needs. This inefficient stage is being passed with the use of large sources in the Andes, the focus of new work swinging dramatically from the smaller Pacific-slope rivers to the great Amazon tributaries, where Russian technology is being employed. A new line distributing power is being laid between Lima and Chimbote. Reversal of flow from Atlantic to Pacific is being employed at some plants like the Huinco station above Lima, which also helps irrigate the Rimac valley. The Mantaro valley supplies are being harnessed by diverting water to cut off a great bend in the river and run it through a 15 km tunnel. Substantial development of the Santa river above Chimbote is used to power its steel mills and other related engineering industries. The Olmos project on the north coast is another large scheme with both irrigation (100 000 ha) and power (520 MW) uses from a diversion of the Chotano and Huancabamba rivers.

Petroleum

Oil resources are still incompletely known, but are large enough to make Peru an oil exporting country with exports of about 6 000 barrels a day. South America's first oil was extracted in the north Peruvian coastal oilfields of Talara, after the War of the Pacific. Talara has continued up to 1974 as the main producing area, and old wells there have even been reopened following the 1973 increase of oil prices, while new ones have been drilled to expand output. But a redirection of effort to oil-bearing regions on the Ucayali, Marañon and Aguaytía tributaries of the Amazon, deep in the Peruvian selvas, has been taking place, under the control of Petroperu, the state agency which has taken over the concessions formerly held by international firms. There are small refineries in the east at Pucallpa and Iquitos which are now being expanded, but most oil will be taken out via the Nor-Peruano pipeline opened in 1976 from the lower Marañon region, 855 km across the Andes to Bayovar where an oil terminal for large tankers allows ready export of oil (fig. 17).

Iquitos, as a commercial and transport base for the foreign oil firms and for PETROPERU, the national oil company, has had a boom comparable to that of the nineteenth century, when rubber was exported and grand hotels and theatres constructed. The river Amazon is still its main means of transport, and there is no road connection, but an airport capable of handling jet planes links it to the outside world.

Bayovar

It is perhaps appropriate that Peru, supplier to the world of fertilizers from guano, nitrates and fishmeal, should have a massive phosphates resource. In the northern desert of Sechura there are an estimated 10 000 million tonnes of phosphates, one of the world's largest deposits. A planned development of these deposits as fertilizers has begun at Bayovar. As the Nor–Peruano pipeline also ends at Bayovar, a massive energy-based industrial development is possible too, and a new port, oil refinery, metals refinery and petrochemicals complex is coming into being. These, with the phosphates industry, must attract a rapid urban development, and the whole has been placed under a regional development agency for Bayovar.

TOWNS AND INDUSTRIES

The Costa

Peru's urban population is scattered through a multitude of small towns, a few cities of medium size, and the metropolitan area of Lima–Callao. Urbanization, and indeed population growth generally, is most rapid on the Costa, with its varied processing industries and ports. Urban-industrial development has been heavily concentrated at Lima, despite the 1964–66 laws creating industrial parks at Arequipa, Cuzco, Trujillo, Ica, Chiclayo and Tacna, and tax reductions or exemptions for industrialists locating outside Lima. In 1976 the capital had 70% of the nation's industrial establishments and 74% of industrial employment.

Without attempting complete coverage, some of the more important towns may be discussed further.

Chimbote (population 145 000)

This is Peru's steel town, with a state-owned mill since 1957, the only one in Peru. Chimbote uses local hydroelectric power from the Cañon del Pato dam on the Santa river. Its coal and iron ore must be brought by sea, and its products also sent out in the same fashion. Chimbote produces high-cost steel because of these transport costs, but also because of the small size of the national market for steel; yet with recent expansions it can produce wire, tinplate, steel stampings and structural steel. Heavy engineering is also appearing at the city, to produce pipeline for the booming oil industry. Chimbote is also the country's leading fishing port, followed by El Callao and Supe. The 1970 earthquake hit the city tragically, but it has been partially rebuilt some 20 km to the south, though the industrial structure remains dominated by the two main industries of steel

18 *The old and the new, Sicuani, Peru. Modern vehicles and the age-old peasant system of a shawl for carrying goods*

and fishing with its related boatbuilding and canning factories. The growth of the city in recent decades has been so fast that over 50% of the population live in the shanty towns, *pueblos jovenes,* and urban planning has been a conspicuous failure. Local estimates of the population size are about double the official figure of 145 000.

Trujillo (population 539 000)

This town has had changing fortunes. As a former sugar-milling town it lost its importance when sugar milling became part of a vertically integrated industry and was done on the estates rather than in town. Trujillo however attracted paper factories and a newsprint factory, using in part the cane bagasse of the estates. An industrial estate was started in 1966 and attracted various firms — making machine tools, motor cycles, diesel engines, tractors — but this failed to develop after 1975 and the industries have been managed mostly from Lima, producing for Lima or for foreign markets.

Lima (population 4 600 000)

Cuzco soon ceded to Lima after the Conquest, a more central and strategic site between the northern cities at Piura and Cajamarca and southern foci around Cuzco. This new site was also symbolic of the change in orientation away from the interior, towards the sea and Europe. Institutional bases were strong, including the archbishopric from 1545, university of Saint Mark from 1551, administrative centre of the viceroyalty of Peru, and jurisdictional centre with its Audiencia from 1543. These established and maintained Lima's primacy as collecting centre monopolizing trade with Spain from the Viceroyalty. The South Seas Armada took all official trade from El Callao to Panama, where it met the Spanish (Atlantic) Armada for trade. By 1600, the town had nearly 60000 inhabitants, half of them negro slaves for wealthy citizens. Manufactures, spices, fabrics and jewels were brought from Europe and exchanged for native silver.

The old city, along with the port El Callao, was virtually destroyed in 1746 by a violent earthquake, and present architecture entirely postdates this time. Central, colonial Lima with its historic churches and wooden balconies (where these have survived) has been kept intact

as a result of conservation measures. The modern city centre, with skyscrapers, has had to be built further west, towards Callao.

Perhaps the finest visual aspect is the great Plaza de Armas (plate 19), central square flanked by cathedral and government offices. After booms and depression in the last century modern growth (figs. 18 and 19) has been dramatic, using up nearly all the flat land of the Rimac delta, linking Lima to El Callao (plate 20), and spreading up adjacent hillsides, a growth stemming both from rural poverty and from industrial growth in the city. The shanty towns have been forced onto the barren land on hillsides around the Rimac delta, or far out into the desert north of the city. Ninety per cent of the national textile industry is located here, and in Lima-Callao is half the fishmeal industry. The port is by far the most important in Peru, with

19 Wooden balconies of the Archbishop's Palace in the central Plaza de Armas, Lima. Most wooden balconies like this have now disappeared, and the one shown is a replacement

three-quarters of its imports, and one third of its exports. Allied to the fishing interests and the port are shipbuilding industries and shiprepairing. Lima has a major industry in car assembly works, and has attracted most of the light industrial investment from overseas. The commercial role of the city as main port and administrative centre is also dominant, and its links to the Sierra are the best in the country, making Cerro de Pasco and the mineral industries part of its industrial hinterland.

Apart from the topographic difficulties, Lima's growth is checked by its lack of water. With virtually no rainfall, it depends on the Rimac river and its recharging of subterranean supplies which are increasingly tapped by wells around the city. A permanent solution is only to be found when the city can afford a major diversion of water from the Mantaro, an Amazon tributary, towards the Pacific, a huge scheme which will be combined with HEP stations in the Rimac valley.

Cuzco (population 208 000)
This was the Inca capital, lying on a small river, the Huatanay, which the Incas had tamed, running its clear water in stone culverts through the paved streets of the city. It was built in traditional Inca megalithic form, with the solid appearance that results from lack of knowledge of the arch, instead of which massive lintels were employed in gateways and doors. Inca buildings were mostly low, roofed in thatch, the largest being the palaces around the central square.

The essential lines have been preserved in the Spanish colonial town, because Inca stonemasonry proved too difficult to change to the orderly geometric lines of the Spanish planned towns. Streets remain narrow despite the Spanish love of open, wide avenues. The central square, Aucaypata, surfaced by the Incas in fine gravel, remains, but the palaces have gone, to be replaced by churches and public buildings. The old central walls of diorite and andesite still stand as well as the fortress of Sacsahuaman

20 Landscape near Lake Titicaca. Urban growth results partly from rural overcrowding as in these minifundia. Here women are weeding a field of quinoa

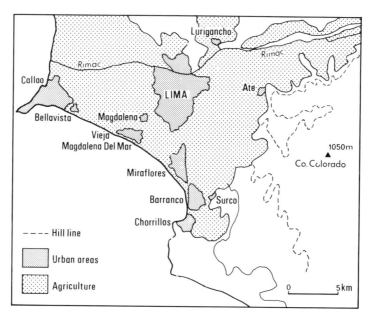

Fig. 18 Lima and surroundings in 1928

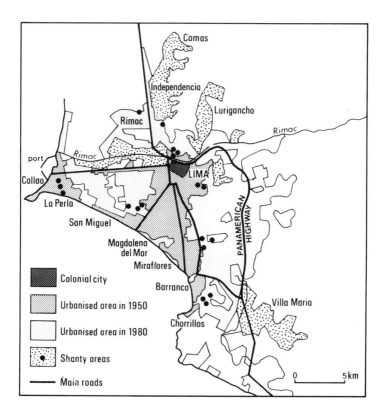

Fig. 19 Lima and surroundings in 1980

outside the town. Within the city the Temple of the Sun, Coricancha, once clad in gold which was stripped for the ransom of Atahualpa, is marked by remaining walls of interlocking masonry, although overlying Spanish work has crumbled from earthquake damage.

POLITICS, ECONOMICS AND GEOGRAPHY

This chapter cannot be concluded without some reference to recent political history in Peru. From 1968 to 1980 there was a unique kind of military government, one which at least initially had reformist aims and well-organized economic and social ideas; it was followed from 1980 by a reversion to civilian government and long-discarded ideas of an open export-based economy.

The military government's aims included wholesale nationalization of industries (steel, fishmeal processing, banking, mineral processing, transport and communication systems); small manufacturers were to form Yugoslav-style worker-managed enterprises, and industry was generally to be protected by high tariffs. A second line of attack was agrarian reform, which was intended to increase production of foodstuffs as well as to revive the community spirit in the countryside.

Between these two measures, coastal development, especially at Lima, was fostered. Many thousands of peasants, displaced by the radical restructuring of the agrarian reform, moved to Lima and other towns. Mining, mostly in the Sierra, was stagnating as foreign firms were discouraged from investing and world metal prices declined. In the meantime, import substitution industry flourished, but mostly at Lima, where markets and infrastructure were adequate.

During the succeeding period of the 1980s, the spatial impact again changed. Under Belaùnde, re-elected to the presidency in 1980, the agricultural focus was made frontier colonization in the Oriente and further development of the Carretera Marginal de la Selva. Agrarian reform had ground to a halt before his election, and now the cooperatives formed were allowed to disintegrate into private *minifundia*. Apart from farmers, there has been encouragement for private capital investments in large schemes of timber extraction and cattle ranching, comparable to the Brazilian development of Amazonia.

In the Costa region, a more open economy with low tariff barriers has meant a wholesale decline in those industries formerly protected, such as textiles and car manufacturing, which were reduced to half their previous volume. In mining, there has been little effect from the governmental changes because world markets remain depressed.

In sum, these wide fluctuations in policy have had a substantial spatial impact which could be greater if they are allowed to continue for decades instead of a few years as at present. They do not, however, seem to have had much impact on the complex and deep-rooted problems of the Sierra. Here there is a shortage of resources, a dense population living in cultural isolation, underemployed and poorly provided with services. The 1980s governments in particular had had no real solution to the Sierra problems. An index of this has been the growth and spread of the Sendero Luminoso movement, which as a radical, Maoist form of communism has spread from its starting point in Ayacucho in the poor southern part of the Sierra in all directions and constitutes a challenge to central government which is more serious than the old unorganized peasant uprisings.

9. Bolivia

Bolivia's landscape is to many the most striking in the continent. In the southern altiplano, there are desert regions resembling the surface of the moon more than any terrestrial landscape, dry white salt flats reflecting harsh sunlight in the rarefied atmosphere, and contrasting with the naked black rocks of island mountains sticking up through the lake-flat surface. Further north, and nearer to lake Titicaca, the landscape is less bleak but still barren-looking. Long low adobe huts covered in thatch are the northern farm houses, with an occasional new corrugated iron roof indicating new influences from abroad. Around the southern desert there are only igloo-like round huts bearing silent testimony to a natural poverty. Despite its bleakness, the altiplano has attracted most Bolivian population since before the Conquest. Within the plateau, though admittedly sheltering within a deep ravine on its edge, is La Paz, the capital, a solitary indicator of prosperity and active development, excentric to the country but not to its economically and culturally determined core area, crowding its constricted valley and climbing up its sheer surrounds in a shanty town sprawl.

On the edges of the altiplano are sharp contrasts; a few kilometres from La Paz's cold, luminous landscape is a zone of subtropical rainforest, the Yungas, a wild medley of palms and hardwoods interspersed with little farm clearings, and constantly bathed in warm air and Amazon rains. Further east, there are luxuriant forests in the Upper Amazon tributaries, parkland savanna in the central plains and semi-desert in the Chaco to the south.

PHYSICAL FEATURES (fig. 20)

In the central Andes, a western range, the Cordillera Occidental, and an eastern Cordillera Real enclose the altiplano. The Cordillera Real is Palaeozoic in age, much eroded so as to expose the granites which form its core, as well as the important minerals of magmatic separation, tin, bismuth, silver, lead and zinc. The Cordillera Occidental is of Tertiary age, and has had less of its cover rocks stripped off, so that minerals are less important, except for some copper. Volcanic peaks form the greatest heights, at 6000 m rising well above the altiplano's 4000 m. Peaks over 5000 m are generally above the snow line, though snow is often absent because of low precipitation and direct evaporation under strong dry winds. Pleistocene glaciation has left its marks down to 4000 m, as near Potosí and around Chorolque, with glacial lakes, moraines, rock striations and other marks. There is also evidence for a great interior lake, lake Ballivián, an expanded lake Titicaca, from the Ice Age's periods of greater precipitation and less evaporation. Today, lake Titicaca is fed only by small streams and drains out through the Desaguadero into a salt lake, lake Poopó. Salt flats further south are occasionally filled by exceptional rains.

The altiplano has a vigorous climate for man, with slight seasonal changes but strong diurnal change, and cold winter nights. The writer

21 Alto Pacagua, a squatter settlement bordering La Paz, is high above the city. It is without proper roads or water supplies

22 Llamas and alpacas grazing on the ichu *bunch grass above the limits of cultivation on the Bolivian altiplano*

remembers a night in an unheated train crossing the altiplano, during which the local peasants' habit of taking a blanket on all travels was made completely intelligible! Minor hazards are the very strong sunlight, deceptive in the cool air, and *soroche*, the altitudinal effect which attacks those who arrive suddenly from low altitudes but which wears off after a week of acclimatization. For agriculture the climate is more difficult; in the south, a large region has 50 mm or less precipitation, and rainfall is only sufficient around lake Titicaca for cultivation without irrigation water.

Oriente
Below 1000 m, the land slopes away to the Amazon and Paraguay, though the water divide between the two is imperceptible and the whole plain is flat with few interruptions. Summer rain brings huge floods from midsummer to late autumn, floods which are particularly noticeable in the Beni section of the north where the rivers are held up by the rock outcrops around the outlet of the Beni to the Madeira; these outcrops are responsible for the rapids or *cachuelas* of this section. Above the rock barrier the water and silt is impounded on a completely flat plain between

Beni and Guaporé, where water surfaces are more common than land during the flood season. In some parts of the flat lands, poor drainage and seasonal flooding induce a savanna vegetation except for isolated gallery forest on river levees and terraces. To the south, the shield rocks come to the surface and form the rolling Chiquitos uplands with a dry woodland cover. Further south still, the Chaco Boreal has a desert climate and no permanent streams though there are many wide dry river beds used by seasonal floods. Along them grows a thin gallery forest of palms such as Caranday, *Copernicia cerifera*, carobs, quebrachos and other xerophytes.

Valles and Yungas
Between lowlands and altiplano, intermediate altitudes belong to the Yungas in the north, to the Valles in the south. Annual rainfall on the Yungas is over 3500 mm, and their steep slopes have near-selvas vegetation. Further south are the Valles which are drier with a long dry season. Because of this, and also because of gentler slopes and the clearing which has been done for cultivation, they present a much more open aspect.

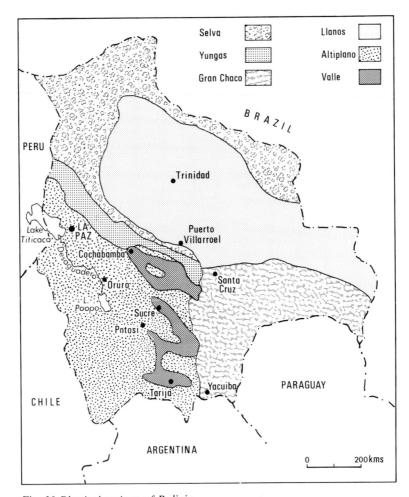

Fig. 20 Physical regions of Bolivia

HISTORY OF SETTLEMENT

Bolivia's pre-Conquest history is closely tied to that of Peru, outlined in the last chapter. In fact, the political boundary between the two countries runs through the very heart of the old culture region, for lake Titicaca, which it bisects, was the Incas' holy lake; north of Copacabana lie the famous islands of the Sun and the Moon, sacred to the Indians.

There was a dense population on the northern altiplano, based on settled and organized agriculture and using only the *chakitaclla* (digging stick) as a tool. The older civilizations left little more than their presumed language, Aymará, and even this was partially replaced by Quechua, the speech of the Incas who spread their influence rapidly over the region during the two centuries before the Conquest. Inca policy was to move loyal soldiers and farmers out from the centre to areas of dissidence or disaffection, and thus Quechua became dominant in the Valles and Yungas and in the south, while Aymará remained uppermost in the central lands around lake Titicaca.

In the Oriente, there were peoples living at an intermediate level of civilization, in the chiefdoms. These were the Arawak chiefdoms and other groupings of the Beni. They built no great architectonic monuments of stone to match Cuzco or Tiahuanaco, but used very considerable civil engineering skills and organized labour to overcome flood problems by placing fields and villages on artificial mounds, laying causeways and canals across the plain, and ridging fields to plant on the ridge tops, over thousands of hectares. This mysterious civilization offers an exceptional example of the possibilities of farming the tropical savannas without the aid of the plough, and it may have supported half a million people before the Spaniards; its affinities to the altiplano cultures are still uncertain.

The Spanish

A large Spanish contingent in Alto Peru, as the land became known, was never necessary or possible. Here Spaniards came only as land-owners, merchants or miners, and the dense Indian population suffered only moderate miscegenation, so that about half the present population is classified as pure Indian, another 35 per cent as mestizo. Since no European immigrants were ever brought in, pure Spanish blood is the only other important component of race.

Changes wrought under the colonial system were gradual, and only occasionally radical. Some new towns were created: La Paz, the capital, was founded on the all-important road from Potosí to Lima in 1584. Its name, meaning 'peace', signified the celebration of total conquest of Inca territory in Peru, a premature celebration in point of fact, for resistance movements were to continue for a long time. To the south, Chuquisaca, Cochabamba and Tarija were all founded in the sixteenth century, and prospered in the reflected light of Potosí, supplying it with food, manufactures and services. Chuquisaca also achieved a certain prominence as juridical centre, with its Audiencia or High Court from 1559, a powerful authority because it was remote from Lima, centre of the viceroyalty. Potosí itself grew up from the silver find in 1545 as a true boom town, with world-wide fame for the wealth and extravagance of its inhabitants, endowed like any Wild West town with its whore houses and gambling dens, populated by hard-drinking, financially reckless and quarrelsome miners. Fortunes were made and lost in a day by these men, though the silver boom continued for over a century, serving thus to fill the Spanish royal coffers through the tax of a fifth, more than any miner's individual pocket.

In the Oriente, Santa Cruz was first founded in the far southeast on the Chaco edge, then progressively moved 320 km west to the present position, to form an agricultural centre and trading post for the region. To the north, only missionaries attempted colonization. Jesuit control from 1668 to 1768 in the province of Mojos allowed some development of an exchange economy, centred on mission villages, and producing surpluses of cotton, rice, sugar and cacao for upland miners. In the longer term the Oriente's economy was to see a decline, in the face of a continual increase in the focus on the Pacific coast, making this region increasingly isolated. After the departure of the Jesuits much of the region became ranching country with a tiny population.

PROBLEMS OF POLITICAL GEOGRAPHY

National identity

Political geographers have long recognized the need, to ensure the survival of any state, of some cohesive force such as a well-defined territory or a state idea such as religion or language, to bind together the nation. Bolivia came into existence in 1825 with little in the way of unifying principles. She was certainly well isolated from centres in Lima or Buenos Aires, and there was a separate Audiencia. But this was not a unit which normally formed an independent state in the nineteenth-century divisions of the continent under independent rule. The name Bolivia is itself somewhat ironic, for Bolivar, Liberator of northern South America from Spanish rule, himself firmly opposed the idea of a state created out of Alto Peru on such flimsy historical bases, and indeed looked to the day of a multinational federation of states in South America. Only the outspoken attitude of the *criollos,* the American-born Europeans of La Paz and Chuquisaca, and support from General Sucre, who defeated the last Royalist armies in the area, established Bolivia as a separate state.

Such inauspicious beginnings were matched by difficulties in holding together the state newly created. It was large, at 2.2 million sq km twice the present size, and its four provinces, La Paz, Chuquisaca, Cochabamba and Potosí, showed persistently individualist tendencies. In particular, there was a rivalry which lasted the whole century between Sucre (Chuquisaca) and La Paz city, for leadership. Sucre had been the old administrative and ecclesiastical centre, but La Paz at independence was already the economic key and had best access to the important Pacific coast, so that it was finally to be confirmed as capital in 1898. The problem of size was to be partially solved in a drastic manner, through the nibbling away of peripheral territories by Bolivia's neighbours on all fronts.

Exit to the sea

Under the nineteenth-century economic system, it was important for countries to have access to the ocean, sole means of long-distance transport. Bolivia could only claim a narrow appendage out to the southwest (fig. 21) from the Loa to the Salado at about 26°S. This fact had mattered little in colonial time because other ports catered to Alto Peru, and Arica especially was the port to Potosí, linked to it by mule trails.

During Bolivia's century and a half of existence, a series of excisions of Bolivian territory have been made by neighbours attracted to minerals or other riches, provoking a revanchist attitude in Bolivian politics, under the name of claims for a *salida al mar* or exit to the sea. On the west, Bolivia tried to build up a port at Cobija, but it was too far from La Paz and not provided with fresh water. Arica, the main port, maintained its dominance until the construction of the Antofagasta and Bolivia Railway in the 1880s, following the nitrate boom in the desert. Nitrates cost Bolivia all her coastal strip, but paradoxically at last gave her access to the sea in the southwest, by the Antofagasta railway, which was long but with easy grades. In addition, as compensation for loss, Chile financed the Arica–La Paz railway, unfortunately not of great value because it had excessive gradients which enforced the use of rack and pinion track. Further north, yet another railway, the Mollendo–Puno line built by Henry Meiggs for Peru gave yet another outlet to Bolivia, though again its value was diminished by the need to cross lake Titicaca by boat and transfer goods from rail to boat and back again.

To the east, Bolivia never had any access to the great rivers, but this did not prevent her raising claims. On the Paraguay, Portuguese missionaries and merchants trickled in long before Bolivian attempts at settlement, and in any case Brazil, Argentina and Paraguay were hostile to Bolivian use of the river and effectively controlled it. From eighteenth-century claims to a Spanish front along the whole upper river, Bolivia was reduced to a tiny window onto the river above Bahía Negra, 50 km long.

In the northeast, the rapids on the Madeira isolated the Beni river from the Amazon which was opened to trade by Brazil and, when value was finally attached to the region with the rubber boom of the 1890s, and settlements came to the Madeira, the Beni, Madre de Dios, Orton and Acre rivers, Brazilian dominance in numbers of settlers soon meant a Brazilian takeover in what was known as the Acre territory. Again, repeating the Chilean events of the War of the Pacific, a rail access to the Amazon was promised by Brazil in part-compensation for the loss of the Acre in 1903, and indeed was built by 1913; again, as in the case of the Arica–La Paz railway, it proved to be of little use, in this case because by the time it was finished the rubber boom was already collapsing with the competition from other regions.

In all, the present-day Bolivian quest for a *salida al mar* may be viewed as something different from a simple recovery of the lost lands. It has been, rather, a political slogan to unite a country with little natural coherence. It has also been a way of putting pressure on neighbour states for good ocean access through free ports, but without any real attempt to recover land. Bolivia has good access to the Pacific, considering her difficult topography, provided by her western neighbours at modern ports. She is also promised access to the Atlantic and Plate, something she has never enjoyed.

Geopolitics

The *salida al mar* campaign can be seen as part of a broader programme of geopolitics, seeking to defend national territory. Another aspect of the same concept has been the action of governments in the Santa Cruz area (Rivière d'Arc, 1979). This includes the government involvement in iron ore mining at Mutun, near the southeastern

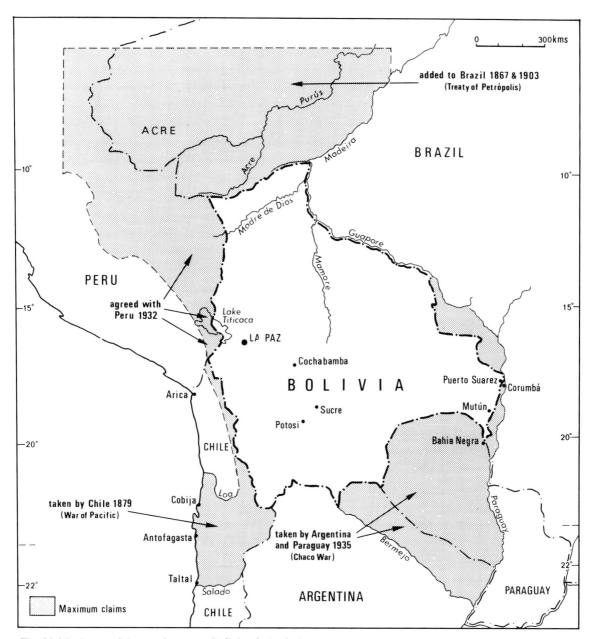

Fig. 21 Maximum claims and present Bolivian boundaries

border with Brazil (fig. 22), under a specially created government agency. This would confirm Bolivian occupation of the frontier and would ensure national security, a major aim, by linking the iron ore mine to a Bolivian steel mill. Other government actions in the area have been a pro-gramme of village creation, to make for a more stable settlement of the frontier area, and, for the same broad purpose, an army-sponsored colonization project, just south of Santa Cruz city, using crops such as soya and wheat on the edge of the Chaco.

THE AGRICULTURAL ECONOMY

Bolivian agriculture is, overall, at a very low technological level, and most particularly in the altiplano. Bolivia is self-sufficient in food, however, and has increased her basic food production in recent years. This is not primarily a result of the agrarian reform — yields and areas of altiplano crops remain poor. After the reform there was indeed a period when production fell because the peasant population ate more of what it produced and because the marketing system was disorganized. A slight dip up to 1955 was followed by expansion up to the late 1970s, mainly through the expansion of cultivated areas in the Oriente.

The altiplano

In the northern altiplano rainfall could suffice for Northern Hemisphere commercial farming of grains like barley, wheat and oats, and these are in fact grown using dry-farming techniques, in particular barley, which is used for malting and beer making in La Paz. Small farmers however are more concerned with the traditional subsistence crops of potatoes and quinoa, the latter growing under similar conditions to barley and replacing it where subsistence is more important than commercial sale. Its richness in protein helps eke out the miserable animal protein supply from a few scraggy chickens or the rare sheep or llama. Quinoa grain is made into biscuits, porridge, soups and steamed puddings, and the leaf is also eaten as a vegetable by country folk. *Canagua* (in Peru *cañihua*) is a related grain of the chenopod family. Both *quinoa* and *canagua* are grown on plots following potatoes, which latter may be fertilized. Near the margins of cultivation at 4200 to 4400 m, the land is rested after the *quinoa* crop for 10–20 years.

Altiplano peasants live in conditions which are still very primitive, despite some improvements since the 1952 revolution which overthrew landlords' power. Adobe huts and a few hectares of land are still their main possessions, though more western clothes, radios and bicycles are appearing everywhere. Goods are still carried to market, without any animal or machine aid, in many places. Most peasant families have three or four llamas and perhaps some alpacas for their wool and meat; the llamas can carry light loads. On high slopes above the limit of cultivation, herds of llamas and alpacas may be seen, minded by full-time shepherds with fifty or more animals. Towards the south sheep are most important, their degree of dominance being indexed by the gradual decline of mutton in price along the Antofagasta railway. Their coarse wool is important for the making of carpets, rugs and ponchos to sell in La Paz. A good deal of the trade in llama and alpaca wool, skins and garments goes as contraband over the high lonely passes to Peru, Chile and Argentina, unrecorded by national customs posts.

This is probably even more common in the case of the vicuña and guanaco skins, which are obtained by hunting in the high *puna* grasslands of *ichu* bunchgrass, near the snowline. Vicuñas, once protected by Inca laws which only allowed royalty to wear their ultrafine wool, twice as fine as the wool of merino sheep, have been subjected to increasingly intensive hunting to the point where in 1969 it was estimated that only about 10000 survived, mostly in Peru but with some in Bolivia, Argentina and Chile. Now it is hoped that the vicuña will be saved, for national parks have been created in all of these countries with special concern for their preservation, and all hunting and trading in vicuña was forbidden for a recuperative period of ten years from 1969. Illegal hunting still goes on, but guards in the mountains are at least ensuring a steady increase in the vicuña population.

Valles and Yungas

In the Cochabamba and Tarija valleys, intermediate levels of 2000 to 3000 m with strongly seasonal rainfall of 400–600 mm produce wheat and maize, potatoes, oats and alfalfa, in part under irrigation using small private irrigation schemes. Farming here is more prosperous than on the altiplano, but there remains the problem of the subdivision of farms to minifundio size, and most farms are under 10 ha. Commercial crops are important and cotton, flax for seed, and market garden products are sent by road to Potosí, Oruro and La Paz. Cochabamba has a relatively advanced dairy cattle industry, importing Argentine Holsteins to improve its stock, and has a growing cattle-feeding function. Oxen replace the altiplano llamas as beasts of burden in the region.

The Yungas, with good access to La Paz for those parts near the roads, has developed a strong commercial agriculture, based on coffee and coca. Coffee is a new crop and covers some 7000 ha in the region. It meets local demands and could be extended for export, but the marketing is not well organized and profits go to middlemen rather than to producers or transporters. Citrus fruit, bananas and vegetables are also brought up to La Paz to be sold on the streets or in the central market by the peasants who bring their loads and often their families on lorries from the production areas.

Coca, from the leaves of which the drug cocaine is extracted, is the most carefully tended crop of the Yungas, produced on tiny plots of less than quarter of a hectare, cleared of all weeds and precisely terraced on the steep slopes. Its high value/weight ratio and steady markets — it is still chewed by the Indians as a stimulant, pain-killer and reliever of hunger, as well as being bought by foreign pharmaceutical firms — make it an ideal crop for the Yungas farmer. Illegally exported cocaine, some through Colombia to the USA, and some through Brazil to Europe, is Bolivia's largest export in value, exceeding tin.

The coca leaf is harvested in the Yungas up to 1000 m above sea level, and is processed locally to concentrate its cocaine content, before being shipped out by various methods. Much goes by light aeroplane — the high value/weight ratio means expensive transport means are acceptable and there is less chance of detection. A main collecting place is Colombia, where intermediaries manage the business and move the product on by plane or boat across the Caribbean. From the Dominican Republic or its vicinity, it is an easy matter to move through the 800 kilometre chain of islands, some unpopulated, in the Bahamas, to reach to southern United States. Bolivian farmers do not become rich through the trade, but some governmental officials have been implicated in the traffic.

Oriente

Extensive ranching is dominant here except for islands of intensive crop cultivation. Cattle ranching is especially important on the Llanos de Mojos, which sends its cattle upriver to the city markets; the cattle are a mixture of tough Spanish longhorns with zebu stock for extra insect and heat resistance. Many cattle are lost in the annual floods, though their numbers are unrecorded on the great unfenced latifundia, the *fincas*. On such ranches there are no capital installations apart from the ranch house itself, and the cattle receive little attention.

Santa Cruz growth pole

One of the changes introduced recently has been the upgrading of cattle and of ranches, and attempts at flying out beef by air. But the most important changes have not been on the *fincas* at all, but among the modern colonies in the Santa Cruz de la Sierra region. Here too the colonial economic scene had been more prosperous than in the nineteenth century, with commercial production of sugar and rice, but transport means declined in relative terms with the arrival of the western railways onto the altiplano. In 1954 the big change came to this sleepy backwater with a road to Cochabamba built with U.S. financial aid, allowing lorries to ship goods in a day to La Paz and Cochabamba, instead of the week or more formerly necessary. Settlement has been by a mixture of altiplano Indians, Okinawans and Japanese, and Mennonites. These people receive plots of land of 10–50 ha, and grow rice, mostly without irrigation, on seasonally flooded land. Sugar cane, cotton and maize are also important.

The district has effectively become the Oriente's regional growth pole, with not only the road to La Paz, but rail links to Argentina, at Yacuiba, Corumbá on the Brazilian frontier, and the soon-to-be-realized rail link to the altiplano. Agriculture feeds industry, with rice mills, sugar mills and farm machinery at the city of Santa Cruz, which had a population of 42 700 in 1950 and 177 000 in 1975, a growth rate faster than that of any other Bolivian city. An industrial park has been created with aid from the IDB, and has over 120 firms operating, almost half of which are timber processors based on the forests to the east. There is also food processing, textiles, chemicals and plastics manufacture in an industrial park separate from the residential areas.

The oil industry is another local booster to the economy. It should be remembered however that this is not the only area of opportunity in the

23 Street vendors in La Paz who travel in daily from the altiplano to sell food

east. The Upper Beni has also been colonized, with roads leading out from La Paz and, although there have been many setbacks in the programme of colonization, its closeness to La Paz may prove a deciding advantage over Santa Cruz. On the flat plains further out, mechanical means for drainage might well make available a new major agricultural resource.

THE MINERAL ECONOMY

Bolivian dependence on ore extraction for export is of long standing. In Potosí, a literal mountain of silver ore, the Cerro Rico de Potosí, attracted immediate attention from the Spaniards who brought Indian miners, first as paid volunteers, then as forced labour, to work under frightful conditions in the mines, already in 1600 reaching a depth of 200 m, bringing out ore painfully on ladders made of hides, after shifts at work lasting several days (including breaks for rest and meals). The death rate was phenomenally high, including losses from exhaustion, accidents on the ladders or in the mine, and lung diseases like pneumoconiosis. Ore smelting was initially carried out by means of tiny furnaces using wind

funnels, a slow and irregular process. The discovery and use of mercury from Huancavelica allowed a speedier and more effective smelting process.

Potosí and some smaller mines acted as a powerful vortex of economic activity, employing thousands of Indians, in the transport of silver out to the ports, and in bringing mercury, food, fuel and mules from a distant hinterland. The whole area of Alto Peru, including the Oriente, and places such as Arica and northwest Argentina, were all part of this hinterland (Chapter 2, fig. 4). The city itself grew to have a population of 120 000 by 1600, the largest city of the Western Hemisphere. From 1572, the demands for power to grind the ores led to the construction of an elaborate reservoir and aqueduct system to bring water to Potosí, based on the cirque and other glacial lakes of mountains east of the town. Some of these lakes are still used by the city today, for the dry climate, with 600 mm annual rainfall which is concentrated in the summer, means long periods of drought and potential shortages.

Silver mining flourished until the late eighteenth century, to be followed after a gap of

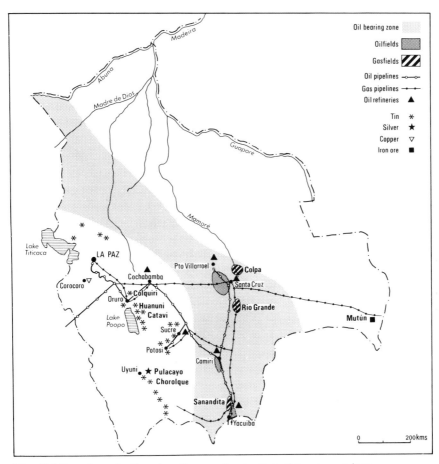

Fig. 22 Mineral production, locations and potential oil-bearing regions

poverty by tin, suddenly in demand for new industries in the late nineteenth century. Simon Patiño was the central figure in this industry, gaining possession of the great Catavi deposit which long yielded over 50% of Bolivian tin. The tin belt (fig. 22), following lines of silver mineralization north–south through the Cordillera Real, was developed at many points in small and large workings. At Potosi, tin ores were found below the silver levels and still provide employment to its miners. Today, the industrial structure is one of very large firms, reflecting the heavy capital costs and economies of scale in the industry. Mines in the mountains far from civilization have caused whole mining towns to be created, which by their isolation and distinctive management were real enclaves of foreign powers. Three firms only, Patiño, Hochschild and Aramayo, owned most of Bolivian tin resources before 1952.

The requirements of organization for tin mining, large firms and large operating units, led both to the rise of the great capitalists and to the overthrow of their power for, despite rigid company controls in mining towns, miners' unions led the movement of 1952. The Movimiento Nacionalista Revolucionario (MNR), initiated in 1939, based its policies for change on the support of organized labour, which in 1952 armed itself, defeated regular army forces, and instituted something quite different from the palace revolutions that have been the hallmark of South American politics since independence. Mine nationalization and agrarian reform were both undertaken by this government.

Comibol, the national mining agency, holds all the big mines and over half the total production, from the main mines at Llallagua (Catavi), Colquiri and Huanuni, in the zone east of Oruro (fig. 22). Hundreds of small enterprises are still privately owned, including primitive peasant —miner workings of short adits and alluvial gravels. The central importance of the industry, as a primary employer and as an earner of foreign exchange, continues to colour any discussion of national development, and much anxiety must derive from the industry's position of high-cost production, compared to Malaya with easily worked gravels as her main source of production.

Taking the minerals industry as a whole, i.e. including byproduct or even main product workings of silver, copper and zinc, a slight tendency for diminishing reliance on the sector is evident from the table, though this is of little comfort to Bolivia for such trends are to be expected in the absence of major wars and the stockpiling they engender. Diversification is the watchword of the day, more and more urgently as mining spreads from the deep mines to old tailings which are reworked as ore at under 1 per cent tin content, and as old machines are allowed to fall into disrepair without any replacement. One form of diversification is the growth of processing. Concentration plants for ore have been built at Potosí and Oruro, and tin and antimony smelters operate at Vinto near Oruro. Bismuth is to be smelted and there are plans for lead, silver and zinc processing. Comibol is also interested in diversification into other minerals, especially wolfram, copper and lead, and in moves away from the altiplano to use the alluvial ores of the Oriente. Copper development, if it could be induced, would cause a genuine geographical dispersion of mining, for the ores are low-grade disseminated coppers all along the Cordillera Occidental. The only major mine today is Corocoro, for competition from foreign producers and lack of local capital has hindered expansion.

Minerals in the east

Petroleum is the counterbalance to the depressing story of Bolivian metals. A major petroleum zone (fig. 22) runs at the foot of the Andes, and within it a number of producing fields have been developed around Santa Cruz and to the south, starting from the U.S. investments of the 1920s at Camiri, taken over by the state in 1937, as an embittered and impoverished Bolivia sought funds to recuperate from the Chaco War of 1932–5, fought with these same oil deposits in mind. The industry was small in scale until 1952, when the revolutionary government rapidly expanded Camiri, followed by Caranda and Madrejones. In 1970, a second expropriation of US interests led to temporary decline in the industry, but this has been followed by expansion and continued discoveries. Associated refineries at Camiri, Santa Cruz and Cochabamba handle oil for domestic consumption, while exports of oil go by pipeline to Yacuiba and Argentina. Gas is also piped out to Argentina, moving from the gasfields near Santa Cruz through a processing plant at Colpa and then to Yacuiba. Gas exports to Brazil on a large scale are now also planned through new pipelines. The oil pipeline to the Pacific at Arica is less important and has remained idle for much of the time recently.

MINERAL EXPORTS EXCLUDING PETROLEUM*

Year	Mineral value in millions of US dollars	Minerals as percentage of total exports
1952	138	97.5
1960	60	88.4
1964	108	94.8
1968	139	79.1
1972	194	80.8
1978	488	76.3
1980	617	59.7

*It should be noted that illegal exports of cocaine in recent years are estimated to exceed the total value of other exports.

In the far southeast, a recent interest has also developed in iron ore. The deposits of Mutún and Urucum, which are huge masses of haematite and manganese ores spreading over both Bolivian and Brazilian sides of the international boundary, may be mined opencast, and their only major disadvantage is transportation cost. Bolivia hopes to send the ore downstream to Argentina through Puerto Busch, though the existing port at Corumbá on the Brazilian side would be more logical and already has rail connections. The advantage of Mutún would be greatest for Brazil, and she has no need for new iron projects. It must of course be admitted that neither oil nor iron ore of themselves can provide a secure base for massive settlement in the east, for they will never employ large numbers.

TRANSPORT NETWORKS

The lack of a good rail and road network is both a symptom and a cause of underdevelopment. In Bolivia's case it is perhaps more the latter in the wide plains of the Oriente, and more the former on the altiplano where there are social and historical roots to poverty.

The rail network is quite thin, and covers only 3542 km. Perhaps the most peculiar feature is that the western sector on the altiplano is quite separate from that in the Oriente, so that regional isolation has been compounded. A link between the two is of some interest, for it would also be a transcontinental link, a long-dreamed-of project in Bolivia and, when completed, a link between Arica and other Pacific ports, and Santos on the Atlantic, a line of 3952 km. To the north of these lines, there is no rail network. The only line is the notorious Madeira–Mamoré railway, from Pôrto Velho to Guajará Mirim, first attempted and abandoned as a project in 1878–9, and finally built only in 1909–12, by an American firm contracted by the Brazilian government. The history of the line's building shows some of the reasons for the lack of other rail extensions in the area. Many died from malaria, from beri beri disease caused by poor diet, dysentery carried in the rivers and even from Indian attacks. By the time of its completion, the fine grade of rubber from the Bolivian trees had become less desirable a commodity since lower grades could be used, and plantations in the Far East were already providing competition. Thus the railway, abandoned for some years and now run at a loss by Brazil, has little function, for it does not connect to any important centre in Bolivia, only to river navigation on the Ichilo and Beni, a steady trade worked by small steamers, but unconnected to the altiplano.

The older links to the exterior, mentioned in the section above on Political Geography, can only handle a very limited traffic. To the north-west, the Mollendo–Matarani outlet is not viable unless good rail or road links round lake Titicaca are found. To the west, the Arica railway is very difficult. Southwest, the Antofagasta line carries most Bolivian trade, and a spur joins the Argentine system at La Quiaca–Villazón, but the distances are very great. In no case are the lines adequate, with narrow gauge and single track, and using outdated rolling stock, though they are being replaced by modern Japanese and German equipment. The writer has seen carriages built at Gloucester in 1910 alongside Japanese stock of 1968 and later.

Roads are notoriously bad, but are in heavy and constant use by open lorries carrying goods and passengers, often together, over long distances at relatively low cost. Roads in fact carried 55 per cent of ton-km freight traffic and 78% of passenger-km in Bolivia during 1965–9. Of most striking importance has been the Santa Cruz–Cochabamba paved road, initiated in 1954 and completed in 1963, a link between the eastern and western transportation systems capable of handling heavy traffic and providing a key to agricultural development at Santa Cruz.

BOLIVIAN OUTLOOK

Reviewing Bolivia's inauspicious first century and a half of separate existence, one might be tempted to conclude that the questions of sea access and lost territory would be most in need of solution. But these have been shown to be somewhat unreal problems, for Bolivian sea access is better than it has ever been, perhaps as good as it could have been had Bolivia in fact retained a coast. As to territorial parings, these may be claimed to make Bolivia today a more coherent and united country and to give her greater credibility as a political unit; no more than a shadowy control was ever exercised over the peripheries.

There are of course problems, but they are of another order: one serious question concerns the *campesinos*, as the altiplano peasants are officially termed, their lack of education, their lack of integration in ideals and way of thought into the national life, their separation, marked by language and culture, their extreme poverty. Related to this matter is that of a failing mineral source of wealth in tin mining and related activity, in the absence of massive international investments; agricultural resources which are totally inadequate to feed the population, requiring periodic injections of North American wheat and other foods; and the lack of any sound manufacturing development. Alto Peru, once the colonial jewel in the Spanish king's crown, has become, finally, the Sick Man of South America. This weakness, combined with a strategic pivot position in the geography of South America, makes it dangerously likely that Bolivia may fall into total dependency on one of her stronger neighbours.

THE MIDDLE LATITUDES

10. The Pampas Countries: Argentina and the Pampas Core Region

INTRODUCTION

Over the middle-latitude grasslands of both Northern and Southern Hemispheres, during the course of the last century, there occurred sweeping changes in landscape, reflecting other changes in economy and society, changes linked to the rise of early industrial nations and to the new technologies these countries introduced. What had been the untamed Prairies and Great Plains of the United States and Canada, the almost unsettled Ukrainian steppes, and the little known grasslands of the South African *veldt*, of eastern Australia or New Zealand, rapidly became settled, prosperous farming regions tied in to a world economy. In South America, the same phenomenon occurred in the Pampas region in Argentina and Uruguay, possessing like the other regions a plains topography ideal for mechanized agriculture, or for transport by railways, fine deep black or near-black soils, and a climate eminently suited to the production of wheat or other grains as well as for grass.

For this South American zone, the settlement and economic rise of the Pampas meant a substantial reorientation of the space-economy of young nations. The economic concentration on the Peruvian altiplano and Lima throughout colonial time, emphasizing the role of northern and western provinces as providers of raw materials to the centre, now changed to a new

focus on the river Plate, with direct access to a new Europe. The political creation of Uruguay, an economic nonentity, to serve as buffer between Argentina and Brazil, was now seen to have economic significance as the little country became part of the growth region in the Humid Pampas. Over the last hundred years, the dominance of Pampas society and economy in the life of Argentina and Uruguay has stamped a special imprint on these countries, distinct from any other Latin American group. They have shed some of their colonial structures of society and economy, and in the central area of the Pampas a totally new socio-economic being has emerged, neither European nor *criollo*, though in terms of physical race almost entirely European since the Plains Indians, as in America, had to be eliminated rather than incorporated into a new life which they totally rejected. The immigrants from Europe of the nineteenth century did not entirely displace traditional socio-economic structures, as will be seen, but they modified them in various ways, helping the advance of education, of democratic government, of intensive agriculture on owner-operator farms, of small industries and urban life in general.

The Indian word *pampa* refers to any kind of a plains surface, and in reality it is more appropriate to speak of the Humid Pampas in respect of the area undergoing the transformations just mentioned. These Humid Pampas, in central-eastern Argentina and Southern Uruguay, are the core area of the river Plate basin today, concentrating most farm and manufacturing production for the region. Round the core are grouped a set of drier, poorer lands, each individually linked in more or less well to the core but with few direct connections between them. These are the regions of Patagonia in the far south, Cuyo in the west, the northwestern provinces in Argentina, the Chaco in both Argentina and Paraguay, eastern Paraguay, northeastern Argentina and northern Uruguay.

The country is large by any standards, covering 2.8 million sq. km or, if its claims to the Falklands, S. Georgia, S. Sandwich Isles and a slice of the Antarctic between 25° and 74° west are recognized, 4 million sq. km. Within these bounds, there are all kinds of physical environments, from subtropical to arctic, and it might be expected that some pronounced regional divisions would occur. The most important is that between the Pampas, including Buenos Aires, and the Interior, which is covered in the next chapter. Another important division might be made between Buenos Aires city and the rest of the country, for in population, economy and culture the capital is of comparable importance to all other regions combined, and is certainly distinctive, if only occupying a tiny fragment of the area of a great country.

The Pampas–Interior division has its roots in physical differences, emphasized by the colonial policy of concentration on Peru and Lima, which brought only the northwest into prominence. The division continued into Independence times despite a complete changeover of relative importance with the development of the Pampas region for agriculture. Integration of the two macro-regions is still in progress, after a stormy period in the nineteenth century when even political unity of the Argentine provinces was threatened. Integration has been in terms of links to the single city of Buenos Aires, and this in itself has been a weakness for the national unity of Argentina, and has converted Paraguay into an entirely dependent state which must reach the outside world through a foreign capital acting as its outport. Neither economic nor cultural integration has been entirely possible, for there are deep gaps in level of education, of income, and employment prospects, between the poor lands of the Interior and the wealthy littoral provinces.

THE LAND

The Pampas landscape is a comparatively new one, with little of the overlay of history, old cathedrals, churches, university buildings and *cabildos*, nor the brown mestizo skins and bright garments of the people of the northwest. It is a landscape of flat fields, straight fences and roads, mechanized farms and small uninteresting towns, more reminiscent of the North American Midwest than of South America. Even the city of Buenos Aires, spreading over an enormous area with its low flat dwellings, great open expanses and straight streets, is an expression of the abundance of flat land and of its recent ordered occupation by man.

The Humid Pampas is a low plain, interrupted by hills in the sierras of Tandil, Ventana and Córdoba. It has been formed as an enormous surface of deposition, crossed by broad modern alluvial floodplains, occupied by sluggish streams and frequent shallow reedy lakes, the home of marsh birds and frogs, and described vividly by many a nineteenth-century writer in the period before it had been tamed and cultivated:

> Around Huincul, the country spread untilled and undivided, with its traditional air of pastoral *latifundio*, with no other visible sign of human appropriation than some flock of sheep, or the cattle scattered around a rustic hut. It was the almost untouched prairie of the recent conquest, not long ago the Indian frontier, where now any tiled ranch might occupy an Indian campsite . . . the monotonous landscape offered its few accidents in the form of nominal streams, endowed with an ephemeral existence by yesterday's rain, destined to die tomorrow, leaving only the bed in which they ran. More permanent, the lagoons filled by the flood, displayed their liquid mirror, occupied by widgeons and shrieking *teruteros*, dusty *chajas* and rose-coloured flamingos, and all framed deeply by the jonquils and reedmace on their banks.

> *Paul Groussac,* Relatos Argentinos *(Victoriano Suarez, Madrid, 1922), p. 131*

A higher portion of the plain is that in Entre Rios, with a rolling landscape and generally better drainage, while the other extreme, a dead flat and permanently ill-drained plain, is that of the Salado river in central Buenos Aires province.

Climatically the region is comparable with the southeastern United States, hot and humid in summer, temperate and wet in winter, with little frost but a constant succession of frontal storms from depressions moving north up the east coast, giving frequent changes in wind direction, humidity and cloud cover such as are common within the world's west-coast middle latitudes. Climate sets the limits of the Humid Pampas near the 500 mm annual isohyet, an approximate limit to continuous grass cover and to cultivation on the west, while in the north the winter (July) isotherm of 15°C is a limit for tropical forms of vegetation and land use, between Pampas and Chaco.

The natural vegetation of the Pampas is a thick grass sward, perhaps not a true climax vegetation but the result of frequent fires during dry periods. Now this grass cover has gone from most areas, either to cultivation or more frequently simply improved by grazing of cattle and the introduction of European grasses and especially clover. The maintenance of a good grass cover has meant less erosion problem on the dry margins than in the North American equivalent on the Great Plains margin of cultivation.

SETTLEMENT AND COLONIAL ECONOMY

A South American frontier

Figure 23 shows the progress of settlement through time, from a linear and river-tied occupation in early times, through the occupation of Entre Rios and southwest Uruguay, to a final swift march across the remainder during the nineteenth century. This settlement and its expansion is of interest as presenting the only large-scale case of a true frontier in South America. In other regions the Spaniards normally occupied pre-existing towns and thus extended their control over the surrounding territory without actually having to occupy it in person; they merely replaced the upper echelons of administration and set the Indians or mestizos to work for them.

In the Pampas there was a frontier, because no settled Indians were to be found over whom control might have been extended, and because the Pampas Indians were actively hostile, requiring stockaded buildings for the *estancias* surrounded by deep ditches to hinder Indian attack on horseback. In this region a direct confrontation was made, over three hundred years, between untamed Indians and Spanish settlers. This confrontation, and the final expansion of the frontier, did not however lead to a new democratic society forged by frontier life, as was claimed by Frederick Jackson Turner for North America. Here in the south, great landowners held the land privately before the wave of settlers arrived, there was little public land, and in any case they came too late to experience much frontier life. Instead, Argentina's 'Wild West' was experienced by only a scanty old-established Spanish population, soldiers defending little forts against Indian attack on the frontier, coaches and coachmen carrying mails or carters with high-wheeled slow oxcarts taking wine or textiles across the plains, ranchers with their primitive *estancias*, any and each of these groups liable to sudden, unannounced attack by marauding Indian horsemen from the *desierto*, the untamed interior. Settlement was thus based on an insecure tenure of the land.

Trade in mules, hides and leather to Peru, and contraband trade out through Buenos Aires were both important, and required only the maintenance of the overland routes to the north of the main Indian concentrations in the Pampas. The land base was the unfenced and unoccupied plain, where cattle and horses, introduced by the Spaniards, multiplied rapidly, leading to a peculiar industry, that of cattle-hunting. This had begun with the *cimarrones*, but it expanded to include any wandering cattle in the interior, for cattle were not always marked and in any case they were not to be brought back, merely slaughtered in the field.

The system adopted was for a number of horsemen to hunt down a herd of cattle, incapacitate them while still at the gallop by cutting their tendons with long knives on poles, until a sufficient number had been brought down, after which they would return to kill off and strip the hides from their victims, leaving the carcass as a useless byproduct of the operation except for some delicacy they might eat themselves, lightly cooked and eaten alone, apart from a little *yerba mate*, which they considered the only necessary accompaniment of their meal.

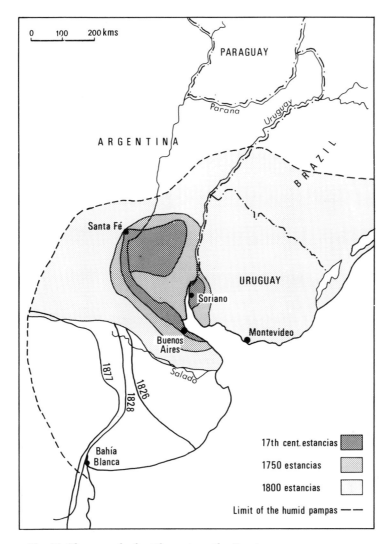

Fig. 23 The spread of settlement on the Pampas

ESTANCIAS AND SALADEROS

Limits on this primitive form of economy were set by the cattle, which eventually became scarce and moved out of the hunting range and into Indian country. This forced some care in cattle husbandry and more *estancias* were set up, temporary gathering places for the animals often conveniently placed in a curl of a river or some other site which confined the herd. From these semi-permanent sites, both hides and tallow could be obtained, and in the eighteenth century meat too became important. It was sun-dried, forming *charqui*, and often in addition salted at the *saladeros*, which brought salt from Patagonia or from the interior for the industry, exporting the product to the slave colonies of Cuba and Brazil. The frontier was extended gradually from the Paraná–Plate line, occupying

Entre Rios from an early date and then reaching out to the Salado, a defensive frontier against the aggressive Pampas Indians from about 1770 to 1820.

Trade

While the cattle kingdom expanded and became more sophisticated in techniques and products, towns grew little. Spanish hegemony in foreign trade meant that all colonial exports and imports went through Lima. This trade monopoly was a serious drawback for Buenos Aires, three or more months' journey overland from Peru. Naturally, a large contraband trade grew up on the Plate, utilizing the city's natural accessibility to Europe compared to Lima. British, Dutch and French vessels were involved in the trade in gold and silver, hides and tallow, all commanding good prices in Europe.

NINETEENTH CENTURY: THE TRANSFORMATION OF THE PAMPAS

The drive to settle the southern Pampas after Independence came initially from military leaders, but was taken up and given a true frontier atmosphere with the mass arrival of European immigrants after 1850, coming not as *estancieros* but as small farmers to cultivate the virgin soil of the Pampas. The colour and romance of the frontier and its savagery were fleeting moments captured by only a few writers who knew and could describe the primitive grasslands. Here is a description of an Indian raid:

> Soon afterwards Indians and cattle galloped over the line of frontier forts, through the virgin pampa equidistant from Trenque Lauquen and Guaminí, an area covered in *puna* grass and thickets of low brushwood. At the noise of this avalanche, the ostriches and deer fled in close-packed groups as did the wild cats which lived among the tall grasses . . . . It was like an undulating river of backs and rumps, an immense mass, sombre against the sun, illuminated here and there by the manes of the white, bay or roan horses.
>
> *E. Acevedo Diaz,* Cancha Larga *(Editorial Sopena, Buenos Aires, 1939), p. 201*

Successful settlement by the small farmer began in central Santa Fé and Entre Rios, then quickly extended to all the Humid Pampas. Tenure systems varied; in a minority of cases, notably in Santa Fé, ownership of the land was conferred on the small farmer, because the provincial government aided settlement and overlooked early debts of the settlers, and because of basically favourable physical conditions. Elsewhere, similar colonies failed, sometimes for want of effort on the part of farmer, owner or colonizing agent, sometimes through total ignorance of the problems of the region, such as locust attack spreading out of the northern deserts, droughts and floods, lack of roads or transport. Many colonists were not farmers at all but recruited in towns and ignorant of any kind of farming. In many places migrants were brought in merely as tenants, cultivating the land for four years and then handing it back with planted alfalfa to the owner, who thus had land rents plus a ready-made pasture of improved grass for his cattle at the end of the contract period. Under such conditions, expansion of the frontier and introduction of small farmers had no democratizing influence on society, as had been hypothesized for North America. *Estancias* continued to grow into the present century, and to control a subordinate labour force of considerable size.

Tenants had a special role in improving pastures. They were part of a technological revolution, which began in the 1830s with Merino and then improved British breeds of sheep, followed by British breeds of cattle, imported to replace the Spanish longhorns and provide good quality meat for European markets. They required good pastures to fatten well, and the tenants would plant alfalfa for the purpose at no cost to the owner of land. To avoid mixing their pedigree cattle with others, and to control pasture use, fencing was needed and this was introduced during the 1870s in massive imports of wire. Railways were extended across the plains to bring the animals to market, and ships using steampower to take them to Europe. For a while there was an active trade in live cattle, but it was superseded in the 1890s by the frozen meat ship, the result of yet another technological development, the use of refrigeration.

Railways also helped the cultivation of crops, and were essential to ship out the wheat surpluses from the 1880s onwards. Rosario was the first port with good rail access to its hinterland, but it

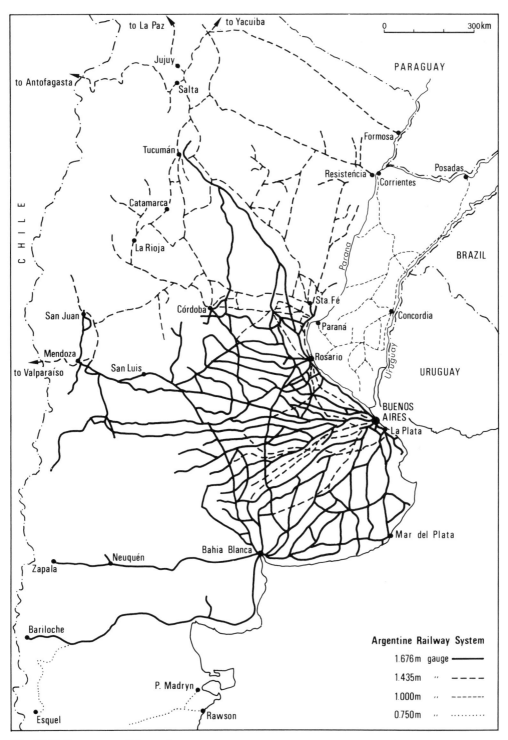

Fig. 24 Railway map of Argentina

was soon overshadowed by Buenos Aires, which gained the termini of most rail lines through commercial advantages and influence with the British constructors of railways. Figure 24 shows that the centrality of Buenos Aires is not as great as might be supposed. There are five different gauges of railway and most interior provinces are on metre-gauge lines, unconnected to the capital.

PRESENT-DAY POPULATION

Argentina is today a largely urban country. Buenos Aires alone had 9.93 million in 1980 (2.91 in the Federal District, which is now losing population), or a third of the total national population. This urban concentration is remarkable in a large country where many other major urban regional centres have long been powerful, and is to some extent an expression of the country's ties to foreign markets, and of the fact that national administration is based in the same place as the national port and manufacturing centre. The Argentines have contemplated the removal of their capital to an interior site for some time, in the interests of spreading development and asserting interest in the provinces, but until now the pull of the coast has proved too great.

The outside world thinks of Argentina as a farming country, of the *gauchos* and the great *estancias,* but in fact agricultural employment is low and declining, from 18% of the 1965 labour force to 13% in 1981, while manufacturing itself seems to have passed a peak of 34% in 1965 and was 28% in 1981. Services have risen over the same period from 48 to 59%.

Even in the rural areas there is little truly dispersed population. The relative dispersal of the nineteenth century has been generally replaced by concentration of farmers in the small towns, from which they travel by car to their work. Most families have either a pickup or a car, an index of an agricultural system standing above the normal Latin American level.

Racial makeup in the Pampas is also distinctive, with no Indian or Negro component. Indians were eliminated in fighting, while the few negroes imported in colonial time were mostly domestics who never mixed with the rest of the populace. Spanish and Italian immigrants of the nineteenth and early twentieth centuries are the largest contingents, Italians having provided

some 55% of the 3.4 million immigrants during 1860–1910, a total reduced to a still impressive 2.5 million if those who returned, the *golondrinas* or swallows as they were called from their seasonal habits, are subtracted. Small minorities of many European nations, English, Scots, Irish, French and German, are also found in both town and country, having come in to take up cheap land offered by railway companies, or with commercial enterprises from Europe. Today immigration from Europe has ceased, but for the capital at least has been replaced by a large flow from the interior of Argentina and from the poor neighbouring countries, Bolivia, Chile and Paraguay.

Modern migration from the interior to Buenos Aires is usually done by stages. Rural people move to small towns in their region, then to large cities and so to the capital, where they form an active, energetic group, poorly educated but not without skills, so that unemployment is not a primary problem. As a rich city, Buenos Aires has also been able to tackle vigorously the housing problem of the immigrants, upgrading and replacing shanty towns, the *villas miseria*, with solid economical housing. The map (fig. 25) shows the effect of the modern development of the Pampas core area and the metropolis, Buenos Aires, in terms of per capita income, which far outstrips that of all interior provinces apart from Patagonia, where the population is tiny and much of it in high-waged industries such as oil extraction.

AGRICULTURE

The governmental body in Buenos Aires which deals with farm matters is called the Ministry of Agriculture and Livestock, firmly separating the two. This Spanish language distinction is an index of the continuing differences between cattlemen and cultivators; there is little mixed farming for a region where it might well be expected, and those who belong to the *estanciero* class regard themselves as a separate class whose dignity might be lowered by bringing arable cultivation into their ranches. This distinction however is between individual farmers and farm types, and not between land-use regions and, as fig. 25 shows, a mixture of farms may be found in many parts, of great *estancias* with small farms producing grain, vegetables or milk.

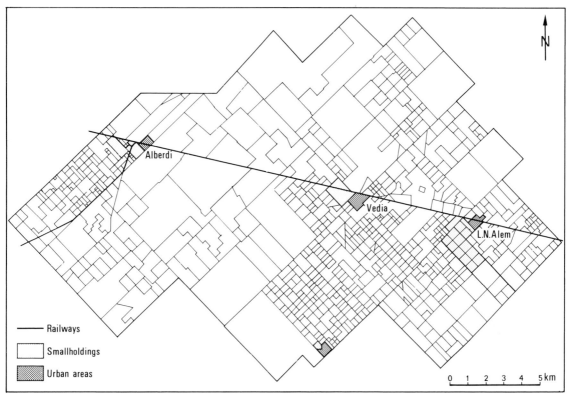

Fig. 25 Agricultural colonies and estancias *in Leandro Alem* partido

There are certain areas of specialization within the agricultural system predominant on the Pampas. Up to the 1930s, a division could simply be made between zones of beef cattle breeding or fattening, and zones of grain production. These are still present as a northern wheat and maize belt, running west from Buenos Aires to Córdoba, and a southern wheat belt east and west of Bahía Blanca, though changed in form and reduced from their maximum extent. There are however large areas under new products, symbols of a new transformation of the Pampas. Dairy regions have sprung up in several places, while potatoes, fruit and vegetables have all made incursions onto Pampas land; such changes are partly in response to growing urban markets, partly a result of the difficult world markets for traditional wheat and beef. The grain and beef producing zones continue to hold most of the area, fluctuating with world markets, but they give way to the new crops wherever small farms are available, where there is a good transport network and dense rural labour force, and where organization of farmers in cooperatives has been successful.

On the traditional *estancias*, and on many medium-sized farms, grain-farming tends to expand with good prices and a stable political situation. During more difficult times, such as that of the Perón government of 1945–55, cultivation is replaced by ranching and tenant farmers by cattle, the land being turned over to a small labour force of *gauchos*, or cowboys. At all times farming is extensive with minimal inputs, a system that shows land to be the cheap input and the one that can still be squandered. Low inputs of capital in buildings or machinery are of course useful to the Pampas farmer in giving him flexibility; he may change easily from one form of farming to another, having invested little in specialized equipment. The system's disadvantage is that production is low and tends to rise only slowly over pre-Second World War levels. Wheat provides an example of this feature.

WHEAT AREA, PRODUCTION AND YIELD

Year	Area 000 ha	Production 000 tonnes	Yield tonnes per ha
1934–8	6783	6 634	0.98
1948–52	4487	5 175	1.15
1955	4062	5 250	1.29
1960	3599	3 960	1.10
1965	4601	6 079	1.32
1970	3332	4 250	1.28
1975	5339	8 560	1.60
1980	4998	7 830	1.57
1984	6120	13 000	2.12

Source: FAO Production Yearbook, *various editions, United Nations, Rome*

INDUSTRY AND CITY DEVELOPMENT

In the twentieth century Argentina has become an industrial power, most of her industry collected in Buenos Aires and other Pampas cities. Industry began with the processing of farm products for export, specifically the freezing and chilling of beef in the great foreign-owned *frigoríficos,* slaughterhouses and meat-packing factories. This first stage of foreign-led industry was added to through the 1920s and 1930s by all kinds of consumer goods industries in the drive for import substitution by domestic production. Nowadays industry has a well-rounded aspect, with not only these consumer industries but those of a third stage of industrialization, including steel, chemicals, heavy engineering and other capital-goods manufacturing.

The geography of industry is simple. Three-quarters of it is concentrated in and around Buenos Aires city. Within the city there are several industrial districts, but the major one is from south of the modern port area to a big zone on the south side of the Riachuelo, in the industrial suburb of Avellaneda. Light industries have come into some old residential sites in the older parts of the city, while large modern industries like car assembly have taken up open-field sites around the peripheries of the capital.

Southeast of the city, there is another industrial concentration at Ensenada, a port originally developed for La Plata, but now with large petrochemical works and an oil refinery. On the northwest side, industry continues upstream with Rosario (955 000), third city of Argentina and a major industrial centre. It is still the port outlet for part of the northern Pampas, milling and shipping much grain, and processing gas and oil from northern Argentina and Bolivia (fig. 26). Further upriver there are other industrial districts, most notably at Santa Fé (287 000) and Paraná (156 000), now closely linked by a new tunnel under the river Paraná. Santa Fé is another port with terminus facilities for grain, but Paraná has only a minor port. Below Rosario, San Nicolás is Argentina's steel city, lying within easy reach of Buenos Aires markets and accessible too, to ocean steamers bringing raw materials.

Far to the south, Bahía Blanca (221 000) has port functions and provides the main outlet for the southern grain belt; its port has bulk-handling facilities and new grain terminals, and suffers less from silting than the muddy Plate estuary. Bahía Blanca also benefits now from the oil industry, lying at the confluence of lines from Neuquén and Patagonia, and it is building up new petrochemical and derivative industries.

The only major Pampas city not on the coast or with ready access to it is Córdoba (982 000). In fact, Córdoba is not strictly in the Humid Pampas region if we judge solely by the 500 mm rainfall line. Historically it has had an intermediate, transitional situation, as the great interior routeway focus and point of contact between the Northwest and the Pampas. Appropriately enough with this situation, it has large transport-machinery factories, making cars, buses, railway rolling-stock and locomotives. Unfortunately for Córdoba, much of this industry, including Fiat, General Motors and Ford plants, has transferred back to Buenos Aires in recent years.

OTHER URBAN FUNCTIONS

Apart from manufacturing, the administrative function is important in the provincial capitals, especially in La Plata (560 000), capital of Buenos Aires province, richest of the Pampas provinces. This city came into being by governmental fiat in the 1880s, as a replacement for Buenos Aires city which had become a federal district and could not at the same time govern a province. La Plata is thus a planned, open, clean city, with no industry and with its university, of high reputation, the only competitor to government. Provincial government in the other cities, Santa Fé, Paraná, Córdoba and Santa Rosa (La Pampa), is a less important but not negligible industry, linked in to a regional service and marketing-centre function.

Another distinctive town function is tourism, again evidence of Argentina's sizeable middle class, for the tourist resorts, apart from the capital, are fed by domestic holiday makers rather than foreigners. Mar del Plata (407 000) is the largest tourist centre, with good road and rail links to Buenos Aires. It houses an increasing number of permanent dwellers, mostly retired persons, who are changing its character from a purely summer resort to an all-year centre and a large city. Other smaller resorts crowd the coastline to the south from Mar del Plata, on uncrowded beaches of fine sand.

Tourists can also go to Córdoba for open air, as the city stands under the Sierra de Córdoba, a

24 The cathedral at Tucuman. This city is not only an industrial centre but a cultural one of long standing

hill range with open country, forests and some old colonial settlements. The city itself provides much of interest to the traveller for, as the colonial centre of trade and administration, it has many old buildings, including a baroque cathedral, and many monasteries. It boasts the country's oldest university, though it was scarcely more than a school, under Jesuit supervision, until the nineteenth century. Santa Fé has similar colonial origins and some old architecture, but its subtropical heat and the marshlands near the Paraná do not attract many tourists.

BUENOS AIRES

This city cannot be classified as industrial, administrative or commercial, for it has all these functions. It grew up, however, as a commercial rather than a manufacturing centre, and its manufacturing function is still limited to port-related industries such as flour-milling and meat-packing, plus a wide assortment of consumer industries such as textiles, shoes and furniture. Steel manufacture is outside, at San Nicolás up the Paraná, and oil refining near the port of La Plata. Administration is important in the life and landscape of the city; the Congress building and the Casa Rosada, the rose-coloured presidential palace on the Plaza de Mayo, are twin symbols of administrative power and, on the same plaza, the old colonial *cabildo* or town hall remains as a reminder of the fact that this was one of the first foci of colonial revolt against Napoleonic Spain. Governmental power is strongly held in Buenos Aires, although the country is constitutionally a federation of provinces.

Governmental control is matched by the private industries, which all have their main offices at Buenos Aires, even those with little association with the capital. In addition, there are the financial and management companies, and those of transport and communications networks, most with offices near the Plaza de Mayo in the centre of the city.

Culturally, Buenos Aires has always been a world apart from the interior. In the nineteenth century, the city and its province were only precariously linked to the rest of the country. The city was the home for all those with any kind of literary or intellectual aspirations or pretensions, because of its associations with Europe, as culture followed trade. Today the city still houses most of the theatre, opera and artistic life of the nation. To its residents, the distant interior is still an uncivilized region, the land of barbarity that people of vision such as Domingo F. Sarmiento, educationalist and nineteenth-century president of the country, sought to change through the civilizing influences of the city, and by replacing local feudalism with a nationally effective government. The viewpoint of city dwellers is no doubt extreme; but it remains, and still has some basis in reality.

11. Argentina: the Interior

A second Argentina lies beyond the city of Buenos Aires and its Humid Pampas hinterland. This is an open, empty land, much of it desert or semi-desert, where man has never had a firm hold. Its landscapes, however, are not monotonous for, apart from the Dry Pampas, the western extension of the Humid Pampas plains, there are many mountain ranges standing up from alluvial piedmont fans at their foot, like cliffed islands in a grey—brown sea, displaying rock formations in sharp contrast of colour and form to the dun of the plains. The cities, whose intense activity stands in contrast to the thinly-peopled countryside, differ from those of the Pampas and from each other. In the northwest and west, they have darker-skinned people, some remnants of old traditions in custom and dress, and are architecturally distinct. Their social milieu is not quite in tune with the twentieth century.

An Argentine joke is that 'God is in all places, but his office is at Buenos Aires', and this expresses something of the relative poverty and resentment of the inhabitants of the Interior towards the richer littoral and especially Buenos Aires. The interior provinces vary in their degree of poverty (fig. 26). The poorest, with average per capita incomes one tenth that of Buenos Aires, are the northwestern ones. Patagonian provinces have some oil and mineral wealth, and in the centre Mendoza has a happy combination of a rich irrigation and power from HEP and oil.

PATAGONIA

The land south of the Rio Colorado is a high plateau region, standing generally over 300 m above the Atlantic, to which it slopes gradually down, a harsh windswept environment with scanty vegetation, the desert increasing in strength rather than diminishing towards the coast. Here and there tabletop mountains or volcanic cones break the monotony of the pebble-strewn flat surface, and the through-flowing rivers, the Chubut, Colorado and Negro, have deep, almost canyon-like valleys. The Andean fringe of the region is a lower and less impressive range than further north, but has spectacular scenery in the region of Bariloche, an Argentine Lake District with similar origin to the English Lake District in scouring by Pleistocene glaciers.

Historical factors

This region was claimed by Chile in colonial times, but no control was ever exerted, and no exploration made apart from the visits of a few missionary priests. It held neither settled Indians nor, despite many rumours, any gold or silver that might have attracted settlers. The few inhabitants were warlike Indians who lived on hunting guanaco (a wild relative of the llama), and the little American deer, mostly in the vicinity of the Andes where there is most moisture and vegetation. In the far south, some

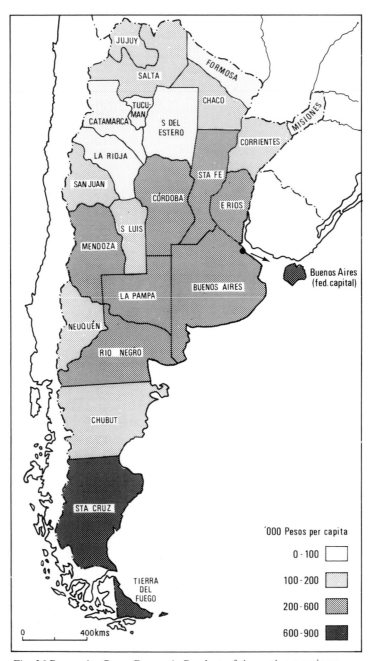

Fig. 26 Per capita Gross Domestic Product of Argentine provinces

of the world's most primitive economies were to be found, among them the shellfish collectors of the Magellan Straits.

After Independence, the question of ownership became urgent, but Patagonian Indians could not be dominated until the 1880s, when Argentine troops conducted the 'Conquest of the Desert' campaign, which effectively secured them the right to all land east of the Andes, and virtually eliminated the Indian population of the region. Colonization of the distant shores of Patagonia by Europeans was not attempted, except for a Welsh group which was enticed by poorly informed leaders to the lower Chubut, where it nearly came to total grief because of misconceptions about the environment and possible farming methods. Meanwhile, most of Patagonia was given away in great grants to landowners who had bought bonds, to be redeemed in land, for the financing of the desert campaign, or given in smaller blocks to soldiers of this campaign. Such grants merely extended the traditional estancia system into a new area.

Modern economy

Mineral resources are important to modern Patagonia, with oil, gas and coal as fuels, and iron ore in the north. The coal of Rio Turbio (fig. 28) is of low grade, unsuitable for steel-making except for a small percentage mixture in the coking ovens, but useful for heating purposes, and its production is expanding under government plans, from under one million tons

in recent years to over four million; the coal is shipped out by a narrow-gauge railway to Rio Gallegos, a little port from which freighters take it to the river Plate.

More important than coal are the oil and gas of Comodoro Rivadavia, an area developed since 1913, the oil again moving north by coastal tankers, the gas by pipeline to Buenos Aires. Large gas fields have also been discovered in Neuquén and Tierra del Fuego. The iron ore of Sierra Grande is a lowgrade (under 50% iron) deposit, but in ore-deficient Argentina is of great interest and is now being developed with foreign aid at a highly mechanized extraction and concentration plant.

Water resources have considerable importance for the region's energy supply. There is now emerging a whole staircase of lakes and power stations on the Limay and Neuquén, the two arms of the upper Rio Negro (fig. 27). On the Limay, there are Alicura, Piedra del Aguila, El

25 The Iguassú Falls, formed where a Paraná tributary leaves the basalt plateau. At present they are a growing tourist attraction on both Argentine and Brazilian sides of the frontier

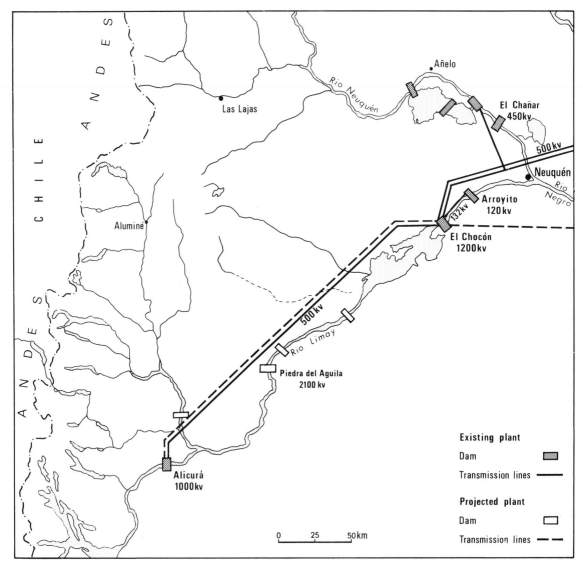

Fig. 27 Hydro-electric plant on the Rio Neuquén and Rio Negro. These new dams are transforming the upper Rio Neuquén into a chain of lakes

Chocón and Arroyito, with others under study. On the Neuquén, there is the Cerros Colorados complex. The total power installed when all projects are completed in the 1990s will exceed 6000 megawatts. No local industries have been built up to use this power, and so it is sent into the Argentine grid through a 500 kV connection to Buenos Aires, providing over 20% of national electric power. This system is ecologically a soundly based one, as sedimentation rates and problems associated with large water bodies are much less serious in this zone than in the tropical lowlands, and the flooded areas are a cool desert environment. River flow is now under control and could be applied to irrigation, but this is a marginal area for agriculture, like the USA's Columbia plateau, and development must therefore be slow.

The other important Patagonian river is the Colorado. In this case an interprovincial dispute between the riverine provinces has held up utilization for decades, the principal contestants being Mendoza, which would divert water for use in its own irrigation system, and Buenos Aires, which already uses a substantial flow for supplementary irrigation in the lower valley. No large dams or hydroelectric projects were attempted because of the disputes between upstream and downstream users, finally solved by a compromise agreement in 1976.

Another river development of importance is that of Futaleufú, on the upper tributaries of the Yelcho, a river running out to the Pacific. Power from a new scheme here is to be sent via 330 kV lines to Puerto Madryn on the Atlantic, and used there for manufacturing aluminium.

Agriculture

In the dry Interior, agriculture tends to polarize into two extremes, intensive cultivation on irrigated land and extensive pastoral land use on dry land. In Patagonia, the irrigated lands are mostly those of the upper Negro valley, where some colonization by small farmers has taken place in this century and marketing of the product in Buenos Aires is possible, using trucks on a modern asphalt road all the way to the capital, or the General Roca railway which runs up the valley to the regional centres, Neuquén, Plaza Huincul and Zapala. Apples, cherries, pears and even grapes may be produced in the warm summers of the protected valley, and cooperative organization aids an efficient marketing of the product.

Outside the irrigated valleys, only sheep farming is practicable and even this is excluded from the true deserts of the northeastern half of the territory. Grass cover is best in Tierra del Fuego and near the Andes, and in both areas there are great *estancias* with hundreds of thousands of head of sheep, some of them Merino and Merino cross-breds.

Industries

There has been little basis for urban growth in Patagonia, and the little towns of the region are either ports, like Puerto Madryn and Rio Gallegos, handling export of wool and some frozen mutton, coal or oil; agricultural or oil centres in the upper Rio Negro valley, Neuquén, Zapala and Plaza Huincul, Neuquén province's oil centre; or the tourist centres of the Argentine Lake District, especially Bariloche itself, which has attracted some permanent retirees as well as

the summer visitors for camping, fishing and hiking in the mountains.

Another tourist attraction which is growing in an urban country concerned for conservation and wildlife is the Valdes Peninsula, an island linked by an 8 km isthmus to the coast of Chubut. Its two great shallow bays, north and south, are a seasonal or permanent home to whales, killer whales, dolphins, seals, penguins, and an unusual range of land species is preserved in the virtual island isolation of the area. The provincial government is trying to control tourist activity and preserve the resource.

THE CUYO REGION

North of the Rio Colorado, the plateau aspect of the landscape gradually disappears and the bunch grasses of Patagonia are replaced by thornscrub, a still more difficult environment for farmers than the arid grasslands to the south. The region of Cuyo comprises the three provinces of Mendoza, San Juan and San Luís; its historical basis is a province of this name, held by Chile until 1776, when it finally became part of the river Plate viceroyalty. Before the Spaniards came, this land had had a certain unity under the Huarpe Indians, settled agriculturalists on the fringe of the Inca empire and with a modest irrigation system, which attracted the sixteenth-century Spaniards exploring from Santiago in the 1560s.

Under the colonial regime, Cuyo developed a prospering vineyard economy and also fattened cattle for driving over the pass of Uspallata to Chile, but the region was economically independent to a considerable degree, as it had to be with the high passes blocked by snow for at least six months of the year. Leather and ironworking, textiles, pottery and woodworking were all practised here because of the impossibility of relying on outside supplies.

This economy declined with the nineteenth-century attachment to Buenos Aires, for the port became the centre, Cuyo part of a remote periphery, and transport over the plains by lumbering oxcart was almost as painful as crossing the Andes to Chile. The rescue came in 1884 with the rail line from Buenos Aires to Mendoza, which allowed vineyards and olive cultivation, as well as alfalfa production, to expand rapidly in Mendoza, sweet grapes for

26 *Careful cultivation is apparent in the vineyards of Mendoza, which now provide a surplus of wine for export from Argentina. Lines of poplars provide both a windbreak and a useful source of wood for fruit packing cases*

drying into raisins in San Juan along with olive groves, though this province was always a little more isolated and less well provided with irrigation water.

The other mainstay of Cuyo's development, besides the rail, was the building of new concrete dams, and general upgrading of the whole irrigation system from a primitive colonial state, in which a multiplicity of water owners had their own derivatory canals taking a little water from rough partial dams of loose stones. Irrigation was organized centrally under a provincial authority which ensured rapid development and reasonably equitable provision of water to farms. No colonists were to be attracted to frontier lands, but there were new settlers, mostly northern Italians who came in during 1880–1900.

Loss of autarchy

The development of vineyards, olive orchards and alfalfa fields was a help to Cuyo but placed her in a subordinate position relative to the new centre and market at Buenos Aires, which acted as importer of goods from Europe, entirely dis-

placing the old craft wares of the Interior. Mendoza, San Juan and San Luís became the home of wine and olive merchants, traders and shopkeepers, not of the host of small manufacturers who had formerly been so important.

Modern economy

Cuyo retains this agricultural orientation to the present, with a still expanding area under vines and alfalfa as well as new intensively irrigated areas with vegetables and fruits. Added to farming is a variety of light manufacture in Mendoza which gives the city a fairly rounded economic structure.

Water and agriculture

Water is all-important, for rainfall in most of the region is under 300 mm annually, insufficient for any unirrigated crop. The rivers, San Juan, Mendoza, Tunuyán, Atuel and Diamante, provide five-sixths of the farm water, pumped ground water the rest. The river water reaches maximum flow in late summer, as it derives from snowmelt in the high Andes, and this is useful for agriculture, though water control leaves much to be desired as sudden floods and long droughts can still cause havoc.

The Rio Atuel has high dams already controlling its flow and helping electricity production in a province which has important power-based industries. Now high dams are being constructed on the Diamante and in the south of the province, and will soon be built also on the other rivers.

Using the river water and increasing amounts from wells, Mendoza continues to concentrate on her vines, used for wine production which serves all national markets and a growing export trade (plate 26). There is a dynamic vegetable production sector too, for sale as quickfrozen, canned or dried food. Most of the farms are small, under 5 ha, but there are also large estates of over 2000 ha, implying enormous wealth when it is remembered that this area is all under irrigation. San Juan is more conservative, and has progressed little towards crop diversification away from the traditional vines and olives. Western San Luís has a more primitive economy, some of its isolated oases producing at a semi-subsistence level. Outside the irrigated lands, throughout Cuyo, there is at most only pasture for goats, whose meat is sold in local markets.

Towns and industries
Mendoza is largest of the Interior's towns, with a population of 600 000 in the urbanized area, extending far beyond the administrative limits of the city. It functions as major regional centre to Cuyo, for retailing, administration and government, with a large state university, and for manufacturing. The *bodegas* producing 80 per cent of Argentine wine are in or around the city, largest among them a government-owned one which acts as price guarantor to the small vineyard owners.

The city also has power-based industries, electrochemicals and explosives manufacture, using local hydroelectric power and also that from a big new oilfired plant, fed by oil from Mendoza's own oilfields; these fields are of growing importance to the nation, and the province has become the largest producer in the country in recent years. A large oil refinery is located at Luján, to the south of the city.

San Juan (290 000), the other large town of Cuyo, is economically less important, and more dependent on farm-based industries, as are San Luís and San Rafael, in southern Mendoza province. These cities are not major tourist resorts; Mendoza attracts some travellers, lying as it does on rail and air lines between Buenos Aires and Santiago, and this city has considerable attraction in its well-kept streets, tree-lined for shade and with ornamental parks and squares, all kept verdant with constant irrigation. San Rafael and San Juan are not so accessible, nor have they so much to offer.

Both San Juan and Mendoza are old colonial cities, but nothing remains of this period except ruins, because of disastrous earthquakes, Mendoza's in the 1860s, San Juan's as recently as the 1940s. In consequence they are modern cities in appearance, most modern construction being in reinforced concrete capable of withstanding some earthquake activity.

THE NORTHWEST

This is a landscape of alternating hills and enclosed basin flats, of dry forests and grasslands, and of old cities with a largely mestizo population, the centre of fertile irrigated lands. The Indians of the region were the most advanced of those in Argentine territory, settled farmers growing maize, beans and squash, and rendering tribute to the Incas of the altiplano.

Colonial links
The region became tributary to Lima in political terms, and in economic terms too, for it was a supplier of materials to the mining industry of Alto Peru, sending up mules and cattle, horses, carts and leather, much coming from Córdoba or even the Pampas and passing through the northwest in an enormous trek to the plateaus of the north. Principal centres to emerge included Salta, where great fairs were held each year for the sale of mules and saddlery to Peru. Salta was also centre to a rich agricultural region with many settled Indians. Jujuy was another centre, a transhipment station on the route to Peru, where oxcarts and carriages had to be exchanged for pack mules and horses, as above the town there is the long climb from the plains to the altiplano, through the dramatic canyon of the Quebrada de Humahuaca, the narrow valley of the Rio Grande. Jujuy at the foot of the valley was also a military site of some importance,

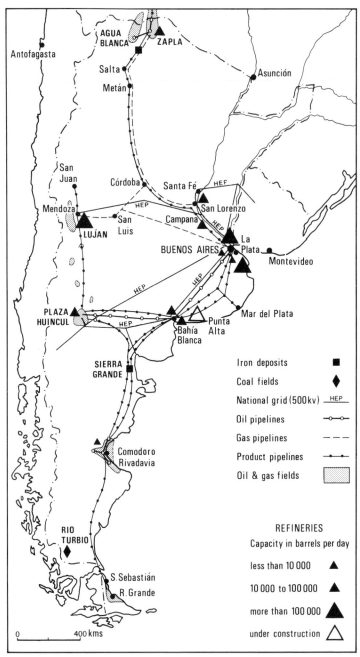

Fig. 28 Argentine mineral resources and the oil industry

guarding the approaches to the altiplano. Santiago del Estero and Tucumán were other important colonial centres, and there were many smaller towns with Spanish settlers, located wherever Indians formed dense rural populations capable of supporting overlords. Some of them had important craft industries as in Cuyo, such as leather and textiles, which declined in the nineteenth century.

Reorientation to Buenos Aires

Changes in this scheme of things came with the rise of Buenos Aires and the decline of mining in Alto Peru in the late eighteenth century. The region was no longer an essential contributor to the altiplano, and was separated from it by a political boundary.

Instead, it became a remote area in a new state based on Buenos Aires and geared to new markets in Europe. Industry and commerce declined until, as in Cuyo, the railways arrived in the 1880s, allowing a new commerce. Tucumán's sugar, important under the Jesuits in colonial time, was revived in this period and exported to Buenos Aires from big new plantations and mills, while crops of tobacco and cotton were possible in the fertile valleys. Few settlers came in, and the population thus retained its mestizo flavour and to some extent its poverty, for the amount of irrigated land did not expand much and few new ideas to change the economy or society arrived from abroad.

MODERN ECONOMY

Infrastructure
The northwestern oil is located in the Chaco plains of Salta, near the Bolivian frontier, with considerable amounts of natural gas, which is sent by pipeline down to the Paraná river at San Lorenzo near Rosario, where there is a large petrochemical industry. There are old silver, lead, copper and other mines in the sierras, but little of commercial interest.

Water resources are relatively poor, for even the highest parts of the Andes in the subtropical latitude are arid, and there is no snowmelt water as a result. Major dam-construction projects may improve the situation, and one big plan is that for the Bermejo, but for the most part there will never be enough river water to supply new irrigated lands and, though subterranean sources may help, their contribution is not likely to be permanent in such an arid environment.

Agriculture
Sugar is the key to Tucumán's economy, and is also the most important crop in the northwest. It is grown on large factory-owned estates, and the concentration of production in a few hands is a long-established feature of the economy, with severe social effects. Small farms are to be found, but they are necessarily dependent on the mill owners. An economic problem for sugar producers is the degree of monoculture, which has led in crisis years such as those of the late 1960s to large-scale searches for new alternatives.

Sorghum for cattle feed has had some success in recent years. In the smaller irrigated oases, there are more varied crops: in La Rioja vineyards are prominent, in Salta maize and vegetables, in Jujuy tobacco, and there is much semi-subsistence farming in the *minifundio* farms, which can barely support their owners.

Urban centres
Tucumán (497 000) is the main centre of the northwest, and has a considerable colonial past, with an old cathedral and other religious monuments, though most of the city is of recent construction. Part of the tourist current to the northwest enters the city and the hills behind it. It is financial and commercial centre to the sugar trade, and even in the heart of the city one may see an occasional tractor followed by a line of six or more rubber-tyred carts of sugar cane, rumbling through to the mills during the cutting season. Derivative industries have also been located around the city producing alcohol and sweets, and newsprint from bagasse. A few other industries, such as domestic electrical goods, shoes and clothing, have been attracted to the city on account of special tax credits given to encourage new industry, and the availability of a large labour force; Tucumán retains the unenviable position of having the highest level of unemployment — over 10% on average — for any large Argentine city, a feature that is related to the cyclical nature of employment in the sugar mills which work for only half the year.

North of Tucuman, Salta (176 000), Jujuy, Catamarca and Santiago del Estero (148 000) are smaller urban centres, with only modest functions as regional agricultural centres. Jujuy and Catamarca attract some of Argentina's domestic tourist trade. At Salta there is a large cement works, and in northern Salta oil-related activities. At Palpala near Jujuy, the Zapla ironworks set up after the Second World War to provide castings for the army, using local iron ore and tree plantations to make charcoal in place of coke, have been expanded to produce sheet steel. Jujuy also has paper works using timber and sugar-cane bagasse as raw material.

The upper Bermejo
A study conducted in 1972 under the OAS made the remarkable finding that the upper Bermejo tributaries, in Salta, Jujuy and Tarija (Bolivia), produce nearly 75% of the total silt carried by

the Paraná–Paraguay system. This led to an action programme formulated on the basis of up to 11 dams to produce irrigation water for the commercial tobacco, citrus fruit and sugar cane crops, power, and sediment control. Six of these have been built, but three problems are apparent. First, the main benefit was to be HEP, which was to be absorbed by the existing cement works, steel works and paper factories, as well as by new industries to be created in an industrial decentralization programme. Since 1975 industrial growth has in fact been slight and the programme has been abandoned. The actual power generation is mostly from private sources — cane factories can use their own bagasse, the iron works has its own plantations for charcoal — so that the value of new power is limited.

Secondly, the dams will act as sedimentation basins, collecting the silt and keeping it from the lower river so as to reduce the need for dredging. But erosion is going on unchecked, at a rate for the whole basin of 2000 tonnes per sq. km, because it is mostly natural erosion, occurring on the dry uncultivated western part of the basin, so that conservation measures in the agricultural area have little effect. The filling-up of the reservoirs in 30 years brings back the original problem. Thirdly, the poorest sections of the population, living in Tarija and the canyon of Humahuaca from subsistence agriculture, are unlikely to benefit from any aspect of the scheme.

THE CHACO AND NORTHEAST

Crossing the desert of the southern Chaco, vegetation becomes thicker and greener again towards the Paraná river. Quebracho and other hardwoods form an open forest on high land, and swamp savanna of palms occupies the floodplains. Further east there are plains too through the province of Corrientes, with swamp forest and grasslands where forests were easily cleared from the sandy soils. The swamps have made this some of the most isolated country in South America, and seasonal flooding makes any kind of habitation around the swamps difficult. Further eastwards, Misiones is a province of rough hill lands and a tropical hardwood forest vegetation.

These northern lands were little occupied till the nineteenth century. The Chaco Indians were always hostile and deterred any settlement in what was in any case a physically difficult region, with no resources for agriculture. In Misiones, settlement came earlier, for Jesuit missions, pushed out of the Paraná plateau region of Brazil by the marauding *bandeirantes* from São Paulo, crossed over into the region during the seventeenth century. After a period of prosperity, the mission villages declined and their churches became ruins in the forest, when the Jesuits were ejected from South America by the civil authorities in the eighteenth century.

Most of Misiones and Corrientes came under large landowners who either had no use for their lands or maintained herds of lean cattle on the grasslands. Another stage of occupation came to Misiones with the nineteenth-century expansion of the *yerba mate* industry, based on wild plants, trees related to our holly to be found as an element in the understorey of luxuriant *selvas* vegetation in narrow, protected valleys of the region. Because of the isolation of the area, poor labourers could be enticed into the industry, then held there under fierce overseers with the pretext that they could not leave till their debts to the company for clothes, food or drink were repaid. This exploitation of manpower only ended with the better transportation means available in this century.

Modern economy

The northeast is not in general a water-deficit region, and Misiones receives throughout more than 2000 mm of rainfall annually. Temporary droughts may affect production but are not severe enough to warrant irrigation schemes. Water for power is present as an enormous resource on the middle Paraná; the gorge section of the river ends just above Posadas, and here, at Yaciretá–Apipé, a large hydroelectric plant is being built in conjunction with the Paraguayan government.

Fossil fuels are not known in the northeast, but there is a very considerable timber resource in the forests of Misiones, useful to Argentina as a country poor in forests. The natural mixed tropical hardwood forest is being replaced by eucalyptus and pine plantations, which grow exceptionally quickly in the region and reach cutting size for use in paper mills within fifteen or even twelve years. Given Argentina's perennial shortage of paper, a priority scheme, inaugurated in 1982, has been a paper pulp plant near Posadas, built by fourteen Argentine paper companies. The plant will feed them and also provide some exports. It uses 3000 tonnes of wood daily, half from its own 20 000 ha of forest plantations. Quebracho trees in the Chaco provide another natural resource, but they are in effect irreplaceable, for the tree requires over a hundred years to reach commercial size, so that no planting programme is contemplated by quebracho extractors.

Agriculture

During the 1920s cotton production in the eastern Chaco began a rapid expansion, under a government-sponsored colonization scheme which attracted some immigrants, but also many migrants from other parts of the country. Cotton farming on the small farms set up then is still flourishing and the area under cotton has undergone considerable expansion, with associated industries such as cotton-ginning and cotton-seed pressing. There are long-term problems in its production, including salinity of the water and soil resulting from poor drainage and the high evaporation rates of this hot region.

Subtropical agriculture in Misiones has a special place in Argentine markets. The province reaches into subtropical latitudes where crops such as tea can be grown. Tea is a comparatively new crop for the country, and is carefully cultivated on small estates and farms, among others which produce citrus, tung nuts or *yerba mate*. Tung, tea and *yerba* all require some processing before transportation to markets, and thus there are a variety of small industries in the region.

Settlement and towns

While the remaining *estancia* country retains a traditional flavour, with no new blood or important changes in the economy, colonization has had some impact through Corrientes and Misiones. In the latter province, many colonists are immigrants, having come to the country during 1900-20, and many are from eastern Europe, Poland, the Baltic countries, European Russia and eastern Germany. The colonists came to small farms on colonies set up with national encouragement on land which in some cases was available simply because of mistakes in surveying the old latifundia which allowed open ground between them! In Corrientes colonies were planned all along the rivers Uruguay and Paraná, but few came into real existence; these have been colonized in recent times by a mixed small-farmer population, including Japanese, who are usually the most hardworking and successful of the farmers, producing citrus crops and vegetables.

There are no large cities in the northeast, though two agglomerations are being brought into being by new bridges at Resistencia (218 000) and Corrientes (180 000), on either side of the Paraná, and at Posadas-Encarnación, where the twinned towns are forming an international conurbation. In both these twin cities, the industries currently serve only an immediate hinterland, and there are no larger industrial complexes, but the new links and industrial promotion efforts may be able to change this.

The traditional isolation of the Northeast is also being broken down further south, where a key link has been made through Entre Rios, linking Buenos Aires to Uruguay. A rail and road bridge at Zarate, 5 km north of Buenos Aires, crosses the marshy Paranà delta, linking an existing rail line to Concordia and the great Salto Grande HEP project which is crossed by rail on the dam wall into Uruguay. Salto Grande makes electricity available from an 1860 megawatt installation for both Uruguay and Argentina. Further power comes from Brazil via international links further north which have recently been constructed.

PLANNING AND THE REGIONS

Argentine central government has made only tentative steps towards encouragement of regional development, with simple financial incentives to move out of Buenos Aires before the Second World War, followed by more complex credit schemes and industrial estates at Córdoba and Rosario in the 1950s, and in the 1960s the creation of some growth poles for focussing the development process. In the north, there were to be three growth poles, at Resistencia-Corrientes, Posadas-Encarnación, and Salta-Guemes, with special treatment for the problem city of Tucumán, with its pool of unskilled labour. In none of these centres was there much attraction for industrialists, who found social and psychological drawbacks to a location so far from Buenos Aires, quite apart from the material economic disadvantages such as transport costs.

Three further centres were designated in the south, another peripheral area but with a quite different order of problems from that in the north. Here Puerto Madryn–Sierra Grande is seen as one focal area, with aluminium refining and ore extraction. Another is the upper Rio Negro centre at Neuquén–Zapala, and in the far south there is Rio Turbio with its coalfield. These centres must be judged as having contributed only in a very limited way to regional development. Their key industries being in the area of mineral extraction and power production, gives them few local links to other industries, and favours the movement of their commodities to Buenos Aires instead. In addition, the designation of three centres in the distant south, virtually unpopulated, suggests a strategic function was seen by the military government of the time, rather than social or economic improvements. New centres in peripheral zones could help consolidate Argentina's claim on lands she conquered only a hundred years ago.

Under the second government of Juan Peron/Isabel Peron, 1973-6, there was a concentration on industrial and energy sectoral planning, effectively abandoning the regional planning and allowing concentration in the centre again. Huge growth plans for the steel mills at San Nicolás are typical of this last phase. It must be admitted that regional deconcentration from Buenos Aires has to some small extent occurred; but it has very largely been to the other cities of the Pampas, and not to the distant interior, helping places such as Bahía Blanca, Córdoba and Rosario. The old problem of strains and divergence of interest between littoral and interior continues to plague the modern nation.

PROSPECTS FOR ARGENTINA

A considerable wealth of resources and a favourable population–resource balance make Argentina the wealthiest country in the subcontinent, on most reckonings. As old ties to European markets are thrown off, and the national economy achieves a certain maturity, one is tempted to expect a smoothing out of the old regional imbalances between Interior and Pampas, or even between Buenos Aires and the rest of the country. That the imbalance has not been corrected, despite the measures that have been taken, shows that deep-rooted processes causing polarization on the capital and vicinity are continuing to operate.

Apart from the internal processes of migration to the capital in search of work opportunities and advance, and the concentration at the city of all important industries, there are external reasons for the Pampas and Buenos Aires to maintain their leadership now and in the near future. In LAFTA, the favoured products of Argentina will be those of the Pampas, middle-latitude farm products and manufactures. The subtropical food products of the north will have to compete with cheaper production from more truly tropical regions, in Paraguay, Bolivia and Brazil.

Superficially, it might seem that there was scope for a flourishing exchange between Interior and Pampas — the latter's manufactures and farm products could be exchanged for the power and minerals of the Interior. This is in fact being done, but the point to be noted is that mineral and power exploitation do not have any regional multiplier effect, that the products are too easily exportable, and that the ultimate gainer from the process remains the central city.

12. Uruguay — the Small State

Uruguay has suffered for many years from its smallness, sitting as it does between two large neighbours and coming into being as a political body to form a buffer between them rather than because of any solid cultural or economic identity. Smallness, and the lack of any strong historical tradition, are in fact sometimes given as excuses by Uruguayans for their failings as a nation, and in particular for the lack of progress in recent years.

National area is in fact quite large by European standards (186 900 sq. km), but very small compared with Argentina or Brazil, with 2.8 million and 8.5 million sq. km respectively. Uruguay suffers however more from the smallness of its population of three million, and the smallness of its development in resources or population skills, than from any lack of land, which by most standards is in abundant supply. Small population and small purchasing power mean a small market, which might not matter had Uruguay been able to trade with other South American countries, and export manufactures to them, but, under the prevailing conditions of trade only with Europe, has hampered development of anything but a traditional agricultural economic structure, set up under British influence in the last century.

The theme of smallness is echoed in the resource base. Uruguay totally lacks coal, petroleum and gas, and has only limited hydro-electric power potential, because of its gentle topography. Among useful minerals, only building materials have been produced on any scale; commercial timber is scarce and metal ores virtually unknown. This still leaves a vast agricultural resource in the soil of the Pampas, but this wealth has yet to be properly tapped and its development will require a new attitude to the land on the part of both farmers and townsmen.

PHYSICAL FEATURES

The geological base of Uruguay is unremarkable, for the most part consisting of a southern extension of the Brazilian Shield, covered thickly in the north by sediments and the Paraná Plateau basalts which reach a thickness of 540 m in the northwest corner. Sedimentary cover to the shield increases to the river Uruguay, covering also the basalt which dips west under the river, except for local exposures such as at Salto Grande above Salto city, where rapids formed by the resistant basalt provide the physical basis for new hydroelectric development.

In the south, rocks of the shield complex are at the surface, except for a loessic cover which has been reworked by streams and deposited thickly in the valleys of the rolling countryside. Because of the crystalline rock influence, southern Uruguay has a slightly hilly topography, with ridges and swells, not the monotonous flatness of the central Argentine Humid Pampas. Along the Atlantic and Plate fronts of the country, recent marine deposition gives rise to flatter land and a fertile base for arable farming. For great distances along the Atlantic coast, there are lagoons, most notably lake Mirim, retained on the seaward side by sand dunes of great size. The landscape is thus one of table lands in the north-west, formed by the sandstones or basalts, and including most notably the Cuchilla de Haedo (fig. 29), and rolling country in the southeast, where the principal ridge is the Cuchilla Grande.

In terms of climate, the country is halfway between the midlatitude climates which may be experienced in eastern Argentina, with their definite winter, and the subtropical conditions of southern coastal Brazil. There is a cool season, but it is insufficient to allow a real rest period for

vegetative growth, and does not eliminate many insect forms of life, so that for example tropical ticks are a constant trouble to European breeds of cattle. Rainfall is around 1000 mm over the whole country, with a fairly even distribution through the year. This means that droughts are an irregular but recurring problem, for summer temperatures are high and any shortfall in precipitation is soon felt in water supplies to plants. Few farms have proper water-storage tanks and they suffer severely when real droughts come, so that cattle may have to be slaughtered *en masse*

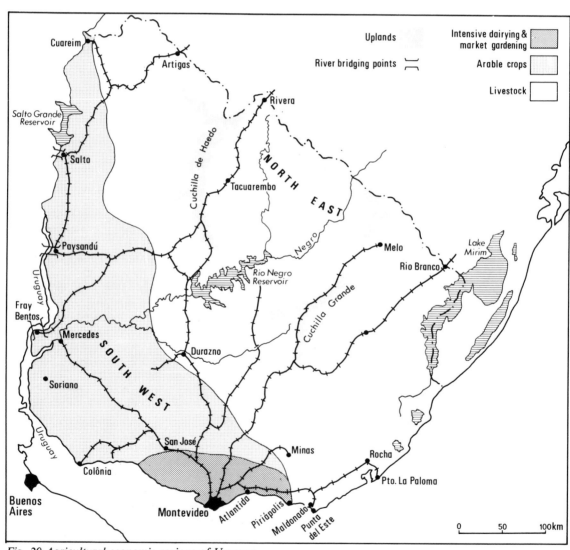

Fig. 29 Agricultural economic regions of Uruguay

or left to die by their owners. Temperature and rainfall are adequate for tree growth, but much of the country has been grass-covered since Europeans arrived, while other areas have been cleared for charcoal making or for construction, leaving an almost entirely herbaceous cover today.

SETTLEMENT AND ECONOMIC GROWTH

Uruguay's aboriginal population consisted solely of a number of nomadic tribes, of which the best known were the fearless Charruas, hunting Indians like their neighbours on the Argentine side. These fierce men forbade early settlement in what was the Banda Oriental, or eastern side (of the river Plate), until the founding of Jesuit missions at Soriano in the southwest around 1625, in a region isolated from the main mission country lying on the Paraná Plateau within Brazil, but probably quite accessible to sources of cattle and cattle hands from the Entre Rios area of Argentina.

In the seventeenth century, Portuguese expansion out of São Paulo led to an early settlement in Uruguay, at Colônia do Sacramento in the 1680s, set up as an advance post against Spanish power in Buenos Aires and staking the Portuguese claim to cattle lands in the rich Pampas. This settlement finally goaded the Spaniards into action in the founding of a rival settlement, Montevideo, in 1726, though Colônia remained a thorn in the Spanish side and indeed changed hands frequently between Portuguese and Spanish in the course of the eighteenth century. Meanwhile, the economy of most of the interior was restricted to cattle hunting for the *cimarrones* and direct robbing of owned cattle from the unfenced *estancias* in the settled southwest of the country.

The wildness of the country districts was notorious, occupied as they were for the most part by *gauchos*, a group which was romanticized and to some extent legitimized in the next century but which had its beginnings in vagabonds and escapees from prison or military service, who lived here by robbing either Spanish or Portuguese of cattle to sell to the opposite side. Most of the contraband trade in cattle went to Brazil, finally reaching the great fairs of Sorocaba near São Paulo, and through them the

gold-mining settlements of Minas Gerais, a food-deficit region where the gold boom brought in thousands of Negro slaves under their masters to work the mines, without any corresponding development of farming. The *gauchos* were paid in money, in clothes or in alcohol, but obviously such a trade had to be irregular as a source of income and at other times the *gauchos* attacked *estancias* or settlements. Vigorous measures had to be taken against them, such as that recorded at the little village of Las Víboras, in 1801, where attacks of *gauchos* on the village were followed by their capture, beheading and the setting up of their bleached skulls at the village entrances as an awesome warning to their like.

The opening up of the interior during the late eighteenth century led to the founding of most of the nation's inland towns. In general, this was an expansion northeast from bases along the Uruguay and Plate rivers. At the end of the century, the Banda Oriental came under Buenos Aires and it was in part the pressure of Argentine estancieros which led to the inland expansion. However, in the wars for independence from Spain, the Uruguayans led a separate campaign for independence under their own national hero, Artigas, who maintained a slender Uruguayan independence from all parties, and claimed the support of Argentine provinces west of the river Uruguay. With the fall of Artigas, Brazil and Argentina warred over Uruguay until a settlement was reached in 1828, leaving a tiny new republic with 70 000 inhabitants, with only an externally determined raison d'être and quite poor prospects for future development or even independence.

RECENT DEVELOPMENT

Montevideo grew immediately after Independence, attracting French and Italian immigrants who formed a merchant class and stimulated the town's commercial functions and administrative centrality. The interior was still quite untamed, because of isolation and the primitive cattle economy, and because of political instability. Civil wars between the two political parties, Colorados and Blancos, only ended in the 1900s and, as campaigns were conducted in the rural areas, were a considerable deterrent to economic advance. The economic base was still cattle, either hides or *charqui*, until a transformation began in the 1860s with the first meat-extract plant of the Liebig company at Fray Bentos. This kind of processing was particularly well suited to the primitive transport conditions of the time. Its raw material was the lean longhorn cattle, which could deliver themselves to the factory without road or rail, and its product was a liquid or solid extract relatively unaffected by storage and with a high value/weight ratio well able to stand the cost of movement to Europe. As an industry it was largely replaced in the 1890s by the *frigorífico,* relying on good-quality steers for freezing and thus on a whole new technology which could fatten such animals and bring them easily to the processing plant. Introduction of new breeds, conversion of estancias into surveyed and fenced ranches, the improvement of pastures, were all applied as in Argentina, though only a limited labour force was brought in and in fact labour needs in the country declined in many regions relative to the previous system.

Even taking into account the size of the country, Uruguay seems to have had a much smaller influx of migrants than Argentina, to judge by population growth from immigration. It is not immediately apparent why this should have been so, but one factor is likely to have been official and private attitudes towards migrants. In Argentina, the establishment of independent farmer colonies was found to be almost impossible without considerable financial and organizational aid, and various disappointing experiments in Uruguay which failed for want of such aid may have deterred further attempts. Tenant farmers could be brought in for wheat farming as in Argentina, on four-year contracts, but even these migrants were less important than in Buenos Aires, where wheat speculation went hand-in-hand with railway development.

A somewhat different pattern was established in the hinterland of Montevideo. Near the city are most of the small independent farmers and many tenant arable farmers, a great number immigrants of the 1900–30 period, when most of Uruguay's immigrants arrived. Some of these farms are quite prosperous, especially in dairying and vineyards, though near the city the *minifundio* has arisen and the dispersed rural population suffers from underemployment most of the year.

The most notable demographic phenomenon is of course the growth of Montevideo itself, which has become centre of all economic activity. Its population of 1.5 million out of a national total of 3.1 million is exceptional even within the Latin American context. It is not approached by any other town, for the next centres in order of size are Salto and Paysandú, each with about 60000 inhabitants.

THE ECONOMY

Metropolitan dominance

There are many reasons which might be advanced for Montevideo's dominance, among them the necessary concentration of settlement on the coast because of links to foreign markets and suppliers, which makes the major port city also the metropolis. In this light Montevideo is just an intensification of the general trend of all Uruguayan population to locate itself near either the Plate or the Uruguay river shipping axis. Another factor is the smallness of the country; given a wholly rural economy and the relatively small distances from any part of the country to any other, only one centre might be expected to emerge for trade and administration of the country's interests.

Contrast between city and *campo* (country) has long been a focus of interest for Uruguayans themselves. Martinez Lamas, a Uruguayan economist, likened the relationship between the two to a suction pump, operated by the city in order to draw off the lifeblood of the *campo* for its own parasitic growth. He claimed that traditional arguments about the poverty of the *campo* as being related to poverty of resources, lack of transport, *latifundio* dominance or the like were unfounded, and that all these could change given the appropriate encouragement from the government.

In fact the government, for most of this century, has indeed discouraged farm production, by export taxes which hit Uruguay's traditional exports of wool and meat, while manufactures have gained from a policy of tariff walls to protect them as young industries against foreign competition. This tax structure has no doubt been responsible for some of the metropolitan dominance, as it has for the general malaise which has increasingly affected the Uruguayan economy.

This divergence in regional fortunes between

city and *campo* may seem odd in a country with a reputation of democratic government better than that of any other Latin American country, dating back to the beginning of this century, when Jose Batlle y Ordoñez, leader of a government independent of both urban and rural pressure groups, introduced a variety of welfare measures with a very modern flavour, such as pensions, farmer credits, unemployment pay and an eight-hour working day. The truth is that this welfare state never penetrated very deeply into the social structure of the country, because of the absence of central government funds, in a state where from 1905 to 1961 there was no real income tax and where the stamp tax on official papers still yields more than income tax. Under these conditions, it is impossible to reduce the gap between rich and poor to any significant extent.

AGRICULTURE AND INDUSTRIES OF THE CAMPO

Agriculture in Uruguay is largely devoted to live-stock production rather than crops. Crop production is increasing, as the table shows, due to governmental encouragement and internal demand, but it is still small and little integrated with livestock. Argentina, it has been noted, has a Ministry of Agriculture and Livestock (Chapter 10, p. 134) but Uruguay has a Ministry of Live-stock and Agriculture! The dominance of the *estancieros* is expressed in the title. A regional division of farming may be made between the southwest, including Montevideo and surrounds, with 85% of annual cropland, and the remainder of the country.

Uruguay is in fact a country in which von Thunen's theoretical patterning of land use may be observed with little distortion, as has been shown by Ernst Griffin (1973). The most intensive farmland with market gardens surrounds the city. Further out and up the transport axis of the Uruguay river are the grain lands, and further afield there are cattle and permanent grasslands. The pattern is apparent because of the lack of topographic or other physical variations, and the uniformity of the transport system centred on Montevideo. Elsewhere in the continent such patterns are lost because of powerful physical controls, as well as social factors which have determined, for example, the pattern of land-holdings.

The southwest

This region (fig. 29) is one both of grain farming and cattle fattening. The *estancias* in the *departamentos* of Soriano, Colônia and San José in the southwest have a third of national rotation-grass area, used for fattening local calves and steers brought in from the northeast, driven along cattle tracks or by rail. Fattening is largely on alfalfa, rye grass and hybrid sorghums, giving a slow maturing animal which is sold at four to six years of age. Dairying is also practised in this zone.

Cash grain farming is for wheat, mostly grown by medium-scale farmers with 50–100 ha. Wheat came into prominence after 1945, with the ploughing up of open plateau lands along the middle Uruguay in the Paysandú and Rio Negro *departamentos* (fig. 30). Mechanized farming and the use of dry-farming techniques in places to conserve soil moisture and fertility are typical. Oats is an important secondary crop on the plateau, though not grown in rotation but used on poorer land as a dual-purpose crop, for grazing in early months, then harvesting if and when other feed becomes available to the cattle. Oilseeds, especially sunflower and flax, are important and were also originally expanded to relieve post-Second World War shortages of vegetable oils.

The metropolitan hinterland

The region around Montevideo differs from the rest of the country in the intensity of farming and in a focussing of all production on city markets. In San José and Canelones *departamentos* there are many minifundios producing vegetables, maize, fruits, milk and potatoes, without the aid of machinery. Most farms are operated by their owners, many are less than five ha in size, and they suffer from soil erosion due to overworking and a lack of fertilizers to maintain soil structure. Some have already been abandoned through soil destruction. On larger farms, sugarbeet and dairying, which are both linked to industrial processing, are more common.

Towns

There are no large towns in the *campo*. The urban network is denser in the southwest than elsewhere because this region is densely populated and has some commercial products. Mercedes, San José and Fray Bentos are small

Fig. 30 Administrative divisions of Uruguay

centres with services to their hinterlands and rural industries such as flour milling, sugar milling and oil extraction from seeds. Fray Bentos has in addition meat packing and grain terminals.

Some towns are becoming tourist centres, a little surprisingly for a country with little tradition in this direction. Uruguay now earns over 10 per cent of her foreign exchange from tourists, a figure as high as anywhere in South America. Montevideo itself is the major attraction, but Punta del Este, at the limits of the Plate's brackish waters, is fast growing up as a resort town. La Paloma, Atlantida and Piriapolis are other resorts growing up along this coast. The most important tourist current is from Argentina, now coming by ferry to Colônia, and the bridge to be built over the Uruguay at Fray Bentos and coastal road improvements should enhance the attractions of the country. There are distinct possibilities along the coast north towards the Brazilian frontier, to be realized with new road improvements linking into the rapidly expanding Brazilian road network.

Well up the Uruguay river lie Salto and Paysandú. Salto is a city of small houses trimmed in local marble, one of the important industries of the town. Apart from this it has the usual complement of mills for processing agricultural goods. Paysandú has a more industrial aspect with its breweries, cotton milling, leather working, cement factory and distilleries, and has a small but active port.

Salto's name comes from nearby falls on the river Uruguay, which have now disappeared under a huge lake behind a dam built in a joint Argentine–Uruguayan project, named Salto Grande, over the period 1974–81, and having an eventual power output of 1.8 million kW. This dam also provides for industry and domestic supplies, irrigation for 130 000 ha of land, navigation through lateral locks for vessels up to 2.5 m draught as far as the Brazilian border. With this installation the Argentine and Uruguayan electrical distribution systems are effectively integrated, with high tension lines to Santa Fe and Buenos Aires in Argentina as well as to Montevideo. It is also a means of transport integration because the crown of the dam is used for new rail and road links between the two countries.

The northeast

Three-quarters of Uruguay is still open Pampas, a landscape little altered by man. In the far northeast there are good cattle lands and the region has become important for beef production. Over the remainder sheep are more important, monopolizing in particular the heights of the basalt and sandstone escarpments in the northwest, and *cuchillas*, low ridges, in the crystalline rocks of the east, where lack of surface water makes beef production difficult. Sheep are produced primarily for wool, so that rustic types with good drought resistance can be bred on poor pastures. Often sheep are grazed on the same land as cattle so that proper management of pastures and herds is impossible.

Cattle raising is also extensive in style, with little care for improvements or advanced forms of technology. Agricultural planning by the government now includes finance for improvement of breeding, pasture and fertilizer use, but land productivity remains low and many diseases are endemic, including foot and mouth and many parasitic diseases.

Islands of more intensive agriculture are appearing, notably rice growing in the ill-drained saline lands around lake Mirim. Sections of the flat plain have been drained for rice production in the last decades, and areas under rice grew from 17 800 ha in 1961 to 340 000 ha in 1982. Expansion of the rice-growing area has been helped by the use of underground water supplies in the north which have a high temperature (over 40°C) and thus aid production in a climatically marginal area. Like sugar, which has been introduced on a big scale in the northwestern *departamentos* on cane lands owned by large landowners, rice has come in with capitalistic forms of exploitation using machinery rather than labour wherever possible. Another move in the same direction has been with citrus crops, though these can also be grown on small farms with little capital. Over all these subtropical crop developments, a big question mark must be placed as LAFTA tariff reductions and the improvements in transportation means now coming into being may make Brazilian production more competitive and even eliminate the local crop which is in a physically marginal position on the edge of the tropics.

MONTEVIDEO

Montevideo is a city of parks and squares, an open city of relatively low buildings, a result of its relative youth and of its planned expansion with liberal allowances of space, only possible in a situation where new urban land has encroached only on open pastures and on flat land with no particular building problems. The aspect of openness and space is enhanced by the expanses of sandy beach to the south, a major summer attraction for tourists and local workers, and a special advantage over the muddy estuarine condition of Buenos Aires's front.

This is of course the economic hub of the country, housing within its *departamento* limits three-quarters of all manufacturing in the country. Its port is a vortex of transport routes, for the old city grew out of port trade and manufacturing has always had close connections to this trade, using the transhipment point between interior and foreign ports. Traditional industries are thus tanneries, flour mills and *frigorificos*. To these have been added under tariff protection a variety of other manufactures for final consumption markets. Textiles have come in through such protection, as have a number of light engineering industries producing for example electrical domestic appliances.

Montevideo maintains its industrial dominance party through a superior infrastructure: its railway network, built from the 1860s by British companies which started work from Montevideo outwards, and its road network which was built (rather unimaginatively) to the same pattern, the roads often running right by the railway for many kilometres. This road network was built up after the First World War with the idea of providing competition to the railways; while not really doing this for a long time, it did help to consolidate the centrality of Montevideo. Now there is the further centrality provided by air services. Electricity supply is assured to Montevideo from the large hydroelectric plants on the Rio Negro at Rincón del Bonete and Baygorria, brought to the city by a 150 kW line. Since 1981 a large increase in power output has come from Uruguay's share of the Salto Grande scheme.

Apart from industrial strength, Montevideo is administrative and cultural centre to the country, monopolizing university education, national government, hospitals, libraries, museums and theatres. Socially, this is a complex city, its largely European population an amalgam of upper-crust merchant and *estanciero* families, a large lower middle class of office workers, some factory workers, and a last group of *marginados*, migrants from the country occupying peripheral areas of the city or old central residential sectors where they live in *conventillos*, rambling old houses converted into slum quarters. Immigrants to the city serve to complicate the geography of poverty for in earlier decades poor people did not typify the city. Now the *campo* has come to the city to remind urban government of a social responsibility yet to be wholly accepted.

CONCLUSIONS

Uruguay is still a country of opportunity. Despite resource limitations it still has enormous possibilities for intensification of agriculture where the basic resource is under-used to date, though proper use will only come with a thorough going reform of agriculture. Specifically, the Uruguayan pampas can produce much more grain and other arable crops, and this they should be made to do whether or not industrial development is fostered. Concerning the latter, there is a total lack of decentralized industry, or any growth points outside Montevideo, though again government action could bring change.

Wedged between Brazil and Argentina, with favourable treatment from LAFTA it should have a key position on the axis from the river Plate to industrial São Paulo, and already the beginnings of transport improvements to aid connections between the two giants are helping Uruguay's own economic development. With this geographical situation and a relatively well-educated workforce, Uruguay's future as an industrial corridor country is not assured but becomes a definite possibility.

13. Paraguay

Paraguay holds a position much like that of Interior Argentina with respect to the city of Buenos Aires and the Pampas. It is poor, short of water over the greater part of its national territory, and dependent on the regional metropolis, Buenos Aires, for manufactures which it exchanges for its own raw-material exports. Paraguay, however, merits separate discussion on the basis of its independent status, as well as on the grounds of its distinct cultural and historical identity, stemming from such factors as the exceptionally complete mixing of Indian and white blood here, the special position on the Paraná–Paraguay river system, and the bitter history of national mismanagement since 1811, the year of its declaration of Independence.

PHYSICAL GEOGRAPHY

Geologically, as in many other respects, Paraguay is composed of two sections. The eastern two-fifths of the country is a rolling, grassland and forest region, formed basically of Brazilian Shield rocks, though these are covered by thick sandstones and basalts of the Paraná Plateau series. The western limit of these rocks and the hilly topography they produce is roughly at the Paraguay river.

Beyond the river, and immediately visible from the heights of Asunción, the Paraguayan capital which is built on outliers of the eastern hills, there is the vast, unending plain of the Chaco, spotted with palm trees or quebracho near the Paraguay, but open and uninterrupted desert scrub further west, with no permanent water courses.

The climate is difficult for middle-latitude man. Given the subtropical latitude and location in the interior of a continent, and altitudes under 600 m, very high summer temperatures are to be expected, and annual maxima well over 36° C are experienced throughout the Chaco. In the east, temperatures are a little lower, but equally uncomfortable because of the higher humidity.

These conditions are alleviated in spring and autumn by the occasional cold fronts which sweep in from the south as the continuation northwards of the Argentine *pamperos*, associated with cyclonic depressions deriving their energy from the Atlantic seaboard and passing along the coast into Brazil. *Pamperos* cause temperatures to fall 10–20°C within a few hours. In winter, temperatures are very comfortable, between 15°C and 25°C, attracting tourists in increasing numbers from Argentina, especially Buenos Aires.

Rainfall is fairly evenly spread over the year, decreasing a little in the cool season; the annual total declines from highs over 2000 mm on the Brazilian frontier, through moderate levels around 1500 mm in the longitude of Asunción, down to levels which are quite insufficient for agriculture, (between 1000 mm and 500 mm), in the Chaco.

HISTORY

Asunción was an old core of Spanish settlement

in the continent. It had one important advantage which attracted settlement, its peaceful and dense agricultural population, capable of supporting Spanish overlords and producing a further surplus for sale. The first settlers on the lower Paraná in Argentina organized excursions upriver in search of riches during the 1530s, and Asunción was founded as a result in 1537, its importance soon confirmed when the lower river settlements had to be abandoned in the face of Indian hostility.

Despite several expeditions made from this base, no finds of gold or silver were made, and the Spaniards merely discovered that there were great deserts between them and the fabulous land of Peru, deserts capable of killing through the simple effects of heat and thirst, or through the actions of their hostile and treacherous Indian population. Asunción became an early backwater with the rise of Peru, its Spanish lords becoming impoverished and marrying or mixing with Indian girls, to form a unique *mestizo* race, in which the landlords, just as much as the poorest peasants, belonged to one new amalgamated stock, so that racially based class differences are less important in modern Paraguay than in other countries of the continent. An index of the historico-cultural importance of the Guaraní Indians is the strength of Guaraní as a language, still spoken by 95% of Paraguayans, though Spanish is increasingly the language of private and official business, and is the language now taught in schools.

The Jesuit impact on the country was also of substantial historical importance. In the eastern borderlands of Paraguay, Indians were gathered into mission villages, called *reducciones,* and fine stone churches and other buildings were built as centres for economic units which produced important surpluses of cotton, *yerba mate*, cloth, tobacco and hardwoods.

From the 1767 expulsion of the Jesuits, their centres were abandoned and their laboriously cleared farmland reverted to woodland, a disaster for the regional economy. Soon Buenos Aires, declared centre of a viceroyalty of the Plate region in 1776, imposed itself as commercial as well as administrative centre and Asunción, the inland river town, was made an insignificant gathering point for its own poor agricultural region.

In the nineteenth century, development was in a negative direction. The effects of Independence in opening up trade possibilities with Europe were brought to nothing by the works of several dictators, Dr Francia (1815–40) and the two López presidents, father and son — the latter brought Paraguay into the War of the Triple Alliance, 1865–70, versus three powerful allies, Argentina, Uruguay and Brazil. Paraguayan military prowess was of no avail against these three and war devastation reduced the national population from 525 000 to 219 000, in addition causing much damage to agriculture and town settlements. A large part of the country was given up to the victors, in the northwest Brazil taking a section between the Paraguay and the Paraná, and in the south Argentina retaining land south of the Pilcomayo.

This war aimed at finding an independent access to the sea for Paraguay, but this could never be tolerated by neighbours who owned the seaboard. Expansionist aims also came to the forefront in the 1930s, finally exploding in the Chaco War with Bolivia in 1932–5. This was fought for possession of the barren Chaco country, and won by Paraguay, though it was truly a hollow victory, for the territory won proved to have no current value, the only oilfields to be found to date lying on the Bolivian side of the modern frontier, though hopeful exploration is in progress on the Paraguayan side.

In 1954 General Alfredo Stroessner took power in a military coup to set up what is effectively a military dictatorship, behind a façade of representative politics including obviously fraudulent elections which have maintained him in office ever since.

PRESENT SETTLEMENT PATTERNS AND POPULATION

Over 97% of the population live in Eastern Paraguay, though this region has only 40% of national territory. The Chaco has only some 80 000 inhabitants, including about 20 000 Amerindians. These hunting peoples constituted a hostile obstacle to settlement until this century. Mennonite settlers from Canada and Russia changed this, founding over 100 villages in the central Chaco from 1926 to 1948. Much Chaco land has now been taken for ranches, leading to loss of the natives' traditional hunting grounds. The Mennonites and other religious groups have purchased land on which to settle the remaining Indians, while over 6000 have moved into Mennonite colonies as labourers, and have also settled as farmers in villages built for them.

In the east, in Paraguay proper as it has been called, lives the great majority of the population, concentrated very largely in the southwest corner of the country near Asunción. The character of this population is homogeneous, 95% of it being the old *mestizo* group, with a minority of Japanese in some rural areas. Typical of an underdeveloped country, it has a very broad population pyramid, 42% of the total being under 15 years of age, so that the growth of population, 2.9% per annum, is very high. Despite this youthfulness of the population, indicating improved medical conditions and protection of young children, there is a high level of infant mortality (49 per thousand); another index of backwardness is the low level of literacy, with 20% of the adult population unable to read, though this is changing rapidly with the advent of universal education and better school facilities.

Settlement concentrates especially around the city of Asunción, which has a population of 602 000 (1978). Despite its size, it presents the aspect of an overgrown country town, with predominantly low buildings and a function which is more administrative than industrial. The old colonial type of chessboard street pattern still remains here super-imposed on a fairly hilly topography which makes it less than ideal; the spread of settlement is confined to the hill site, for there is the river to north and west, and marsh land to the southwest. Urban migration is apparent in the shanty town developments which occupy large areas, especially in the localities along the floodplain edge.

27 Shanty town at Asunción, subject to flooding from the Paraguay river

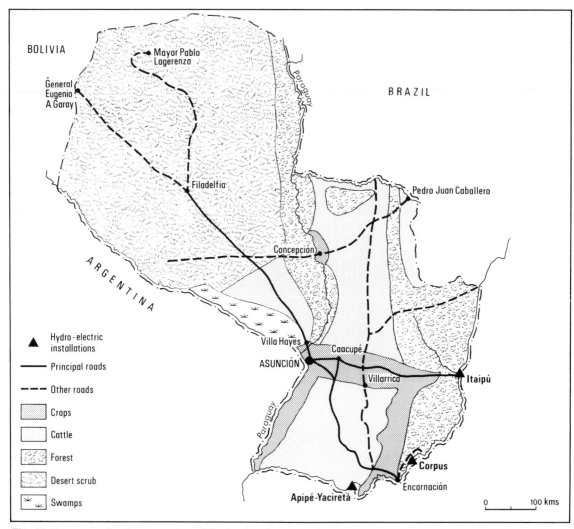

BOLIVIA

Mayor Pablo
Lagerenza

General
Eugenio
A.Garay

BRAZIL

Paraguay

Filadelfia

Pedro Juan Caballero

A R G E N T I N A

Concepción

Villa Hayes

Caacupé

ASUNCIÓN

Villarrica

Itaipú

Paraguay

▲ Hydro-electric
    installations

— Principal roads

- - Other roads

  Crops

  Cattle

  Forest

  Desert scrub

  Swamps

Corpus

Encarnación

Apipé-Yaciretá

0   100 kms

Fig. 31 Paraguay : land use, roads and hydroelectric power sites

THE ECONOMY (fig. 31)

Asunción today gives us a fair idea of national economic status. Rather than skyscrapers there are two- or three-storey buildings. In place of organized bus services there are minibuses, converted trucks and the like, overstaffed with conductor and driver though only carrying half a dozen passengers. Disguised unemployment is rife and many people hold two or more jobs, since a one-job salary does not suffice to support a family.

Underemployment and unemployment are themselves indices of rapid urbanization, equal to anything on the continent, and forming a fast-growing town population which stretches public services beyond breaking point. Urban growth is due, not to urban boom conditions — the only boom industry is the government — but to the lack of any rural opportunity, so that migrants are constantly moving into town in the hope, not the sure knowledge, of finding jobs.

Land tenure

In the 1820s lands without proper title became state land, church holdings were expropriated, and in this way the whole Chaco as well as half

28 President Stroessner bridge across the Paraná, linking Brazil and Paraguay

the eastern region became state property, including all the yerba mate and timber resources. From the 1880s great blocks of land were sold to individuals, and Paraguay became a country of latifundios, 60 individuals owning nearly the whole Chaco in 1900. Colonization schemes existed but attracted few farmers (fig. 32).

As a result, in 1960 only the area east of the Paraguay and close to Asunción was densely settled. On the eastern (Paraná) frontier, there were huge forests exploited only for timber and yerba mate. This area was the focus of an agricultural colonization movement which is still going on. No agrarian reform has however taken place and there are still many great estates. The colonization has been mostly unguided, and not provided with roads or definitive title to plots, let alone farmer credit, extension services, educational or other infrastructure. The massive clearance of the forest constitutes an ecological danger, with increased soil depletion and erosion (Kleinpenning, 1984).

Agriculture
No arable land production of note comes from the Chaco, except some cotton and vegetables from Filadelfia, marketed out to Asunción along

the rough road. Most of this land is unused, or only used on a very extensive basis for beef-cattle production, supplying canned beef factories which constitute one of Paraguay's more important export industries. The Chaco cattle comprise about 40% of the national stock. Production techniques are geared to the ultraextensive use of land; few attempts are made at cattle selection, for fences to guard cattle are not in use, nor rich grasses to feed them. Serious diseases including foot and mouth are endemic to the country and can scarcely be controlled using present techniques.

In the east, agriculture is a mix of various food crops produced on small owner-operator farms (46% of all holdings are under 5 ha) interspersed with a few large *estancias*, the remnants of old *latifundia*, where cattle are reared on a more intensive basis than in the Chaco. Maize, cassava, beans and other vegetables, as well as cash crops such as cotton and soya beans (see section on the Paraná Front), are grown on the small farms. These two last crops now provide Paraguay with her main exports. Where there are alluvial soils, tobacco and cotton are remunerative, but for most of the east, despite the usual guidebook references to fertile soils and great potential, soils are thin and, as is common in continental subtropics, yields decline rapidly with continued cultivation.

ECONOMIC INFRASTRUCTURE

There is no road or rail network in Paraguay. The only railway, apart from some private lines constructed on the quebracho properties, is a single-track, standard-gauge line from Asunción to Encarnación, so slow that lorry transport competes successfully with it even for heavy freight, and poorly supplied with antiquated rolling stock.

There are two well-paved roads: between Asunción and Encarnación, and from Asunción east to the international bridge over the Paraná and into Brazil (plate 28). The Encarnación road is to be continued by a bridge into Argentina, linking to Posadas, while the eastern road already leads through Brazil to Paranagua where Paraguay is given free port facilities.

The Transchaco highway, begun in 1964, runs 800 km from Asunción to the Bolivian border,

and half of it is asphalted. In its neighbourhood, more intensive ranching has been encouraged, and the highway also gives good access to the farming colonies nearby. The Paraguay has been bridged to link the road to Asunción.

River transport has historicallly been of overriding importance and continues to be of much use for the settlements above Asunción on the Paraguay, not currently served by road. For long-distance movements, however, this river is not so useful, for it is a long haul of 1640 km from Asunción to Buenos Aires, and there are substantial disadvantages in its great variation of seasonal level and heavy silting. The Paraná is much less used, but its potential may be improved by the Yaciretá dam, with bypass locks that overcome the rapids section at that location.

Power and minerals

Within the country, the plant at Acaray is the largest HEP installation in operation, its 90 MW capacity being doubled in 1975 to 180 MW, and supplying electricity to both Brazil and Argentina. The Acaray river is a tributary of the

29 Nanduti, a traditional Indian craft weaving industry, at a roadside site near Asunción

Paraná, whose main stream has much greater potential. Yacireta–Apipé, with 3 300 MW, is being built jointly with Argentina. When finished, it will be the world's longest dam, at 69 km. With Brazil, Paraguay has built Itaipú on the Paraná just above the Iguasú mouth, with a flooded area of 1400 sq. km, comprising a reservoir which reaches back over the whole 200 km canyon section of the Paraná and drowns the famous Guayra Falls (Sete Quedas). Its power output is 12 600 MW.

The need for these great power projects is not self-evident. Paraguay has no coal and as yet no oil worth extraction, despite continuing exploration. But neither does she have any industrial development capable of absorbing huge increases of unstored power — even Acaray's moderate contribution must be exported at present. Power development along the river seems rather to respond to the aims of the two big neighbour countries, and to provide a field for active competition between them, in which Paraguay is

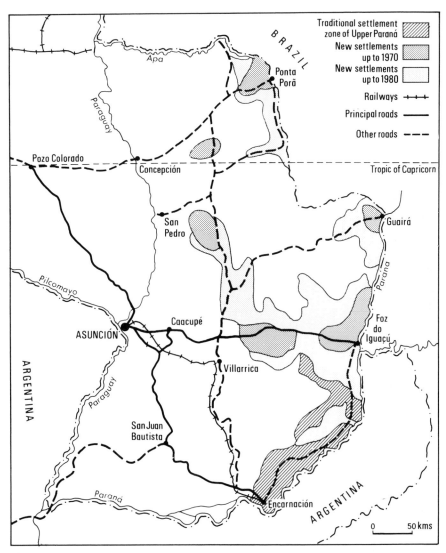

Fig. 32 Colonisation areas in Paraguay. The map illustrates the rapid spread of colonies along the main east-west axis and from the Paraná westwards

likely to be a pawn, though now benefiting greatly. I return to this matter at the end of the chapter.

Most of the saw timber comes from eastern Paraguay. Beyond the Paraguay river there is a separate resource in the red quebracho tree, *Schinopsis balansae*, a particularly tough hardwood with over 20% tannin content. Tannin has been extracted on a large scale since the 1880s, by cooking chips of the heartwood in great boilers. Much of the industry belongs to an Argentine firm, Casado, which alone has 3 million ha of land in the Chaco. An enclave economy has been operated along the east edge of the Chaco north of Resistencia in Argentina, with company villages, private railways into the forest, and provision of water and electricity.

In recent years, competition from some synthetic tannin sources makes this a declining industry. In any case, the trees themselves provide an irreplaceable reserve, for they grow extremely slowly and once gone are replaced only by low scrub of very little value. Conservationists see much advantage in leaving the remaining trees and concentrating on the alternative tannin sources.

Industries

Manufacturing industry and urban development are very slight in Paraguay. Timber provides some material-oriented industries such as sawmills on the Paraná and the quebracho extractors on the upper Paraguay, but the tannin industry is not healthy and saw-milling suffers from Argentine unwillingness to receive prepared timber rather than raw logs.

In Asunción itself and on the road axis out towards Caacupé to the east, there are industries designed to make use of cheap labour. Apart from meat processors, the city has cotton mills, cigarette, glass, soap and various food and drink manufacturers, items typical of first-stage industrial development, and using little advanced technology (plate 29). As university town and administrative centre the city also has printing and publishing industries. There are no true industrial zones in the city, only a tendency to concentrate near river or railway, and in the suburbs.

Outside the capital, besides the timber-based industries, small-farm product processors occupy the small towns, making tung oil and soya oil at Encarnación, *petit grain* oil from the wild orange, and vegetable oils from cotton seed, coconuts and oil palms. Asunción dominates the urban structure, with no other towns having more than 40 000 inhabitants, but Encarnación, Puerto Pres. Stroessner, and the towns between these two and Asunción, are beginning to grow.

THE PARANÁ: AN ECONOMIC AND POLITICAL FRONT

Along Paraguay's eastern frontier a remarkable process is in operation, making Paraguay an economic satellite of Brazil and threatening even her national integrity. The process has two main aspects which may be outlined here — the colonization of farm lands and the building of the world's largest HEP dam at Itaipú.

The map (Fig. 32) shows the process of colonization taking place, based on the studies by Gaignard (1972) and Kohlhepp (1984). The Paraguayan government began encouraging new colonies of small farmers in the 1960s, along the line of the road from Asunción to Port Pres. Stroessner, though the exercise was not well managed nor enough finance put in to ensure prosperous colonization. But from the 1950s, Brazilian land-dealers had been buying land on the eastern fringes, from the old yerba mate companies or from government officials who had been given land, to sell off to big coffee farmers anticipating the advance of the Brazilian coffee frontier moving westwards through Paraná state in Brazil. Frost damage checked the coffee frontier in Eastern Paraguay in the 1970s, and the land was re-sold to colonization companies. The best-organized land companies were Brazilian, and these brought in many thousands of new settlers, colonizing further inland and both north and south of the east–west highway. Brazilians were encouraged to enter as part of the Paraguayan regional development scheme, and Paraguayan landowners could make good profits from sale of land. International companies from Britain and the USA have also bought large areas for large-scale commercial soya bean production, but the Brazilians still dominate. In population, Brazilians number 320 000 (1981), 60% of local population in the eastern provinces.

The lead crop driving the westward push in the 1970s was no longer coffee but soya beans, doing well in rotation with wheat on the relatively rich volcanic soils, and these met a rising world market demand. This crop has become so important (over 700 000 ha) that Paraguay is the fourth producer in the world. It is marketed entirely out to the east through cooperatives, going to the free port of Paranagua and avoiding Brazilian export taxes.

This strong Brazilian orientation and the colonization is reinforced by the Itaipú project. This could only proceed from 1973 because Paraguay agreed to drop her claim to the strip of land adjacent to the Guaira Falls (Sete Quedas). Itaipú, 170 km downstream, is forming a lake of 1460 sq. km that has drowned these falls, and the first of 18 turbines are in operation. Paraguay provided only a small (15%) proportion of the inputs to the dam, and cannot absorb its share of the huge output of 12 600 megawatts, which it will therefore sell to Brazil at what are regarded as very low prices (Nickson, 1982). The dam has brought still more Brazilians to the area as construction workers, increasing pressure on the area.

More important is the position of economic dependence on Brazil by Paraguay, a country committed to great projects she cannot herself supply or demand. The position is further complicated because Argentina seeks to build dams further downriver, which may be affected by Itaipú, at Yacireta-Apipé and at Corpus. The very height of the dam at Corpus (yet to be started) has been restricted by the need to let Itaipú operate.

Paraguay has been promised considerable development aid from Brazil and Argentina, as a reward for cooperation in these great schemes, including road and rail links, aluminium and steel plants, but these may be poor compensation for the loss of national control that is now apparent. The power in particular must be sold to Brazil as there are no alternatives and no grid structure to move the power to different markets.

14. Chile

One version of the origin of Chile is that at the Creation, after God had finished His Labours, as a final task, He asked the angels to sweep some leftover pieces behind a high wall in an out-of-the-way corner of the globe; the wall was the Andes, and the leftovers, a motley assortment, formed Chile. The story is doubtless apocryphal, but it does underline a real state of isolation, as well as the diversity of the Chilean landscapes. Inevitably, in a stretch of 4300 km from north to south, there is room for physical contrasts; but even across the country, in the narrow 150–300 km width of Chile, there are profound contrasts between Andes, Central Valley and Coastal Cordillera. Corresponding to the major physical divisions, there are significant cultural and economic differences between the old-settled Mediterranean core and more recently occupied peripheries.

THE LAND

Structure and landforms
Structural units in Chile run north–south, parallel to the shield edge of Brazil and Patagonia. The Andes, backbone of the whole country and maintaining an impressive height throughout, are deepseated igneous masses, with some volcanics, rather than fold mountains; recent faulting and uplift have given them their present height, leaving the great Longitudinal Valley to the west as a fault-lined trough or graben. This igneous origin is responsible for the abundant mineral deposits, originating at the edge of the magmas and consolidating in contact zones. Continuing fault-line movements make earthquakes a constant peril and there has been repeated destruction of major cities throughout the country.

First of the three longitudinal elements of physical geography are the Andes. Because of their great height it is sometimes forgotten that they are also a broad mass, generally over 80 km wide, and composed of several parallel ranges. In the north, they open out to enclose high desert basins like the Salar de Atacama, with salt flats the only outlet to small streams. The Southern Andes are lower than the north, ranging around 3000 to 3500 m, and, in contrast with the northern deserts, are well carpeted with forests. They are dissected by deep valleys, carved out by glacial action during the Pleistocene era. The mountain chain continues beyond the mainland into Tierra del Fuego, of which Chile owns a half.

West of the mountains, the Longitudinal Valley has varied form. In the north it is a high desert basin with drainage into the salt flats of the Pampa del Tamarugal north of the last permanent river, the Loa, and is marked by typical desert pediment slopes. From Copiapó it disappears, to re-emerge at Santiago and form the enclosed basins of the capital and, to the south, of Rancagua, then open into a low trough reaching south to Chiloé Island, covered increasingly to the south by glacial and proglacial deposits giving a hilly or rolling topography.

The third element is the Cordillera de la Costa, another hilly or rolling topography, lower than

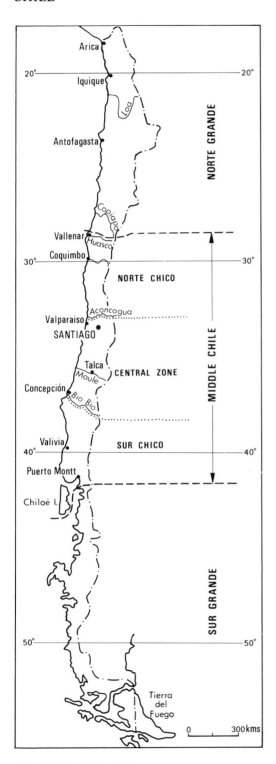

Fig. 33 Chile: the regions

the Andes, and generally under 3000 m, but for all that a continuous barrier and negative factor for transportation. Marine terraces all along the coast of Chile, and cut into this Cordillera, are a reminder of the rapidity of geological events here.

Climate, soil and vegetation

The fame of the northern desert is as one of the world's driest places, if not the driest of all; on the coast there are long records, covering over twenty years with fair accuracy, which note no rainfall. There was once a vegetation cover inland, however, in the desert country of the Longitudinal Valley, probably fed mostly by ground water seeping through from small mountain streams. The woods were *tamarugos* for the most part, a kind of mimosa which gave the name Pampa del Tamarugal to the northern desert.

The northern desert land is called the Norte Grande by Chilean geographers. To the south of 30° S, there is the Norte Chico, the Little North; this region is a patchwork of contrasting extremes, with long runs of open desert like the Norte Grande, alternating with deep transverse valleys, green and lush in comparison to the uplands. From an airliner, seen through the cloudless desert skies which are nearly always found in these latitudes, the Norte Chico shows such valleys as the Copiapó, Huasco and Elqui as clearly as if marked out by pencil on a map.

From the river Aconcagua south to the Bío Bío is Mediterranean Chile, a land similar to the Mediterranean in climate, soil and vegetation, though the natural dry forest has been eliminated gradually by urban and agricultural expansion. Rainfall increases continuously to the south in this zone but a winter concentration typical of Mediterranean climates is found to the south in Valdivia and beyond. South of the river Bío Bío in the Sur Chico, this high rainfall combined with seasonality gives a unique vegetation of mixed Mediterranean and temperate forms, a dense evergreen and deciduous mix.

South Chile is temperate forest with podsolized soils, and a vegetation which includes some useful species in the northern margins, notably the 'larch', *Fitzroya cupressoides*, and the 'oak', *Nothofagus obliqua*. The Chilean monkey-puzzle tree is a member of this southern mixed forest, but its quality as a good construc-

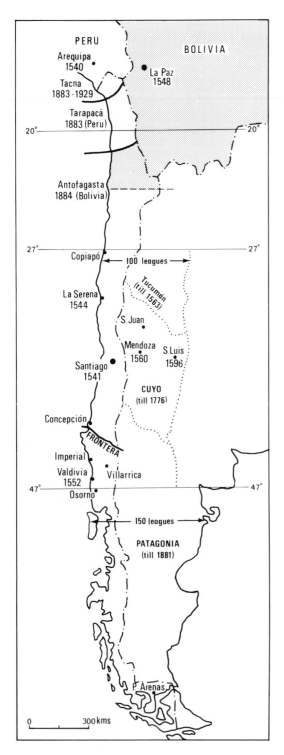

Fig. 34 Chilean boundary changes and claims

tional timber and the old Indian practice of collecting its cones for nourishment have made it a rather scarce species in its country of origin. Further south, extreme wind velocities, and lack of sunshine and heat, mean an impoverished forest cover of scrubby nature. In its extreme representatives in the far southern islands and coasts, it is a mat of ground-hugging vegetation; there are interesting descriptions of how exploring parties have had to crawl over the woods rather than walk through them in this zone! In the lee of the mountains, there is a small section of Chile which belongs to Patagonia and thus has a completely different physical aspect, dry, open and treeless.

THE SEA

To Chile, the ocean, producing food, providing employment, acting as road and railway, tempering the climate, is as important as to any small island in the Pacific. Most notable among its features is the Humboldt current, actually composed of two elements, a coastal section of cold, green-brown water moving at only 1 kph, and an outer section beyond 50 km out of deep blue, warmer and faster water moving at 2-3 kph. The coolness of the coastal water is due to upwelling more than its southern origins, for the cold spots are those where upwelling is strong, and temperatures scarcely rise before it reaches Peru.

Historically, the current was an important separator of Chile and Peru; and Juan Fernandez Islands, still in Chilean hands, were named after their discoverer, a pilot on the Valparaiso–El Callao run seeking to avoid the current by going out to sea on his return voyage. Today, the current is most important for the quantity of nutrients brought by upwelling and mixing into the life zone near the water surface. Hake and sea bass are important in the south, *anchoveta* and sardines in the north, while shellfish are found throughout. Mussels were the staff of life for the primitive Indian populations living around the Magellan Straits until recently.

OCCUPATION OF LAND

Claims and realities (fig. 34)

The effective occupation of Chile was by Pedro de Valdivia, lieutenant of Francisco Pizarro, conquistador of Peru; he was sent out in 1539 to found a colony, and soon made its base at Santiago, founded in 1541 in the centre of a prosperous agricultural region where there were many settled Indians and where gold could also be gained from placer workings on the rivers.

Valdivia's colony, later the Captaincy General of Chile, had pretentious claims to a hundred leagues of country from the Pacific inland, a claim which made it trans-Andean and extending well into present Argentine land. Northern and southern limits were set only in vague terms, for no solid occupation of the north and south could be considered.

In reality, occupation was only of a central *oecumene*, the core area of Mediterranean Chile, where settled Indians, good land and security were possible. Across the Andes, the province of Cuyo, with the cities of Mendoza, San Juan and San Luís, formed a linked section, but the high passes over the Andes meant that the links were tenuous and could not be held indefinitely.

Trans-Andean territories in fact were gradually given up, starting with the area of Tucumán, already lost to Argentine interests in the 1560s; passing to the loss of Cuyo, in 1776, when the Viceroyalty of the Plate was formed; and ending with the loss of Patagonia in the 1880s when Argentina finally subdued the southern Indians and incorporated this territory.

On the other hand, cis-Andean lands could readily be maintained against all comers, and expansion was possible; to the north, it was easy to extend Chilean hegemony over the northern deserts in the War of the Pacific, using the open road of the sea for access; to the south, there were no other claimants to the land besides the Indians, and once these were defeated the land was Chile's. Thus in all cases, territory and frontiers were defined by the natural wall of the Andes, to which decrees and claims had to defer; only in the southern extremities, where a substantial difference between mountain line and water divide existed, and where in addition the mountains were lower, did a serious transgression of the Andes occur and become a supported political frontier. In this case, Chileans had settled through the low glacial valley troughs into Patagonia in the nineteenth century and had anticipated Argentine settlement. On this substantial basis they were allowed to remain east of the mountain peaks, in a treaty celebrated in 1901 between the two countries.

Colonial economy

A typical Latin American colonial economy and society came quickly into existence in Chile. The land was divided into great *latifundia*, leaving only small areas for the Indian and mestizo villagers. From the *latifundia*, cattle produced tallow and hides, which were sent to Peru from the earliest days. While Peru was supplier to Spain, Chile, with its abundant farmland and temperate climates, could be supplier of middle-latitude products to Peru's urban populations. A chain of dependent relations existed from the *inquilino*, semi-serf on the great estates, through owners and merchants all the way to the Spanish metropolis.

Nineteenth-century economy

This hierarchical economy was not broken by the advent of independence for the country, but later, by the arrival of migrants from the overcrowded farmlands of Europe. Immigrants were attracted to the Sur Chico, between the river Maule and Chiloé Island to make clearings in the dense woodland and cultivate small farms. Chile never received large numbers of migrants but those who came had considerable impact, coming as they did into new, unsettled lands, and able therefore to maintain their own institutions and technology.

The colonists started from bases around Valdivia and Puerto Montt, first Germans, who had a tradition of forest clearing in eastern Europe which suited them well for this task. It is of interest to ask precisely why the migrants were successful here, when they were so unsuccessful in other places. One factor must have been their title to land, given freely or for a small sum, so that there was no fear of permanent indebtedness for land, or clouded title which might come from previous purchasers in the area before it was surveyed. Another factor was the plot size, 75–100 ha, big enough to support any reasonable farming family in this area. Finally, one must give credit to the group spirit and cultural provenance of the people. Their traditions, and the way they were permitted to retain them in Chile, meant no creeping demoralization such as could occur to a lonely family in a strange country elsewhere in the continent.

In a sense, the Germans (there were also some French and other European groups later) were allowed to preserve their identity so well because of the Indians; to the north of them, between 38° and 40° S, the Araucanian Indians, the Mapuche, had led a guerrilla war against the Chileans to the north for a 150-year period, only ending in 1883. This area, the Frontera (fig. 34), formed a *cordon sanitaire* between traditional, colonial Chile, and a new small-farmer, immigrant and democratic society to the south. Historically and even today, there is something of a duality between Spanish Chile, the centre, and the northern and southern fringes whose culture is from other sources, Indian, European, even North American in the case of the mineral workings.

Modern economy

Colonial Chile sent farm goods to Lima; today, the man—land balance has changed and Chile is a food-deficit country; the new key element is mining. Extractive industry employs only some 3–4% of the work force, but it brings in 90% of national export earnings. Such lopsidedness in the national economy is matched by regional imbalances, for the variation in means of support of the population is extreme, between mining and smelting, logging, manufacturing and urban employment, and farming. Chilean economy cannot be discussed without reference to these regional contrasts.

NORTE GRANDE

Nitrates

In colonial times the Peruvians mined silver at Huantajaya (fig. 35) and a host of smaller mines in the coastal hills north of the Loa. To break up the ores, explosives were made from the *caliche*, hardpan on the edge of the *salares*, desert salt flats. This *caliche* was locally in high concentration and directly used by the Indians for fertilizer with good results. In the first decade of the last century, the royal powder mill at Lima was desperately short of saltpetre for gunpowder production, and while sodium nitrate, the product from *caliche*, was not immediately usable as a replacement for true saltpetre, potassium nitrate, a formula for converting it was obtained and the ore began to be extracted on a modest scale.

The first crisis in the nitrate industry came after the end of the Revolutionary Wars, when no further use could be found for the mineral, and the problem was enough to close down many of the small-scale operations; a longterm solution came when its properties as a fertilizer were recognized abroad. Peter Aikman was a Glasgow merchant with trade in little ships to South America from 1825. In 1829 a ship of his put in to Iquique for ballast, and was given nitrates which it brought to Liverpool. The port authorities were determined to throw it into the sea as a dangerous and explosive material, but Aikman became curious and took ten sacks of it away to give to farmers around Glasgow, thus beginning a new era for the Chilean nitrates.

Swiftly Chilean and British enterprise moved in to the Tarapacá deposits all along the salar edges (fig. 35), using first a primitive technology of melting down the caliche or desert hardpan in great copper pans, with the aid of *tamarugo* wood, both standing and as trunks found under the desert sand by 'wood diviners' amongst the Indians; this was the only fuel available. Soon technical advances in refining and the use of coal brought back from Europe in the nitrate vessels, allowed much more rapid production and use of thinner nitrate ores further south.

In the desert section claimed by Bolivia, between the river Loa and 24° S, and the Chilean section to the south of this, development was slower than in the north because there was little earlier mining industry, the nitrates sector poorer, and water was a constant problem. Thus the Bolivian sector only saw extraction from 1869, the Chilean from 1879.

The nitrate boom

The rise of the industry was particularly rapid after 1860, when nitrates began to take the place of guano. A growth centre began to emerge in the desert, with mines and ports both attracting men. Iquique, Antofagasta and Pisagua became important ports, populated by a largely Chilean miner and merchant group; in 1878, Antofagasta, in the Bolivian sector, had a population of 8500, of which 6500 were Chilean. Besides the influx of men, inflowing food and material came from many quarters. A large and constant movement of cattle, trekked over the mountains from Salta in Argentina, and originating from the Gran Chaco and Córdoba

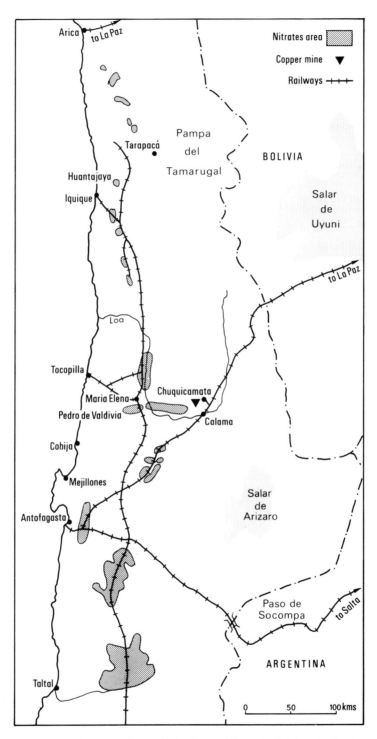

Fig. 35 The nitrates regions of Northern Chile and neighbouring lands

as steers, came to the mining camps where no food was produced. Vegetables were grown also on local patches of irrigated land, flour and sugar brought on coasting steamers.

Politically, the industry was subject to international frictions: in 1875, Peru nationalized her nitrate industry to finance railway construction, a move she had previously made in like manner with the guano industry; soon after, the Bolivian sector of the desert fell under Peruvian control. Such events alarmed Chile, for the nitrates industry was in the hands of Chileans whose livelihood was now threatened. Chile also rightly suspected a secret alliance between Bolivia and Peru, which could turn against her. For Peru, the progress of Chilean enterprise was menacing, and for Bolivia, there was an additional irritation over the political boundary with Chile, set at 24° S but with a band from 23° to 25° S in which mineral rights were shared.

New focus: copper

The War of the Pacific settled the disputes conclusively, and allowed the industry to go to new heights. Control passed very generally out of Chilean hands, a pattern followed with the copper industry, and British firms made good profits till the rise of synthetic fertilizers in the 1920s. Now the nitrate workings are reduced to one *oficina* in Tarapacá, and two in the sector south of the Loa; ghost towns remain as reminders of former wealth. A new industry was soon found to replace nitrates, copper, from the giant open-cast mine of Chuquicamata, known and worked since before the War but never developed. This now became a growth industry, replacing nitrates, with associated smelting, refining, and power production industries. Chuquicamata itself grew to over 25000, endowed with modern housing, electric lighting and modern plumbing. The mine, a huge hole 3 km long and 300 m deep, has reserves to maintain its present rate of extraction, 100 000 tonnes of ore daily, for a hundred years, so that it may be expected to dominate regional economy for some time. Today, of the four great mines which produce most of Chile's copper, Chuquicamata contributes over 50%, far more than the second mine El Teniente, inland from Rancagua.

Apart from copper, developed with private funds, various manufacturing industries, notably chemicals, electrical goods and car assembly plants, were fostered at Arica in the Norte by government action from 1953. At this time import duties were lifted in Tarapacá province and in the southernmost Chilean provinces. This move, it was hoped, would promote economic expansion and help political support for the regime, as the peripheries were centres of anti-government voting.

Car assembly was particularly boosted from 1958 by the virtual prohibition on location at other places, so that by 1963 there were 20 different companies in operation at Arica, producing in no case more than 2000 vehicles per annum. Inefficiency in scale of operation was compounded by distance to Santiago, whence came an increasing percentage of components, poorly made by national firms but up to ten times the price of unavailable imports. As well as bringing up components from Santiago, trucks had to be used to take the finished cars back to Santiago, the main market. Finally, the ban on assembly in Santiago was lifted and much of the industry moved, quite rationally, to that city. Arica's car factories became electronics works, of which some have remained.

What next as the export base?

Douglass North* and others have contended that many pioneer regions did not develop gradually out of a subsistence economy into commercial production as did the European countries, but depended from the start on finding and utilizing viable export base industries, the mechanism being that these basic industries would bring in capital, labour and enterprise via local multiplier effects, and that these new factors of production could then promote further growth in a snowball effect. The local or regional multiplier effects were those indirect effects of an industry on the local economy, growth because of the need to establish accessory or supply industries, growth of local demand from the labour force and its own needs for service industries, construction, etc.

This theory of the export base has application to the Norte; here a capitalist, exploitative economy was set up from at least the eighteenth century with silver as the export base, followed by nitrates, then by copper, and finally, spasmodically, by manufacturing industries. The

*Douglass C. North, 'Location theory and regional economic growth', *Journal of Political Economy*, Vol. 63, 1955, pp. 243-58.

earlier bases had however only limited regional multiplier effects. Chuquicamata has had little impact for, though there are links to the high Andes via pipelines, electric power comes from Tocopilla, and copper moves out along the Antofagasta railway, the mine does little for the region; employment is small because of heavy mechanization, and supply or market industries are absent. The same applies to silver working, to guano or nitrate mining in previous booms.

The 1953–67 policy of tax incentives to industry might have provided a better export base because regional multipliers would have been bigger, from larger labour forces and supply industries, but the lack of permanent control over industrial location meant this could not be. As an alternative agriculture has been put forward as an export base, using water from elsewhere. Since 1950 there have been discussions with Peru and Bolivia over possible diversion of lake Titicaca waters west into the coastal desert; in 1971 a longterm plan to bring water from Chile's own South, paralleling plans on the Pacific coast of North America, was announced, though no source of funds has been apparent, and this plan can scarcely be made operative in the near future. Thus the search for a viable export base remains a problem for the Norte.

NORTE CHICO

Farms and mines
Economic activity in river oasis Chile, from Copiapó south to the river Aconcagua, is a mixture of farming and mining. Historically copper mining was concentrated in the Norte Chico's interior, especially in Coquimbo province, and mostly in small and medium-size mines, forming over a thousand separate enterprises. As these mines cannot afford their own smelters there are government smelters at Paipote, Copiapó and Ventana near Valparaiso, which purchase ores and process them in competition with the big smelters. Iron ore is regionally more important as an export mineral. The industry is located in the Coastal Cordillera between Coquimbo and Chañaral, owned by both Chilean and foreign, including North American and Japanese, enterprises.

Most population and agriculture is concentrated in the valleys, owned in part by large farmers, who use the irrigated meadows for feeding cattle with alfalfa, to complement hill grazing above. Some areas also have small farms producing a wide variety of crops: maize and vegetables on valley floors, vineyards and orchards on the dry slopes. Traditional Indian *comunidades*, communal agriculturalists, are a third element, working tiny plots which afford little surplus. Outside the valleys, dry scrub provides a little grazing for the *comunidades* and for big graziers, and grain is grown in places along the more humid coastal hills, the Coastal Cordillera.

MEDITERRANEAN CHILE: THE CORE AREA

Farming
Here all land may be put to some farm use, except on the steepest slopes, and a landscape of straight irrigation ditches and poplar avenues, dispersed houses of brick and tile or *ranchos* of mud and cane, framed by stark eroded hillsides, forms the scene. Until recently, a sharp contrast was to be seen between the large *fundos* and small farms, the minifundia growing subsistence crops. Prior to the agrarian reforms which limited farms in the irrigated belt to under 40 ha, the big farms often had more than 1000 ha of irrigated land, used in many cases for alfalfa, rather than for intensive crops of grain, fruit or vegetables. Darwin described this traditional economy when he saw it in the Quillota valley near Valparaiso in 1834, on the round-the-world voyage of the *Beagle*:

> Each landowner in the valley possesses a certain portion of hill country, where his half-wild cattle, in considerable numbers, manage to find sufficient pasture. Once every year there is a grand *rodeo*, when all the cattle are driven down, counted, and marked, and a certain number separated to be fattened in the irrigated fields.
>
> *Charles Darwin,* Journal of Researches in the Natural History and Geology of the Countries visited during the voyage of H.M.S. Beagle round the World *(New York, Harper, 1846), vol. 1, p. 329*

Now the important farming sector has become the intermediate group of farms, between 50 and 150 ha, producing fruit and vegetables, flowers and wine. This has been partly the effect of the agrarian reform which split up the larger estates, and in part the result of the Pinochet government's fostering of foreign trade at the expense of domestic markets, at least up to 1983. As Chapter 3 has shown, however, agricultural food production has not kept up with population, though Chile's performance has been better than Peru's. Chilean vineyards are among the best in Latin America, and the best among them are found in conditions matching the northern Mediterranean prestige areas, on dry, even stony, alkaline soils, with moderate rainfall and high insolation. European vines may be used here without the need for grafting onto an American wild vine rootstock, as phylloxera has not travelled over the Andes, and is not a problem in Mendoza in any case. Quality in wines owes much to care in manufacture, and in Chile there is careful government regulation of quality and control over the use of particular names when the wines are labelled for the important export markets. Some 30 000 vineyards cover 110 000 ha.

On the Coastal Cordillera's dry lands, large farms are operated with machinery to grow wheat by dry-farming techniques, on the broad gentle slopes of marine terraces and piedmont slopes of the mountains. Amongst such farms, occupying steeper slopes and areas with access to stream irrigation, there are clumps of small farms producing sometimes at a semi-subsistence level. As they depend often on water from streams that have only a seasonal flow and cannot build dams to store water, their livelihood is always subject to risk and few such farms will indulge in the further risk of commercial production for marketing in the cities. This is a landscape where the dual economy is directly visible, commercial and subsistence sectors side by side.

Santiago de Chile
The site (fig. 36) of the capital is a gentle, westwards-sloping piedmont, within a small hill-ringed basin. The city is sprawling, low,

30 *Wooden and corrugated iron housing of a* callampa *in Santiago. In the background is a new three-storey housing scheme, part of the government's plan for increasing urban residential densities, while improving housing conditions. Chile's record in dealing with rural-urban migrants is better than that of most Latin American countries*

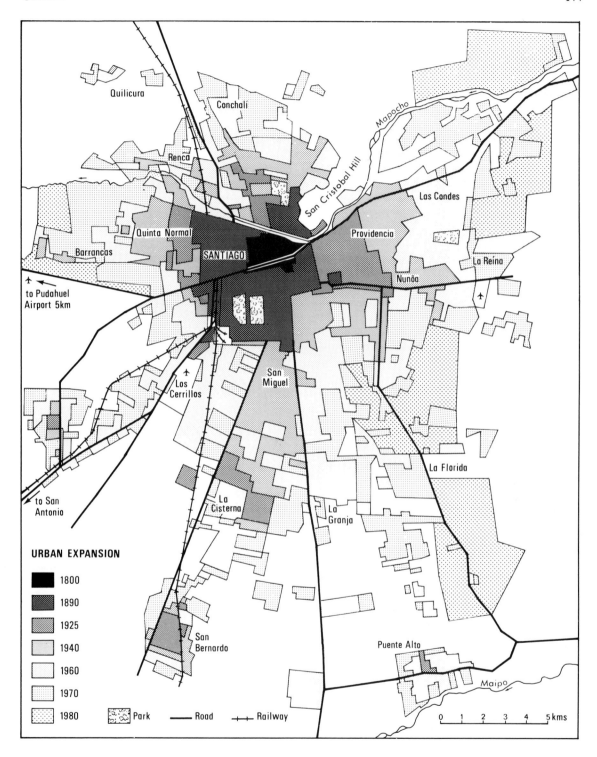

Fig. 36 Santiago city and environs

composed mostly of single-storey buildings, and occupying as much land as Paris which has twice the population; earthquake hazards have caused a fear of high buildings. The city, growing out of the colonial chessboard on the south side of the river Mapocho, has spread mostly to the south, to the river Maipo. To the northeast, the Cerro San Cristóbal presents a barrier, though construction is encroaching on its lower slopes.

The city's economic structure is reflected in its buildings. Nothing remains of colonial architecture, for earthquakes have destroyed it. Nineteenth-century expansion was as a residential, commercial and administrative centre, with fine housing and offices near to the centre. Industrial growth came later, in the twentieth century for the most part, as a result of crises in the nitrate industry and in agriculture, which forced the setting up of manufacturing industry under tariff protection, to provide for home markets when no foreign exchange was available to pay for imports. The industrial structure established in this way was largely of consumer goods, using few local resources apart from labour and some foods.

Economic growth continues apace in the city, for 800 000 immigrants came during 1950-70 to be housed in the *callampas,* the 'mushroom towns', as Chileans call their shanty towns, as well as in government-built flats west of the city to balance middle-class extension up the piedmont to the east (plate 30).

The metropolitan region
Santiago is the core of a metroplitan region which concentrates within it much of the national economic activity. The city's population has grown from 2.7 million in 1970 to 4.1 million in 1983, and the whole urbanized area probably holds five million, out of a national population of 11 880 000.

Around the city are other important centres of industry, Valparaiso (267 000 in 1983) developed as port to Santiago in colonial time, growing rapidly in the nineteenth century when trade to the Pacific was expanding and the Cape Horn route had to be used. It has grown on a narrow coastal terrace which has constricted its growth into a north–south line. Like Santiago, its growth benefited from the expansion of consumer industries under tariff protection, many of

them set up by European immigrants, but also from classic port industries processing tobacco, sugar and other foods, and from engineering and shipbuilding. More recently, a major oil refinery has been built a few miles to the north at Concón. Its immediate northern suburb is however Viña del Mar (299 000 in 1983) which has become a commuter suburb of Santiago and developed residential and tourist functions. The Viña seafront, with its 15-storey hotel-apartment blocks, is reminiscent of popular Spanish coastal resorts. Immediately west of Santiago there is another port, San Antonio, which handles some general trade and exports copper from El Teniente mine. To the south the economic region of the metropolis stretches beyond the Santiago basin to the Rancagua basin where Rancagua (142 000 in 1983) has car components plants and a Fiat car manufacturing plant. However Santiago remains dominant within its region and in a general sense within the nation, and efforts to decentralize activities have failed both under planning-oriented and laissez-faire governments.

SUR CHICO

The economic structure of the South is generally, like that of the north, dependent on minerals. In the case of the Sur Chico, coal mines and forests are the leading resources, though agriculture is also important and gives rise to a distinctive landscape, especially around Puerto Montt and Valdivia, in what Weischet called *Waldrodungs-Chile,** 'Forest-clearing Chile', a near-European landscape of small hedged fields, stumps marking old clearances, a hilly land of glacial deposits and little lakes, spotted with the neat wooden houses of small-farmer settlers.

This is prosperous farm country, with 50–100 ha properties producing beef, wheat and barley, milk, cheese and butter, and middle-latitude fruits. To the north of it is a different land, in the old Frontera zone, where a major socio-economic problem has arisen in the reservations set up for the Mapuche and other Indians, because of their rapid population increase and lack of land, so that takeovers of nearby estates

---

* W. Weischet, *Chile* (Darmstadt, 1970), p. 11.

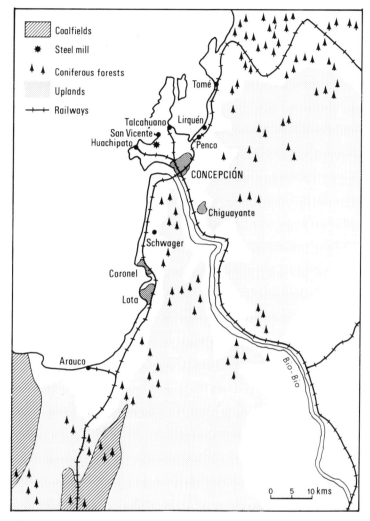

Fig. 37 The industrial region of Concepción. This city, with Talcahuano and Huachipato, forms a single urbanized area of over half a million inhabitants

have been made, anticipating government action. The regional centres in the Sur Chico include some agricultural market towns, notably Osorno and Valdivia; Osorno is sometimes credited with a German atmosphere, but little apart from shop names and social clubs remains of this; Valdivia is more industrial and has many small wood-based and farm-processing industries as well as a university. The city was badly hit by an earthquake in 1960, its wooden buildings then being replaced by new wood or concrete ones to form a smart centre, but the loss of economic status that

occurred through this disaster only helped on its longer term relative decline, as one of the provincial towns, compared to overweening Santiago.

Forests

The region's forest resource is large but still under used. Good stands of single species and rapid growth rates under high regular rainfall are physical advantages, but economic backwardness is holding back the industry. Afforestation is important near Concepción, where Monterrey pines have been introduced from North America and planted on eroded farmlands for soil conservation and as feed for the paper pulp mills in Concepción, Valdivia and on the river Bío Bío. Further south, as for example on Chiloé Island, there is primitive lumbering on a small scale and poorly organized, often on the basis of hired temporary workers during the summer months and using little machinery. Much forest land is in the hands of the National Forest Agency, CONAF, although under the Pinochet government policies some three million hectares have been sold to large private firms.

Industries

If the Norte Grande's economic base is exports, raw or processed, that of the Sur Chico is goods for the home market. During the period 1930–73, Chile's industries enjoyed a high level of tariff protection, and several examples of this are found in the area around Concepción. This industrial district grew up from 1840, from copper smelting originally using the small local coalfield of Lota-Schwager (fig. 37) and then building a variety of industries in the high-tariff period, to feed the home markets. The coal supplies encourage a woollen industry at Tomé, cottons at Chiguayante, glass at Lirquén, pottery at Penco, refractory bricks at Lota. Other industries were sugar milling at Penco, Talcahuano's fish canning and freezing, and ship repairs at San Vicente.

Concepción, the central town, had administrative functions until 1950, when the government, through CORFO, set up an integrated iron-steel plant at Huachipato. This industry demonstrates how Chile's peculiar geography is quite manageable from the point of view of coastal industries. Iron ore comes from near Coquimbo, 800 km to the north, limestone from Guarello island in the Madre de Dios archipelago 1500 km south, coal is local, mixed with N. American coking coal. Local coal is in thin seams, dipping deep under the sea, and mining has virtually ceased, but new supplies may now come from discoveries in the far south. Steel capacity is sufficient to feed all the home market. Water supplies from the Bío Bío river, and HEP from three plants in the river's headwaters, Antuco, El Toro and Abanico, totalling over 500 megawatts, complete the inputs. Besides national markets, the steel is used in local ferroalloy and steel fabricating industries.

Valdivia is the second industrial town, still further south, but its regional industries have stagnated as Concepción grew to compete in brewing, leather and footwear, as well as taking over the steel industry which had begun in Valdivia with a blast furnace.

In the recent period of free-market economy, virtually all the Little South's industries have suffered as the tariff barriers which sheltered them were dismantled. Textiles factories have closed at Tomé, as have the potteries at Penco and the leather-based industries (Gwynne, 1985, p.223). There is a definite spatial effect of a free-market economy, which has been the concentration of industrial strength in the capital city. It must be pointed out that this economy does not necessarily harm regional development — the North has been relatively favoured, as its industries, principally copper, do not rely on protection and already feed world markets.

SUR GRANDE

Beyond Chiloé, the island archipelagoes and the fjord country of the adjacent mainland, steep tree-covered slopes and deep water, form a region of scenic grandeur and extreme isolation. The railway line ends at Puerto Montt, and further south there were only short unmade roads, until a new road was recently built south into Aysén. Settlement is sparse and either scattered over fertile patches at low level, or clustered in the little ports. The only really useful farmlands are strips along the glacial valleys cutting through the Cordillera, linked thus to coast and interior but isolated from one another. Much land is in the public domain, though in the post-1973 era forests, islands and fisheries have been sold off in Aysén and Magallanes.

Wool

On the opposite side of the Andes an abrupt change of landscape occurs, to Patagonian steppe with prosperous sheep farming. Mineral exploitation has become the economic base here, both oil and gas being important on Tierra del Fuego and in Chilean Patagonia. In this dry land sheep thrive and produce wool, Merino and Romney breeds being common on the great ranches, an industry that first started in 1878 with immigrants from the Falklands. Most of the grazing is unimproved, carrying only one animal per ha, but improvement and higher stocking rates are in hand and are raising wool and mutton production.

The oil industry

Continuous expansion in oil production has been possible since the first strikes made in 1945 under the impulse of wartime shortages in fuel. Most of the oil is taken out by pipe to ports and shipped to refineries at Concón, serving Santiago, and San Vicente, for Concepción, leaving only little refineries in the far south for local needs. The oil basin around the Magellan Straits where active exploration is still going on has been linked up by modern all-weather roads, and provided with various public services, but its influence on the regional economy is limited. Natural gas is to be liquefied here for export to the USA!

PATTERNS OF REGIONAL DEVELOPMENT

Chile's spatial pattern is one of a wealthy and productive metropolitan region, distant peripheries to north and south which are rich in resources and have slight populations, and in the central, mediterranean area, the greatest concentrations of poverty apart from the capital and a few industrial towns. In the years since Independence, policies and world markets have helped the northern periphery with its nitrates and copper, while the centre stagnated, apart from those towns given tariff protection for industrial growth.

A first major effort at regional policy was in 1939, when CORFO, the Chilean Development Corporation, was created, financed by part of the taxes on copper. Its remit was to move some of the wealth created by copper into manufacturing industry. This could have been of great value in promoting a better regional distribution of industries, but tended, apart from small exceptions and notably the promotion of steel at Huachipato, to increase Santiago's dominance both through the support of industry, and through CORFO's own creation of a large bureaucracy of office workers administering the programmes. In the 1960s another policy, of free ports, led to the creation of car manufacturing facilities at Arica, but this must be termed a failure and a misdirected venture in view of the relative wealth of the north.

Allende's 1970–73 government had no direct regional policy; agrarian reform could have been the key to growth in rural central Chile, but ended in limited benefits to a minority group of medium-sized farms. Since 1973, Pinochet's government has also failed to enact any regional policy, but national monetarist policies of *apertura,* opening to the exterior, have constituted a major change from protectionism. This has caused a major decline in the import-substitution industries and has been catastrophic for the Little South.

Thus centralization continues, and is aided by foreign relations. Chile is isolated from her Andean neighbours who might have helped the border area development, and from Argentina and Brazil, whose own industrial programmes are based on domestic markets. Dependency on foreign countries of the Northern Hemisphere, which take Chile's exports, and local isolation work together to promote a highly centralized pattern, functionally based on the export industries, regionally on those areas engaged in production for export.

BRAZIL AND THE GUIANAS

15. Introduction to Brazil

Brazil is a country of continental proportions, occupying 8.46 million sq km, over half of South America. In spite of her size, Brazil has a certain unity, and there are not, for example, the sudden contrasts to be seen while travelling through the Andean countries, between high plateaus, mountains and selvas, and lowland deserts. The entire Brazilian landscape displays the mark of its firm foundations, the crystalline shield mass which has changed little over recent geological times. This shield produces a landscape of flat horizons, with few imposing mountain peaks. Homogeneity extends into climate and vegetation, with only gradual change from forest to wooded savanna to open plain, and the whole area is under the constant influence of tropical atlantic air apart from the occasional cooler wave along the east coast.

Man's use of this giant territory has also exhibited a certain homogeneity; Portuguese occupation has been dominant and has imparted Portuguese language, religion and culture to the country. Far in the interior there are islands of pure Indian communities, scarcely affected by the European invasion, but they are dwindling and now only preserved by governmental decrees protecting tribal land from further incursions, decrees which can only delay, not prevent, the eventual incorporation of all the land into the national culture. Unity is emphasized by the political integration of Brazil with few active separatist interests. It is a feature commonly remarked on that the many races of Brazil have all been absorbed into the national entity, a remarkable accomplishment considering the size of the country.

A second feature of Brazilian human geography is the fact of its rapid and recent settlement, for the population has grown from 9.9 million in 1872 to 136 million (estimate) in 1985. A growth rate of over two million inhabitants per annum has been matched by enormous strides in industrialization, the building of cities, roads and power schemes. Inevitably, large sections of the country have experienced lesser growth and remain backwaters of subsistence agriculture and poverty, for agriculture has not been able to modernize in the same way as industry.

THE LAND (fig. 38)

The two elements of physical unity, shield structure and tropical climate, deserve some further detailing. Shield rocks do not occupy all Brazil, for in the north there is the Amazon valley, a giant rift valley separating the Guiana and Brazilian shields, and part of the Guiana shield in Amapá and Roraima also belongs to Brazil. The Brazilian part of the Amazon valley is not all alluvial floodplain, or *varzea*, as might be imagined; *varzeas* only occupy 1–2% of the Brazilian part of the Amazon plain, though this still makes them very large in absolute terms, perhaps 65 000 sq. km.* Over large areas there is low rolling topography, as suggested by some old

* H. O'Reilly Sternberg, *The Amazon River of Brazil* (Wiesbaden, Steiner, 1975), p.17.

Fig. 38 Physical regions of Brazil

explorations. Road construction on the Trans-amazon highway from 1970 has been made difficult by the continuing alternation of hill and dale encountered.

Over the southeast half of the country the shield rocks, gneiss and schist, are near the surface, determining landforms. These forms are of broad plateau type, lightly dissected by the rivers which cross them. On the Paraná (fig. 38) and locally elsewhere, geological events of more recent time have produced the still more level plateaus of basalt and interbedded sandstones. Both sandstones and basalts are rimmed by imposing cliffy scarps, hindering road and rail construction, but presenting great hydro-electric power potential. In a line parallel to the coast from São Paulo northwards, the eastern edge of the shield loses its plateau character with ancient fold mountain systems now exposed through uplift and differential erosion; such are the Serra do Mar and Serra da Mantiqueira near Rio.

The low general level of the land allows deep penetration of humid Atlantic air, and gives a tropical or subtropical climate to broad expanses. Rainshadow effects are slight, except perhaps in the Nordeste, the northeastern bulge of Brazil, where mountain slopes are wetter or drier according to their orientation, and vegetation and agricultural potential follow the same pattern. Climatic homogeneity is most impressive over the great Amazon lowlands, where the thick mass of tropical air enters with no topographic hindrances. The products of tropical humid climates on the plateau surface in soil and vegetation are also found over wide areas. Weathering is rapid because of the acidity of the vegetation cover, and penetrates deeply, producing a clay regolith which accumulates because stream erosion is so much slower. Soil fertility is low because of rapid decomposition of humus and solution of mineral bases, except where erosion locally outpaces weathering or where alluvium is brought regularly to flood-plains.

Figure 38 presents a physical regionalization of Brazil into zones of different potential for man. The open grasslands are: those of the *campanha*, in Rio Grande do Sul, an extension of the Uruguayan pampas; the Rio Branco country, which also has some wooded savanna; the Pantanal and Campos de Vacaria in Mato Grosso; and the savannas of Marajó island in the Amazon delta. These grasslands occupy flat plains and owe their grass cover to poor drainage and floods rather than lack of rainfall. The intermediate region between forests and grasslands is shown as *campos cerrados*, wooded savanna which covers huge areas of Central Brazil on the plateau surface with 1000–1500 mm rainfall and a short dry season. The *campo cerrado* becomes wetter and more forestlike to the west and north, but is increasing its extent with the progressive burning and depletion of soil fertility by colonists. There are two high-rainfall tropical regions, the Amazon selvas and the Eastern Mountains extending from São Paulo state through the rugged and forested coastal mountains of Espirito Santo to the Nordeste, with a narrow discontinuous coastal plain to the east. Within the selvas the lower basin has the more tolerable climate for man, with frequent dry spells and lower humidity, while the west is continuously humid and hot. The Caatinga region is one of low irregular rainfall and has thin scrub forest, covering the whole interior of the Nordeste. Finally, the only middle-latitude type of forest region is the Paraná Plateau, with its cover of Paraná pine and strong seasonality of climate.

Early settlements

The second element of Brazilian unity is its people and culture. Brazil was discovered by the Portuguese soon after the first Spanish arrivals on the South American mainland; in 1500 Pedro de Cabral voyaged down the east coast by error, after losing his course to the East Indies. Cabral's trip and the Treaty of Tordesillas, however, laid the basis for a Portuguese claim to a vast territory, over which little effective control could ever be maintained in the colonial years.

There were substantial differences between Spanish and Portuguese forms of occupation, relating to their different motivations. Spanish religious fervour was never matched in Brazil — the first bishopric was not established till 1546 —

and the Portuguese came with fewer illusions and a less emotional attitude to colonial enterprises, with the political maturity of over 200 years' independence and colonial experience in West Africa and Madeira. In Brazil, all had to adapt themselves to a region with little mineral wealth and few inhabitants, the main resource being the land, not an easy prospect in a tropical climate where no previous agricultural advances had been made. The hardheadedness of Portuguese settlers reflects itself in the very name of the land, Brazil, named after the wood which was the land's first export commodity, sent as a valuable dyestuff to Portugal and northern Europe. This name replaced the early names of Santa Cruz and Vera Cruz.

The focus of this merchant and agricultural settlement was at first very much on the narrow coastal plain. While the Spaniards had won half a continent to the west, and were free from major attack throughout the colonial period, Brazil was always subject to attack from envious European powers, because it was so much easier to reach. First France, joining in the brazil-wood trade, then Holland, setting up coastal factories or trading stations, threatened Portuguese hegemony and forced the settlers to guard this coast with walled towns and castles, which are not seen in Spanish South America except along the Caribbean coast where pirates always lurked. Thus until the eighteenth century, Bahía and Rio were both walled towns. This forced focus on the coast was a blessing in disguise, for it kept the people together in an identifiable culture group, in touch with one another and with Portugal, instead of dissipating national energy in occupying the interior.

The form of settlement was in great grants of land, *donatárias,* given to landowners from Portugal to work in exchange for one-tenth of the harvest and one-fifth of the metals but, although these stretched indefinitely inland, their effective occupation was confined to the 16-km band next to the coast.

The sugar cycle

Brazilian economic history consists of a long series of speculative and dynamic waves of expansion in agriculture, leading to subsequent depressions when markets or production fall. Lucio de Azevedo, a Brazilian historian, termed these 'cycles', and recognized the sugar cycle,

31 A colonial sugar engenho, *from an engraving by Rugendas*

followed by those of gold, cotton and coffee. Sugar growing proved the only long-term successful economic basis for settlement in the sixteenth century, for the brazil-wood supplies were soon exhausted. By 1560–70 there were at least 60 sugar mills or *engenhos* spread out over the long coast from Pernambuco to São Vicente, the island near São Paulo in the south, and sugar was earning twice the income of brazil-wood. The old *engenho*, powered by oxen or by water (plate 31) with three wooden rollers, was placed close to its supplies of cane, from a plantation which usually formed part of the enterprise. In the seventeenth century the industry concentrated in Pernambuco and Bahía and, as it could never be carried out by the few Portuguese and settled Indians, thousands of Africans were brought into the Northeast, forming to this day a large element in the racial makeup of the

Nordeste. The industry was associated with a particularly strong plantation type of society, highly stratified, and dominated by the owner, who with European or mixed-blood foremen dealt in a patriarchal manner with the slave labour force. To some extent, this society has survived to the twentieth century in the Northeast.

While sugar was the Nordeste's driving force in the seventeenth century, in the Southeast, the *bandeirantes*, explorers, cattle men, and slave traders and capturers, were opening up the interior of São Paulo. They started activities as slavers around 1600, seizing and deporting Indians to the coast, especially those from the Jesuit missions in the state of Guayra, which they occupied. The attack of the *bandeirantes* on these missions between 1628 and 1638 was so fierce that the missions were eventually forced to move across the Paraná into Paraguay proper and Argentina. Once having cleared the territory, it was ready for repopulating with gold miners and cattle.

Some of the expeditions were *bona fide* mineral searches, and it became increasingly important for Brazilians to find minerals as the sugar boom declined with European favour given to their own colonies' supply of cane. Gold was found in alluvium on the Rio das Velhas, in 1698, and diamonds in 1728. Further west in Goiás and Cuyabá, gold was found in the early eighteenth century. The effect of the gold rush was in the long term to re-orient economic activity from the old northeast into the southeast, a re-orientation confirmed by the removal of the national capital from Bahia to Rio de Janeiro.

Cotton and coffee

In the late eighteenth century, gold declined in importance and cotton became important, re-

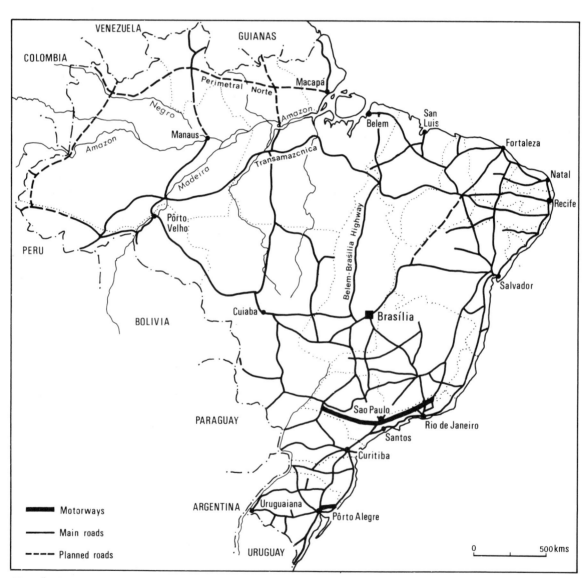

Fig. 39 The Brazilian road system

emphasizing the Nordeste, but the focus in the Southeast was fixed more firmly, from the early nineteenth century, by iron, which replaced gold as a mineral resource, and by coffee. Thus, while in 1700, 70% of the population of 200 000 was in the northeast, by 1800 the southern states had over 50% of a 2.5 million population. At the time of independence from Portugal, effectively reached when the Portuguese monarch was forced out to Brazil in 1808, Brazil was a country with substantially single history and culture, despite its mixed population. No region had enough sectional consciousness to separate and the giant nation held together. The kingdom lasted till the 1880s, by which time São Paulo was becoming established with Rio de Janeiro as joint metopolis, at the centre of a core region with both industrial and agricultural strength. The coffee, first planted on a large scale in Rio de Janeiro state, spread out into eastern São Paulo, then westwards to the Paraná river, and into northern Paraná state. Its commercial focus remained in São Paulo where great mansions were built around the old city by the new coffee barons.

The twentieth century

The eighteenth-century *sertão,* the back country, was reached by the tracks of the *bandeirantes.* In the nineteenth century the coffee boom depended on rail-line development, though railways were never flexible enough to meet the demands of a moving coffee frontier. The present century seems likely to be recorded as the century when peripheral areas were first brought into effective occupation, and the key is the new road network, accomplishing linkages never possible before. Figure 39 shows the crossing of the Amazon basin from east to west, linking to Peru and Ecuador and the Carretera Marginal de las Selvas, and at the other end to the poverty-stricken Nordeste. There are also north–south roads, linking the industrial core to the Amazon, especially along the Belém–Brasília road, intended to promote both agricultural colonization and trade. Much has been done in the 1964–72 period, during which period the national highway department tripled the federal highway network in terms of paved roads, while the state and *município* (county) roads grew at almost the same rate.

Even on the edges of the industrial Southeast, there are large areas never before reached by real roads. These areas, in western Paraná, eastern Mato Grosso and Goiás, are experiencing sudden upgrading into potential small-farmer land, using the modern roads to truck out goods to market. The roads are not all paved, and most still turn to dust in the dry season, and impassable mud in the wet, but they are all graded from time to time by heavy machines, and are capable of handling heavy traffic under normal circumstances.

CORE AND PERIPHERY

The comments above on the physical integration of distant regions into the national life by road improvements do not mean that economic and social differences have been eliminated. The process of development in the Core Region of the Southeast has been so rapid that peripheral regions have been left behind, indeed southeastern growth has been partly at the expense of the other regions, because of the migration of people, capital and resources to the growing point. Roads may even hasten the movement by allowing a more rapid migration to the big cities, and greater flows of information about the opportunities available in the cities are liable to reach the peripheral areas as a result of the same improvements.

A measure of income disparities is given by the data for broad regions in the accompanying table. An obvious pattern is that the states of the Southeast and South (Regions I to III) plus Brasilia have high income levels; taking Rio as representative of the Southeast, its 1970 per capita income level was nearly three times that of the Northeast, Region VII. In 1980 the position was substantially more equitable, through a process of smoothing of the interstate disparities. Using Williamson's index of regional disparities, a coefficient of variation weighted by the population size of each region, or $V = \sqrt{[\Sigma(x - \bar{x})^2 (f/n)]}/\bar{x}$, and put into percentage form so that 100% means maximum disparity and 0% means equality, then the value for 1970 is 39.35% and, for 1980, 30.63%.

Within each state, however, the process is in reverse; the Gini index of concentration shows a rising concentration of income, and the top 10% of earners earned a higher proportion of total income in 1980 than in 1970. The inequality seems to be worst in the northeast, where the top 10%

took 50.3% of earnings in 1980. In other words, while inter-regional differences have been alleviated by rapid development in the periphery, there are gross local inequalities, such as those between urban and rural dwellers, between industrial and agricultural workers, between traditional and modern sectors.

Some other significant distinctions between peripheral and central regions may be brought out from the demographic table which shows that the periphery has most of the area but a minority of the population, and that its population is growing at a rapid rate. There is a high level of urbanization in the periphery which suggests lack of agricultural development rather than the high overall development which is usually associated with urbanization.

On the basis of the phenomena hinted at in these two tables, it may be seen that a broad division between the centre and the various peripheral regions is the most important one to be made. In the following pages some analysis of peripheral regions is given, followed by the central region.

BRAZIL: INCOME OF ECONOMICALLY ACTIVE POPULATION

Socio-economic regions	Year	Income (1981 cruzeiros)	Gini index*	% of all income accruing to segments of population	
				Lowest 20%	Top 10%
I Rio de Janeiro	1970	24 844	0.511	4.6	43.6
	1980	39 922	0.572	3.7	47.9
II São Paulo	1970	23 399	0.513	4.4	43.2
	1980	35 382	0.522	4.3	42.3
III Paraná Sta. Catarina, R. Grande do Sul	1970	15 230	0.474	4.6	41.0
	1980	29 199	0.555	3.8	46.8
IV Minas and Espirito Santo	1970	11 783	0.558	3.5	46.0
	1980	23 316	0.560	3.6	47.6
V Maranhão, Piauí, Ceará, R. Grande do Norte, Paraíba, Pernambuco, Alagoas, Sergipe, Bahía	1970	8 503	0.520	4.2	45.4
	1980	16 119	0.583	3.4	50.3
VI Federal District of Brasilia	1970	25 399	0.494	4.4	41.4
	1980	44 748	0.584	3.3	47.6
VII Rondonia, Acre, Amazonas, Roraima, Para, Amapá, Mata Grosso, Mato Grosso do Sul, Goiás	1970	12 284	0.454	5.6	41.1
	1980	24 476	0.548	4.0	46.7

Source: Anuario Estatístico do Brasil *(1983), p. 796*
*The Gini index shows degree of concentration. If incomes were homogeneously distributed among all groups, it would have a value of zero. A value of 1.00 would indicate complete concentration.

DEMOGRAPHIC DATA FOR BRAZILIAN REGIONS

Region	Per cent of area	Per cent of population 1980	Population (000s) 1960	1980	Percentage growth 1960–80	Percentage urban in 1980
Norte	42	4.0	2 562	5 880	92	49.9
Nordeste	18	29.5	22 182	34 812	63	47.4
Sudeste	11	41.9	30 631	51 734	68	83.8
Sul	7	18.3	11 753	19 031	91	49.0
Centro-Oeste	22	6.3	2 943	7 545	165	54.4
Totals	100	100.0	70 070	119 002	76.5	63.5

Source: Anuario Estatístico do Brasil, 1983

16. Brazil: The Peripheral Regions

These are lands of great difficulty, with problem areas of two principal kinds. One of these is the vast population desert occupying the whole of the west and north (fig. 42). Here the problem stems not so much from lack of resources as from a total lack of infrastructure for development. The very size of the area imposes great isolation and resultant lack of progress. The other type of problem is in the Nordeste, where there was once prosperity and wealth, but where the situation has changed, leaving the region with few resources apart from its impoverished people.

THE NORTH

The land

In hydrographic terms the Amazon Basin covers 56 per cent of Brazil, but the north region is confined by the statisticians to the northernmost states (fig. 42), about 42% of total area. This region is still effectively a demographic desert, despite a rapid growth of population since the Second World War, from 1.84 to 4.49 million over 1950–77. Most people live near the watercourses which are both roads and sources of food, and many live in the few Amazon towns, Manaus, Santarém, Belém, leaving the interior empty apart from sparse and dwindling pure Indian groups.

Some of the foreigner's preconceptions regarding the Amazon have a good foundation in facts. The region is one dominated by the action of nature: tree growth is amazingly rapid and strong on the fertile alluvial *varzea*, the floodplain, where forest giants provide a deep shade to lower storeys of vegetation, and sometimes nearly exclude it. Land is named according to its relation to water level, *terra firme*, upland, *várzea,* floodplain, and *igapó*, frequently flooded land, divisions which are strong because of the enormous variation in the river level, ten metres average from high to low season, and sometimes far more. Structurally, the *terras firmes* are low terraces, of which the most widespread is a bench of sands, sometimes silts or clays, of probably Tertiary origin. The *igapós* occupy islands in the rivers, or backswamps, and the *várzeas*, only 1% or 2% of the total but still an area of perhaps 65 000 sq. km, are the floodplains over which the rivers are actively working, eroding laterally and depositing a part of their load.

The river itself can only be described in superlatives. Accurate measures of the Amazon's flow date only from the 1960s, and show its discharge, at over 160 000 cubic metres per second, to be far greater than ever thought, and four times greater than its nearest competitor, the Congo.* The depth of channel is maintained at the astonishing depth of about 50 metres over a 2-km width, at the Obidos narrows; at the mouth of the tributary Rio Negro, the water reaches 90 metres depth. The Amazon's suspended particle load, carried out to sea, exceeds 1.3 million tonnes per

* H. O'Reilly Sternberg, *The Amazon River of Brazil* (Wiesbaden, Steiner, 1975), p.17

diem, serving to clog the Guiana coast for hundreds of kilometres to the northwest with a fine cloying mud.

Most of the load is carried by only a few tributaries — 12% of the basin, the Central Andean section, provide 82% of the solid load, coming from steep slopes and powerful streams cutting into soft sediments. These are the 'white water' streams, their colour derived from the clay load, such as the Madeira, Solimões, Purús and Juruá. Black water streams are those derived from sandy soils developed over hard rocks, where tannins colour the water but there are few plants or fish. Clear water streams, the Xingú, Tapajós and Tocantins, come from the plateaux of central Brazil, and have very little load or colouring.

Life is everywhere adjusted to the river, the farmer on the *várzea* particularly working to harvest a crop from land that may be underwater during the high stage of the river, or grazing beef cattle on the meadows which are temporarily available, moving his manioc crop, which needs good drainage, to new sites as the river cuts away his field on an old terrace. Fishers and farmers both cling closely to the river banks, leaving the interior a near-desert.

Some parts of the north have a different aspect, like the Rio Branco country in Roraima Territory, a savanna land, its inhabitants living from the rearing of scrub cattle on the flat plains, like their neighbours in Venezuela's Llanos. *Campo cerrado* occupies the south of Pará and Amazonas states, and there are even substantial mountain ranges. the Tumac Humac on the Guiana border and Serra Pacaraima on the Venezuelan front, with an altitude of over 1200 m. On Marajó island in the Amazon estuary, an extensive cattle economy is found in the savanna covering half the island.

Settlement
Historically this region had a distinctive identity, and at one time even the makings of a separate state. Difficulties in reaching the rest of Brazil, because of the long east–west coast of Maranhão along which both wind and current set westwards, allowed a separate state of Maranhão to come into being for a while in the seventeenth century. Isolation of the interior was made complete in the hands of the Jesuits who set up *aldeias* where they protected the Indians from slavery and encouraged spice production for export. Later, isolation by land was discovered to be a fact, by explorers seeking overland routes between southeast and north; these hardy men, penetrating up the great southern tributaries of the Amazon, the Tocantins, Xingú and Araguaia, found falls and rapids barring their path, forcing portages around them and permitting no access for heavy craft.

After the expulsion of the Jesuits in 1757–60 by civil authorities fearful of their growing power, the Amazon was virtually abandoned till mid-nineteenth century, for many Indians retired inland away from the rivers to escape slavers. After 1850, the rubber boom revived trade for a while, based on the inefficient collection of wild rubber by the poor *seringueiro,* sent into the forest to collect latex from trees which he had to discover for himself, on company credit he could ill afford. This made him a debt serf, feeding the growth of a new aristocracy of 'rubber barons' at Belém and particularly at Manaus, where rubber wealth built an opera house, theatres, ballrooms and fine stone mansions, 1600 km from the nearest outpost of civilization on the lower river. Belém and Manaus were centres of control from which agents went out to collect new workers by trickery or bribes and take them upstream to the rubber lands; they were also centres to which the cured rubber was brought, via the river.

Manaus thus grew up from an obscure Portuguese slaving trade base at the outlet of the Rio Negro, to boom town and capital of a new state, Amazonas. Vital to its growth was the new steamer service on the river, inaugurated in 1853. The town lost all vitality in the early twentieth century because of a change in the form of rubber production, from wild-tree collection to plantations. The rubber plant, *Hevea brasiliensis,* was smuggled out to London and thus to Malaya, where it flourished as well as in its homeland, and the irregular and wasteful process of tapping, and thereby destroying, a declining number of wild trees was replaced by the much more efficient method of controlled tapping of the growing trees by plantation workers in Malaya.

Manaus' economy was revived in 1957 by the declaration of a Free Trade Zone, which encouraged the setting-up of some high value/weight ratio industries, such as electronics and clothing. However, they were unrelated to local resources and largely assembly-type industries, the products being flown out to the Southeast or abroad. From 1967, with the creation of SUFRAMA, the Superintendency for the Free Trade Zone of Manaus, more planning, co-ordinating and provision of infrastructure has allowed projects such as steel-making, ship-building and engineering, and agro-industrial projects such as timber, jute and rubber process-ing, using local resources, to go ahead. Manaus has new high-rise blocks in the city centre, and its population has grown from 250 000 (1968) to 613 000 (1980).

Manaus's growth still leaves Belém as main city centre to the North, with 800000 population in the metropolitan area,* 1975, and an impor-tant function as administrative centre and gate-way to the region. The city of Our Lady of Bethlehem (Belém), a Portuguese foundation of 1615 on the river Pará, not on the Amazon, is not really well-placed as outlet to the river, and it is possible that the Portuguese founded their city here in mistake. But in any case it attracts most shipping, and ocean-going ships can proceed up the passages connecting it into the Amazon main channel north of Marajó island.

Mineral development
Up to the late 1960s it was thought that mineral resources in the Amazon were slight, and hopes were pinned on agricultural settlement in the pro-jects of SUDAM and along the Transamazon Highway. With the failure of these projects in the early 1970s, official eyes were turned to some remarkable mineral discoveries, notably in the Serra dos Carajás between the Xingú and the Tocantins rivers, where a gold-mining boom comparable to California's 'forty-niners' took place. This was followed by government deci-sions to develop iron ore mining, through the CVRD, a mixed government-private firm. High-grade ore is already being shipped out along a 800 km railway to a new port 10 km from São Luis in Maranhão. The initial movement has been with diesel locomotives but the railway will soon be using electric power from the project at Tucuruí.

* Population figures of cities refer to city *municipios* only unless otherwise noted. Metropolitan areas cover much more land than the cities proper.

Another mining development has been aluminium. Bauxite from the Trombetas river area is brought to a smelter near Belém, while another smelter owned by ALCOA is at São Luis. The large electric power requirements of smelters and the railway can both be met from the HEP at Tucuruí on the Tocantins river. Here a 19 km dam with a reservoir of 2000 square kilometres, reaching upstream nearly to Maraba, will have a power output of 8000 MW, making it second only to Itaipú. (fig. 40)

There are enormous environmental problems in these developments. The CVRD, which is responsible for the iron ore project, has ex-perience of pollution control from its activities in southern Brazil, and is capable of controlling pollution at port and mine sites. But the large reservoir is a problem, and freshwater lakes created in rainforest environments have a poor record generally (see Chapter 1, also Caufield, 1985). Brokopondo in Surinam produced pro-blems of vegetation decomposition which may be matched in Tucuruí, because the dam was being built before extraction of forest timber was con-templated, and only some 10% of the total was taken out before the reservoir flooded the land. Acid water resulting from this decomposition may corrode equipment at Tucuruí just as at Brokopondo. Another problem is that of vegeta-tion growth on the reservoir, such as the water hyacinth which has been so difficult at Broko-pondo. Nor do Brazilian authorities seem to have anticipated the erosion and silting possibilities. Land near the reservoir has been converted to ranches, and in this land of sharp slopes — not the Amazon plains once thought to exist here — and heavy rainfall, the soil may be swept rapidly into the reservoir.

Apart from the physical problems there are direct human ones, including the danger of spreading diseases into the area, especially malaria, endemic in Brazil. Other likely diseases are schistosomiasis or bilharzia, a serious debilitating rather than killing illness carried in slow-moving fresh water. The common child-ren's ailments, influenza, measles, along with venereal disease, are other illnesses which most affect the native Amerindian population. Local tribes have also witnessed a many-sided on-slaught against their culture, including relocation in reservations, when construction began in 1977. There followed an invasion of the reserves by the Transamazon Highway, which involved cutting down the forest habitat, as well as physical attack by gangs sent by landlords to clear the Indians out. There are also about 25 000 non-Indians who, though spared the trauma of attack in any direct form, have needed to be re-settled out of the reservoir area.

Agriculture: a question mark

Farming peoples are already entering the region in fairly large numbers along the fast-advancing Transamazon Highway, and it is expected that agricultural use of the region will soon be very general; but, though shifting agriculture has long been practised, there remain serious difficulties in settling large numbers of colonists in the forest region.

Bragantina

An example of the agricultural problem is presented in Bragantina, an area which is productive and well settled, between Bragança and Belém in the lower basin. In 1848, when H.W. Bates, the naturalist, visited Belém, it was little more than a village, though already with 15 000 inhabitants, and he commented that the forest reached to the very outskirts of the settlement. Intensive land use came after 1900 along the railway line between the two towns. Shifting agriculture has eaten its way through all this land so that no natural, fertile selvas soil remains, only secondary forest and brush and low amounts of humus. The ancient slash-and-burn technique is still practised by shifting farmers who must expend continuous effort on clearing as their staple food crops, manioc, corn and beans, suffer a 50% fall in yield from first year to second. The short dry season from September to November allows complete burning which gives good ash fertilizer for the first crop, but also burns out humus and exposes the soil directly to the burning action of the sun. In this way, the whole zone was degraded by the time the railway closed in 1936, and would support only about eight persons per square kilometre.

Commercial farming in Bragantina is confined to *malvas* (a vegetable fibre, *Urena lobata*, used as a successful jute substitute), tobacco and black

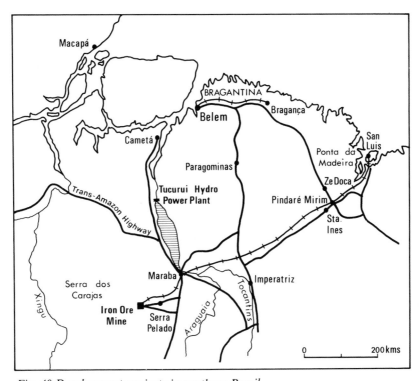

Fig. 40 Development projects in northern Brazil

pepper, introduced by Japanese settlers in the 1940s. Below the Bragantina zone, on the flat alluvium near the river, there is also jute grown on a commercial scale. Pepper has become an export crop of some magnitude, though there are some undesirable features. Profits go partly to merchants and middlemen who advance credit to farmers. Prices are so unstable that the smallest farmers must always be dependent on this kind of credit, in the absence of other financial institutions. Tobacco is sometimes grown on plots fertilized by cattle kept for the purpose; this may look like a rare case of mixed farming in the tropics, but it differs in that cattle are quite subordinate in the system, brought in solely for their fertilizing dung.

A third land use is rubber, developed after 1950 when Brazil was suffering acute shortages of this strategic material. In 1927 the Ford Company had attempted rubber plantations in the lower Tapajós, a commercial failure because of disease and labour problems. At last modern technology has succeeded, and Pirelli and Goodyear own large plantations of several thousand ha, where the soil is preserved by ground-cover plantings, and by avoiding burning of the forest as a preliminary to planting, because this destroys soil humus. Disease is controlled by trained agronomists. The problem in this sector is not economic success but ownership; much land, skills and capital are retained in the hands of a trained group which manages the estates, not disseminated among other producers.

One major attempt to tame the Amazon has become world-famous; this is the Jari venture, D.K. Ludwig's project based primarily on silviculture of pulpwood trees associated with an industrial complex and some cultivation of rice. Investment was justified in this case by the tax concession offered by the government through SUDAM, the regional development agency for the Amazon. Ludwig's 1967 land purchase of over 1 million ha was in Pará state and Amapá territory, most development taking place in Pará. Felling of native forest and its replacement with the quick-growing exotic species *Gmelina arborea* began in 1969. First plantings were on sandy soil and some areas had to be replanted with Caribbean pine from 1973. A large pulp mill was set up downstream, fed initially by native forest, but later from the plantations. Hard-

woods have also been planted, for a sawmill which will process them. The project proved of dubious viability financially and Ludwig sold out in 1982, to a group of Brazilian companies backed by government money. Perhaps more important, there is doubt too as to the physical possibility of monocultures of trees or other crops in this region. Heavy rainfall of 2500 mm annually leaches out nutrients, and biomass is greatly reduced by the removal of forest. Insect and fungal attack on the trees has already affected production, as it did the rubber plantations of a previous generation.

THE WEST

The three states of Mato Grosso, Mato Grosso do Sul and Goiás, with Brasilia, cover nearly 1.9 million sq. km. Mato Grosso do Sul was separated from Mato Grosso in 1979 in an attempt to speed up development. Like the north, this is an empty region with few permanent settlements of any kind, and most people live in the southern part where the vegetation is *campo cerrado* rather than selvas. Northern Mato Grosso, on the middle courses of the Xingú and Tapajós, is still one of the least known parts of the inhabitable world, occupied by a thin population of Indian cultivators and hunters who have never had real contact with white populations.

The dominant land use is cattle rearing, throughout the *chapadas*, the dry flat uplands lying at 1000 m on natural or improved grasslands. There has been a rapid build up of cattle numbers in the West, which had 10.5 million head in 1960, and 19.5 in 1975. However, the region has a very low carrying capacity, especially in Goiás, where a third of the cattle are maintained on pastures with under 15 head per sq km, compared with Rio Grande do Sul, itself an extensive cattle district, where 50 per sq km is typical. In Mato Grosso there is a higher density because of the Pantanal, the upper Paraguay river flood-plain with a 160-km width of seasonally flooded meadow producing fine natural pastures. The Pantanal is also the world's largest remaining natural wetland, and conservation measures are urgently needed to protect its wildlife, as the agricultural frontier is already encroaching on it.

Outside the Pantanal, the West has infertile soils, often lateritic, sometimes poorly drained, except for the valleys cut into the surface. These expose fresh minerals which plants may use, and allow agriculture to develop for local markets.

From the 1940s the federal government has promoted colonization, especially in southern Goiás, in forest lands of slope and valley bottom which were ignored by the cattle *fazendas*, pre-emptors of the open lands. In the 1970s, the expanding agricultural frontier hit southern Goias and Mato Grosso do Sul with full force, expanding particularly the areas under soya beans, which dominate among the crops, often grown in alternation with wheat, the second crop. These commercial crops come from medium-sized farms. Smaller farms with a near-subsistence economy grow rice, manioc and beans.

Regional isolation

The West, incorporated into Brazil in the eighteenth century by the expeditions of *bandeirantes*, had no direct connections with the coast, and communicated with it more via the Paraná–Paraguay system of rivers than overland on the long and difficult trails. Only in the present century was there a rail connection to the east, from Corumbá to São Paulo, effectively bringing the region into the national ambit. The region's isolation and the urge to fill what appeared to be a dangerous void on the borders of Spanish lands led to the *Marcha para o Oeste,* the westwards march, a popular phrase in the government of Getulio Vargas in the 1930s. In order to assist the growth of the West, new federal territories were created out of isolated portions of states, in a Vargas decree of 1943. These included Amapá, Rio Branco (now called Roraima), Guaporé (now Rondonia), taken out of Mato Grosso and Amazonas, Ponta Porã from Mato Grosso, and Iguaçu, from Paraná and Santa Catarina. The two last were returned to their states in 1946, but the others remained federal districts which received special aids to development. Since the federal lands were mostly peopled by Indians with little knowledge of white men, the Indian Protection Service was utilized to attempt a gradual transition of the life the primitives had known into something compatible with modern farming and to protect their hunting grounds until they could be educated for other employment.

Indians

The treatment of Indians on the farming frontier has become something of an issue for Brazil, because of allegations by foreigners, by the Church and by anthropologists and others within the country, that Indians have been mistreated, even shot at like animals, in order to move them away from estates which have acquired value for their owners with the gradual advance of the farmer frontier; even the Indian Protection Service has been implicated in criticisms of Indian treatment, along with cattlemen, farmers and prospectors. The most useful work, now terminated by the government, was that done by the anthropologist brothers Vilas Boas, in teaching the Indians and preparing them for the cultural shock of Western civilization. This is the most that could be done, for complete isolation in National Reserves, desired by some anthropologists to prevent the irrevocable destruction of their culture, is a hopeless ideal.

The Polonoroeste project illustrates some of the problems. This is a vast colonization project involving 400 000 sq. km of land, the strip being accessible from the improved road between Cuiaba and Porto Velho, the capitals of Mato Grosso and Rondonia. Only about 8000 Amerindians live in the area, but they belong to over 20 tribal groups. These vary greatly in their level of acculturation, some farming and even owning tractors, other scarcely known or uncontacted by Western civilization. The programme involves careful survey and demarcation of their lands so as to form reservations and evict illegal settlers from them. Help in education, health and agricultural production is being introduced while trying not to break up the traditional society, though the very contact with outsiders brings new diseases, changes aspirations and inevitably breaks up traditional society. Even the land demarcation is dubious as an exercise because of the wide-ranging movements of tribes which live from hunting and collecting.

Brasília (411 000)

Part of the urge for westwards movement, to fulfil Brazil's 'continental destiny', expressed itself in the move to locate the capital in the west, an idea dating back to the eighteenth century and the rebellious miners who sought freedom from Europe and a symbolic turning inland away from the coast. Brazil's Federal District is located symbolically at the headwaters of the three major rivers, Amazon, Paraná and São Francisco, indicating Brazilian dominion over all three. Brasília's interior location symbolizes the conquest of the *sertão,* the backwoods which have been the continuous challenge to Brazilians. At the same time, the idea of an implanted, created city is scarcely new or original. Belo Horizonte, capital of Minas Gerais, was inaugurated in 1897, a new city to replace the old, picturesque but overcrowded town of Ouro Prêto. In this there is something of a parallel with Brasília and Rio de Janeiro, which it replaced; there is also a parallel in the opposition to the transfer by established interests in the old settlement. Teresina and Aracaju in the northeast are other nineteenth-century created capitals; nearer to Brasília, in Goiás, Goiânia was made state capital in 1937, replacing Goiás city. There are, then, antecedents for a move of the national capital.

A long time lapsed between initial proposals and movement, which only began under the Kubitschek government and, since public programmes have a habit of falling by the wayside if not completed under a single mandate, was to be completed in five years. In fact the basic structure of the capital was laid out in this period, following the superbly monumental design of the architect Lucio Costa.

QUESTIONS
In spite of being a largely administrative city (itself a potential problem though government is currently a growth industry), Brasília has suffered some of the usual growth problems of Brazilian cities. The *favela* has been a feature here as much as in Rio, for many people have been attracted in by job possibilities. In the mid-1960s, it was estimated that 100000 people, a third of the population, were in substandard housing, for the most part *favelas*. These were the migrants, hungry for jobs in the construction industry, in service industries, in anything open to uneducated *caboclos*. They occupied land near the Pilot Plan which centres on lake Paranoá, in areas which became known as the Social Security Invasion, Vila Tenório, Candangolândia and Taguatinga. Blocks of flats had been built in the initial planned areas, but they were too expensive for penniless migrants with absolutely no resources. Towns outside the capital but within

the District could also have been used to house the *favelados*, but there was no system of organized public transport to bring them in from these places, nor housing to accommodate them. Brasília's grandiose design, expressive of high aims and excellence, it must be concluded, was not built for the poor who were to constitute a large part of its inhabitants.

Another question which must be asked about the city is whether it has been worthwhile for the nation. It was constructed at enormous expense by a nation with limited public funds, in a region which was not the main problem area of the country; its employment possibilities were not great for the untrained, nor were its industries capable of stimulating much local development. Martin Katzmann (1975, 1977, Ch. 3) assessed the developmental role of Brasília by estimating its impact on the growth of population in Goiás state, within which the Federal District lies. By 1970, he calculated that Brasília's effect as a market for farm goods and services had been at most 150 000 new migrants, i.e. only 5% of the state population or 15% of the 1960–70 growth. This was considered a weak effect in view of the investment and efforts made. Parallel calculations made for the Belém-Brasília road indicate similarly poor effects in attracting new settlers.

THE NORDESTE

This region, a fifth of Brazil, includes the northern marginal state of Maranhão, Piauí, Ceará, Rio Grande do Norte, Pernambuco, Alagoas, Sergipe, and Bahía on the southern margins, with in 1977 an estimated population of 33.6 million, or 30 per cent of the total. If we were to look for a rough parallel to the Nordeste in the developed world, it might be among the old coalfield regions of North Britain or Pennsylvania. In such areas, development has come many years ago, promoted prosperity for a while, and then gone to leave a dense population with a shortage of useful work, with the unemployment that breeds discontent and rebellion. In the Nordeste the sugar cycle brought prosperity to the rich *massapé* black-clay soils of the *mata*, the coastal belt, during the seventeenth century, cotton prolonged it to the nineteenth, but no new resource was found for the twentieth century. Given the social structure of the region, the phenomenon is perhaps predictable: a region with successive agricultural export bases, when these are no longer viable, has no ongoing dynamic source of ideas or entrepreneurs for a new export base, and relapses into poverty.

The culture of rebellion

The Nordeste is defined not only in terms of poverty, but also in its distinctive culture, identified by historians and celebrated in literature. Especially since the decline in regional fortunes in the nineteenth century, various kinds of outburst, functions of the internal stresses in the system, have occurred here.

Early antecedents were the establishment of runaway slave colonies, notably the Republic of Palmares (1630–97) in the backcountry. In Maranhão a peasant revolt took place in 1838–40. In 1896-7 a religious movement under the ascetic Antonio Conselheiro brought together bandits and fanatics in what seemed to some a threat to the new Brazilian Republic, at Canudos in northern Bahía. In fact this was never an organized threat to authority, but it showed the difficulty of governing the *sertão*, for whole brigades had to be sent to take a village of a few thousand determined fighters, and many lives were lost both to these defenders and to the drought and inhospitable environment of the interior.* Throughout the centuries, Robin Hood characters, half-bandit and half idealist, have entered into the folklore and history of the *sertão*. In more recent years, Peasant Leagues, first formed in 1955, among the sugar mills of the coast, have focussed the bitterness and the aspirations of the labourers.

The expression, almost caricature, of the *sertão* type is the *vaqueiro,* the independent cowboy who is no one's master and nobody's servant. He watches the cattle on a share basis with the owner, taking one calf in four, and is trusted to do this without overseers. His clothing, adapted to a hostile environment of spiny bushes, is more like that of a medieval knight than that of a cowboy, with tight leather leggings, leather gloves, shinguards, leather jerkin and vest. Physically he may be a

mameluco, mixture of white and Indian, or a *cafuso*, Indian–Negro mix.

Coastal society

On the coast, there was a more settled, stable, less nomadic society, allowing harder lines to be drawn in the social stratification.

> The cane culture of the Nordeste aristocratized the white man into a lord, and degraded the Indian and principally the Negro, first into a slave, then into a pariah. It aristocratized the house of stone and cement into a mansion and degraded the straw into mucambo. It inflated the plantation and depreciated the *mata*, the virgin forest.
>
> Gilberto Freyre, Nordeste, *edited by J. Olympio, 1951, p. 124*

Tradition centred on the *senhores de engenho*, secure in their rich lands and the leaders of their society, but so conservative that they allowed Cuba to steal the advantage when the age of improvements came for sugar, with the introduction of steam-powered mills in the nineteenth century. Another tradition, more independent like that of the *sertanejo*, is that of the small fisherman on the coast, with his fragile *jangada* which takes him out almost literally in search of tomorrow's food (plate 32).

Racially this is another mixed region, but with a strong current of African blood, some of it from the higher civilizations of West Africa, metalworkers and of Moslem faith, rather than the more primitive Bantu tribesmen. These skilled workers were of use in developing and working the little mines of the interior, and were also experienced herdsmen. African culture, despite the deliberate mixing of tribal groups to avoid formation of communities, has survived in a variety of dances and semi-religious rites, kinds of food and cooking, and clothing, which seem to be of Moslem origin.

Land use

THE SERTÃO

Physically the interior of the Nordeste has enormous difficulties for man. This land of ancient gneiss and schist rocks, or dry sandstones, is cut through by a great river, the São Francisco, running first northeast then cutting southeast to the sea. This northern elbow of the river and the plateaus, hills and mountains to the north, suffer

---

* The Canudos campaign, and the *sertão* environment, are admirably portrayed in the work of Euclides da Cunha, *Os Sertoes,* first published in 1902, and in shortened form in English as *Revolt in the Backlands,* translated by Samuel Putnam (London, Victor Gollancz, 1947).

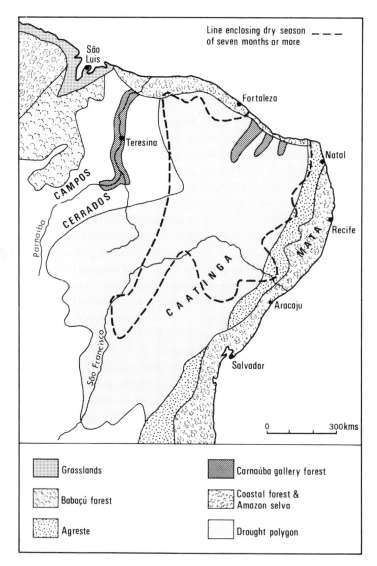

Fig. 41 Vegetation zones of the Nordeste and the Drought Polygon

from drought, not a continuous lack of water — most of the land has over 600 mm and some 1000 mm annually — but a more dangerous phenomenon, a dry season which sometimes lasts four months, sometimes for twelve, when it causes disaster, famine and emigration of countless thousands of *retirantes*, quitters, leaving the land and going to the coast, to the towns, anywhere in order to survive. The Drought Polygon, as it is called, is roughly defined by the region with seven or more months' drought (fig. 41). It

lies in the interior, reaching the coast only between Fortaleza and Natal. Along the east-facing coast, there is adequate rainfall of 1500 mm or more, and often thicker soils with alluvial material. This is the *zona da mata,* literally the forest zone, which it was when first met by Portuguese explorers. Inland, there is a belt of transitional country with thin forest, the *agreste,* and further in the *sertão* (fig. 41). Both *agreste* and *sertão* may be affected by drought. In the driest country of the *sertão* the vegetation is *caatinga*, the scrub forest dominated by thorn trees, cactus and bromeliads.

Here drought is not easily combated with irrigation schemes; the water of the São Francisco is too far below the northern plateaus to allow simple diversion with dam techniques for irrigation, and in any case the area is isolated and cannot well compete in the provision of irrigation crops to the urban markets of the coast. Thus most of the *sertão* is cattle land, used for tough unimproved beef animals which only reach slaughter weight at six years, and then only achieve a carcass weight half that of a North European animal. In the driest parts sheep and goats are kept on pastures that are virtually useless for other animals and have been progressively degraded by overgrazing and cultivation in the course of the century.

In the northern part of the Drought Polygon, the rivers dry up in the dry season, their flood-plains occupied by carnauba palms in gallery forests, feeding on the groundwater and rich soil.

The wax formed on the leaves to prevent evaporation loss of water is an important commercial product, increasing output now coming from Piauí, Ceará and Grande do Norte, where the tree is also used for its edible nut and its strong wood.

AGRESTE AND MATA

The densest population in the Nordeste is in the *agreste* and *mata*, and the coastal belt is still occupied by sugar plantations, especially in Pernambuco and Alagoas, leading sugar states in the region. Cocoa is also an important estate crop on the Bahia coast, and oil palms have become successful in this area. Apart from plantations, there is a large body of subsistence farmers cultivating small plots for beans, rice and maize, and making ends meet by seasonal labour for plantation owners who may indeed own their land, making them completely dependent.

Minerals have also favoured the coastal *mata*,

32 Jangadas, *primitive fishing craft, at Prainha, Ceará, in the Brazilian Nordeste*

where oil has been produced in substantial quantities since 1950. Bahia's Recôncavo basin of Mesozoic rocks accounts for nearly all Brazilian natural gas and 80% of her petroleum. Sergipe, neighbour state to the north, produces most of the rest. A new coast road being built between Rio and Salvador (Bahía), in addition to the existing one which runs inland, should help the coastal developments, especially the potential lumbering and cocoa-producing country of southern Bahia and Espirito Santo state to the south. Fishing is practised along the whole coast, from villages standing in the shade of palm trees behind the long beaches. The fish catch is not enormous, only a third of Brazil's total, but the industry is labour-intensive and takes little capital, points to recommend it to a country where men are less scarce than money. The fishermen work from tiny boats without motors which they re-make themselves every year when the wood begins to crumble away.

Urbanization

Towns now hold the majority of the regional population. There are three major foci: Fortaleza in the north with 1.1 million population; in the centre Recife 1.2 million (2.2 million metropolitan area), capital to the Nordeste in general; and Salvador (1.5 million). Because of waves of immigrants from the countryside in recent years, there is high unemployment in these cities and in the many smaller towns of the interior. Port processing industries are still, as in colonial times, important in Recife and Salvador, but tax concessions have brought a host of unconnected light industries to the Aratu industrial estate at Salvador and to the suburbs of Recife, such as electronics, electrical hardware, synthetic fibres and petro-chemicals. Not all of these industries can use the migrant labour force, with its skills oriented to an earlier stage of industrial development, to weaving, basketry and leather-work, craft industries which are rapidly declining in the country. Many migrants end up in the already overstaffed tertiary sector where wages are minimal.

Maranhão

A fourth region of the Nordeste is the Amazon fringe, mostly in the state of Maranhao, a region which is physically transitional from the dry zone of the *sertão* to the humid environment of the selvas. Some writers have even referred to the Maranhão–Piauí area as a separate region, the Middle North, a distinction that has some justification on economic, physical and cultural grounds. It has an easily cleared selva cover, replaced by secondary growth of the babaçu palm also found to a lesser extent throughout the Nordeste. This region differs in an important aspect from the rest of the Nordeste, in its lack of population. It has been able to act as steamvalve for the Nordeste, accepting over the last century untold thousands of migrants leaving the dry lands during hard times.

Culturally the region was typical plantation country, focussing on the colonial centre of São Luís, and producing rice, sugar and cotton in the seventeenth century. Thereafter it fell into complete decadence so that fossilized townships are to be found scattered throughout the coastal plain. The small population turned in part to a primitive existence, living from hunting and fishing with traditional techniques, and growing only subsistence crops of rice and manioc. To earn money salt, fish and animal skins were sold in small quantity. In the present century the babaçu became a new source of some wealth, because of its valuable vegetable oil; it is collected in nut form by tenants who must sell to the landowners in return for a small payment, and the lack of organization of collection or marketing means poor quality at times and irregular supply.

In recent years the local economy has been stimulated by large numbers of migrants from neighbour states of the Nordeste, coming spontaneously or in government-sponsored schemes which have had varying fortune. Over most of the interior however, cattle are raised with little help from man, on an ultra-extensive basis of zero provision of improvements. The cattle must often migrate great distances because of floods in the low plains of western Maranhão, or droughts in the east.

STRATEGIES FOR THE NORDESTE

The Nordeste's vicious circle of poverty starts with impoverished and often landless farmers and labourers: they cannot invest in land improvements because of poverty and because they do not own the land; their production is thus meagre, and their living conditions are insanitary; their crops are often sold to their landlords at low prices, thus they earn little and remain poor. In Brazil, however, different diagnoses of the problem have led to new strategies being adopted. An early approach was to assume the main problem was physical, and disaster relief was attempted in the towns, waiting for the problem to go away. In the first half of the twentieth century, the 'hydraulic approach' was adopted, attempting to overcome the drought by means of dam construction and wells. From 1959 to about 1970, a broader economic approach was adopted under SUDENE, seeking to widen the economic options for the area. Finally, in recent years the problem has again been bypassed by focussing regional development on the Amazon lands where drought sufferers would be taken.

The attack on drought
For a considerable period the drought problem, the *secas*, has been treated as the central one. As early as 1877, Emperor Pedro II was moved to set up an investigating committee after the terrible drought of that year which killed half a million people in Ceará. By 1909 a permanent Inspectorate for Droughts had been created, still in existence today as the National Department for Drought Measures (DNOCS). This federal agency has provided emergency relief in food and work for the *flagelados*, those scourged by the drought, and has built over 250 reservoirs in the Drought Polygon. These were intended to retain water through dry seasons, and feed irrigation canal systems, but lack of funds and poor planning have meant that the canals, except for a very few, have not been built. Reservoirs were often too small and dried out in the dry season, to expose a strip of good soil round their edge for cultivation, sometimes the only useful function of the dam. Since 1964 DNOCS has had more money available and doubled the public reservoir capacity from 6.8 million cu m to 11.7 in 1971, though no growth has occurred since then. Many wells were also drilled in this decade.

The drought programme of DNOCS has not been totally successful, either in a narrow technical sense or as a broad solution for the Nordeste. Only in terms of employment for workless farmers was it ever of vital importance, and even in this matter, it could be queried whether it would not have been better to let the *flagelados* migrate to better-endowed regions. Corruption and mismanagement have been a constant companion of the planners, and an Indústria das Sêcas grew up, whereby exaggerated claims of drought brought in government money when it was most convenient to local political leaders. Basically, however, the failure is one of specialization, of concentrating on infrastructural measures rather than using a broader approach to social and economic problems.

The regional development authorities
A river-basin approach was first attempted in the São Francisco Valley Authority, created in 1948. The northern quarter of the valley lies within the Drought Polygon as officially defined for the DNOCS measures. However, the hands of this agency were tied from the beginning because hydro power was placed outside its control under a separate and successful federal agency which developed the Paulo Afonso Falls site on the river, producing power for the first time in 1955. Only electric power production, which offended no vested interests, could readily be planned.

Up to this time the policy for the Nordeste could be classified as a *política hidráulica*, a policy based on hydraulic engineering measures. Now a move towards comprehensive development planning was made with the setting up of SUDENE, Superintendency for Development of the Northeast, in 1959, as an autonomous agency for coordination of planning throughout the region. The multiple attack on the problem envisaged a) industrialization to diversify the economy, b) agricultural concentration on foodstuff production as a protection against famine and c) colonization of areas outside the densely peopled Nordeste in transitional Maranhão and Goiás.

After 1964, the SUDENE programme was progressively altered by military governments that have controlled Brazil since that year and which have limited the autonomy of the regional agencies. Private industry has continued to be attracted into the area by substantial tax concessions, which in the most favourable cases meant that an investor only had to contribute 12.5 per cent of the capital cost of a new venture. In 1964–9 this served to double the fixed industrial capital in the region. Some economists have expressed doubts about the effectiveness of this approach. Most investment went to the fine new Aratu industrial estate at Salvador, to main road sites around Recife, or to Fortaleza, in other words to places where a good infrastructure for industry was already present. Elsewhere there was little to attract the industrialist, and the small states of the Nordeste were bypassed, in a process of concentration of economic advance on the big cities. Industrial structure was also less than optimal for the purposes of regional policy, because the links of the new industries in the region were not to other local industries, but out and back to the mother companies which were in the Southeast or overseas, and to market and supply industries in the Southern–Southeastern complex. Little in the form of local, regional multiplier effect from the industries could be discerned.

In agriculture, food-crop production expanded according to plan. Over 1950–69 rice production expanded to 8.6% annually, beans 7.2%, maize 6.0% against 3.8% for sugar, 3.2% cotton and 1.4% cocoa. There was however a realization that this did not solve any long-term problems, or even some short-term ones, since food crops could avoid famines only if they were grown successfully in the famine areas, and in any case famine was only one facet of the Nordeste problem.

The relief valve approach
From 1970, a year of severe drought and in a period of tightening military control, the orientation changed again. Now the central project was President Medici's National Integration Programme, the PIN, aimed at national integration and national security, which in practice meant pushing new roads into Amazonia to tie it into the rest of the country. The best-known road was the Transamazónica, crossing the whole Amazon east–west along a line near the edge of the Brazilian Shield, south of the Amazon. Along the road, it was planned, thousands of Nordestinos would settle, the road providing a relief valve for land-hungry peasants. These settlers would then start producing for the nation — the Amazon was to become the breadbasket of

Brazil. Such a programme was of course a political choice, of colonization instead of the more difficult land reform which might cause antagonisms, and also served geopolitical aims, as mentioned in Chapter 6.

The colonization project was in fact an abject failure, settling only 6000 in four years instead of the 100 000 forecast. It was quietly dropped after 1974, another failed attempt to cultivate the *terra firma*, the non-alluvial land which had never permitted intensive long-term farming. The settlements had been carefully planned in geometric designs with a hierarchy of settlement sizes: villages (*agrovilas*), towns (*agropolis*) and cities (*ruropolis*). However, not all the important feeder roads were built, so marketing was difficult. More important to Moran (1981) was the failure to choose and train the settlers. Nordestinos had no experience of this kind of environment. The most successful were local backwoodsmen, *caboclos*, who could identify the best soil areas by tell-tale indicators in the environment, such as the presence of certain trees. They also knew how to supplement the protein-poor diet of the Amazon by fishing in the rivers and hunting small animals. The Amazon is a varied environment, and local knowledge and experience was valuable.

From 1970, year of a severe drought, the orientation of effort changed again under the military government. Now the central point was to be President Medici's National Integration Programme (PIN), aimed at linking in to the centre all the peripheral regions, and thus bringing development and maximum national security. Two roads were to be of importance, the Transamazonica and the Cuiabá—Santarém (fig. 39), along which colonization by farmers was intended, both to aid the development of the North and to act as a safety valve for the still overpopulated Nordeste. Many other modern highways were to be built, in a programme which seems more concerned with strategic and security interests of the military than with regional economic development. It is true that the Transamazonica now provides a fine paved road-link from the river Madeira near the Bolivian frontier to the east coast 3500 km away, and that the road will link to the head of navigation on many southern tributaries of the Amazon, thus incorporating this river into the transport system. But for the farmers who must use the land a less than optimal choice has been made, following the well-drained but infertile uplands above the *varzea* plain. Possibly only the stretch south of Santarém will provide a long-term basis for farming.

In particular, the programme would seem to be a poor second choice to putting through a thoroughgoing agrarian reform in the Nordeste. Such a reform has never been carried out because of the effective power of the landlords in areas such as the *mata,* where they control both rural land and industries. Agrarian reform has been made a priority in three northeastern states — Pernambuco, Ceará and Paraíba — but the reform proposed is not complete, for it offers payment in compensation for land lost at commercial rates, an expensive proposition which can scarcely be afforded by the government; there is in addition no enforcement of complete breakup of latifundia, only reduction to half size. Finally, breakup is not to be practised on the productive lands at all, so that large sugar estates, with their high production, escape altogether, and only poor cattle lands of the *sertão*, totally unsuited to new small farmers, are likely to be available.

OVERVIEW OF THE PERIPHERAL REGIONS

The Nordeste is obviously the main problem region in the Brazilian periphery. It has a large, poverty-ridden population with few hopes for improvement. The atmosphere of the region is one of tension; this has even been expressed by such conservative elements as the Church. Dom Helder Cámara, Archbishop of Recife and Olinda, has argued that significant reform of Nordestino society has yet to be achieved, and that more than lip-service to change must be given by the government. Dom Helder's voice has considerable weight among the people and he is supported by his bishops and clergy; his voice has not been silenced, but those of leftwing agitators who sought to rouse sugar workers against their masters have been quieted, leaving the tension bottled up and still seeking an outlet.

The problems for Amazonia and the west are of another character and perhaps less obvious; for these regions there are the questions of conservation. How is it possible to press forward with farmers into the selvas without destruction of much that is useful? Indian cultures and the Indians themselves are being killed by the advancing wave of occupants in the Midwest. At the same time there are the proposals for national roads through the north and west and farmer-colonization of huge areas along them — without the experience of trial and error to guide them. Possibly the colonization will be successful, though some reservations about this have been expressed. But there remains the destruction of the forest, a secular process in Brazil but one which is now accelerating and which may constitute not only a Brazilian but a world problem, since this forested region is one of the last biological sinks for the atmosphere, controlling to an unknown but large extent the carbon dioxide and oxygen content and balancing it naturally. Once the selvas cover is gone, it has been observed that replacement is extremely slow because of the close relation of soil and vegetation; this makes destruction all the more serious.

17. The Core Region of Brazil

The Southeast and South are taken together as a core region (fig. 42), distinguished from the rest of the country primarily on the grounds of their greater wealth, and secondarily because they have a more urban and industrial makeup. The map shows that their trade links make all parts of Brazil, except the Nordeste, tributary directly to the metropolitan southeast, but distance and the differences in economy and society which typify the periphery make it desirable to treat them separately.

The south is distinguished by a more rural population, and by an economy based mainly on mining, minerals and farming; the southeast is threequarters urban already, and is the industrial–commercial centre to the country. The problems of the periphery, outmigration, lack of rural employment and poverty, have their counterpart in the city: immigrants in the city slums and *favelas*, lack of urban employment opportunities for the new arrivals, and consequent poverty for the *marginados,* those living on the edge of society without secure employment, sometimes without secure lodgings for themselves and their families.

THE SOUTHEAST

Physical geography
All southeast Brazil is shield country, forming a series of tablelands or *chapadas* at different levels but sloping generally down to the west. The hydrographic net is thus composed mostly of Paraná tributaries, flowing away from the coast, a factor that long retarded exploration and settlement of the interior. Only short streams flow east, apart from the Paraíba which occupies a longitudinal valley between the Serra do Mar and Serra da Mantiqueira. The first of these ranges is still a forested wall of land rising sharply from the coast, a steamy blue–green in the usual humid atmosphere. Climates are subtropical rather than tropical, modified by altitude on the plateau and on the coast by occasional depressions which bring cooler air from the south. A ride by bus from Santos via the superhighway up the Serra do Mar to São Paulo, taking only half an hour, serves to bring home the differences in temperature; in August this writer has regretted the lack of a jacket in the city on the plateau, having been perfectly comfortable in shirt-sleeves in the port.

Historical background
In early colonial times the capitania of São Vicente was able to develop as a commercial centre because of the active trade of São Vicente island, near the modern port of Santos. The trade products included quinces (*marmelos,* basis of the original marmalade), and sugar from the few plantations; a relative abundance of settled Tupi Indians allowed successful farming of the traditional slave-based type. This was not however Brazil's early core region, that honour falling to the Nordeste. In this latter region there was a much greater development of slaving, of sugar, and of trade with Portugal's Oriental Empire — Bahía became a frequent port of call

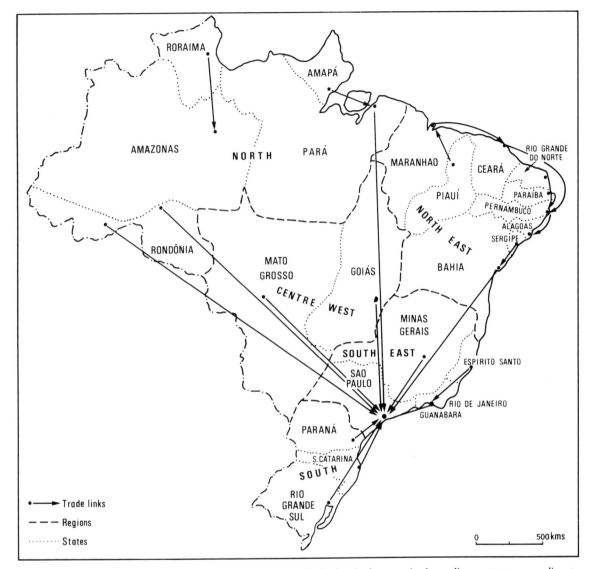

Fig. 42 Brazilian regions and trade linkages: each stage is linked to its largest single trading partner, according to internal trade statistics

for the India fleet, absorbing its silks and spices before they had a chance to reach the Portuguese markets.

In the São Paulo region, appropriate to the city's plateau rather than coastal situation, there arose a definite tradition of exploration and exploitation of the interior, under the *bandeirantes*, groups of men who went first to look for gold or slaves. Enslavement of the Indians was illegal, but a pretence was made of going to exchange slaves for captives already taken in war. Other men went on a more permanent basis from São Paulo to open up cattle lands in the *campo cerrado* and savannas of the interior, in western Minas and in the São Francisco valley. Gold was found in the late seventeenth century and formed the basis of eighteenth-century wealth, a wealth to which the old city of Ouro Prêto (plate 33) testifies: this was the capital of the mining kingdom and, with the transfer of its administrative functions to Belo Horizonte in the 1890s, has been fossilized

33 The city of Ouro Prêto, fossilized in its eighteenth-century form, its architecture protected as an ancient monument

in its narrow valley, the purest example of Portuguese Baroque architecture in Brazil.

Gold, and also diamonds from northern Minas Gerais, were the basis for an economic cycle that attracted new settlers, including Nordestinos with their troupe of slaves, to the mines of the Southeast. The decline of mining in the nineteenth century was followed by the coffee cycle, giving rise to a new coffee aristocracy which built its ornate mansions around São Paulo, matching those of the gold and diamond merchants in Rio. Finally, over the last hundred years the rise of industry, using in many cases the capital won in trade from coffee, has confirmed the central position of the Southeast.

The rural economy

Market-oriented commercial farming has long been established in the Southeast. In some remote areas or on difficult sloping land in the Serra do Mar or Serra da Mantiqueira there are semi-subsistence farmers growing more for themselves than for the market, but these are the exception, not the rule. Important commercial crops include coffee, cotton, and sugar, for this area has replaced the Northeast as centre of cane-sugar production. São Paulo produces 40% of Brazilian coffee, and is responsible for the surpluses that have allowed Brazil to diversify her foreign trade. In 1985, coffee accounted for only 10.2% of export value, sugar for 0.6%. Food crops are maize, rice on the wetter lowlands, and fruit and vegetables of a wide variety in the suburban market gardens.

Mechanization and technification of farming is advanced, as compared to other regions, as the table opposite suggests. While the North and Northeast have about 250 workers per tractor, the South and Southeast have 20, and produce far more of the national farm product with a smaller labour force.

Part of the secret of the Southeast's agricultural success is in the general background of education and capital availability, part is in the connections of farming to industry through processing. For example, one advantageous factor for cotton growing is a market location, feeding the local textile industry, for most of Brazil's cotton mills are in the São Paulo metropolitan area, and edible cotton seed oil is also processed here. Cotton is also a useful accompaniment to coffee in its ability to occupy the dry sandy soils that coffee will not tolerate. Other products, like rice and milk, may be seen essentially as responses to the vicinity of great urban markets, and to the competition for land near the cities which ensures that only intensive farming may be practised. The once-marshy valley of the Paraíba, between Rio and São Paulo, is spotted with rice fields along its whole alluvial floor. Yields from the well-tended and irrigated fields are higher than in the Nordeste, because of better management and fertilizer use.

COFFEE

This crop has long been the great dynamo of Southeastern agriculture, and it is still a lead product, occupying over a million hectares. It was introduced commercially in the Paraiba Valley in the early nineteenth century, but the centre of the producing area shifted westwards into São Paulo state where, as the table shows, it was dominant from 1940 to after 1950, when Paraná became the top producer.

BRAZILIAN COFFEE PRODUCTION: PERCENTAGE TO MAJOR STATES

State	1940	1950	1960	1970	1980	1981
Sao Paulo	65	45	35	29	39	30
Paraná	6	14	47	56	16	22
Minas	17	20	10	9	19	34
Espirito Santo	8	16	4	4	15	8
Others	4	5	4	2	11	6

The extension into Paraná state was into a land of good soils, but land that was climatically marginal, located on the Paraná plateau and liable to occasional frosts from cold waves

moving north up the Brazilian coast from Argentina. After 1970, coffee was pushed back in part into São Paulo and Minas.

In coffee-growing there has been a cycle of production, starting with forest-clearing by subsistence pioneers, for maize or manioc, followed by coffee for 15 to 20 year, then sometimes abandonment of the land, or ejection of the first settlers by large land companies for ranching. This kind of phenomenon in São Paulo state was observed by the famous North American geographer Preston James. He termed it the 'Hollow Frontier' in reference to the lack of solid, permanent occupation after the coffee wave had moved through. James's view may have been true for the 1950s and 1960s, but today it seems less tenable. Katzmann (1977) argues that the frontier is only temporarily hollow, and that over time the pressure on land is filling in everywhere, with dairy farming zones, for example, being created to meet growing urban demand from some interior cities in lands formerly occupied by coffee.

One well-documented exception to the tendency for hollow frontiers is in North Paraná, where a private land colonization company has maintained stable settlements since 1924. In that year the N. Paraná Land Colonization Co. was formed in London, and purchased 2.5 million ha of public land on the Paraná Plateau at around 1000 m altitude. This was an area of good *terra roxa* soils, and the soils were based on the volcanic materials of the plateau. The company built up an infrastructure of 5000 km of roads and also new railway lines, as well as urban service centres for the farming lands. Village centres at 15 km intervals, with nearby market gardens, helped consolidate the settlement pattern. This became a successful and permanent settlement with 1.7 million inhabitants in the area by 1968. Physically it is not strictly comparable with James's frontier further north, as the southern soils are better, but the climate, with its frost liability, is a problem. In terms of agrarian structure the N. Paraná has problems too; family farming was the intention, replacing the traditional *fazenda* system, and the labour force was 47% composed of family members in 1940, but only 27% in 1960, as larger farms began to reassert themselves.

There is a final chapter in the coffee cycle, when soyabeans, a tiny crop in 1960, began to assume importance and replace coffee as the lead crop. Soyabean farmers, growing a rotation of soyabeans and wheat on commercial farms of 50–150 ha, are replacing the coffee farmers as world markets have favoured these crops. Coffee at 2096 million dollars (1983) has been replaced as the Brazilian lead farm export by soyabeans in the form of beans, milled soya flour, and oil, valued in all at 2563 million dollars (1983), or 11.7% of all merchandise exports. The 'soyabean frontier' has been pushed westwards by land companies, through Paraná, Rio Grande and São Paulo into Paraguay (see Chapter 13), where Brazilian companies have bought much land. One unfortunate feature is that mechanized soyabean farms use less labour than coffee farms.

Industries and cities

The resource base for heavy industry here in the Southeast is good. Minas has rich iron ores of near-pure haematite, adjacent to Belo Horizonte and to the Rio Doce valley. Of the 30 million tonnes annual production most goes down the valley

by railway to the port of Vitoria in Espirito Santo. Manganese, a useful alloy with steel, is also produced. Besides iron ore, there is abundant energy, from the Paraná river sites, such as Jupia and Ilha Solteira, but especially Itaipú. Brazil now has international transmission links to Argentina and can export some of her power surplus. Apart from hydroelectric power there is nuclear power in a programme which has been delayed for many years, starting with a plant near Rio. Offshore there are also new oil discoveries, especially in the Campos basin 100 km offshore in water nearly 1000 metres deep, one of a string of potentially oilbearing basins which could eliminate Brazil's external dependency on oil by the 1990s.

THE STEEL INDUSTRY (fig. 43)

Although textiles are still the main employing group of industries in Brazil, steel is more important in terms of its wages bill and links to other industries. Many of the dynamic growth industries, owned by foreign firms or multi-national corporations, are dependent on this steel in-

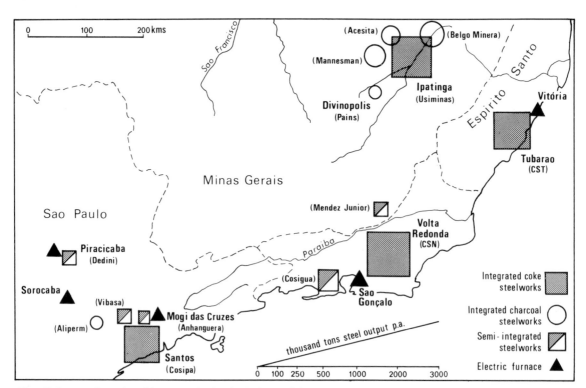

Fig. 43 Iron and steel making capacity in the Industrial Core, 1984

dustry and located in relation to it. The map pattern may be systematized as follows:

1. The non-integrated steel furnaces, rolling and shaping mills, in an aureole around São Paulo city; these were often set up as backward linkages by engineering firms which sought their own supply of steel. For example, one firm set up a steel works to make steel for its sugar-mill machinery industry. Many firms make special steels, requiring electric furnaces and using the abundant hydroelectric power supplied from stations on the escarpment to east of the city.

2. Fifty small blast furnaces making pig iron in the west of Minas province, based on cheap charcoal from plantation forests.

3. The large integrated iron and steel plants, government-owned in part, modern plants gaining economies of scale and through their use of modern technology. The main mills are CSN, at Volta Redonda, COSIPA at Santos, and USIMINAS at Ipatinga on the Doce.* The pull of urban markets has been important for COSIPA and Volta Redonda, charcoal and power for Ipatinga, but the main location factor has been the political pull of each state, São Paulo obtaining the Santos plant, Minas Gerais the Ipatinga one, and Volta Redonda representing an earlier (1940s', rather than 1950s') compromise between Rio and São Paulo, with a special mission in solving unemployment problems of the depression-hit Paraíba valley after 1930.

AUTOMOBILES

State intervention is equally if not more important in the automobile industry, which has grown up in the Greater São Paulo district. This started in the 1920s as assembly of American Ford and GM cars. In the 1950s laws were introduced which forced manufacturers to use local parts for cars sold in Brazil, and by 1960 over 90% of inputs were Brazilian. Through the 1960–80 period the industry blossomed, making 1.14 million vehicles in 1980 (World Bank, 1983). Volkswagen is the largest firm, with over 40% of the vehicles built, and the three great American firms, Ford, Chrysler and GM, with Mercedes Benz and Fiat, are all represented, as well as

* CSN is the Companhia Nacional Siderúrgica; COSIPA is the Companhia Siderúrgica Paulista; USIMINAS is the Uniao Siderúrgica de Minas Gerais.

small specialist car producers. This industry has been a major contributor to Brazil's new role as exporter of manufactured goods. In 1980 14% of production was exported.

The main concentration is at one suburb, São Bernardo do Campo, south of São Paulo, with six automobile plants. A slight dispersal has occurred because of urban congestion, into the Paraiba valley at São Jose (GM), and Taubate (Volkswagen), as well as to Campinas (Mercedes). A more distant move has been Fiat's new plant at Betím near Belo Horizonte, and its success at this distance from the main markets and from parts suppliers remains to be seen.

SÃO PAULO

Figure 42 shows the centrality of the two cities (of São Paulo and Rio de Janeiro) to all Brazil apart from the distinctive Nordeste. Of the two metropolises, São Paulo is the younger, an upstart of only 30000 in 1872 when Rio had 275000 inhabitants, but since about 1955 São Paulo has been the larger, with 7.2 million in 1975 to 4.9 million in Rio (metropolitan areas had 10 million and 8.3 million respectively). São Paulo is a visibly dynamic city, with great concrete skyscrapers in the centre and constant rebuilding on old sites (plate 34). São Paulo has always looked to the interior, as its plateau position suggests, depending on products from a wide hinterland, and producing goods for that hinterland and for itself. Industrially it is complex, but the car industry stands out as one notable concentration: Volkswagen plants here produce over half the Brazilian output of cars. Textiles, electrical goods, chemicals, paper, cement and leather working are all large industries, both in the city and in a number of industrial suburbs.

The city's population is varied in origin: many of the Paulistas are immigrants who came penniless to the coffee fazendas in the nineteenth century from all parts of Europe. These Spaniards, Germans, Jews and other groups from eastern Europe have been joined by an important group of Japanese. All migrants are represented in the city's commercial and industrial middle classes. Apart from this human resource, the city has advantages in its infrastructure for industry, including excellent transport connections to the interior of the state and along the coast to Rio, its own outlet in the

34 São Paulo — the city centre, with its many levels of vertical development, a result of its explosively rapid growth

port of Santos and a better power supply than any other Brazilian city, including Ilha Solteira and Itaipú on the Paraná.

RIO DE JANEIRO

This is a city of greater dignity, with a tradition of culture and the sophisticated society proper to a capital with long links with Europe. Its wealth grew on the sugar mills and naval garrison of the seventeenth century, and was augmented in the eighteenth by trade in gold and diamonds, which were brought out from the hinterland in Minas. It finally came into glory with its designation as capital in 1763, replacing Bahía. It still has some aspects of the traditional colonial city in its social patterns, including a large number of luxury dwellings near the centre rather than in the suburbs.

Compared to São Paulo, Rio exhibits only steady growth rates though it is still in second place in absolute population growth. The process of giving way to São Paulo was already begun when it was accelerated from 1956 by the beginning of Brasília, which quickly took away its federal government function, the last ministry to leave, protesting as it did so at relegation to the uncivilized interior, being the Foreign Ministry. Banking and financial operations, as well as the home offices of many large companies, remain in the city, and would seem more likely to move to São Paulo than to the interior.

Rio's industries are widely diversified, with textiles, clothing, printing and publishing, and food industries, employing the largest numbers, though even in publishing and printing São Paulo exceeds Rio in quantity if not in quality, with a larger circulation volume for her dailies and a larger list of books published every year. Though not comparable with São Paulo's, Rio has a small steel industry, the Cosigua company, which is to be built up to 1.5 million tonnes per annum maximum, using seaborne coal as does São Paulo. But Rio's energy base is weaker than that of her sister and this situation will change only marginally with the building of two more nuclear power stations at nearby Angra dos Reis, following Brazil's first such venture which is already in operation there.

As in São Paulo the suburbs, mostly in the area beyond the old federal district, have most of the new industrial growth, which seeks the open space totally unavailable in crowded Rio. Heroic efforts have been made to overcome the awkward geography of Rio's site: swamps near sea-level; *morros*, the sharp steepsided sugar-loaf mountains typical of tropical erosion eating into a long-weathered plateau surface; and connec-

tions to offshore islands — all have been conquered by means of tunnels, bridges and pumping systems. The new bridge to Niteroi across Guanabara bay is the latest in a long line of similar feats.

FAVELAS
Rio's shanty towns have an interesting relation to topography, occupying as the map (fig. 44) shows the edges of *morros* throughout the city. In contrast with other South American cities, *favelas* are not peripheral, but are scattered through the city, spreading out with it through time, and growing with particular strength from about 1940, so that they now hold over 10 per cent of the urban population, despite clearance

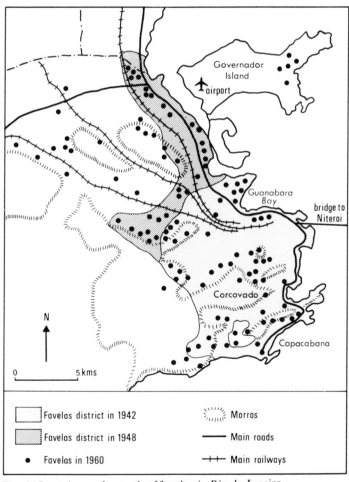

Fig. 44 Location and growth of favelas *in Rio de Janeiro*

programmes. *Favelas* are often grouped near industrial zones, where their occupants may work, near the rail lines on land undesirable for building, and on marshy land, as well as on the *morros*, in fact wherever there has been unused and accessible land in the city. *Favelas* are a symbol of the life of the poor in Rio and in all Brazil; the *cariocas* (Rio dwellers) also have other expressions of their interest and vitality, notably the February carnival, essentially and in origin a feast of the poor of the city, with many African elements in its dances and songs.

THE SOUTH

The southern panhandle of Brazil may be treated alongside the Southeast because of several similarities it has with it, including its high per capita wealth, good resource base, and situation on the important river Plate–São Paulo axis, which ensures its long-term importance for trade and industry.

This is non-tropical Brazil, and because it lies mostly above 200 m altitude, frost and snow are possible as well as changeable middle-latitude weather brought in along the coast from the south. Climatic uniqueness in Brazil, the resource of the south, allows temperate crops, such as wheat, soya beans and potatoes, to be produced, middle-latitude grasslands in Rio Grande do Sul which support large beef herds of cattle, and middle-latitude forests of Paraná pine (*Araucaria angustifolia*) and other species occurring in single species stands. Temperateness of climate no doubt helped in attracting the immigrants who came to the southern states during the nineteenth century and allowing their successful settlement. It must be admitted however that the immediate coastal belt where the immigrants first landed was subtropical in character and more suitable for crops of tobacco and sugar cane, still grown there, than for North European crops.

Landforms are dominated by the great Paraná plateau, with its sharp east-facing scarp and gentle tilt to the west. The coastal plain is tiny in the north but in Rio Grande prograding has built out the plain and forms the Lagoa dos Patos, behind sand bars and dunes, and the Lagoa Mirim which extends south into Uruguay. Behind these shallow lakes, the southern plain is continued as the campanha, an open prairie.

Settlement and agriculture

Original settlement was very thin in this border region. A few trading posts were scattered along the trails used to bring cattle north to the great fair at Sorocaba near São Paulo, from the southern grasslands, including some essentially military settlements, to consolidate claims on this southern territory, which was also claimed by Spain. Colônia do Sacramento in Uruguay was the southernmost of the line of posts marking Brazilian pretensions.

Agricultural colonization dates only from the early nineteenth century, and had a slow start, with a few small settlements in favoured parts of the Rio Grande and Santa Catarina coast, first by Germans, then by Italians, who were forced to take up the nearby areas of the plateau after 1870 when the valleys were filled, followed by Slavic groups who moved still further inland and into Paraná state. Though the numbers of settlers were small, their influence was important, for they established in Brazil for the first time a small-farmer and owner-operator type of farming, on plots of 20-50 ha, an economy quite different from the great cattle *fazendas* of the South.

MIGRANTS

There was something of a mutual exclusion between cattle men and cultivators, for the new settlers chose the woodland, unwanted by the cattle ranchers who relied on natural grasslands for their herds. The new men did more than change land use; they introduced their own types of house construction, as in southern Chile, and built carefully, with fences, windmills, sheds and other buildings designed for permanent occupation, in contrast with the shifting agriculture which was hitherto the only common form of cultivation by small farmers. Crop rotation and the use of animal manure allowed this permanent occupation of a single plot of land. Wandering into the interior, some of the new immigrants eventually gave up their European way of farming and became *caboclos* like the mestizos of the region, using no capital or machinery, but these were a minority and the region as a whole has a high level of productivity and farm organization; farm cooperatives are a good index of farmer education and technical levels, and the South has 500 of them, or 30 per cent of the Brazilian total. Extension agencies also provide a better service in this region than in any other.

RANCHERS

Estancias have remained the dominant land users on the *campanha* of Rio Grande do Sul, great cattle ranches worked like their neighbours on the other side of the Uruguayan border by a few *gauchos* (the term of all the Pampas lands for the cowboy, rather than *vaqueiro* as further north) who herd the animals but provide little in the way of hygiene or care. Some *estancieros* have improved their herds with pedigree stock but the grass quality is low as it is natural cover in a subtropical environment with little attempt at seeding or improvement. Carrying capacity is very low, less than one animal per hectare on many ranches, and the economic size of ranch is thus many thousands of hectares.

FORESTS

A major mineral resource is the southern forest. This is of commercial value because generally composed of large stands of only one species, and the Paraná pine forests, on the cool dry heights above 1000 m, are of particular interest, forming the basis of a useful export trade in timber. All three southern states produce large quantities of wood, though the most valuable, and much of the Paraná pine, is from Rio Grande. Paper mills are most important in Paraná, though new developments are extending this industry into Santa Catarina. All Brazilian forests have a 'collecting' economy, based in the Amazon on Brazil nuts, in the Northeast on carnauba palms or babaçu. In the South it is Indian tea, *erva mate* (in Spanish *yerba mate*), which is still collected from wild trees in Rio Grande do Sul, and to a lesser extent in other southern states, as well as from plantations of the tree in a few places.

Another mineral resource is coal, and all of Brazil's five million tons' annual production comes from the South, mostly from Santa Catarina, secondly from Rio Grande. Production is being encouraged to try to reduce Brazilian dependence on imports of fuel from overseas. More important than the coal is the hydro power, available on the Paraná tributaries such as the Iguacu, soon to be tapped at Salto de Santiago and Salto Osorio on this river.

The cities

Pôrto Alegre, Florianopolis and Curitiba, the three state capitals, are thriving cities, particularly the first, a city whose metropolitan area

has 2 million, and where construction is proceeding at a rate only exceeded in São Paulo and Rio, much of it being factories for the budding industries. Pôrto Alegre is a town of relatively rich people, compared with the rest of Brazil, with many cars and few shanty towns. Its factories make engineering products such as wires and cables, machine tools, items using special steels, as well as products for a growing farm sector, such as farm machinery and fertilizers. It has access to the coastal trade via a six-metre channel. Caxias do Sul, a few kilometres north of Pôrto Alegre, Novo Hamburgo and São Leopoldo share in this industrial growth, with engineering works, textile mills, *bodegas* and flour mills. These industries have grown up from the capital investments of the small independent farmers, who have thus proved the advantage of their type of farming over one dominated by large landowners with tenants.

Florianopolis is a more provincial centre, with a population of 154 000, an administrative rather than industrial centre, and a hinterland which is nearly all plateau, having little of the rich coastal plain. Curitiba (844 000), state capital to Paraná state, is well-placed to administer the plateau section, though its position (at 905 m altitude) is a disadvantage for the coastal region, and a separate major urban centre has emerged at Paranagua. This port has recently seen a new burst of activity because of the new trade from Paraguay, which country has free-port facilities at this site. Passengers can also travel by bus from Asunción in one day to this point. Much of Paranagua's trade is now international and the value of trade makes it second only to Santos in Brazil. Other transport links are also being developed in the Panhandle, never formerly well connected to any other area. The rail link Pôrto Alegre–São Paulo is being improved and shortened in length, and the coastal road has been paved over its whole distance to São Paulo. The international road and rail links to Uruguay, Argentina and Paraguay are all being rapidly upgraded.

PROSPECTS FOR THE CORE REGION

A Brazilian megalopolis?

In terms of physical resources, the Core Region, South and Southeast, is better provided than other parts of the country. Even its soil, located in more temperate belts, is less prone to erosion and depletion than further north. These resources, but more the human resource which is conveyed in the names of the great cities, serve to reinforce the centripetal dynamics of socio-economic evolution in the country. Both labour and capital are evidently attracted more readily to the centre than to any peripheral region. The reasons for this dynamism of the centre cannot be investigated in detail here, but they are the same as those noted for other countries in the continent, and some account of them is given in the chapters on population and industrial development.

Looking ahead to predict future population and related patterns is particularly difficult in a country like Brazil, where population growth rate is nearly 3 per cent, where the modal family size is 6–9 persons, and where migration to cities is continuing apace. It is confidently, and by many Brazilians proudly, predicted that the present population of 125 million will reach 210 million by the year 2000. Of these, some 70 million are likely to be in the Rio–São Paulo–Belo Horizonte triangle, the Megalopolis of Brazil, with three of Brazil's millionaire cities. The others are Recife, Salvador and Pôrto Alegre, and one vision of the Brazilian Megalopolis is a 1600-km stretch along the coast including all these cities, but this seems to distort the idea of Megalopolis too much; the urbanized area loses its unity.

On the other hand, to think of this triangle as a single conurbation would be wrong; it is 550 km on the longest leg, São Paulo to Belo Horizonte, and there will be open ground over large areas for farming, recreation and forest in the Serra do Mar and Serra da Mantiqueira. It may quite definitely be thought of as a unit for considerations such as atmospheric pollution, sewerage disposal, water supply and consumption patterns, and land use competition, like its North American equivalent on the New York to Washington axis, and it will present equal problems in congestion and planning optimal land-use patterns.

It is perhaps disturbing to think of a basically centripetal growth of population and economy when the oecumene of the nation is being stretched out to new frontiers in the west and north. Yet this centrifugal movement is to be viewed as part of the same process of growth which causes massing in the centre; the higher the pyramid being built, the broader must be the base. This metaphor is not the ideal one, for the shape of the curve of population densities, from distant frontiers to metropolitan areas, is likely to be strongly concave; more appropriate then is that of the giant selvas tree, for example the Brazil-nut tree, with a narrow but very high peak, flourishing in the sunlight and nourishing itself from roots spreading over a great area of the forest floor.

18. The Guianas

Perhaps the most obvious examples of colonial economy in Latin America are to be found in the Guianas. In these countries, there was a straightforward, uncomplicated development of plantation economy from the time of earliest European settlement, to feed European mouths with American sugar and other foodstuffs. There was never any need to modify this economy by adjusting to local labour availability or local customs, nor by any orientation to local urban markets or commercial centres. Instead, in the Guianas, European capital and African labour were brought together in a new land where all social and economic options were open to them. Logically, they chose the best land for production and for accessibility from the coast, and established the plantation economy, an efficient means of producing commercial surpluses of valuable tropical farm products. The forms and organizations established in the plantations are still responsible today for many patterns in the man-made environment of the Guianas.

SETTLEMENTS: FROM INTERIOR TO COAST

To the first explorers, Guiana was a name given to all the lands from Orinoco to Amazon, but within this great stretch of country only the three former north European colonies, British, Dutch and French Guiana, are considered here. By their political and cultural attachments to northern Europe, these countries have come to have a distinct identity, and are certainly quite different from neighbouring territories in Brazil or Venezuala.

The principal Spanish base on mainland South America was at Darien, in Panama, far from Guiana, where there were no strong attractions, either in the form of docile Indians or as gold or precious metals. The Darien base was early confirmed by its accessibility to the Pacific and by the discovery of Peru, leaving the Guianas without action till the 1590s, when Sir Walter Raleigh, hearing of gold in the interior, explored the Orinoco in search of a hidden El Dorado; in all probability this mythical source of gold was rumoured by the Spanish to divert Raleigh's attention from more profitable areas such as the Peruvian wealth which they were exploiting themselves in the Andes. In any case, no gold was found, and no further luck was had in English attempts at settlement in the decade from 1600 to 1610, made on the river Oyapok.

Permanent settlements date only from the 1610s, when Dutchmen established themselves on the Mazaruni, incorporating these colonies with others elsewhere in the Indies under the Dutch West India Company, which used the *patroon* system. This social—administrative institution gave feudal rights to any merchant or landowner who would bring in settlers and buy land, and operated as well here as in New York State area within what was to be the United States. Dutch settlement centred first on the island fort of Kijk-over-al, in the Mazaruni river, and produced sugar and tobacco. Settlements grew in 1640s, with the colonists driven out of Brazil, and the Pomeroon and Essequibo rivers were settled and put to sugar. In these lands, the coastal area, a flat and lowlying malarial plain with frequent flooding, was shunned from the beginning. Instead, settlements were made on the edge of the plain or even within the sterile White Sands zone behind it.

In Surinam, attempts were made by the English and French to settle in the 1630s, but permanent colonies date from 1650. Here the success factor seems to have been management by men with experience of the tropics, for the founder was Lord Willoughby, governor of Barbados, who made a start by establishing good relations with the Amerindians.* This had been a major stumbling block in previous settlement attempts. An important contingent of colonists was the Jewish one, coming from Brazil along with the expelled Dutch.

The coastal frontier

By the eighteenth century, flourishing colonies on the rivers, especially those of present-day Guyana, the Essequibo, Pomeroon, Berbice, and Demerara, but also the Surinam, were established under Dutch rule. In the French section no poldering or irrigation was carried out as in the other areas, and agricultural production was slight. In the second half of the century, growing demand for sugar and cotton required good soils and African slave labour was employed on a large scale to extend coastwards the polder and irrigation system. At the same time, the poor soils of the White Sands zone could not support prolonged intensive exploitation and the land here was abandoned and reverted to forest. The centre of economic activity thus moved downstream, Stabroek (Georgetown from 1812) on the lower Demerara becoming capital in 1783, to replace Kijk-over-al, while on the Berbice, settlement moved down eighty km to New Amsterdam in the same period.

Effectively, the move downstream onto the new polders was a colonization towards the coast, the opposite of that conducted towards the interior in most of the other countries of the

continent. It may be regarded as a technical frontier, subject to poldering abilities, rather than a small-farmer spread in search of open lands, and for this reason it had no democratizing influence in terms of land ownership and frontier society. The polders were all taken up by plantations, excluding the small farmer even if he had been present in numbers sufficient to demand more farming land.

Ethnic mixture

Population structure began to change with the large slave influx (over 300000 into Surinam alone) and with additions of European origin. Dutch colonies were open to all nationalities from 1738, in contrast with Spanish and Portuguese areas which excluded foreigners. In the nineteenth century abolition of slavery forced a search for new labour, as the ex-slaves often left the plantations as soon as they were free to do so. This labour crisis was solved by bringing in indentured servants from southeast Asia, poor peasants who were willing to accept tough conditions of work. They came on five-year contracts, passage paid but with no pay until half the contract period was over. Indians, Chinese and Javanese all came to Surinam in great numbers. In French Guiana, few labourers could be attracted because of the evil reputation of the colony, which was used as a penal settlement. A few indentured labourers came to the Guianas from Europe, most notably Portuguese from Madeira; these soon moved from plantations to town, as did the Chinese, becoming shopkeepers and merchants. In all, this influx of migrants pushed the Amerindian population far into the backcountry, where it forms a small and independent minority living a semi-subsistence economic life and enjoying its own non-western culture.

PHYSICAL GEOGRAPHY

The Guianas are formed out of the ancient Guiana Shield, a block once attached to the Brazilian Shield but separated in the Tertiary when the Amazon basin came into being. There is little evidence of tectonic activity, for the most ancient sediments, the sandstones of the Pakaraima mass, have been flatlying since their deposition in Precambrian times. These sandstones are responsible for *mesa* landforms, with sheer rocky

---

* The term Amerindian, used in Guyana, will be used here to distinguish American Indians from the immigrants from the Indian subcontinent who came into Guiana as indentured servants in the nineteenth century.

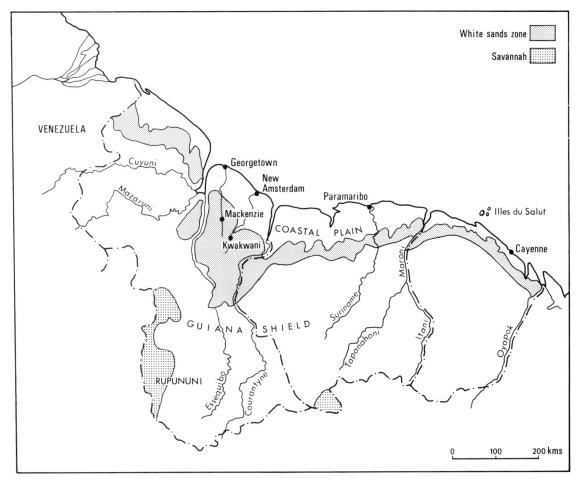

Fig. 45 Physical map of the Guianas

cliff edges, overlying a crystalline plateau which forms most of the interior, a hilly, heavily forested land. Fringing the shield is a narrow coastal plain, formed of marine mud, much of it washed along the coast from the Amazon mouth, a belt 15 to 80 km wide (fig. 45). It is in this narrow plain that 80% of the people and practically all agricultural land is located. Locally there are savanna areas, on the White Sands and far into the interior, in the Rupununi.

Climatically, the region is equatorial, with year-round high temperatures and rainfall. Near the coast, the combination of heat and humidity is tolerable while sea breezes blow, which is for most of the time as the trades are fairly consistent here. In the interior, both rainfall and humidity are lower. Whereas 2250 mm annual rainfall is common on the coast, interior mountains have around 1500 mm and the Rupununi savanna 1000 mm per annum.

RESOURCES

Agricultural land is concentrated near the coast because of the problems of erosion on steep slopes inland, and poor lateritic soils on the flatter areas, or unproductive soils of the White Sands region. Isolation and lack of any infrastructure are other obvious drawbacks. Mineral resources of the shield are however substantial. Over much of the interior there are broad surfaces of deep weathering and laterization, forming in some cases bauxite, a laterite with large amounts of aluminium oxide. Currently these ores are mined only on the edge of the plain, but their existence is known from surveys of the interior as well. Apart from bauxite, there has been irregular working of other minerals though generally without any mechanization and thus not tapping major ore bodies.

The mountains harbour another resource, hydroelectric power, already tapped at dams for alumina and aluminium production in Surinam. A major difficulty here is the lack of natural deep basins to contain reservoirs, at least in areas accessible to the coast. Fossil fuels are not found, though there is mounting interest in offshore deposits of petroleum which have already been identified.

GUYANA

The neo-plantation economy

The former colony of British Guiana became a sovereign state in 1966, remaining a member of the British Commonwealth till 1970, since when it has been a republic with a markedly Socialist regime. Like the other Guianas, one obvious characteristic of the nation is its varied population, dominated by Creoles or Africans who make up some 30% of the total, and Asians who form 50%, though exercising less influence in the community than their numbers suggest. Portuguese and other European peoples form small minorities. Amerindians are about 5% of the population, geographically isolated from all other groups in the interior. Guyana is the most important of the three former colonies, in terms

of population size and economy, with a fair variety of export products though dominated by bauxite and alumina.

Physically this is the most diversified of the Guianas, sharing with Venezuela the large region of dissected sandstone tablelands which present superb cliff scenery and waterfalls such as the famous Kaieteur Falls, and many still little-known ones in the deep interior. There are four principal physical regions, the first being the coastal plain of alluvium and marine mud, with associated backswamps and lakes. Behind this lies the leached White Sands belt, with savanna and scrub forest, at its widest on the Berbice river. Behind this again is the forested shield country, with overlying sandstones of the Pakaraima and other ranges. In the far southwest the Rupununi forms a last region of open savanna plains.

The human landscape

The drama of nature cannot be matched by man's efforts in Guyana, restricted to a narrow strip of land, but making a definite impact in this limited zone. Flat land has suited the plantation economy based on sugar which has proved more stable here than elsewhere in the Guianas. A landscape of ordered, straightline patterns, both for settlement and agriculture, is the norm throughout the plantation area. The city of Georgetown is similarly on an open, rectangular plan of precise lines, though its houses are not for the most part of any great age, as fires have repeatedly destroyed the light wooden buildings on low brick bases. In aspect, the town is like a

COMPARATIVE STATISTICS FOR THE GUIANAS

	Guyana	Surinam	French Guiana
Population (1983)	918 000	351 000	70 000
Area (sq. km)	215 000	163 000	91 000
GNP per capita (dollars, 1982)	520	3 520	3 230
Infant mortality (%, 1982)	41	34	29
Exports f.o.b. (million US dollars, 1982)	241	429	33
Imports c.i.f. (million US dollars, 1982)	280	511	250
Crop land (%)	2.3	0.4	0.1

Sources: UN Statistical Yearbook (*New York, 1983*), UN Demographic Yearbook (*New York, 1983*), World Bank Atlas (*Washington D.C., 1985*).

southern United States county town, with two-storey verandahed houses, spacious treelined streets and a slightly somnolent air.

Economic infrastructure

A principal infrastructural element is the water system, including sea wall, drainage and irrigation ditches. Flooding by the sea is possible for eight or more kilometres inland, and further inland still, river flooding must be guarded against. The present sea wall was built between 1874 and 1882, its concrete and stone replacing and augmenting earlier earth walls. Through the sea wall, sluices or kokers allow the exit of fresh water from drainage ditches; they open at low tide to allow drainage and close to keep out the sea at high tide. In addition, steam pumps replacing nineteenth-century windmills are used to eliminate excess river water. Behind the sea wall, estates run back in long lines from the sea and river fronts, backed by a second wall to keep out excess river water. Behind the back walls, accumulated river and rain water form shallow lakes, known as conservancies since they are a water reserve for the irrigation of the plantation lands.

Control of all water works comes under a separate government department which coordinates all local systems. This department has recently been active in increasing the reserves available in the conservancies, with the special aim of extending the land area for rice fields. This policy is certainly increasing production, though only absorbing a small part of the excess rural labour force.

Apart from the water works, infrastructure is sadly lacking. Only one decent road is in existence, along the coast, and even this is not completely paved. Inland, transport depends on the rivers, or on state air lines which use light aeroplanes and makeshift airfields. A railway, claiming to be the oldest in South America, runs from Georgetown to a point opposite New Amsterdam, and private lines run short distances between mines and rivers, but these do not add up to a system.

Agriculture

While most agricultural land is in small farms, typically under four hectares and worked by peasant farmers, about 20% belongs to twelve great sugar plantations of over 400 ha; these are the remnants of formerly extensive plantations which occupied nearly all farm land in the colony. They are no longer traditional plantations, but neo-plantations, where few workers are employed and mechanization is well advanced, using modern technology.

Sugar is grown as a monoculture on the great estates. Machinery is used for preparing ditches and ridging the land when too wet and in need of drainage, and fertilizers and pesticides are applied from the air (plate 35). Thus labour requirements are low and irregular, most being needed for cane cutting with the traditional cutlass, when temporary hands are taken on to supplement the small permanent labour force. Sugar-cane is grown continuously for eight to nine years and then put to flood fallow, land being flooded for several months to add new fertile alluvial topsoil. The product, bulky cane, is brought by barge trains along estate canals to the sugar mills within the estate, then coarse unrefined sugar from these mills is taken by coaster to the Sugar Terminal at Georgetown for loading onto ships and export, making a major contribution to national foreign trade earnings.

Most sugar was grown on the plantations of one firm, Booker McConnell, a British company whose interests extend through subsidiary companies into manufacturing and service activities. In sugar, it controlled all production from ditch laying and cleaning to the transport overseas in ocean-going ships. Most of its plantations were concentrated around the lower Demerara river, close to Georgetown. Concentration of plantations under a single foreign owner emphasizes the plantation-orientation of the whole economy, and makes it more dependent, like any colonial economy, on market conditions, enterprise and politics in a distant country. Booker's interests in Guyana have since 1977 been taken over by the government, but dependency remains important.

Rice, a staple of all the coastal peoples and now an export crop as well (though still second to sugar), is produced on 100 000 ha by the Indian small farmers who came bringing the grain from East Asia in the nineteenth century and have always grown it as a subsistence crop. Two crops a year are possible if water is available, or alternatively the land may be grazed over by cattle after a single harvest. Besides rice, there is small-scale market gardening and some citrus production around the towns. All these farming

35 Cane-cutting can be mechanized, but most sugar cane is still hand-cut in Guyana

patterns are however subordinate to sugar, the leading farm product.

Away from the coastal area there are other patterns. In the deep interior forests, the Amerindians live on shifting cultivation just as they do in neighbouring Venezuela and Brazil, in good ecological adjustment to the land, though the balance is now threatened by the advance of commercial farming from the coast. The only commercial area of production is the Rupununi, where there are large ranches shipping out carcasses of cattle reared on the coarse savanna grasses, nowadays using air freight rather than the long overland trail which still exists between this region and the coast.

Minerals

Guyana has a long history as a source of precious metals, and gold is still panned in the interior and diamonds taken out of the Pakaraima Mountains, though in tiny quantities and by single miners, the pork-knockers as they are called because of their former reliance on salt pork rations. In modern times timber has been a modest contributor to exports and there is a large untapped resource of good hardwoods. Only the greenheart, still used in dock and harbour works, is important among the timbers. Manganese is an important modern ore, produced in the Matthews Ridge area of the north, but bauxite is the main mineral of value, developed since the First World War by the Aluminium Company of Canada (Alcan), at Mackenzie, now renamed Linden, on the Demerara river. A smaller unit is on the Berbice at Kwakwani. Bauxite is widespread and other less accessible areas will no doubt be exploited in time. In 1961, an alumina plant was set up at Linden, so that bauxite and

36 A punt train on a sugar estate, which takes the bulky produce to cane mills along the irrigation canals

alumina are now both exported, and rank among the principal export products.

At present Guyana has an agreement with Trinidad to send alumina there to be smelted at a new smelter using natural gas. But longer-term plans would seem to favour smelting within Guyana itself, because of its considerable power potential, and there is a plan to utilize a site at Latipu on the upper, mountain course of the Mazaruni river, for a large dam with hydro-electric output eventually at 1500 to 2000 mega-watts. Even with a Guyanese smelter at Linden, about half of this power would be excess to national requirements and other power-hungry industries would presumably be the market, as neighbouring parts of Venezuela are supplied by the Guri dam on the Caroní, and Surinam with a big new complex planned on the Courantyne can scarcely be expected to import electricity.

Gearing to foreign markets, large units of operation, small labour requirements and limited processing of the minerals, make for a mineral 'enclave' economy comparable to plantation agriculture. Although Alcan and Reynolds were nationalized in 1971, refining and smelting have not been expanded for want of capital and international companies have expanded bauxite operations in other parts of the world.

Social structure and the urbanization process
Guyana was thinly peopled by an Amerindian population base, over which have been laid African and Asian elements, while Dutch, British and other Europeans occupied the towns. Much has been made of the diversity in ethnic and racial backgrounds by observers of the Guyana scene, and the topic has had a political aspect because of some polarization of political feeling

according to ethnic groupings. Currently the dominant ethnic group is the African, which supports the government of Forbes Burnham. Progressive integration of the different groups is being fostered and it is claimed that the old rivalries are now being eliminated.

GROUP MIGRATION WAVES

Following independence, some Europeans left the country. This has created a vacuum in the top echelons of power in politics and commerce, to be rapidly filled by people of African origin, who have moved up out of lower middle class jobs in offices and small shops in the towns, jobs which they have tended to monopolize during the first half of this century. As these urbanites have moved up the economic and social ladder, they have in turn been replaced by East Indians in the small shops and offices, and by the sons of peasant farmers or labourers on the plantations who have acquired a minimum education and who have insufficient land to support them well in agriculture. On the plantations themselves, the large East Indian group is still dominant, itself somewhat divided between Moslem and Hindu groups. These are the most traditional and least educated groups, holding onto a near peasant existence, and with least experience in the new land of America.

Group migrations may of course be seen as nothing more than the general process of rural to urban migration going on all over Latin America, but in this example we can see that the migration is not a disordered mass movement into towns but one affecting specific groups with greater or lesser intensity according to qualifications and group background. Similar regularities of migration patterns may no doubt be seen in the other countries.

THE AMERINDIANS: THE AKAWAIO CASE

Group migrations form a chain reaction involving all groups except the Amerindians, who have been artificially excluded from social interaction by legislation dating from the early part of this century. This legislation was enacted with the laudable intentions of protecting the group from the exploitation of their labour which was then beginning to emerge, but it served in the long run to isolate them both racially and culturally from the newer occupants of the land.

One major question is land rights. In 1966, when Britain handed over to the rulers of the new country, one condition was that the Amerindians be given legal rights to the land they occupied. A commission was set up to investigate and report on this matter, which it did in 1969, recommending title grants to many tribes, but little was done because of a reported difficulty in surveying the lands in question. Among the tribes were the 4000 members of the Akawaio tribe in the upper Mazaruni country, the colourful hill country northeast of mount Roraima. This tribe is threatened by the proposed construction of the new dam referred to above, at Latipu, which if built will have a reservoir of 250000 ha, covering almost all the tribal lands, and the central government seems determined to proceed with the project despite powerful reasons for not doing so. One is the fact that the Akawaio will lose their lands. Another is the availability of other sites, notably one on the lower Mazaruni, generating less power but quite sufficient for Guyanese demands over the next decade and causing no disturbance to Amerindians. Yet another reason for leaving the upper Mazaruni alone is that it lies near a frontier disputed with Venezuela, where there is a moratorium signed in 1970 and forbidding any unilateral action to enhance one country's claims on the land.

Questions concerning Guyana's Amerindians must be expected to arise with increasing frequency now as a policy of integration replaces the former quarantine in which the tribes were placed. So far, as in Brazil, humanitarian concerns in this integration have not been conspicuous and land greed on the part of modern farmers and even central governments must be feared by the defenceless tribes.

SURINAM

A plantation socio-economic structure was established in the mid-seventeenth century in the lower valleys of the Surinam and Cottica rivers. It developed principally after 1667, when the territory was given to Holland as recompense for New York, which the British had captured three years earlier. Today, Surinam shows the hand of Dutch architects and engineers in its tiny settled strip, which has never expanded since the eighteenth century and has even retreated coastwards from the interior edge of the plain.

Paramaribo (182 000 in 1964), the capital, has Dutch eighteenth-century styles in some public buildings, copied faithfully in wood. Dutch influence is also present in the straight lines of villages in the plain, though only the newer properties have truly rectangular outlines, and old plantation lands have been subdivided along irregular division lines.

As in Guyana, a narrow coastal plain is backed by slightly rolling or flat countryside of dissected old terraces, the White Sands zone, with a savanna or scrub cover (fig. 45). The back-country is the gneiss and granite of the shield, thickly forested with hardwoods. Southwards the land is higher and reaches over 500 metres in the Tumac Humac mountains on the Brazilian border. Main rivers in the dense stream network are the Courantyne or Corantijn on the Guyana boundary, the Coppename, Saramacca, Suriname, and on the French Guiana border the Marowijne (Maroni).

Settlement and population

The Dutch plantation colony enjoyed relative prosperity until 1712, when French corsairs raided along the coast and started a negative trend in the colony's fortunes. Negroes were taken from the plantations by their masters to hide from the pirates, and some escaped from slavery at this time, never to return, but forming instead an independent group which raised the plantations and liberated more slaves, thus swelling the ranks of a Bush Negro group which survives to this day. After slavery, indentured labour from India and Java came in, but plantations were unable to progress because of Dutch refocussing on a commercially more interesting area, Java, with its rich soils that could readily be put to sugar. Settlement in Surinam declined, plantations were abandoned in inland parts, and the country came into this century with few prospects, eventually to be resuscitated by a new economic colonialism, that of bauxite.

Population patterns today are somewhat distinct from those of Guyana, for sand and shell ridges break up the settled area of the coastal plain; in addition, settlement tends to penetrate farther up the rivers than in Guyana, for these rivers give quite good access to the interior. In Guyana, they are obstructed at the inner edge of the plain by rapids impeding navigation such as that of the river steamers used in Surinam. Sixty

per cent of the population lives in and around Paramaribo, and in a few small towns linked to it by the coast road. Paramaribo's population is very mixed, including Europeans of all kinds, as well as Chinese, Indians and Javanese. As in Guyana, a selective migration process has taken some groups into the city, leaving others, later comers, in the rural areas, most notably the Javanese, but also many Indian small farmers.

GOVERNMENT POLICY AND RACIAL MIXTURES

In the remoter inland areas there are definite racial groupings, partly because of a government policy which allowed these groups to form villages and take over estate lands when abandoned, in order not to let them revert to forest. Thus, for example, there are villages on the middle Suriname, Saramacca and Tapanahony rivers, inhabited solely by Bush Negroes; in the far interior there are many purely Amerindian villages.

Bush Negroes however make up only 8% of the population and Amerindians only 2%. In general, a broad cultural unity is being imposed on the diverse ethnic groups by modern education and compulsory instruction in the Dutch language for all young people. The melting-pot effect is particularly strong in the urban areas. National costumes and the old slave tongue which was commonly used in the seventeenth and eighteenth centuries have disappeared in the standardization of modern life.

The mineral-exporting economy

Surinam, far more than Guyana, is a one-product economic unit. Eighty per cent of its exports are made up of bauxite and alumina, compared to 45% in Guyana. If Guyana may be categorized as a neo-plantation economy, Surinam has a mining economy organized in plantation manner, that is, production by largely foreign firms, for foreign markets, with heavy investment of foreign capital and relatively little labour. Investment in mining is of course the more striking because in the country generally there is very little capital investment, and the economic infrastructure is tiny. Roads, railways, ports and power from electricity or whatever source are poorly provided. One major hydro-power development has been made on the Suriname river above Paramaribo, but it is in connection with industrial needs for aluminium production and would scarcely have been developed for urban consumer needs. Paramaribo has the only modern port, with improved facilities in recent years, financed largely from Europe because of Surinam's links to the EEC through Holland.

MINING

Bauxite is the lifeblood of the modern economy, providing 35% of GDP but 80% of exports in recent years. Surinam has advanced from being

a mere bauxite shipper to aluminium and alumina manufacturer, which serves to bring some diversification, but still within a framework dependent on one basic product.

Bauxite was first developed at Moengo, near the French Guiana border, after the First World War. In 1941, Paranam (fig. 46) became the principal mining site on the Suriname river, using coastal bauxites as at Moengo. In both areas production is at low cost because the ores are rich, containing over 50 per cent usable oxide, with only moderate overburden. A major change

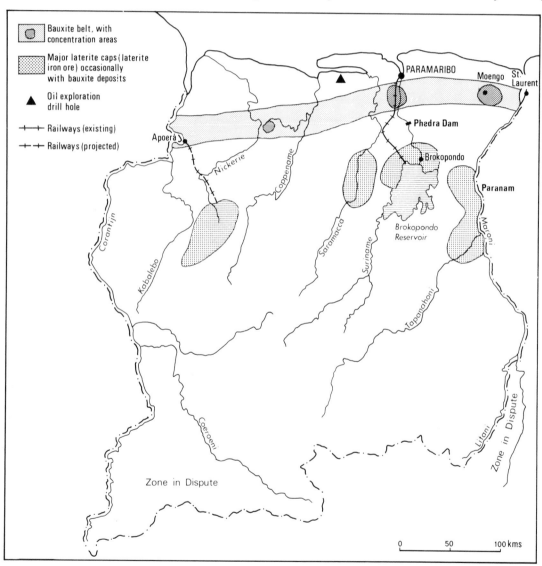

Fig. 46 Bauxite and aluminium industries of Surinam

in the bauxite economy came in 1959, when the big Brokopondo project was completed. This involved a dam on the Suriname river, generation of hydroelectricity for refining and smelting nearby at Paranam, and the production of alumina and aluminium for export, so that these products now far exceed bauxite in value of exports.

Ecological problems

Most recently, there have been important developments in the Bakhuis Mountains, in western Surinam, where a large lateritic cap of 45 per cent aluminium oxide is known and has been surveyed. This is to be developed by the Reynolds Metal Company of the United States, in partnership with the Surinam government. Ore will be sent by rail to Apoera on the Corantijn river and smelted there using hydro power from the Kabalebo, a tributary of the Corantijn.

This project, like the existing Brokopondo one, has a major potential ecological and economic effect, for the associated dams cause flooding of huge stretches of forest country, in the absence of deep basin-shaped valleys suited for storing water in a small space. A general impoverishment of wildlife in the area takes place, while in economic terms the huge lakes could have the effect of sterilizing the whole interior by putting a neutral or negative belt across the middle country, flooding land of little current value and with only a thin population, but possibly important to future generations. It is a symbol of the power of the bauxite kingdom that pre-emption of vast areas has been permitted and even encouraged by the authorities.

The ecological problems are best exhibited at Brokopondo, where a 1500 sq. km lake was formed in rainforest country, the trees being allowed to rot as flooding went on, acidifying the reservoir water and thus rusting the metal components at the dam site, so that costs were greatly increased over the original budget. Water hyacinth and floating ferns also covered most of the lake within two years, and herbicide sprays to control the vegetation caused further problems by poisoning the water and its fish population.

Agriculture

Agricultural production is confined strictly to the coastal strip, and most land is in small farms, principally for rice. The old plantation economy has disappeared. Paddy rice is grown along the whole coast, but most intensively around Paramaribo and in the Wageningen estate in the west, established in 1949 with Dutch assistance as a mechanized unit producing high-quality rice for export. Small farmers operating around Paramaribo for the town markets usually own less than 4 hectares of rice-land. Sugar, once the principal crop, is today grown only by two plantations. Coffee and cocoa, other former cash crops, are now also unimportant, though some commercial production is beginning to reappear, in banana and other fruit production for export to Europe.

FRENCH GUIANA

Beside Guyana and Surinam the French effort in their segment of the Guianas seems slight. Physical reasons for the lack of progress are not at once apparent, since the country continues the same zones found to the west in Surinam, though the coastal plain, the all-important lowland, becomes narrow and somewhat discontinuous. In the interior, the shield country is heavily forested for the most part though with savanna breaks, and access is made difficult by the rapids sections on the rivers.

In the early seventeenth century when British and Dutch Guiana were first settled, this section of the coast seems to have attracted no settlers. From the time the French acquired it in 1667, little was done until the nineteenth century and there are records of poor relations with the Amerindian population. From the mid-nineteenth century the French, in tacit admission of their failure to achieve civil settlement, set up penal colonies, both along the Maroni river near St Laurent and on the Iles du Salut, notorious for their harsh life and the difficulty of escape. The ill fame of the penal colonies was enough to sterilize the land for all further colonization for a hundred years. Some stories about the camps are doubtless inventions,* but it is true that the mainland camps on the Maroni where the workers were forced to cut hardwoods under

---

* The best-seller adventure story *Papillon* by Henri Charrière (translated by Patrick O'Brian, Rupert Hart-Davis, 1970) provides a fine picture of the islands in the 1930s as seen by a deportee who successfully escaped, and a picture which is accurate in all major respects.

terrible conditions, had very high death rates from infectious and deficiency diseases acquired from their poor diet. The islands, high-standing and dry and some ten kilometres offshore, were relatively healthy. In the Second World War it was agreed to close the penal settlements and the last prisoners were repatriated to France in 1946 and 1947. This left only the tiny population of 'Creoles', a Negro–White mix, plus some relatively pure Bush Negro blood originating in escapees from Surinam plantations during past centuries.

Economically the country, now elevated to the status of overseas *département* of France, is weak. Some immediate needs in food products are met, including sugar, manioc, maize and bananas. Fishing, especially shrimp fishing and packing for the United States market, is a relatively healthy industry. Minerals have little economic attraction as yet; gold prospectors have always gone off into the interior to find small amounts by panning, and there is untapped bauxite. In 1969 an agreement was reached between ALCOA, owner of the Surinamese Paranam workings, and a French company, for exploiting bauxite in French Guiana and smelting it in Surinam, a project which helps the economies of both countries.

Another mineral resource with long-term possibilities is the hardwood forest; since the departure of the prisoners in the camps of the Maroni, little is done with the valuable rosewood and other cabinet woods of this zone. Finally, a substantial break away from the traditional exploitative economy has been made by the French in introducing a space centre, constructed at Kourou following closure of their facilities in Algeria in 1967. Kourou, a village-port, has grown up to be a town of nearly 50 000 inhabitants, and is the most dynamic centre in the country.

OUTLOOK FOR THE GUIANAS

It might be expected that the Guianas, only recently promoted from effectively colonial status, would stand at considerable disadvantage in relation to countries with a longer history of independence. In fact, Western colonialism has itself changed in the course of the last century and a half, and the Guianas, benefiting from more liberal and comprehending attitudes

towards colonial territories everywhere, have relatively little leeway to make up. Some educational, cultural and economic advances have been possible in the Dutch and British sectors.

It is obvious that the economy suffers from a heavy one-sidedness, especially in Surinam, and the most urgent current needs are to find new markets, new alliances, and new products to sell. Without them, these little states stand open to all the cold winds of market change in international preference.

On the external front the Guianas would appear to be disadvantaged as non-members of LAFTA. As in the case of internal affairs though, prospects are probably better than they seem for there are links to Europe which may preserve a special position for these countries in European markets. Surinam has had access to the EEC's regional development funds as an overseas territory of Holland and, although she became an independent republic in November 1975, may continue to reap some advantage of her special relationship. French Guiana is similarly provided for as an overseas *département* of France. As for Guyana, the British commitment remains important. Following the end of the Commonwealth Sugar Agreement in 1974, Britain negotiated guarantees of the EEC's intention to continue drawing substantial sugar supplies from Guyana and the Caribbean Commonwealth countries.

It is to the Caribbean that Guyana is now increasingly turning, and she has found an alternative to LAFTA through her membership of the Caribbean Community, CARICOM, which she joined together with the other Commonwealth states of the Caribbean under the Treaty of Chaguaramas of July 1973. Surinam, along with Haiti, has indicated her intention to join CARICOM. This community is far-reaching in its aims, including both a coordination of external and internal tariff levels in Common Market fashion, a regional industrialization plan combining, for example, Guyana bauxite with Trinidad natural gas to make aluminium, and a common foreign policy. This new alignment emphasizes the elements of common culture and economy of the Caribbean and the Guianas, and must be looked on as a promising development, though a doubt remains over Guyana's willingness to accept common cause with island territories whose aims could clash with her own. Her large land area and relatively low density of population must attract migrants from overcrowded Jamaica or Trinidad in the face of immigration restrictions in Britain and Europe. Indeed, the present African-dominated government has suggested bringing West Indians into Guyana, people who with their African background might be expected to support the present regime. But Guyana is numerically dominated by Asians, and this must cause friction if and when the Asian populace achieves political maturity.

THE TROPICAL HIGHLANDS

19. Ecuador

To the north of Peru, Ecuador shares some of the heartland characteristics, though in modified form, and introduces others which are distinctive. Like Peru and Bolivia, it has a core area in the highlands where pre-Columbian civilisations were strongest, though the Inca domination was only for one generation before the arrival of the Spaniards, and Inca remains are few. The Quechua language was extended through the country mostly after the Conquest. This core area in the Sierra is also limited in extent because the two parallel cordilleras are here close together, leaving only a narrow, disconnected upland valley area between them. Like Peru and Bolivia, it has some human groups which are fairly pure Indian, while most of the *serranos* are mestizo, mixed White–Indian. The Sierra economy is like that to the south, one of small subsistence peasant farms mixed with large *haciendas*, though the latter are disappearing through subdivision. Industrial development is slight and artisan industries remain important, most of the Sierra towns operating more as service centres to a limited regional hinterland.

West of the Sierra there is a large lowland which has no counterpart to the south, occupied by the Guayas basin and coastal hills; this region has had an increasingly important role in the Ecuadorian economy since independence, producing a variety of tropical export crops. Some of it is still little developed and is the object of modern colonization schemes. The duality Costa–Sierra is expressed in the rivalry between Guayaquil, largest city of Ecuador, and the capital Quito in the Sierra.

The Sierran landscapes recall some elements of those of Peru, with bare landscapes, eroded soils, eucalyptus plantations and hedgerows, towns with open-air markets made colourful by the red, brown, white and black of traditional woven goods and numerous different vegetables and fruits on sale, in squares surrounded by long, low, broad-eaved houses with red-tiled roofs. Costa landscapes bring in a new tropical lowland element — lush tree-weeds invading fields wherever they have been allowed to flourish, zebu cattle feeding on tall grasses, houses of bamboo built on stilts above the poorly drained flat lands, coffee, cocoa, banana and manila hemp plantations. To the east of the mountains there is an equally tropical and less developed Oriente. Throughout there is however, as to the south, continual evidence of extreme poverty both in rural and urban areas.

PHYSICAL BACKGROUND (Fig. 47)

The Andes form two major cordilleras in Ecuador, Eastern or Oriental, and Occidental. To the east there are low hills adjacent to the eastern Cordillera at 2000–2500 m, and to the west along the Pacific fringe there are low hills which curve back eastwards to die out at Guayaquil.

The Eastern Cordillera is a high and fairly continuous line of mountains, a massive wall of sedimentary and metamorphic rocks crowned by Tertiary and Recent volcanoes such as Cayambe and Cotopaxi, Antisana and Sangay. These are classic cone-shaped volcanoes which have been

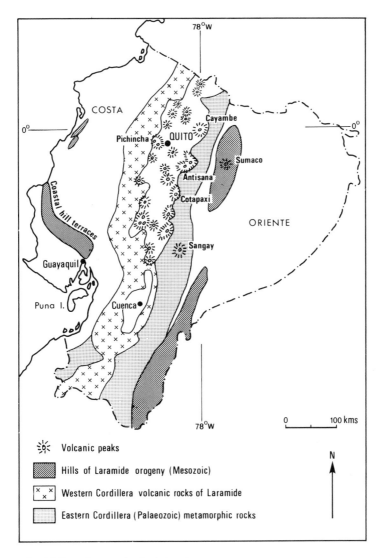

Fig. 47 Ecuador: geological structure

active in the recent past and have filled the narrow Sierra valleys to a depth of several hundred metres in places, with grey-white volcanic ash that produces Loess-like landscapes of cliffy slopes and arid tablelands where it is cut through by the rivers. The peaks rise to over 5000 m (Chimborazo to 6300 m) and thus are permanently snow-crowned. Their activity represents a constant threat to human activity. Cotopaxi erupted violently in 1877, forming a burning gas cloud which melted snow and ice and set off mudflows that reached the town of Latacunga and destroyed large areas of fertile valley land. Earthquakes have also caused disaster; in Riobamba, the 1797 earthquake set off a landslide which killed 4900 people, over half the population at that time. Other major earthquakes of this city occured in 1645 and 1698. Ibarra, north of Quito, was wiped out by an earthquake in 1868. The giant volcanoes, located on the edge of the inter-montane north–south valley, help divide it up into separate basins, *hoyas,* partially isolated from one another by mountain knots, the *nudos*.

To the west, the Western Cordillera is slightly lower, formed mostly of sedimentary rocks and cut into by innumerable rivers running in narrow canyon valleys to the west. Below it, the Costa lies generally at under 200 m elevation, though the break with the Western Cordillera and its steep slopes is reached at 600 m or more in some places. Much of it is a fertile plains land of soft Tertiary sediments covered locally by river alluvium. North of the Guayas valley estuary, there is a tectonic swell near the coast and a belt of higher, drier and poorer land, marked by a flat upper surface probably representing marine-eroded terraces, *tablazos*, and cut into by steep-sided and intricate river valley patterns. The lower Guayas basin around Guayaquil is a flat broad floodplain, poorly drained and without topographic accidents. The Oriente, east of the mountains, is an ever-flatter plain towards the east, formed by the many strongly-flowing tributaries of the Marañon or upper Amazon river.

Climate and vegetation patterns

The typical altitude-controlled variety of climatic and biotic belts characteristic of Andean countries is found, from lowland semi-desert and scrub through palm savannas to rainforest in the lowlands, followed by cloudforest at 2000–3000 m and at higher levels, open grasslands becoming poorer in the *páramos* which lead up to the snowline.

There is a variation not only between Costa, Sierra and Oriente, but also within the regions. On the southern Costa, near the Peruvian border, and again at Manabí northwest of Guayaquil, the climate is dry, coming under the influence of the Humboldt current and the south Pacific high pressure cell, and in these regions the natural vegetation seems to be a scrub forest dominated by the kapok tree, the *ceibo*. In the northernmost Costa, there is rainforest and 1500 mm annual rainfall. Similarly within the Sierra, there are many dry pockets in rainshadow positions, causing sudden transition from well watered to dry zones where there is under 500 mm of annual rainfall and a semi-desert aspect with acacia scrub, cactus and coarse grass. For example, a few miles north of Quito which has 1200 mm rainfall, it is under 400 mm on the equatorial line and crops are only possible with

irrigation. Throughout the Sierra the natural vegetation has long been removed, and tree cover is absent, except for planted eucalyptus and Monterrey pine. Seasonal variations in temperature are slight in the Sierra, where day–night differences of 20°C are of far greater importance. There are rainy and dry seasons however, the wet season on Costa and Sierra corresponding to the Northern Hemisphere winter, when the influence of the Pacific cell wanes and moves further south, allowing unstable equatorial westerlies to enter both these regions. The Oriente does not have an important dry season, but the Cordillera Oriental prevents its humid air from affecting the Sierra at any season.

THE EMERGENCE OF COSTA–SIERRA DUALITY

Colonial development

Ecuadorian civilization seems to date from about 2 700 BC, when settled agriculture and pottery are known from the Costa. Ecuador was probably tributary to the Peruvian coast, or at least developed through the diffusion of technology and culture from the Peruvian centre. A strong social and political organization may be dated to about AD 500, with the emergence of regional states on Costa and Sierra. Inca settlement was delayed by the strong defence of the regional kingdoms of the Sierra, until the fifteenth century, and few Inca remains are found. However, the racial mix was probably modified by some Quechua-speaking people brought in as a conscious policy by the Incas.

Quito was burnt by the Incas to keep it from the Spanish, but was thereafter rebuilt as a colonial city and important centre within the Lima viceroyality. Other cities followed in the sixteenth century occupying the Sierra, where Spanish overlords could settle in the towns and live from a dependent Indian population. Up to 1640, mining was the most important economic activity relating the land to the exterior, and also accounting for some of the new town settlements. But the mineral wealth was never great, and from 1640 to 1740 textiles were central, and *obrajes*, large woollen mills based on primitive technology and Indian serf labour, were important in the Sierra between Ibarra and Riobamba;

they took advantage of the lack of textiles from Spain and the existence of a pre-Colombian tradition in weaving. Compared with this intensive development, the Costa had only great *haciendas* with cattle, cocoa and sugar cane, some worked by slave labour. A mulatto and pure negro population emerged on the Costa, distinct from the mestizo blood of the Sierra. These differences remain in the racial mix today, as the census figures show (they relate to 1950 as later censuses do not ascertain race).

ETHNIC COMPOSITION 1950

Race	Sierra (%)	Costa (%)	Total (%)
White	29.0	28.0	28.5
Indian	28.0	7.0	17.5
Mestizo	42.0	28.0	35.0
Mulatto	0.5	28.5	14.5
Negro	0.5	8.5	4.5

The Costa focus

After 1740 textiles became less important to the national economy than cocoa, produced in the Guayas basin and elsewhere in the Costa, and this latter region now asserted its dominant role in the Ecuadorean economy as well as a leading political and social role. Freedom from Spain was achieved in 1822, Quito Presidency forming part of Gran Colombia with Venezuela and Colombia, but almost immediately, in 1830 Ecuador separated from Colombia and became the Republic of Ecuador. The origin of this name, in a French geodetic expedition sent in the 18th century to measure an arc of meridian at the equator, symbolizes Ecuador's lack of a strong political identity. In spite of having a respectable name, that of the ancient pre-Columbian kingdom and colonial province of Quito, a mathematical, geodetic interest of external powers was made into the patriotic inspiration.

In the nineteenth century, the existing polarization of interest between Costa and Sierra was reinforced by politicians and parties, the Guayaquileños representing the interest in trade and commerce and the exterior, the Quiteños representing conservative, traditional landowners of the Sierra. Guayaquil was export focus for not only cocoa, but also coffee, tagua nuts, hides and natural rubber. Although Quito was the largest Andean city, it did not benefit from any boom in the later century comparable to the guano and nitrates of Peru and Chile, nor yet the industrial surge of Antioquia in Colombia. Cocoa and the other exports of the Costa became competitive in Europe, especially with the opening of the Panama canal in 1915. However, after 1925, cocoa declined because of soil depletion and fungus disease, and was followed by other crops, coffee, rice, and more recently in the 1960s, bananas, to be followed in the 1970s by African palm and *abacá*, manila hemp. During the first half of the century, Quito had become a sleepy regional centre to the Sierra. A narrow-gauge railway was finished from Durán opposite Guayaquil to Quito in 1909, but did not radically alter the way of life in the Sierra. There was no drive from the Sierra to occupy the Oriente, and large areas were lost to Brazil and then, in 1941, to Peru, to form *terra irredenta* for present-day politicians to argue over.

Today's population has changed its focus to the coastlands. In 1780, it was estimated that 81% of the population were in the Sierra, 19% in the Costa. For 1972, of Ecuador's 6 million people, 52.2% were on the Costa, 45.3% in the Sierra and 2.5% in the Oriente. (The 1500 m altitude line is used as demarcator of these zones.) The balance is still moving in favour of the Costa, with a vegetative growth which exceeds that in the highlands, compounded by out-migration from Sierra to the lowlands. Within the Sierra, Quito has been growing rapidly in recent years due to oil-related activity and the growth of central government. The overall population growth in Ecuador at 3.5% annually (1980–3), the highest in South America, is an important problem because this increase is focussed in two cities.

MODERN ECONOMY

Ecuador has an economic structure typical of underdeveloped countries, with a concentration of all export effort on one or two commodities. Thus its development areas on both eastern and western peripheries have an inherent tendency to 'boom and bust' conditions. On the west side there is the costeño agricultural resource, varying from one decade to the next, and currently shared between cocoa (14% of exports in 1979), coffee (13%) and bananas (10%). On the east, febrile expansion in the oilfield regions of the northern Oriente (oil provided nearly 46% of exports in 1979) is also a phenomenon which may or may not bring long-term expansion of the regional economy. Between the two, the Sierra is a region not geared to any export activity and with large pockets of subsistence agriculture, its principal resource being its population, a resource which is scarcely tapped and presents formidable obstacles to change.

Oil: a key sector

In the 1970s Ecuador's fuel and power position was dramatically changed by major finds of oil in the northern Oriente near Lago Agrio (Fig. 48) after many years of fruitless exploration. Four major international consortia drilling here struck rich low-sulphur fields in 1970, and produced 75 000 barrels per diem in 1973, compared to the mere 5000 barrels per diem in the previous sole area of production, on the Santa Elena peninsula 140 km west of Guayaquil.

While the Santa Elena fields, developed and worked by Anglo-Ecuadorean Oilfields Co., a British company, had supplied domestic needs fairly well up to 1960, they could not do so thereafter and oil imports began to drain the country's foreign exchange reserves. Today, domestic supplies plus an exportable surplus of 150 000 barrels a day daily is available, and a pipeline has been built from Lago Agrio to Esmeraldas on the Pacific where there is a tanker terminal, and a major refinery. It is possible that the most important oil and gas region will be not the Oriente but the Costa; in the Gulf of Guayaquil substantial natural gas structures have been known for some time but not exploited. Now they are to be used in a project to use gas for making chemical fertilizers, and as fuel for a coastal steel-making plant. In addition, the oil potential of the Costa is now being explored and it is likely that important oil fields will be opened within the coastal hills and the Guayas basin.

The Sierra benefits of course from the oil

37 A public wash basin, built by community work in the Sierra near Cotopaxi. The Sierra landscape of scattered settlements with eucalyptus trees near the houses and minifundia with tiny fields is typical

development. The national oil company CEPE shares in oil production, and the national government which is centred in Quito relies directly and indirectly on oil for large revenues. Quito is thus experiencing in mild form the oil-based boom of capital cities experienced in the 1920s in Caracas. Oil combines with hydro-electric power to form the basis for electric power generation in Ecuador. Guayaquil has large oil-fired stations, which complement the HEP plant of the Sierra, notably the Paute dam 115 km east of Cuenca, already functioning, which will eventually produce 1500 megawatts. A triangular grid connecting Quito, Guayaquil and Cuenca has been built, though this still leaves many rural areas without a service.

The rural economy

Agriculture's longstanding central importance has had some impact on government thinking, and a colonization agency was founded in 1957, aimed at settling the eastern selvas. The Agrarian Reform Law was passed in 1964, with the purpose of correcting the unbalanced structure in which a third of sierran farms were under 1 hectare, and another half between 1 and 5 hectares. On the Costa the situation was less crucial, for this region had been colonized in large measure spontaneously, by Sierra emi-grants who selected for themselves adequately-sized plots of land. In this region, the obstacles to farmer progress were such matters as access to markets, to credit, to technical advice, and to all kinds of service.

The main criticism of IERAC, the Ecuadorean Agricultural Colonization and Reform agency, must be that much of its attention has been to colonization and not to reform; and that within the set of reform measures, it has chosen the easier ones related to outlawing old forms of tenure such as the *huasipungo* and payment of

38 Community work in the Cotopaxi Sierra. Clearing stones from the bed of a stream

39 Casual street selling in Quito. This has become a familiar scene. Traditional markets are still found here and in the countryside as well

non-money rents, but has not changed the farm size structure and the monopolization of good farm land by the great estates.

Agricultural regions

THE COSTA

In 1950 most of the Costa was still non-agricultural land, and of that land classified as agricultural, half was occupied by forest and wasteland. Much of the landscape was one of old, abandoned plantations, now turned to savanna-like grasslands with interspersed palm trees, the coarse grass being used to feed tough *criollo* cattle for beef. In the Esmeraldas region of the north-west, it was a forest landscape. The population was thin, and in all regions lived dominantly in single houses on stilts constructed of split bamboo cane.

This landscape has been altered locally in the recent decades by population pressure on the Sierra and new opportunities on the Costa. The Guayas basin has become a region of more intensive use, with migrants from both west (Manabí suffered intense droughts in the 1950s) and east, from the Sierra. Bananas became the dominant crop in the 1960s and remain important today, wherever good transport is available, their optimum physical environment being one of very high rainfall, over 2000 mm annually, and a short dry season, plus reasonable soil fertility. These conditions are best met, not in the poorly drained lowlands of the central Guayas valley nor on the dry western edge, but on much of the eastern fringe of the Costa, and in El Oro province south of Guayaquil. Bananas are not grown on estates as in Central America, where foreign control has been typical, but on medium size farms of 50 ha, privately owned and often family farms. Successful marketing is important and depends on co-operatives of farmers or merchants with packing stations for washing, dividing and packing the crop. Successful marketing, plus Ecuador's relative freedom from Sigatoka disease compared to Central America, permitted Ecuador to become the world's largest banana exporter in the 1960s, feeding the USA and Japan. However, banana cultivation as a long-term monoculture has exhausted some soils, as around Santo Domingo which has been colonized since about 1950, and bananas are replaced in such areas by grassland and African oilpalm.

Coffee and cocoa are other export crops. Coffee comes from the banana lands and also from the drier margins to which it is better suited. Cocoa is grown in the Guayas Basin, the main concentration being in Los Rios province about 100 km northeast of Guayaquil. Cocoa is of increasing importance, expanding from 155 000 ha in 1950 to 287 000 ha in 1980. There has been some yield improvement as well as a real expansion, though there is still room for further increases, and often up to 40% of the crop may be lost through disease.

Sugar cane is another commercial crop, mostly for domestic consumption, its location determined largely by that of the sugar mills which own most of the sugar land. There was an expansion of cane land from 78 000 ha in 1960–65 to 110 000 ha in 1975. Production centres around Milagro, a few miles east of Guayaquil, where the largest *ingenios* are found. Alternative commercial crops are *abacá* or manila hemp, cotton, especially in dry Manabí, and African oilpalm, this latter a successful replacement of banana and requiring similarly sized properties for successful management.

Cattle are traditional occupants of the Costa, and improvements have taken place in nearly all herds, with the use of resistant crosses of Zebu Indian cattle with the *criollo* or European breeds that have good beef producing potential. Cattle and grass may be regarded as the dominants wherever there are large estates with little labour available, and also as a follow-on after intensive land use has depleted soil fertility.

Ecuador's dry coasts, in the south and in the westernmost province, Manabí, offer less to the farmer, and more to the fishermen. Ecuador lies on the northernmost coastal section of the Humboldt current, which only sweeps out to sea at the equator itself, at least in the northern hemisphere summer when the South Pacific high pressure cell, and the ocean currents which follow it, are furthest north. This current is notably rich in fish resources. Ecuador also has a very large offshore claim, up to 200 miles (320 km) from the continent, plus a 200-mile radius circle around the tiny Galapagos Islands, which belong to Ecuador and lie 600 miles (960 km) west of the continent. At present the richest fishing grounds are in the Gulf of Guayaquil and near the Peruvian border, and the principal fish resources are tunny and shrimp which latter is fish-farmed in the mangrove swamp areas of the Gulf. Deep-sea fishing is little developed to date, as the fleet is mostly composed of small vessels limited to coastal fishing. In addition, freezing and canning facilities, at Manta and Guayaquil, are inadequate.

THE SIERRA

This region provides the foreigner's usual stereotype of Ecuador: small fields, steep mountain slopes, rows of eucalyptus or agave as field boundaries and larger blocks of eucalyptus planted on estates, poorly surfaced roads, and small market towns (plate 37). The pressure of farm population on the land around the towns often produces a half-bleached fringe effect, in the aureole of fields nearest to the houses from which the topsoil has been totally eroded to show the bare grey-white volcanic ash subsoil. Many farms are tiny, unable to support families without other employment, and rural poverty does not permit education in better farming techniques or mechanization. Much of the produce of the farms under 5 ha is for subsistence, and marketing is in any case difficult because of the lack of farm-market roads and the long chains of intermediaries between farmer and consumer, chains which account for low farm prices and high market prices.

Outdated land tenure is another old feature of sierra backwardness, typified in the *huasipungo*, whereby the Indian farmer had merely the right to use a small plot of land on the estate, in return for several days labour each week from him or a member of his family. This system is officially outlawed though there are recrudescences of it from time to time in various disguises.

Maize, potatoes and barley are the twin staffs of life for the poor and are supplemented by pro-

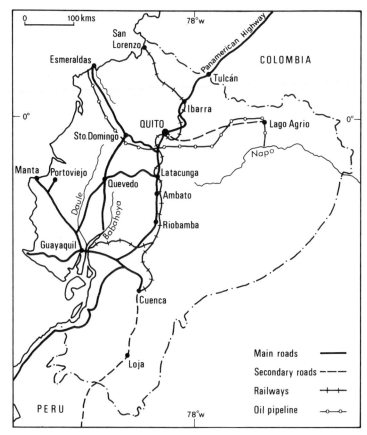

Fig. 48 Ecuador: road and rail transport

tein from beans, lentils, peas, and only a very limited amount of meat or fish. Lack of iodine from seafish or any other source has meant there is endemic goitre in much of the central Sierra, which in alliance with malnutrition produces physical stunting and sometimes mental deficiencies, all affecting the poorest segment of the population. Quinoa, oca, lupin seeds and arracacha are other mior minor crops of the uplands. On the tiny plots of the *minifundio*, intercropping of beans, lupins and maize is often to be seen, an ecologically good choice because the plant variety gives some protection against insects and disease, and because the nitrogen from the leguminous crops helps feed the maize. It would be a more successful system were it not for the lack of sufficient land and consequent overcultivation.

Physical factors account for some differences in farming within the Sierra. On the *páramos* above 3 500 m the temperatures are too low for grain, and grazing is found with occasional potato crops; in areas not exposed to moist air currents from the west, drought forces seasonal grazing where irrigation cannot be applied.

THE ORIENTE

Development of the eastern territories is still hindered by their relative inaccessibility. The Eastern Cordillera provides a topographic obstacle which makes road building costly and tedious. Road building has not been organized by central government but began here and there by Sierra municipalities aiming to expand their influence and area eastwards, only for the work to be abandoned when interest declines after

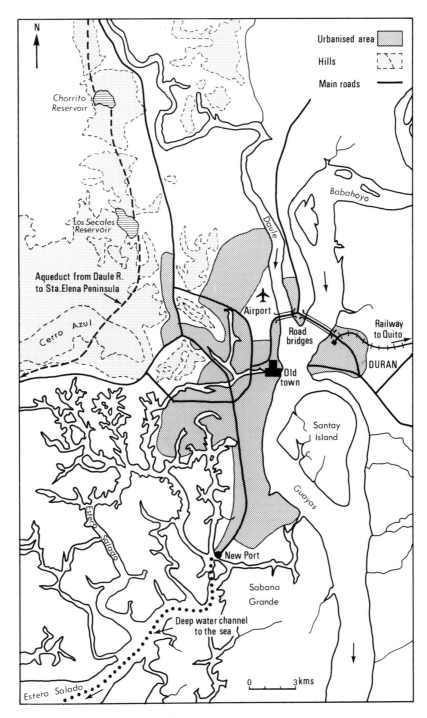

Fig. 49 Guayaquil: site and situation

some years of work. A few links have been made, notably linking Ambato, Loja and Cuenca to the Oriente, but in no case reaching further than the marginal area of piedmont alluvial slopes and relatively fertile soils. Population pressure has however continued to send an important stream of landless farmworkers into the zone, most notably colonizing along the road accompanying the oil pipeline to Lago Agrio in the northeast, completed in 1971.

Agricultural colonization, whether spontaneous or official, has had only limited success in the east, and only in the piedmont zone. For most commodities which it might be possible to export from the region to the Sierra, transport problems have been an insuperable barrier, favouring only beef cattle, with their own means of locomotion to market areas, or such high value/weight articles as *naranjilla*, a tomato-like fruit used in drinks, or *panela*, crudely refined sugar. The national government is interested in colonizing the far east on the Peruvian border, but this project stems more from strategic, frontier occupation motives, than economic or social ones. The frontier areas have no adequate linkages to the Sierra and their soils are generally infertile and have poor drainage.

The government is also interested in pressing forward with the Carretera Marginal de las Selvas, a north–south road through the piedmont zone from the Peruvian frontier to that of Colombia. This kind of transport development seems unwarranted, in that it links, not the complementary zones of Sierra and Oriente, but similar regions within the Oriente, so that the possibilities for trade use of the road are slight.

URBAN STRUCTURE

Like many other countries of Latin America, Ecuador has a markedly primate urban hierarchy, i.e. one that is dominated by its largest city, except that in this case it is two cities that dominate: Guayaquil and Quito.

QUITO (881 000 in 1982)
The differences between Quito and Guayaquil symbolize and are part of the more general differences between the Costa and the Sierra. Quito retains, at least in its centre, a somewhat more traditional and refined atmosphere, as centre of government and historical capital. It attracts

most of the tourists from abroad, for the city is rich in colonial Baroque architecture, with some priceless art treasures decorating the interiors of the many churches and monastries.

The site of Quito is on the western edge of its *hoya* or basin, on a shelf above the main valley floor, and at an altitude of 2 800 m, which gives it a remarkably equable and enjoyable climate with temperatures ranging commonly between 12°C and 20°C from day to night, throughout the year. The western fringe of the city climbs the lower slopes of Mount Pichincha, and the east is cut off by a river gorge, making expansion a dominantly north–south affair. Colonial Quito is still largely intact, a compact town of whitewashed three-storey buildings with red-tiled roofs at the south end of the shelf. Expansion has been an expansion of middle class villas over the north half of the shelf during the last 50 years, dragging out some commercial development with it, and recently flowing right round the airport site which must now be removed to the main valley floor well away from the city.

The urban poor live either in the old town in old mansions converted to tenements, or in shanty towns, the *barrios marginales*, particularly along the western mountain edge of the city. They are less apparent than in other large cities of Latin America as their construction is generally good, of locally hand-made bricks or composition blocks, and they are hidden in the ravine-like valleys cut into the slope of Pichincha. But they may account for 10–15% of the city's population. Municipal policy of maintaining a green belt of eucalyptus along this front, and of not providing water above the level of 2 850 metres, has failed to hold back barrio growth in the 1970s.

GUAYAQUIL (1 279 000 in 1982)
Guayaquil (see fig. 49) is a bustling city combining the functions of national port and manufacturing centre to the nation. It has a nodal situation within the Costa, not in mathematical terms but by virtue of its good access to the most important part of the lowlands. Its hinterland is reached over relatively flat country, and it has good sea links to the exterior; both of these factors constitute advantages over interior, isolated Quito. Roads connect it to all parts of the rich Guayas Basin, and it has good road and rail links to the Sierra. The city has grown from an orig-

inal site at the tip of the ridge where the coastal hills curve in from the west and die out at the river's edge. The site is high and well above the marshy plains on either side. From here the city has grown downstream, the main business centre occupying land just south of the hill ridge. In the last ten years growth has taken the city on far to the south towards the New Port, built on the Estero Salado which is much more silt-free than the Guayas and has a 10 m deep-water channel maintained to it from the open sea some 70 km out. (Fig. 49).

Heat, humidity and occasional floods gave Guayaquil an evil reputation for malaria, yellow fever and other diseases in the last century. Even in 1910 it could be said that:

The lower parts of the town are partially flooded in the rainy season . . . . the old town is in the upper or northern part and is inhabited by the poorer classes, its streets being badly paved, crooked, un-drained, dirty and pestilential . . . . malarial and bilious fevers are common, the latter being known as 'Guayaquil fever', and epidemics of yellow fever are frequent.

Encyclopaedia Britannica, *11th edn., Vol. XII, Cambridge University Press, 1910, p.665*

Now the city is relatively healthy, and has become the largest city in Ecuador, having overtaken Quito in population in about 1950. Its commercial hinterland is more extensive than that of Quito, reaching over nearly all the Costa and into the southern part of the Sierra. Its industrial makeup is diversified, including vegetable oil and flourmilling, sawmills and related woodworking industries, cement manufacturing and other heavy industries, but also light industry such as textiles and electrical goods, and a massive construction and construction-related industry. Guayaquil has a very smart modern centre, where concrete blocks, and some highrise buildings, have replaced nearly all the old-fashioned wood and bamboo buildings that were typical and were regularly destroyed by fires in previous generations. Much of the city's economic activity is associated with the port, which is the principal port for imports and exports, and has a large part of the new port devoted to container traffic, with specialized cranes and warehouses, to replace the older and much slower system still used at smaller ports, of con-

tainer ships using their deck cranes to unload cargo.

Guayaquil is not without its shanty area. The *suburbio* as it is called, has grown out in all directions but most notably to the west of the old city over the swamps around the Estero Salado and onto the Estero itself. The process involves first the building of traditional stilt-houses of bamboo over the water, connected by catwalks to dry land; next there is pressure put on the municipality to improve the area, by filling in the swamps with material from the narrow neck of hill-land mentioned previously. The original owners can then sell their improved houses at a good price to new incomers, who in turn may make their own improvements by replacing the bamboo with bricks and blocks. Unfortunately the first areas filled in are the streets, which leaves the house-backs as unhealthy stagnant morasses until they are filled. Drinking water supplies, sewage provision and storm drainage are only provided later. It is calculated that 40% of the population live either in these shanties, or in central slums.

Other cities: the Sierra

Quito and Guayaquil dominate the urban hierarchy as other cities do elsewhere in South America. After these two, Cuenca is number three with a population of only 151 000 (1982). Each basin in the Sierra has however its own urban centre from Loja in the south, through Cuenca, Riobamba, Latacunga to Quito and further north Ibarra, Otavalo and Tulcan. These towns of 50–100 thousand act as administrative centres to their provinces, and centres for most of the trade of their basin, wholesale and retail. Traditional open-air markets are a conspicuous and colourful visual aspect of this trade, sometimes handling all trade together, elsewhere having two or three separate markets for farm products, for manufactured goods brought in for sale from other regions, and for artisan goods.

Cuenca as the largest, has many representative features of this group of towns. It is a town of two-storey buildings, many in local stone, with a few new ten-storey blocks for offices and hotels to accommodate a respectable tourist trade. It is laid in strict chessboard fashion with a large central square, and is flanked on one side by a river forming a cliff front of the city towards the south. It has a number of modern factories on an industrial estate which represents the efforts of the regional development agency to attract light industry, but in addition a sizeable artisan industry making panama hats (very finely woven straw hats), wood-working and leather working, and jewellery making. Some of these industries are organised on an urban–rural basis, with most of the work being done in the villages around the city, while finishing and marketing are carried out by merchants who visit the villages and take up the production from a large number of families.

The transport network (Fig. 49)
Up to the end of the nineteenth century Quito and Guayaquil were virtually cut off from each other, linked only by mule tracks and a journey lasting many weeks. Today there are rapid air and road links, and it is some of the smaller towns which retain their isolation, notably Loja in the southern Sierra, and the settlements of the Oriente such as Puyo and Tena. The first modern links were, however, by rail: the Quito–Guayaquil narrow–gauge (1.067 m) line was built in 1897-1908. A journey on this line is an exhausting but fascinating passage through Ecuador's landscapes, with the ordinary (steam) train taking 21 hours, i.e. averaging under 22 km/h (14 mph) over the 463 km (288 miles), or half this time on the diesel-powered tourist train. This train has to pass from sea level to over 3700 m, the limits of cultivation, in moving from Guayaquil to Riobamba.

The rail network is very poorly maintained, runs at a loss and carries little traffic today. The line was extended north and south in the 1930s, to Cuenca and Ibarra, but a full network of feeder lines was not built, and the existing line was unable to take much traffic. Its coastal terminal was not even Guayaquil city, but Durán on the opposite side of the 2.5 km wide Guayas river, requiring costly slow ferry services to reach the city. The river is now bridged at Durán, but by road only. Thus the railway is replaced by road carriers, including a very extensive bus service, and trucks for freight. Passengers and expensive freight going to remote areas may use the relatively cheap air services. Air travel is made somewhat hazardous by the lack of bad-weather installations at the main airports, and by airport location. Airports for Quito and Guayaquil lie within the modern cities and are adjacent to residential areas.

REGIONAL DEVELOPMENT

A country as small as Ecuador might be thought to have insufficient regional differences to warrant special attention. But its relatively small population of 8.08 million (1980) has very varied conditions and levels of living.

The are no accurate measures of the distribution of poverty and wealth in Ecuador, but it may safely be said that the twin metropolises are areas of relatively high average incomes and the other regions are poor. Because of the powerful focussing of manufacturing industries, migration, and capital investment in the two cities, there are great disparities between conditions of life in them and in the rest of the country. It may be asked if regional development agencies have not been able to reduce these differences, or if the central government cannot at least focus some of its sectoral policies on the poorer areas.

One problem is that only a few regions have any kind of regional development organization, notably the area around Cuenca, the province of Manabí, the Guayas river basin and the southern frontier zone bordering on Peru. These regional agencies have come into being not because of a national policy for the regions, but as a reaction to specific crises — in Azuay, the province of Cuenca, it was drought in the 1950s, plus a decline in the Panama hat industry; in Manabí, it was successive major droughts; in the south, it was the delicate nature of relations with Peru and the need to guide carefully the joint river basin development of the Puyango and Tumbes valleys.

With the oustanding exception of CREA, the agency for the Cuenca area, the regional agencies have not been concerned with a broad-based development of their whole region, but with a narrow focus on a few projects within one sector. Thus in Manabí, the focus has been on the small river valley of Portoviejo, only 3% of the provincial area. In the southern frontier area the focus has been on a river basin project, the Puyango–Tumbes scheme for hydro-electricity and irrigation, with little spent on other areas although most of the population lives outside this dry coastal frontier zone.

For the Guayas River agency, the potential regional scope is much greater, covering the whole physical river basin, and thus parts of nine provinces, but the sectoral concentration is equally narrow, with the emphasis firmly on water projects, especially at Babahoyo and Daule Peripa, which latter will provide some water for the dry western Costa, as well as reducing floods within the main valley. Only in CREA, centred in Cuenca, where there were no funds initially for giant river basin projects, has there been a useful focus on small projects which provide work for local labour, not only in construction phases but on a permanent basis. These projects have wide sectoral cover from agriculture through commerce and trade to artisan industries, and infrastructure such as rural electrification.

The civilian government brought to power in 1980 after a decade of military rule has promised a strong regional planning function, covering the whole country. This will obviously be an improvement over the present state of affairs, though it will still require strong and clever administration to ensure that the present polarization does not continue to build up. The record of governments to date in controlling the growth of Guayaquil and Quito has been poor, and there has never been any serious effort at removing industries or building up new ones in the regions. On the other hand, agriculture, the backbone of the regions, has always been taxed heavily, as one of the easier types of tax to collect is that on exports of primary commodities. Export taxes on coffee for example, have worked against the farmers and thus against all rural areas of the country.

Economic planning, whether for regions or on a sectoral basis, is not sufficient in Ecuador. It is necessary to begin with social reforms, in order to integrate in some way the poorest rural groups into the life of the country. As these groups are commonly the pure Indian stock of the Sierra, social policy becomes a policy for racial groups. Criteria for such policies have scarcely been examined, but the problem should not been seen as one of simply getting the Indians to adopt western ways and organizations. In Ecuador as throughout the Andes there are remnants of traditional communal organization not based on monetary exchange but simply on mutual aid among members of a community. These pre-Columbian *comunidades indígenas* may well form the basis for co-operative action to develop the rural community, as well as help in slowing the outmigration from rural areas. Outside the Sierra, modern co-operatives may be used to promote the rural areas, though their organization needs some improvement over that commonly found today.

20. Colombia

Colombia is an Andean country like her neighbours, and shares with them a variety of environments from tropical vegetation through temperate environments up to the high *páramos* and snow peaks. Colombia resembles its neighbours also in its backward economic structure, for it is dependent on agriculture for the production of export commodities to sell in exchange for other manufactures. Like its neighbours, a single crop, coffee in the case of Colombia, provides most of the export earnings, and Colombian fortunes rise and fall with the price of coffee on Northern Hemisphere exchanges.

Beyond these broad similarities, differences from the other Andean states are more apparent. Colombia's physical geography tends to divide its people. The country is large (1.14 million sq km), and thinly populated, with under 30 million inhabitants (27.5 million in 1983). More important, the populated highlands do not comprise a united mass as they do further south, but three separate ranges, so that groups of people live in areas more or less isolated from each other by hot swampy lowlands or high mountains. Most of Colombia's efforts must therefore be devoted to integrating the various regions into a whole, efforts which are fortunately aided by a comparative lack of racial divisiveness.

PHYSICAL GEOGRAPHY

Colombia has an equatorial situation which, combined with her adjacency to both Pacific and Atlantic, would seem to ensure constant high temperatures and humidity. Topography, however, and the nature of the northeast trades in this zone, make this not entirely true. The basic relief features, the three mountain ranges named somewhat unimaginatively Cordillera Occidental, Central and Oriental, open out fanwise from the Pasto knot in the south, leaving two major structural valleys between, occupied by the Magdalena and Cauca rivers. West of the mountains is the Atrato river in another structural low between coast hills, the Serranía de Baudó, and the Cordillera Occidental.

Of the three ranges, the Central is the highest, with volcanic peaks of over 5000 m in its central section. It is in this range that the Nevado del Ruiz is located. This volcano was thought to be inactive, but in late 1985 it erupted violently, killing over 25 000 people. The Oriental, east of the Magdalena, is broader, with high-level plateaus created by the infilling of old lake basins. Little lakes and flat grassy plains framed by surrounding mountains, with scattered eucalyptus trees, provide a beautiful landscape where man has been active for many centuries without spoiling the scene. The Sabana de Bogotá, home of the national capital, is one of these upland basins. To the west, the Cordillera Occidental has slopes as steep as the others but is lower and cuts into Mesozoic sediments rather than igneous rocks. West of the mountains, the Pacific lowlands are low hills rather than plains, a difficult and rugged country. The Caribbean coast is flatter but has the great mass of the Santa Marta moun-

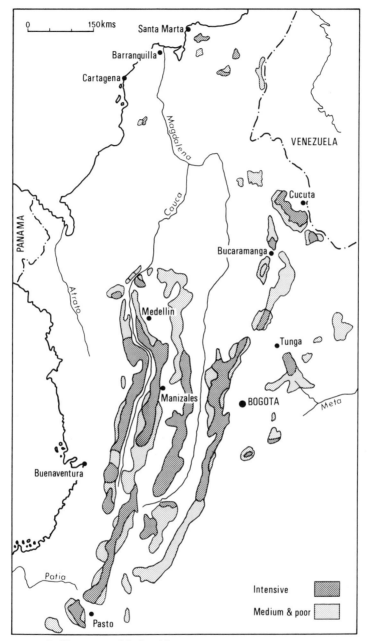

Fig. 50 Coffee zones of Colombia

tains and the upland area of Guajira in the northeast.

Colombia's section of the Oriente, like those of Peru and Bolivia, is inhabited only by a scanty Indian population and by cattle men. There are two distinct sections, in the south a true selvas of the upper Amazon, in the north the Llanos, open grasslands which suffer alternately from flood and drought.

Climate
Altitudinal differences are the most noteworthy, with *tierra caliente* extending up to 1000 m, *tierra templada* between 1000 and 2000 m, *tierra fría*

between 2000 and 3000 m, and *páramos* above this. The *templada*, with temperatures of 17°C to 24°C and annual rainfall of over 2500 mm, is the coffee belt par excellence, usually a narrow strip of land on the steep slopes above the main river valleys (fig. 50).

Rainfall produced by airmasses coming either from the Pacific or from the Amazon valley gives plenty of moisture to the eastern and western flanks of the mountains, but leaves the deep valley floors of main rivers such as the Magdalena and Cauca in a rainshadow with totals around 1500 mm, making supplementary irrigation desirable. On the Caribbean coast there is substantial drought in the tradewind zone, especially in Guajira, where Uribia, on the north coast, has 330 mm rainfall annually, allowing only scrub vegetation.

HISTORICAL ASPECTS

This region lies on the highway between Central American and Peruvian centres of civilization, and while not occupied itself by high cultures such as the Inca or Aztec states, it did boast chiefdoms of several thousand persons and a considerable social organization, appropriate to an area which must have been strongly influenced by its neighbours. Evidence of contact is present for example in the San Agustín culture in the south, which has many stone-carved monuments, art motifs and ceramic decorations comparable to the Central Andes and to Mesoamerica, dating from pre-Christian times to the Conquest. The fine metallurgy of Colombian prehistory also seems to derive from the Central Andes.

Settled Indians were concentrated at the time of conquest in the mountain basins above 2000 m, notably in the Cordillera Oriental, occupied by the Chibcha. Physical remains of the Chibcha culture have been little preserved, for they used daub and wattle rather than stone, and occupied open country where grave looting was easy and profitable in colonial times. They cultivated the potato and other tubers, used irrigation and drainage of the flat plains, and organized commerce in metals, textiles and farm products at town centres such as Bogotá and Tunja, later to become important Spanish settlements. The Chibcha were conquered with ease and absorbed very completely into the mestizo race which

forms modern Colombia, more so than in Peru where the Indian element isolated itself and remained a separate race.

El Dorado
Santa Fé de Bogotá, the capital, was founded by Jimenez de Quesada in 1538, as the culmination of his journey up the Magdalena valley in search of gold, no doubt urged on by the rumours he must have heard of El Dorado, the prince who regularly covered himself in gold dust, and who lived in this region. He reached the Indian centre of Bogotá a little ahead of another party of Spaniards under the leadership of Belalcazar, governor of Quito and lieutenant of Pizarro, moving in from the south, and finally a third force under Nicolas Federmann, a German expeditionary from the colony of Coro in Venezuela which at that time was held by the Welser financier family from Germany, in recognition of their aid to Charles V during his campaign for election as Holy Roman Emperor. The Germans had made many expeditions in search of gold and it must have come as a cruel blow to them to arrive just after another group had found the source.

In the event, the Chibcha gold was found to be small in quantity and not even derived locally but from alluvial deposits in streams to the west. Emeralds were the only valuable local mineral. El Dorado was a real person, a tribal chief from near Bogotá, but the ceremony of coating him in gold dust and dipping him in the holy Lake of Guatavita had died out some seventy years before the Spaniards arrived, leaving no easily accessible gold. To the chagrin of the other claimants, Quesada was confirmed as commander of Bogotá and the region, and the land became part of the Peruvian Viceroyalty, to split off under the Bourbon reforms of the eighteenth century and become the Viceroyalty of New Granada, including Colombia, Venezuela and Ecuador.

COLONIAL AND NINETEENTH-CENTURY DIFFERENTIATION OF REGIONS (fig. 51)

Cundinamarca and Santander
Availability of Indians to some extent determined the colonial economy. In the centre where

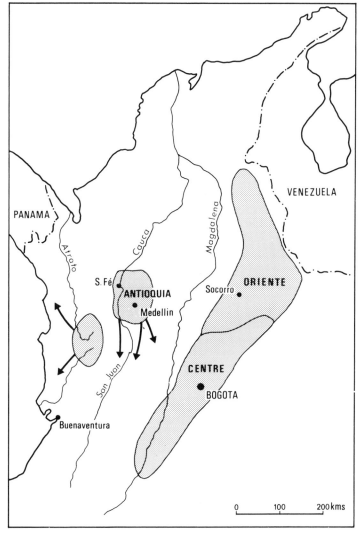

Fig. 51 Colonial foci of settlement and cultural identity in Colombia

there had been a dense Chibcha populace a typical semi-feudal society, similar to that of much of Latin America, grew up with Spaniards occupying positions of power and mestizos operating a near-subsistence farming economy. Bogotá grew as the hub of this regional economy, with a more shadowy role as administrative centre to the whole of the northern Andes.

A quite distinctive set of conditions prevailed to the north of traditional Bogotá and Cundinamarca: in the region called Oriente by Colombians, the present departments of Santander and Norte de Santander, there were few Indians to rely on for farm work and an industrious colonizing spirit developed among the people. Eighteenth-century Spanish immigrants were attracted to the farmlands being opened up at this time, and to the little towns of the region where an artisan cotton industry flourished. Eventually the identity of this region was lost, through colonial taxation, which hindered the development of tobacco farming and removed it gradually in the nineteenth century to the middle Magdalena valley. Competition to the artisan industry from large modern mills in Europe and in Antioquia also caused decline, so that regional identity was almost totally lost, in economic terms, by the twentieth century.

Antioquia

As in Santander, in the Central Cordillera there was a lack of settled Indians and flat land, and enterprising mestizos became responsible for the growth of independent small farming and mining for gold on a small scale. There is something of a myth surrounding the role of Antioqueños in Colombian development; according to some writers there was a peculiarly distinctive Antioqueño character, forceful and hard-working, which made the region a leader, especially in industrial growth during the last hundred years. Another opinion, which seems more acceptable in view of its simplicity, is that straightforward economic factors helped the region's emergence to prosperity. In any case there is little need for special explanations since the Antioqueños were only a little ahead of other regions, such as the capital, and differed from the rest more in the kind of industry than in timing.

The factors that seem to have importance are the old development of mining, which brought some entrepreneurial skills to industry, and, more important, the development of coffee farming on small owner-operator units. Coffee may indeed be seen as the main motor to industrialization from within the region. Introduced quite late into the country, after 1850, production was still small in 1870 and concentrated in Santander on poor soils and marginal climatic regions. A dramatic shift of coffee growing occurred by 1914 as the crop took up the best zones of Antioquia, and already by this time 35 per cent of the crop was grown there, on the well-drained land and fertile volcanically-derived soils. Coffee was grown by small farmers generally with under 10 ha, among other crops on the same farm.

In the period between 1900 and 1914 profits from coffee-growing went directly and indirectly into manufacturing, through the expansion of railways for coffee exports, the development of urban labour forces, and investment in cotton mills by the merchants and farmers of coffee.

The Antioqueños also expanded their influence by colonization movements in the nineteenth century, reaching south into the middle Cauca valley in search of gold and finding instead good farm land for coffee, so that the Middle Valley acquired something of the Antioqueño identity. Large land holdings on the fertile valley floor prevented a total modernization of this region, leaving this to the present day and the efforts of the CVC (see pp. 254–5).

The Pacific coast

To the west of the mountains the isolated hills had few Indians, and these could not be brought readily into mining ventures. The rich colonial mining of old gravels for gold on the upper Atrato and San Juan rivers was thus manned by imports of slaves through Cartagena, and a regional identity was imparted by the Negro slave, forming the dominant element in a racial mix of Europeans, Indians and Negroes. When freed from slavery these people, becoming small farmers, moved out along the coast and, from Panama into northern Ecuador, made it a Negro coast with a primitive subsistence economy.

MODERN ECONOMY

Transportation (fig. 52)

A central factor in any discussion of the Colombian economy is the transport network, for the long high cordilleras and deep valleys present formidable obstacles to interregional relationships and movement. As late as 1889, the British consul in Colombia reported that travel from Bogotá to the Magdalena took as long as from Europe to Colombia. Many routes were only possible for *tercios*, human baggage carriers who could go where even mules might have difficulty.

Transport difficulties were reduced a little by river steamers in the 1850s, but major improvements depended on railways, introduced on a big scale only from the last decade of the last century. Even these were built only as special-

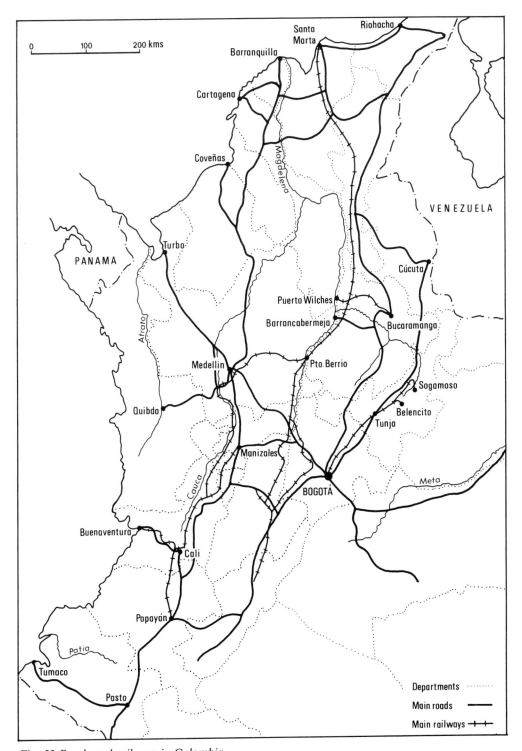

Fig. 52 Roads and railways in Colombia

purpose lines and never comprised a complete network. In more recent time, there has been a drift away from rail and onto road, while air traffic was of considerable importance only in the 1950s before road traffic extended into the northern and eastern lowlands.

Railways and rivers remain vital to some regions, such centres as Barrancabermeja depending heavily on the Magdalena for their trade, and Cali relying on rail connections to Buenaventura and Bogotá. Transport modes here are complementary rather than competitive, road and river filling in the transport gaps where rails are not possible or justifiable.

The most important river for navigation is the Magdalena, carrying more than 90 per cent of all river traffic. On its lower 500 km, navigation is possible at all times for 1.5 m draught vessels. Above this point up to Barrancabermeja, this level is maintained except for two months' lower water, but problems of silting, aggravated by the erosion caused by farmers occupying and clearing the valley slopes indiscriminately, are constantly present. Barranquilla and Cartagena share the Magdalena traffic, the first lying on the river itself 18 km inland from the mouth, the second connected by a 130 km canal to Calamar on the river.

The Cauca is navigable for river steamers for 200 km inland from its junction with the Magdalena, and the Atrato would also be a useful river if its valley were to experience any commercial development. There is a plan of far-reaching significance, to cut an ocean canal through Colombia, using the Atrato and the San Juan on the Pacific side, converting their upper courses into inland reservoirs or lakes, and replacing in function the Panama canal. On the Pacific coast, Buenaventura is Colombia's largest port, handling 40 per cent of all foreign trade, with a protected bay site and 10 m of water at high tide on the entrance bar.

The railways were all constructed to the one-yard gauge, which could make their integration easy in one respect; however, they have never been turned into a national network, despite much infilling, including the major line run down the Magdalena valley during the 1950s. Even this line did not connect to the ports of Cartagena and Barranquilla, but only to the banana port of Santa Marta, and only now is construction being extended to Barranquilla.

Significantly, the most heavily travelled rail links are the east–west ones between the valleys, where river traffic is not possible, and the Medellin–Puerto Berrío line is the most heavily used of all. Long north–south lines such as the Magdalena valley line have not proved a great success as they follow the same lines as road and river. Throughout, apart from the Magdalena line, the equipment and lines are in a poor state of repair and generally single-track.

The road network is also limited, despite rapid recent improvements. Only a few thousand kilometres of paved roads are in use, and the roads, like the railways, suffer from constant landslides and floods in the mountains and must continually undergo repair. Apart from north–south routes, there are some useful transverse roads cutting across mountains and linking outlying settlements. Such are the roads to Tumaco and Pasto in the south, from Bogotá through Medellín to Turbo and Quibdó, and the Rio Meta road in the east. The most noticeable gaps are the whole Pacific coast and the link to Central America, the last connection to be made in the Panamerican highway. The Panama road must cross the *Tapón de Darién* or Darien plug as it is aptly called in Colombia, consisting of the difficult swamp country of the lower Atrato river valley. The completion of this road will no doubt help the Medellín and through it the Colombian economy, though long-distance traffic is likely to be slight.

Agriculture
Colombia remains a strongly agricultural country despite modern industrialization, whether we measure the fact according to employment, output or export value of farm products. Half the population is rural, far more than in most South American countries, and most rural people are on farms. Besides being strongly agricultural, Colombia has the added emphasis on one product, coffee, which together with bananas generates three-fourths of foreign exchange. Despite the importance of farming, only a quarter of the land is used for production, and of this, 5.1 million ha or 5% (1974) of the land total is for crops, the rest being natural and improved pastures; these figures suggest an enormous potential for future expansion of production, but much unused land is either in the east on acid leached soil or in the mountains

where soil erosion is a limiting factor. For much of the unused land heavy infrastructure investment in roads, forest cutting, flood control and drainage would be a necessity. Something of a movement onto lower lands has taken place already, into the Magdalena valley, into the northern lowlands, and into the near Oriente, but this is minor compared to the land remaining unused.

Farm tenure and structure of farm holdings are important problems; two-thirds of the properties are registered as owner-operator, but in fact many are run by administrators rather than by their owners. Owner-operator farms are most common in Antioquia and Boyacá. Tenancy, accounting for 7.4% of land but 23.4% of farms in 1960, is often of backward form, including much sharecropping on coffee farms and tobacco farms in Santander. Cash tenancies are common on the lower river plains. On hill lands public domain has been occupied by squatters, who move off to new homes when their crops decline through soil erosion on the steep slopes.

The distribution of farm sizes is lopsided; a quarter of all farms in 1960 were under 1 ha, while 786 farms, 0.1% of the total, were over 2500 ha and occupied 20% of the farmland. This situation has not been affected by land reform, for the reform agency has only managed to settle some 50 000 new farmers and give proper titles to some squatter farmers.

Farm production

SUBSISTENCE
In the highlands traditional farming is practised without the help of government price guarantees and without machines, either by small owner-operator or tenant farmers. Maize for domestic consumption is common, and on the cooler lands potatoes and beans. In the *tierra fría* such edible tubers as arracacha, oca and ulluco are still common mestizo-grown crops, along with temperate grains. No fertilizers other than animal or human dung are used.

On the Pacific coastlands an interesting variant of the slash–burn system of farming is practised, which has been called slash–mulch farming. Secondary forest is sown with maize seed or rootstocks of banana or manioc, then the rest merely cut down with machetes to form a mulch through which the crops grow. This system is employed rather than slash–burn because of the lack of any dry season on this extremely well-watered coast, while the rapid breakdown of vegetation provides nutrition to the new plants.

Commercial agriculture

COFFEE
The key role of coffee in promoting industrial and commercial development in Antioquia has been noted. Coffee is still a key product for Colombia; for the last forty years it has been the leading crop and, to judge from the renown of Colombian mild coffees which command premium prices on the markets, it might be imagined that coffee covers a large part of Colombia. In fact the *cafetales* are a narrow belt of land (fig. 50) along the slopes of the river valleys, at 1000–2000 m. The crop is grown on small farms of under 50 ha, for steep slopes and difficult terrain do not lend themselves to large properties and mechanization. Much of the crop must be carried on mule back to the mills. Coffee is commonly grown here under shade trees, usually plantains. These give a longer ripening period to the tree, so that berries may be gathered by selecting only the red ones over a period of time — again a process favouring family farm operators — rather than all at once as in Brazil, and the result is the fine mild coffee of the country, without the bitterness induced by green berries which are inevitable in the Brazilian stripping of the tree. Shade trees also help to preserve soil with their leaf litter and shade, and their roots protect against erosion.

OTHER CROPS
Overdependence on coffee is recognized as undesirable and other crops have been given some official encouragement. One is cacao, though poor cultivation and low-yield varieties have hindered interest in expansion in the producing areas, principally the Cauca valley and Antioquia. Cotton has also been of interest because of local demand in the textile industry; cotton lands are widely dispersed, but most comes from the Caribbean coastlands, and production has increased substantially since the 1950s on medium and large farms with mechanization. Sugar-cane is also in good demand, and

production has increased, but most still goes to the production of simple *panela* cakes of brown sugar, a major element of diet among the Colombian poor. Cane is grown all over the *tierra templada* and Atlantic coast, but the best, used in mills in Cali and Manizales for white sugar, is grown in the Cauca valley on mechanized farms. Bananas are another commercial crop and have been a major export, from the Santa Marta region which developed under the United Fruit Company, no longer an owner of land in the country; the Atrato valley and the area around Turbo also has modern banana plantations on good alluvial soils, developed since the 1950s.

Livestock is an important element of farming, raised either on the poor natural grasses of the tropical north or the Llanos, or on rather better pastures in the highlands. On the Llanos cattle are produced only for beef, of relatively low quality, on plains where they must wander far in search of pasture in the dry season, and must migrate out of some regions altogether when the rains bring floods. In the eastern and central sierras small cattle farms are found sometimes occupying deserted coffee lands when erosion

has set in, with a stock of local white cattle, together with some European breeds for milk as well as beef. In the *tierra fría* a fair proportion of pure dairy cattle is found. Compared to cattle, sheep have minor importance with a stock of 1.9 million head against 2.3 million horned cattle in 1975. Fish are yet another animal resource, little tapped to date, as most of the catch comes from the rivers rather than the ocean (plate 40).

MINERAL INDUSTRIES

Minerals as yet contribute relatively little to the economy. A little gold and silver is still extracted as in colonial times from mines and placer gravels in Antioquia, and from the Pacific coastlands where platinum is also worked.

Emeralds, for which Colombia has long been noted, still come from mines in Boyacá, but are not important. More significant are the iron-ore deposits of the Cordillera Oriental, used for the steel mills of Paz del Río in the industrial valley of the Chicamocha, in conjunction with local limestone and coal.

40 *Fishing is little developed in Colombia. These are fishermen's huts at Tumaco, on the Pacific coast*

Coal is found mostly in Tertiary basins within the Cordillera Oriental, where the massive reserves give Colombia pre-eminence in all of Latin America. As geological survey is incomplete there is substantial difference between the 400 million tonnes proved and the 10 to 40 billion tonnes estimated reserves in Colombia. Some coals have been discovered only recently in the far southeast, in the Amazon country. Most of the coal is high-grade bituminous, large amounts of it suitable for coking, a vital factor in a continent where all coal is in short supply, and coking coal is precious; there is also some anthracite, a commodity which is eminently suited to long-distance transport. Within the highlands the greatest concentration of estimated reserves, 50-60 per cent, is in Cundinamarca and Boyacá, north of Bogotá. Another important area is the El Cerrejón field in the Guajira peninsula with 400 million tonnes estimated reserves, now producing coal for electricity power plants, and linked to a new port by rail. Reserves are 3.5 billion tonnes, for the whole region.

Colombia is the only Latin American country with a major potential for coal exporting, though there are substantial problems in taking coal out to the coast. Guajira is best sited for ocean movement, but has no transport infrastructure at all at present. The port of Riohacha would need improvement for this field to be developed. Interior fields present greater difficulties and improvement of the Rio Magdalena railway or of the river navigation facilities would be necessary to expand from the present negligible export levels. Internal markets are however likely to take much more coal than they now do (3-4 million tonnes annually) as declining petroleum reserves are exhausted. Colombia is already importing petroleum.

Oil has long been exploited in Colombia, in small widely-dispersed fields, which have fed home demand and some exports. Production was long in decline through the exhaustion of old fields until 1980, when increased exploration brought production increases and again made the country self-sufficient in oil. The new production areas were mostly in the Oriente. Coal and natural gas have also come into greater use so as to economize on oil. Natural gas supplies were spectacularly improved by the discovery in 1973 of a very large field in Guajira, the field lying both on- and offshore.

Salt, another little-used resource, is mined in Guajira too, at Manaure, and at Cerromatoso in Córdoba, south of Cartagena, a major new development in mining nickel and cobalt is being pressed with Dutch and American participation. It is of long-term significance that Colombia looks much more favourably on foreign participation in minerals extraction than do most of her neighbours, and the growth of the minerals sector may be more rapid because of this factor.

POWER INDUSTRIES

The geography of electric power production is distinctive, for there are two major producing regions with different power bases. In the Andes, a major power source is the river flow, already tapped in part in the Cauca valley and at the new Chivor dam north of Bogotá. This contrasts with the northern plains where power comes from oil and coal, and in recent years from natural gas. Dependence on one kind of supply has its disadvantages in the different levels of response possible to demands which themselves fluctuate through time. Obviously it is desirable to have a national grid to iron out supply and demand irregularities by switching supply from one region to another, and this was achieved in 1985 with a 500 kV connecting line from near Medellin to near Cartagena, 523 km in length. In addition to this line, there is now a 230 kV grid which reaches into the Guajira to bring in thermal power, into the middle Cauca to link in the CVC plant, and tying in the numerous HEP plants of Antioquia and Cundinamarca to the cities of Medellín and Bogotá. Dry season declines in water supply and consequently in HEP can thus be remedied by using more of the thermal plant from the Atlantic coast region.

Seventy per cent of installed capacity and of electricity production is hydroelectric, and this figure is likely to remain high in the future, as the six regional power companies have joined together both in extending a national grid and in building the expensive large dams and HEP turbines. The most significant of these are Chivor (1000 MW) in the Eastern Cordillera near Bogotá, San Carlos (1200 MW) near Medellín, and Cañafisto (1500 MW), being built on the Cauca northwest of Medellín.

INDUSTRIALIZATION: URBAN AND REGIONAL DEVELOPMENT

Origins of the multiple-centre urban network

In most developed countries an urban network of cities of varying size, where rank in the urban hierarchy is matched to city size in a rank–size relationship, is expected and found. In less developed countries the relationship does not generally hold, and is replaced by a city system dominated by one or two major cities. For Colombia the rank—size theory does hold good however, for a variety of reasons. In colonial time, placing the capital city at an inland site meant a need for other cities to act as ports, and Cartagena, Santa Marta and Barranquilla grew up on the Atlantic front. Other cities were important because of regional isolation, Cali, Medellín and Popayán in the highlands, Barrancabermeja as a river port, Bucaramanga as centre to Santander.

A separate cultural and economic identity was possible for each of these towns because of the inordinate cost of transport between them. Nineteenth-century growth modified this scheme of things, but did not overthrow it, and the period of rapid growth after 1850 helped the port cities as much as it did Bogotá and the regional centres of the highlands. Coffee and tobacco exports helped first the Atlantic ports, Santa Marta and Cartagena with its fine natural harbour, then Barranquilla, after construction of a short railway to an outport on the ocean. After 1914 the Panama Canal and a railway from Cali led to rapid growth at Buenaventura on the Pacific. Medellín had its own source of growth, first as coffee emporium, then also as cotton-textile manufacturer to the nation. Only Cartagena lost status during the century, through the disappearance of its special function as port of call for the Spanish fleet. Its population, 18000 in 1825, was in 1905 only 9700.

Recent trends

More recently, the very largest cities, Bogotá, Medellín and Cali, have asserted a tendency to dominate over all others, with more rapid growth of population and industry. Bogotá, with about 2.9 million in 1973, had had a growth rate of 7.5% per annum in its postwar population.

Bogotá's function as administrative and political nerve centre to an increasingly centralized state accounts for much of its importance; administrative centrality has meant growth in employment areas such as printing and publishing, the head offices of private industries, retailing and wholesaling, metals and electrical engineering industries, foreign-owned chemicals, pharmaceuticals, food and drink and car assembly industries, as well as in central government itself and governmental agencies and public bodies.

Bogotá continues its expansion, with government investment to improve its infrastructure in elements such as electric power, a new underground railway system, and roads. Though not primarily a manufacturing city, it is the main market for the steel industry in Belencito, the Paz del Rio steelworks.

The Paz del Rio plant is one of the smallest integrated iron and steel works in Latin America, with a 300 000 tonnes annual capacity, which is far below present world standards. Its advantage is location close to Bogotá markets and to raw materials, local coal and iron ore. But the decision to locate inland was controversial, for a coastal plant would have had access to cheap Venezuelan oil, iron ore and scrap steel. Since the recent gas and coal developments in Guajira, the location seems still more marginal.

Regional planning

During the 1960s regional policy was applied for the first time in Colombia. One arm of the 1960s policy was to restrict the growth of Bogotá and encourage the intermediate cities, but this was sharply reversed from 1970 by policies favouring active urbanization concentrated in the four big cities. This policy runs counter to most modern thinking about city growth, but was sponsored here as a way of generating concentrations of population able to support modern industry in the cities, and leading to modernization in the countryside as the peasants migrated to the towns. In rural areas, agrarian reform had been proposed as a policy, but it has failed to become effective. Another rural policy was that of regional corporations, of which there were nine, though these absorbed only 1% of the national budget, most of it spent on one corporation, the CVC or Cauca Valley Corporation.

41 Bogota's street children exemplify a major problem of rapid urbanization. There is a growth of squatter settlements with few amenities

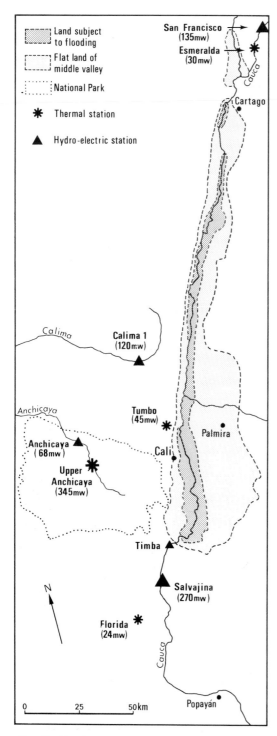

Fig. 53 The CVC: main power projects and the floodable area of the Cauca valley

Cali and the Cauca valley

The Cauca river flows in its upper course through the mountains of the southern Central Cordillera; it forms a long structural trough in its middle section, from the town of Santander above Cali as far as Cartago, beyond which there is a small further island of flat land before a gorge section through the mountains to the lowland section. Central to the middle basin is Cali, which has grown from 100 000 inhabitants in 1940 to about 1.6 million in 1986. This rapid growth is evident in the somewhat irregular skyline, skyscrapers interspersed with areas of 5–8-storey construction, and in the burgeoning *tugurios,* the shanty towns which are relegated to the often flooded lands near the Cauca river. Cali's industries are based on local resources — power and cane bagasse in paper mills, now being supplemented by timber from plantations; and food-processing industries, since the basin produces over 80% of the nation's sugar cane and soyabeans, which are milled in the city. The agricultural area is constantly being expanded with the help of the CVC.

The CVC

Apart from a natural identity conferred by the enclosed valley, a separate identity has been sought through an autonomous public body, the Cauca Valley Corporation (CVC). This body provides a good example of the possible role of multi-purpose river-basin bodies though it has not been successful in many of its stated aims (fig. 53).

It was created in 1954 on the instigation of the local populace, especially Cali interests, who saw a set of interrelated barriers to development which should be solved jointly. A South American TVA was envisaged, covering not only the Department of Valle Del Cauca but also other departments on the river.

The problem was that the river was subject to damaging floods over a quarter of the 400000 ha of flat land in the Middle Valley, where the best soils and irrigation water were available. Flood damage was increasing over time with the depredation of forest cover on the steep slopes surrounding the valley by small farmers. The intensity of small-farmer cultivation was itself in part a consequence of the monopolization of the lower flat land by big farmers, ranchers with great herds of cattle feeding on natural pastures, or by sugar planters; the land was concentrated in the hands of a few owners. Cattle ranching was in turn a natural result of the flood liability of the flat lands.

To improve matters, the CVC was to place high dams on the Cauca river in its upper course above Cali, which would both generate power and moderate river flow. In addition they would straighten the river course with cuts by some 30%, and place levees as further protection. Other dams on the Anchicayá and Calima rivers of the Pacific drainage would raise further power. Irrigation of farmlands and drainage of lowlying land would help to make the land suitable for mechanized arable farming. The mountainous slopes would be relieved of cultivation pressure and be subject to conservation measures. The human resources of the valley would be mobilized by education and improved social services.

The CVC encountered opposition in its plans from other departments, which refused to join it, from central government which saw a challenge to authority, and from local landowners who would have to pay a tax to finance the new corporation. Over the long term the CVC was defused by uncooperative attitudes and limited to its central functions of power generation and river control.

Even given this reduced role, the agency has not been really successful, and there have been substantial ecological problems. A well-known example is the first Anchicayá reservoir, which silted up in 15 years from its building, requiring the construction of a second, higher, dam. Shifting agriculture combined with very high rainfall, over 7620 mm annually as is common all along this Pacific coast stretch of Colombia, has increased the high silt yield in the river basin to dangerous levels. CVC has been practising reforestation using eucalyptus and leucaena, and there are also private forest plantations of pines. The largest company, Carton de Colombia, alone plans 30 000 ha by the year 2000. But these species do not encourage a good shrub understorey to protect the soil, so that the problem seems likely to persist. Protection to the physical environment might also be expected from the existence of the Farallones National Park (Fig. 53), which covers much of the headwaters area, but there is pressure from frontier farmers to have roads built through the Park which are supported by the national government Roads Department, and once the roads are built deforestation and agricultural clearings are likely to spread rapidly.

THE ATLANTIC COAST CITIES

The Atlantic or Caribbean coast is another area where growth industries are beginning to emerge. There are several sources of this growth. First, the push into lowlands by farmers is taking up more of the north coast hinterlands, with tropical fruits, sugar and beef cattle; secondly, there are the thriving power and fuel industries, located in the north and bringing processing to the port cities; finally, there is a nascent tourist industry.

Cartagena profits from all these elements. As an old colonial city with its walls and many buildings intact from the eighteenth century and earlier, it has many attractions for tourists, which will be amplified by the new coast road being built from the Venezuelan frontier through Santa Marta. Its location on the Caribbean should also bring Northern Hemisphere tourists, and Santa Marta is building a new international airport to receive them. Cartagena also has the usual gamut of port processing industries and there is a large oil refinery and petrochemical works at Mamonal nearby, making fertilizers for domestic and export markets.

Barranquilla (690 000) has the advantage of ready access to the Magdalena river valley, though rail access has never been direct. It has large chemical factories and cement works, and a new integrated pulp and paper industry making cardboard packaging for new delicate varieties of banana which must be packed on the farm rather than shipped direct to ports. A new bridge over the Magdalena will link this city more closely to the Santa Marta and Guajira tourist coast and to Venezuela.

21. Venezuela

This country occupies 916 000 sq km, not including 150 000 sq km which it disputes with Guyana, making it one of the region's larger countries, but it has the small population of 16.4 million (1983), mostly concentrated in and around the urban centres of the north and leaving a huge region of minimal density population in the Llanos and Guayana. The republic is divided into twenty states, two federal territories, the federal district of Caracas, and some seventy tiny islands in the Caribbean which are federal dependencies. Effective power is however heavily concentrated in the national capital.

Venezuela is outstanding in the continent for its contrasts and contradictions in economic and social life: on the one hand, a slow-changing, traditional rural economy based on semi-subsistence farming and primitive ranching; on the other, the oil industry providing the impetus for urban and industrial growth in the present century and a source of wealth for a small minority of Venezuelans, many of them city-dwelling executives who live not far from the *barrios*, slums that house people with infinitely lower standards of living.

HISTORY OF SETTLEMENT

Indian cultures

There are still Indian groups living in little modified native communities in Venezuela. For example, the Guaraunos live in parts of the Orinoco Delta region liable to periodic river or tidal flooding, and depend on fish for their livelihood, isolated by a semi-amphibious way of life. Primitive tribal communities are to be found in the remote Andes too, especially in the Sierra de Perijá, where the Yukpa shifting cultivators are protected by an Indian reserve since the 1940s, though their way of life is gradually being changed by contact with outsiders. On the plains below them live the once-feared Motilones, primitive gatherers of the Maracaibo lowlands. There is evidence of more advanced cultures, notably the Timoto-cuicas, in the Andean region of Mérida, who once lived a life more comparable to the Incas or Chibchas than their neighbours. They constructed terraces, knew how to build in stone, how to establish irrigation systems, and store water in reservoirs, against occasional drought. Their farm products, manioc, potatoes, maize, tobacco and cotton, could be stored in great underground warehouses. Manufactures included cotton goods, basketry and metal work, and they had a form of money. They made settlements of up to 800 stonewalled houses. Their relations to the Inca and Chibcha peoples are uncertain, but they seem to provide further evidence of ancient links throughout the whole Andean oecumene from northern Argentina to Venezuela.

Spanish conquest and rule

Spanish interest first focussed in the eastern island of Cubagua, in 1507. In the glassy Caribbean waters of this little island pearls were brought up by native divers, though this resource could

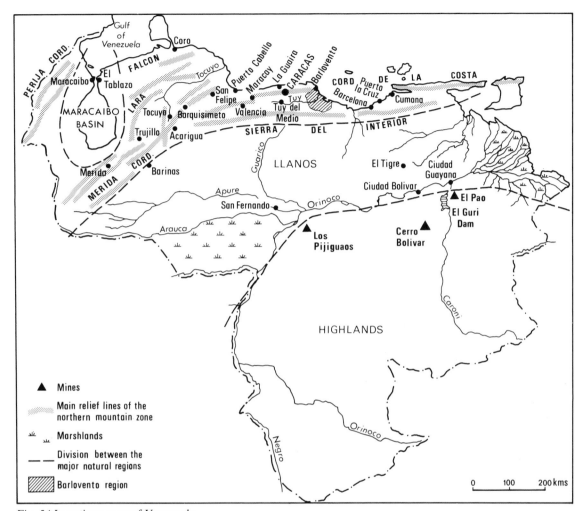

Fig. 54 Locations map of Venezuela

never be longlasting and Cubagua was soon over-shadowed by other areas. In the sixteenth century, the island of Margarita replaced Cubagua as pearl centre and it is now a deserted island, while the whole industry has declined with the competition from cultured pearls.

Around 1520, the Spaniards moved inland to found Cumaná (1520), Coro (1527) and other towns, but then Charles V of Spain leased out the Coro colony to his German bankers Welser, whose material interests led them both to try colonization and hunt for gold. In both attempts they failed and as the Coro colony had become a financial drain on Welser resources, Spanish direct rule returned, with a capital at El Tocuyo

from 1545 (fig. 54). By the end of the century there were 26 towns, including Caracas (1569) which replaced El Tocuyo as capital in 1577, Maracaibo, Barquisimeto and Valencia, all founded on the sites of old Indian settlements, mostly in upland valleys where native labour and fertile soil could supply them with life's necessities.

The process of occupation was slow and diffi-cult compared to that in Peru, because in this zone there were many small tribal groups each fighting for survival in a difficult terrain, rather than a great empire whose nerve centre had only to be attacked in order to disorganize the whole nation. Movement far into Venezuela had to await the seventeenth century, when Salesian and other missionaries entered and effectively pacified parts of the Maracaibo Basin and the Llanos and Guayana regions, paving the way for a trickle of settlers.

Colonial economy and society

The period 1520–1600 was one of exploration without any very stable economic base. Thereafter Venezuela became a primary exporting region similar to others in the continent. We may follow Travieso's outline of the sequence in a table.

Exports	1600–50	1650–1810	1830–1925	1925
Dominant	Cattle Hides	Cocoa	Coffee	Oil
Transition		Tobacco Indigo		

Source: Travieso, F. (1975), Ciudad, Region y Subdesarrollo, Fondo Edit. Comun, Caracas.

Cattle hides and salt meat were a first resource, coming from various parts of the country. They did not disappear after 1650, but gradually declined in importance. Cocoa, of top quality from the Maracaibo basin, from the central region of Valencia and Caracas, became the next dominant export, until the rise in world popularity of coffee in the nineteenth century. Coffee was best suited physically to the subtropical, well-drained and fertile soils of the Andean margins and the central region. Transitional products such as indigo and tobacco were from these same regions.

The Llanos exported some hides, along with exotic goods from the Guiana highlands such as tree gums, gold, egret feathers (fashionable in late Victorian society), all through the port of Angostura. The Llanos achieved some importance in the early nineteenth century, only to lose it through continuous wars, as Venezuela, seeking a national identity, first separated from Spain to join Gran Colombia, then seceded from this new state to form a republic in 1830. From 1830 to 1900 there were 39 revolutions and 127 smaller uprisings, occupying over 24 years of the period, as various regional leaders, the *caudillos,* sought central power.

Venezuela remained a backwater under such conditions until the effective development of oil

from 1917. This caused new regional shifts of the economic base, first from the Andes and central coffee lands to Maracaibo, where the oil was, then back to Caracas from 1925 as the oil companies set up their offices in the capital. The oil economy continued unreined under foreign ownership through the 1930–50 period, making Venezuela the world leader in oil exports. Political dictatorships of Gomez (1908–35) and Perez Jimenez (1948–58) allowed oil to continue as king. Policies for 'sowing the oil', by putting state oil revenues into agricultural colonization and urban development, met with very limited success. A centre–periphery structure was firmly established in this way, and this has remained to some extent to the present, despite a return to democratic government which has been maintained without interruptions since the times of Perez Jimenez.

PHYSICAL GEOGRAPHY

A number of well-defined physical regions may be distinguished. To the north there are two groups of mountain ranges, the Andes, enclosing the Maracaibo Basin, and the Coastal Ranges. In the centre are the Llanos, to the south again Guayana.

The Andes

The Western Cordillera or Andes loses height from Peru northward, and in Venezuela lies at around 3000 m, with peaks to 4000 m. This is mainly a region of vertiginous slopes covered in dense rainforest, deep-gashed valleys and silt-laden rivers. Intense folding has exposed old rocks in the mountain core, and Tertiary folding has made the landscape one of fault blocks rather than fold mountains.

The main topographic features are the narrow Cordillera de Perijá on the Colombian frontier, and the Cordillera de Mérida, a broader mountain mass of several ranges. While Perijá has little flat land, Mérida has many wide alluvial terraces at different levels, the result of recent uplifting, and these flat *mesas,* as they are called, provide good farm land. Mérida and Trujillo are sited on such terraces within the *tierra templada.*

In the north the Andes fade into a transitional zone of low hills and drought, in the states of Lara and Falcón, east of Maracaibo. Drought

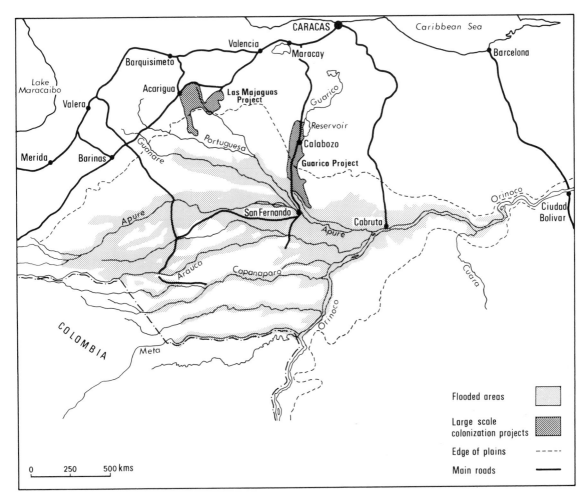

Fig. 55 Flooded area of Apure and Orinoco rivers in June–August 1976. A discussion of this flood and Venezuelan policy is given in the last section of Chapter 1

affects the whole coast, especially the west-facing or lee shores and those projecting far north. To the northwest lies the Maracaibo tectonic depression, partly occupied by the lake, a largely freshwater lake though open to the sea, for it is fed by abundant river water. Poldering may assist in the rapid infilling of the lake which is now occurring naturally by sedimentation.

Northern Cordilleras

These differ from the Andes in their geological history, structure and appearance; they run east—west like the West Indies, breaking away from the Andean directions beyond the divisory depression east of Barquisimeto. Two broad groups of mountains may be discerned, the Cordillera de la Costa (fig. 54) and the Serranía del Interior, separated by the Valencia Basin, the Tuy Valley and the Gulfs of Paria and Cariaco. Behind the coastal ranges there are some of the most important economic zones of Venezuela. Valencia and El Tuy are old colonial lands of tropical farming and they have additional roles today. The coastal landscapes differ from those of the interior hills by their increasing drought to the north, with 400–800 mm of rainfall and scrub vegetation.

Llanos

This plain extends 1000 km east–west and has a regional slope to the southeast and the Orinoco. In the northern and western margins there are broad alluvial fans with coarser and more fertile material than the south, where during the April–October season of maximum rainfall, there is flooding over huge areas of the savanna. Cattle are driven onto slightly higher ground, the old levees of the west and *mesas*, ancient alluvial terraces of the east, during this period. On the southern edge of the plain, the Orinoco is broad and shallow, skirting the mass of hard rock which is Guayana. River flooding and seasonal rainfall give an alternation of drought and moisture which makes tree growth difficult, and coarse grasses are the usual cover except for the *galería* forests of Mauritia palm along the water courses. (Fig. 55)

The Orinoco Delta region is a somewhat different part of the Llanos, under constant threat of flooding from river or sea. Active building out of the delta has been going on in recent years and added about 900 sq km to the delta in the period 1875–1950.

Guayana highlands

This section of the Shield is of metamorphic rock, including useful iron ores, the itabirites, in the north. In the south there are tabular forms, the *tepuis,* pre-Cambrian quartzites which form remarkable vertical cliffs. The south is subject to heavy rainfall, reaching over 3000 mm per annum; this allows a dense selva and powerful rivers which make dramatic leaps as they leave the *tepuis*, including the Angel Falls, 972 m high, at the edge of Auyan Tepui. The Caroní, draining the high southeast of Guayana, is second only to the Orinoco in flow. In the north, lower rainfall gives a chaparral vegetation of low open tree cover and coarse grasses comparable to the Brazilian *campo cerrado*, with under 2000 mm rainfall.

Southern Guayana and Mount Roraima (2800 m) were the inspiration for *The Lost World* of Conan Doyle, a reasonable choice for the tops of the *tepuis*, including Roraima, are ecologically isolated areas, islands surrounded by cliffs up to 1000 m high. Such mountain fastnesses do in fact hold many rare and hitherto unknown flowers, orchids and other epiphytes, and species of birds

not known elsewhere, as has been documented by recent expeditions to Roraima.

> The mystery of the tepuis was more a matter of man's romanticism though it must be admitted that situation, structure, impenetrability of adjacent regions, the primitive Indian groups which live on the riverbanks and look with awe on the heights where they place, as did the ancient Hellenes, the god—demons of their primitive theogony, all this has contributed and still contributes to create round the tepuis an atmosphere of legend and mystery difficult to dissipate.
>
> *Alfonso Vinci,* Los Andes de Venezuela, *Caracas, 1953*

AGRICULTURE: THE DUAL ECONOMY

The problem

Within the long-occupied mountain regions of the Andes and Northern Cordilleras, there are the features common to most Latin American countries, an excessive concentration of land-holdings and of commercial production, contrasting with the great majority of farms which are *minifundios* that can produce little for the market and often cannot even support their owners with food. Many of these tiny farms are sedentary, fixed in location, but in Venezuela an important part of the problem is that of the *conuco*, the shifting farm, and the *conuquero*, its owner. As practised in the Venezuelan Andes, the *conuco* differs little from its relatives in neighbouring countries, such as the *roça* of Brazil, and in its basic form consists of the age-old processes of selecting and cutting a plot of forest during the dry season, burning it at the end of this drought (February–April) so as to clear the land and feed it with the valuable wood ash, then sowing seeds of maize, beans and a variety of other seeds, as well as bananas, plantains, manioc and taro, plants that are reproduced vegetatively without seeds, using simple wooden digging sticks, and harvesting the crop after a few months in which there may be little weeding, especially in new plots. After a year or two the yield may have declined so much that the plot is abandoned and the farmer cuts out another *conuco*. Such farms are found throughout the humid subtropical forest lands at levels below

1600 m and in difficult country with very steep slopes.

This traditional system was perhaps the optimum for low density Indian populations. Ecologically it was well adjusted to the environment because it represented a modification rather than a destruction of the natural conditions. Shade was preserved, an important factor, by leaving shade trees and by planting other trees within the *conuco*. A storied cover and balance of demands on the soil was achieved by intercropping of different crops and use of tiny plots when a single crop was grown. A long forest fallow after abandonment was typical. Now the system is breaking down, with increased pressures on the land. Although population densities are low — in the area of traditional pure Indian tribal lands in the Perijá mountains, there are some 2200 Yukpa and Yuko Indians, giving an overall density of 1.5 persons per square kilometre* — the plots of land chosen for the *conuco* must be of adequate quality, and if possible come from the best alluvial or terrace lands; other lands which they are being forced to use in Perijá are of much lower farming potential. Furthermore, the forest fallow period is being continually reduced, and the soil is thereby depleted and opened to erosion for longer and longer periods, reducing its productivity.

Other kinds of *conuco* may pose even more of a threat through soil depletion, though as they are on lesser slopes they do not lead to rapid erosion. On the north coast in the Barlovento zone shifting cultivation is practised by small farmers whose primary interest is growing cacao trees, and *conuco* is followed by planting of cacao and shade trees. Here commercial production replaces subsistence cropping, and monoculture replaces the ecologically sounder polyculture of the Indians. Another variety of *conuco* is that of the northern Llanos, practised by employees or tenants of land on the big ranches known as *hatos*. Here the land used for the clearing is the gallery forest along the streams. In such cases, the problem is perhaps less an ecological one and more one of tenurial relations, for the *conuquero* is a minifundista who must pay for his land in labour or cash that he can ill afford from his earnings.

* Kenneth Ruddle, 'The Yukpa cultivation system', *Ibero-Americana*, No. 52, University of California (1974), p. 28.

Solutions

An agrarian reform law was enacted in 1960. It was less powerful than the Bolivian or Chilean ones (see Chapter 3) and less effective in some respects. There were, for example, no fixed lower limits on size of holding to be allowed to remain unreformed. In addition, compensation was to be paid to expropriated farmers, at the market value and in cash for farms which were producing under modern tenure conditions. Venezuela paid out in compensation 25 times as much as Bolivia in the 1960s. Most private farming areas were skirted round altogether, because the majority of lands subject to reform were public land, which was more easy to deal with. A large area was involved, 4.6 million ha over 1959-69, compared to Bolivia's 9.7 million in 1953-69 (Wilkie, 1975).

Reform has not decreased agricultural production, which did not falter during the 1960s and has risen well ahead of population increases. But there are many reports of abandoned post-reform farms, and there are too many minifundia (in 1971, 43% of all farms were under 5 ha, compared to 52% in 1956). Increased production would seem to be coming from commercial farms outside the reform sector. And latifundios also continue (farms over 1000 ha still have 67% of all land compared to 71.7% in 1961). Venezuela has also been slow to grant definitive title to lands. Most farmers have only provisional title, and many cases are clouded by tenure changes after reform, so that proper title may not be granted.

Irrigation

Another approach to the small-farmer problem has been via expansion of the irrigated area along with electrification, roadbuilding and education. Enthusiasm for the irrigation approach was enough to double the 240 000 ha of irrigated land between 1950 and 1970, though most was still private schemes.

One major government project, the Guárico, involving over 100 000 ha on a northern tributary of the Orinoco and begun in 1954, illustrates the problems in the main region of irrigation expansion, the Llanos. Construction of the works meant very heavy capital expenditure before any returns were possible, including excavation of a reservoir for water because the river runs over the Llanos where no natural basins are available; canals had also to be dug. Soils, apart from small areas of alluvium, are poor compared to those in parts of the highlands, lateritic and infertile with poor drainage. This has allowed large-scale rice and now forage-grass production, but is of little use for other crops. Rice and irrigated grassland crops are suited to fairly large farms, and small farmers have not had much access to the Guárico. Indeed, from the beginning, land was given to *empresarios,* managers of 150–200 ha farms, rather than to *campesinos.* After some years campesino families came in but only 845 families were settled by 1971. Nor is the size of irrigated area satisfactory, with only 40 000 ha achieved.

In recent years and continuing under present plans, vast areas of the northern Llanos, including Guárico and similar schemes, are being reclaimed for irrigation to provide fodder for cattle, an enterprise that fits in well with the traditional ranching economy of the area as it economizes on the need for sending cattle north to the mountains for fattening, but does not do much to slake the campesino thirst for land. It may be asked whether too much has not been invested in vast schemes, rather than in improvement and extension of small schemes which are working well in the highlands. Irrigation schemes sponsored by government in the highlands have proved inexpensive and highly productive, and government favour seems to be finally turning more to these smaller schemes. It must be emphasized that the primary failure of the big schemes is not in their poor level of production, however, but in lack of settlement. Only 3715 families under government projects for irrigation were settled by 1971, though there are perhaps 200 000 farmers in need of land.

Land pressure is being relieved at present by spontaneous colonization in some areas such as the Maracaibo lowlands, moving out ahead of roads, public service or extension agency aid. Again, with relatively little expenditure such schemes of colonization could become commercially productive and serve many more farmers with a redirection of governmental interest, especially by bringing technical assistance to change subsistence farmers into commercial agriculturalists.

FARMING POTENTIAL OF THE REGIONS

The mountains
In the Andes of northwest Venezuela, commercial farming is restricted mostly to patches of slope land at lower angles than the average. Old river terraces provide the best sites. The region is very productive, yielding some 20% of national farm goods from only 3% of farm area, mostly minifundia holdings. Commercial crops of coffee and sugar-cane dominate the lower altitudes, wheat and maize compete with them in the *terra templada,* and potatoes and cattle, dairy and beef, are important in the *tierra fría,* at 2200–3000 m. Fattening of cattle is traditional in Táchira and Aragua states.

In the northern Cordilleras agriculture is more concentrated, in the intermediate longitudinal depression between the coastal ranges and the Serranía del Interior. Within this depression, the Valencia Basin, lying at 400–500 m, has a fine subtropical climate and alluvial soils, with rainwater supplemented by irrigation sources. Immediate access to markets in the industrial cities of Maracay and Valencia, within the basin, has allowed development of market gardening along with field crops in an intensive commercial system. Sugar and coffee are processed in modern mills in the basin. The lower Tuy valley, Barlovento, is predominant in cocoa production and irrigation has extended the growing zone upstream into the dry middle Tuy south of Caracas.

To the northwest of the mountains are two zones of distinct potential. The Maracaibo Basin, little settled to date, has good potential farm land in its southern half, and with irrigation this could extend to the north. In the 1960s tropical dairying made some impact here, but much infrastructural work such as drainage and roads needs completion first. The other zone is Falcón-Lara-Yaracuy, the dry limestone hills which have long been deforested with their soil often eroded to rock surfaces, the preserve of wandering goats. Only deep valleys between the hills have intensive sugar-cane or maize cultivation.

The south
Traditionally, Llanos land use has been the pasturing of cattle; the Llanero is a cowboy as

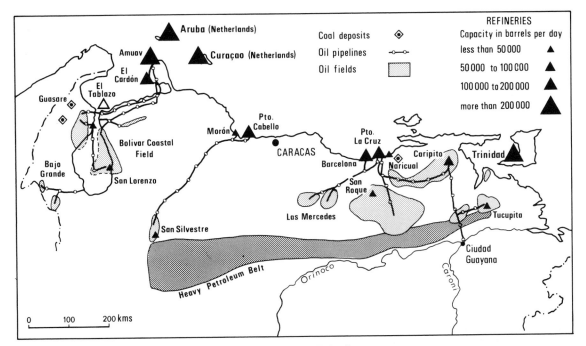

Fig. 56 Coal, oil and heavy petroleum fields, oil refineries and pipelines

tough as his rangy cattle, which are the descendants of Spanish longhorns introduced to the plains in mid-sixteenth century, spreading rapidly in the wild. In recent years these hardy animals have been given still greater resistance to tropical conditions by crossing with the zebu. State irrigation schemes in the northwest Llanos, mentioned above, are now radically altering this way of life. The state of Portuguesa has most cultivated land in the Llanos, centred on the piedmont urban site of Acarigua. The rice-growing area under this stimulus has grown from 41 000 ha in 1948–52 to 150 000 ha in 1975.

Beyond the Llanos, Guayana promises little for farmers, for it is remote, with poor soils. Possibly cattle raising may be extended into the northern chaparral belt, but its grazing capacity is very low.

THE PETROLEUM INDUSTRY

As recently as 1920 Venezuela was tiny in the world's oil league, producing 0.1% of the total: in 1957 it supplied a massive 15%, only to decline again in relative terms through the rise of Russia and the Middle East. Oil is still central to the economy, as may be seen from the fact that 90%

of exports are oil and oil products. The geography of the industry is indicated in Fig. 56. Oil is found in large Tertiary structures in the Maracaibo Basin, both inshore south of Cabimas and offshore under the lake, and to a lesser extent west of the lake. Maracaibo state accounts for 80% of Venezuelan production. Oil also comes from numerous small fields in the eastern Llanos, developed in the 1930s and now declining in production.

Oil movement is generally by pipeline to coastal refineries at Barcelona, Puerto Cabello, and especially to the large refineries on the Paraguaná peninsula where most refining capacity is located. In addition, the Dutch Antilles, Aruba and Curaçao, have refineries catering largely to Venezuelan oil. Refineries were mostly built with a view to demand from the east coast USA, largely for heavy fuel oil for industry. Now Venezuela has deliberately sought new markets worldwide, and the demands are for lighter oil products, so that the refineries have been substantially modified in recent years.

Natural gas is associated with the oil in many fields, but was not used by the companies before the 1950s, being burned off or simply allowed to escape from the wellhead. Now some gas is piped to storage tanks and liquefied for transport in liquid gas carrier ships to overseas markets, though millions of cubic metres are still flared off in a dramatic waste of precious resources.

Alternative oil sources

There are other potential areas for oil development, notably the Gulf of Venezuela, within the reach of modern offshore techniques, though here a dispute over territorial rights has been simmering for a long time between Venezuela which claims the whole gulf and Colombia which claims part of the west side. Other offshore areas of promise are the Caribbean coastal seas — oil has been found near Margarita — and the huge deposits of the Heavy Petroleum Belt of the Orinoco. This latter was discovered in the 1930s but no way of extracting it economically was known. It lies south of the worked fields around Tigre in the Llanos, and extends as a band 40–60 km wide adjacent to the Orinoco and the hard rocks of the Guayana Shield, from the Orinoco delta at least as far west as San Fernando de Apure. Venezuelans prefer the name Heavy Petroleum Belt to the older Tar Belt, emphasizing the new possibilities for these oils using new secondary recovery techniques. The most promising technique, already used successfully in extracting more oil from the old fields of Lake Maracaibo, is of injecting steam at regular spaced intervals into the oil-bearing stratum. This is found to increase the yield from 5% to over 30% of total oil in the deposit, and make the potential reserve in the Belt 840 billion barrels, which may be compared to a present 18 billion barrels of proven reserves from conventional sources in Venezuela. There are other problems with the heavy oils, notably their high content of sulphur, vanadium and some other metals, which must be separated out before the oil is passed to the consumer.

More important as an obstacle to immediate massive use is the availability of oil from the older exploited areas. Since the private companies were granted no new concessions after 1959, and under a threat of nationalization, they made no new investments and let their installations gradually run down in the 1960s and 1970s. But since nationalization in 1976, new exploration by the state firm, Petroven, which has assumed responsibility for the whole industry, has discovered deposits in deeper beds of older

Tertiary and Cretaceous age underneath the presently worked fields. Secondary recovery also maintains some of the older structures in operation, and in any case, Venezuela has reduced her output of oil in a more conservationist attitude towards the leading resource of the country. It is however still planned to have large-scale production from the Heavy Petroleum Belt from about 1989.

Foreign control

Though a national oil company was first in production in the 1880s, a Venezuelan president, Castro, granted concessions which were sold in 1907 to British and North American firms. Reaction against this loss of national control only asserted itself after 1945, when further concessions were withheld, and an increasing share of profits insisted on by the government. Since then, the great increase in oil prices of 1973 allowed Venezuela to anticipate her stated intention to take over oil in 1983, and establish a state oil firm, Petroven, to replace all the foreign firms from 1 January 1976. This has been accomplished peacefully because the firms have been paid large amounts in compensation, and indeed continue to provide technological knowhow. Dependence on foreigners, it might be claimed, has not been reduced by nationalization, since Petroven has no control over the marketing of its product, in foreign countries.

Diversification or oil?

Income from oil royalties, from income tax and company tax on oil companies, local taxes and special exchange rates, have all contributed to sustain the Venezuelan economy in recent decades, and oil is inevitably still strong with profits going directly to the central government, despite a firm control on the physical level of production today. There is a movement away from oil towards diversified production, spoken of since the 1930s as 'sowing the oil' but not really embarked on until after the Second World War.

Arguments supporting diversification can be summarized as follows. First, the ruling party, Acción Democrática, has traditionally had much of its support in the rural areas, and must spend money on farming if only to maintain farmers' support. On an economic level, it is necessary to diversify to avoid dependence on one commodity and its uncertain prices. This argument has always been present though it looks dubious in the present age of high oil prices. Finally, the unassisted expansion of manufacturing industry in the country has been small, so that only some light consumer goods manufacturing and assembly have become established. This means that the state should take a hand through setting up state agencies as in the case of steel, aluminium, petrochemicals and refining.

Against diversification, it can be said that petroleum has in fact proved a very stable and rising source of income especially under the aegis of OPEC with no sign of any future period with low oil prices to come. It is also possible to develop petrochemicals and refining, as Venezuela is trying to do, without moving outside the oil sector. In addition, within South America, and especially within the Andean Pact of which she is a member, Venezuela's forte is not in agriculture or industry generally, but in oil, which she could sell in refined or crude form throughout the continent.

STEEL IN VENEZUELA

Venezuela's first small private steel plant was built in 1950 and used scrap steel. The much larger state-owned SIDOR plant was finished in 1962, as a part of the Guayana investment scheme under CVG the Guayana Regional Corporation, and located just to the west of Ciudad Guayana. It grew out of the massive iron-ore export industries which has been built up from 1950 by Bethlehem Steel and United States Steel corporations, and out of a political promise to make Venezuela more than a raw-material exporting country.

The ore is present in massive deposits at El Pao and Cerro Bolivar within the Guayana massif (see the locations map, fig. 54), totalling 1.8 billion tonnes of high grade ore, with still larger deposits of lower-grade ore. In 1975 the iron ore industry was nationalized and made into another state agency under CVG. Other physical resources are also abundant — hydroelectric power, first from the Macagua dam on the Caroni river adjacent to the city and more recently from the giant Guri Dam further upstream, which has been built in stages producing 10,300 MW and providing 70% of Venezuelan energy needs.

SIDOR, the state steel firm, is rapidly increasing production to 5 million tonnes, using the direct reduction process, which eliminates the need for coke but does need large amounts of heat. This was efficient in Venezuela because of her abundant oil and natural gas, and lack of coke. The sponge iron which is produced goes directly to an electric arc furnace rather than the standard steel converter, again favouring Venezuela's abundant hydroelectric power at Ciudad Guayana. This is a unique case of the direct reduction process being used on a very large scale, and relates to the unusual Venezuelan resource combination. The principal limitation has in fact been the lack of suitably skilled labour. A completely separate new steel plant is now being planned at a site near Maracaibo, to be based on conventional steel-making techniques using coal from the nearby Guasare coalfield, and iron ore from the northern hills (Serranía del Interior) near Barcelona. A coastal site makes alternative ore sources possbile for this plant which will have a 5 million tonne capacity. It also makes transport of the product easier than at the present Ciudad Guayana site, from which huge 60 tonne lorries are currently used on inadequate roads to transport the steel to Caracas region. A projected east-west railway through the Llanos from Ciudad Guayana will alleviate this problem.

URBAN AND REGIONAL DEVELOPMENT

Caracas
The central element of Venezuelan urbanization is Caracas. This city, whose metropolitan area holds 2 480 000 people (1975), dates back to 1569 as a Spanish settlement, and as capital to 1577, and the historical inertia of a long colonial dominance of a region stretching from the Guiana coasts to lake Maracaibo has given it an unchallenged position. It grew up and remained largely an administrative centre for its region until the present century, in a small fertile valley with the climate of an English summer day, 1000 metres above the hot Caribbean coastlands. Despite the growth of a new industrial focus on oil in the distant Maracaibo Basin, Caracas remained the hub of all economic and political activity. Maracaibo's oil made that town a point of ultra-rapid expansion in the period from the

first commercially successful oil well, in 1914, to about 1925, but thereafter the offices of oil companies, which had no pressing need or desire to stay in an isolated provincial town, moved away to Caracas, principal link to the outside world.

Symbolic of the links to foreign markets and capital sources was the fine new motorway built after the Second World War as a four-lane toll-road across the coastal hills to Maiquetia, Caracas's international airport, and to La Guaira, its principal port. This was a great improvement over the old narrow-gauge railway, built 1883, which had been the first modern link to the exterior. La Guaira, despite its poor open roadstead site for a port, has been maintained in its historic role as chief port for the city, handling in particular its substantial imports.

Most city growth has occurred since 1950, and Caracas, receiving huge numbers of migrants from rural areas, has had acute housing problems in its long but narrow and steep-sided valley. It spread out from the confining colonial chessboard pattern of the early city only after 1920 (fig. 57), expanding both east and west along the valley floor, absorbing fertile farmland and by 1966 occupying all accessible land (plate 42). Future growth of population will inevitably be accommodated by higher densities in the existing city, already an urban jungle of motorways and high residence or office blocks — 30% of the populace are flat-dwellers — that is known as the Los Angeles of Latin America (plate 43). Oil revenues and the pressure of land scarcity are obvious factors in the surge of high-rise developments, but they still appear remarkable monuments to wealth in a land where most people are very poor. Some further growth can be taken up on the sharp slopes surrounding the valley, where the *barrios* or shanty towns are found, but the city's plans have been to reduce suburban densities, concentrating population in the city centre

42 *In the background, the twin towers of the Bolivar Centre are a well-known landmark in Central Caracas. This was built in the 1950s by the last dictator, Perez Jimenez. In the foreground is the El Silencio district. Here there is an earlier and more attractive approach to redevelopment of the city centre*

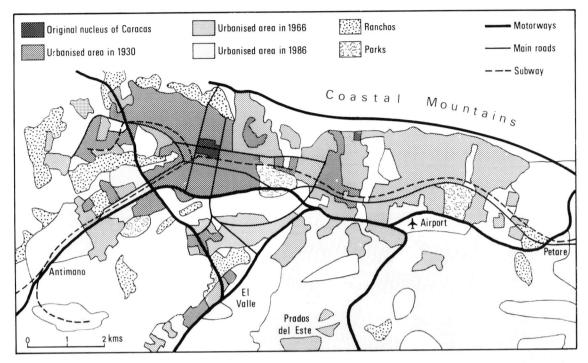

Fig. 57 Caracas city

and at the same time making movement easier there by introducing an underground rail system linking together all inner areas.

The Metro, as this system is called, consists of an east-west line through the valley, confirming the already elongated shape of the city, and will not reach most of the southern suburbs which contribute heavily to the traffic moving into the centre, as there are no important employment centres in these suburbs. The inconveniences of urban pollution by noise, air and water pollutants, and the difficulties of living in a city built essentially for a population of cars, with few areas for walking and with its retailing structure already in the North American mould of shopping centres designed for a car-borne clientele, are likely to persist. Designing a city for car users is perhaps thinkable in North America, but in Latin America a substantial segment of the population is dependent solely on public transportation.

The barrio problem

Exploding city populations have led to shantytown development everywhere. Seventy per cent of Maracay's population, 50% of Maracaibo's and 35% of Caracas's is housed in *barrios,* the growth of which engenders a variety of problems. Municipal services are often initially unable to cope with demand for new roads, sewers, drains, electricity, gas and water, especially as the *barrios* are usually in areas distant from the city centre. *Barrios* supply some of these services themselves, but they have not the capital to make permanent provision. Economically, the inhabitants suffer from their own lack of education and training, and high rates of unemployment are common.

In one view, the *barrios* are a dynamic feature demonstrating the drive in the economy, and their less desirable features are temporary maladjustments, in process of elimination. They represent the attraction of growing cities, of new aspirations and possibilities. The opposing viewpoint is that the *barrios* are collections of the poorest parts of society in one place, a bad form of urban zoning of natural occurrence, and also that they represent a migration of misery from an intolerable rural environment.

Something of both views is acceptable; *barrios* are certainly in part the result of lack of farming opportunity, but they also attract people because of positive long-term job and social prospects in the city. They are useful in a laissez-faire economy, where housing and infrastructure are difficult or expensive for a city to provide. Made of old oil drums, adobe with canes, corrugated iron and packing cases, they cost nothing to the authorities and, for want of funds, have been institutionalized — Caracas has included them in her official plans for housing over the rest of the century.

Cities and regions

Massive population growth in Caracas with its 3 million inhabitants, and to a lesser extent in the second line cities — Maracaibo is second with 920 000 — is both an index of the regional imbalance in the country and the origin of some of the problems associated with imbalance. In the cities there is a lack of housing and urban infrastructure such as roads and sewers, and pollution and traffic congestion are increasingly severe. In the rural regions there is the reverse problem of out-migration. The argument might be made that since 80% of the population is in one third of the area, the northern mountain fringe of the country, regional balance is undesirable — the Llanos and Guayana must remain thinly-peopled resource regions and their intensive development is impossible.

This may be accepted but even within the north fringe there are large differences in welfare. The Andes of Mérida, Trujillo and San Cristóbal are poor, as is the northern Oriente east of Barcelona. They have little part in the industrialization that is going on in the central region. In 1977, 58.6% of value added in manufacturing was in the Central-North Coast region, i.e. the Valencia-Maracay-Caracas axis. In the poor Southern Andes, Mérida, Táchira, and Trujillo had 50%, 53% and 43% of the national

43 A Caracas motorway. Such roads have not solved Caracas's urban traffic problems, for there is no effective public transport system

average per capita regional product, of 2865 Bs in 1961.* In the north east Sucre and Nueva Esparta (the island of Margarita) had 50% and 36%. At the same time, the Federal District of Caracas, and neighbouring Miranda state, had 160% and 143%.

John Friedmann, concerned with Venezuelan regional planning in the 1960s, advocated regional concentrations of an urban-industrial nature, a kind of growth pole policy, to solve Venezuela's overwhelming economic concentration and the continuing centripetal movement of men, physical resources and capital to the Caracas region. His main poles were at:

1 Valencia–Maracay (population 450 000 and 320 000, respectively), using the agricultural wealth of the Lake Valencia basin to support food-processing industries, and well connected to Caracas so that assembly-type industries such as car manufacturing could be developed here;

2 Barquisimeto (504 000), route nexus between the Andes and the Northern Cordillera;

3 Barcelona-Puerto La Cruz-Guanta (284 000 total), an urbanized 20 km long strip of coast with a coal port at Guanta, an oil-refining and general port at Puerto La Cruz, and an administrative and manufacturing centre at Barcelona;

4 El Tablazo, Tuy Medio, and Ciudad Guayana (new growth points). These latter three differ in function among themselves.

El Tablazo was designated a new city in 1967, on Lake Marcaibo opposite Maracaibo city, and intended first as a petrochemical town. Because this was realized as too narrow a base, other manufacturing industries have been sought to help growth. Some of El Tablazo's growth may be seen simply as overspill from Maracaibo across the lake, and it is well linked to the city by a giant road bridge built in 1963.

Tuy Medio is being developed with a comparable role, as overspill receiver for Caracas, providing both jobs and housing and thus becoming more than a commuter suburb. This town is in the middle Tuy valley, 10 km south of Caracas, well linked by road, and in the future by rail, to other regions. But if brought into being as planned, with a population of 500 000 by 1990, it will represent an enormous urban sprawl as it will inevitably link to Caracas to form a single

*J. Chi-Yi Chen, *Estrategia del Desarrollo Regional*, Caracas 1971.

mass. Problems of pollution of air and water are likely to become increasingly severe.

Ciudad Guayana

The third growth centre, Ciudad Guayana, is different in function and in scale from the other two. It dates back to 1960, and has had the benefit of vast financial resources poured into it and a specially created government agency, the Corporación Venezolana de Guayana (CVG) which watched over it and which had the advantage of considerable autonomy of action. Though a regional effort, the developments were concentrated at the junction of the Caroní River with the Orinoco River, where a few small villages had existed, including the iron ore exporting terminal. A new town was built and a bridge crossing the Caroní, economic development becoming based on the steel industry, hydroelectricity from the Caroní, and water transport for ore carriers up to 60 000 tonnes out to the sea by way of a dredged canal. The population of Ciudad Guayana has reached about 210 000 (1981) while 100 km upstream, Ciudad Bolivar, (once known as Angostura because of the narrows on the Orinoco here) has 150 000 population, and is growing almost as rapidly as the industrial city below it.

Steel manufacturing at Ciudad Guayana has already been mentioned. Unfortunately the steel industry has been unable to attract many linked engineering industries, as the principal markets and skilled labour are in the north and industries such as shipbuilding are tied to the coast. Cheap hydroelectric power has attracted some industry, notably pulp and paper manufacture, and it is to supply this industry that a large area north of the river in the infertile acid sands of southern Monagas, has been planted with Monterrey pine (*Pinus insignis*), which may help to bring this whole region into the industrial hinterland of Ciudad Guayana. Another industry using local resources is alumina and aluminium. This is being built up rapidly on the basis of first, the cheap electricity, and secondly, discoveries in 1976 of up to 500 million tonnes of bauxite within Northern Guayana, at Los Pijiguaos, (see fig. 54). A refinery to produce alumina with one million tonnes ore capacity annually is being built at Puerto Ordaz. This will feed into existing smelters to produce aluminium, and replace imports from Caribbean countries.

Industrial growth at Ciudad Guayana may be seen as a success story, in terms of production; whether it is so in regional terms is less clear. The growth-pole effect of the key industries (steel, paper, energy, aluminium) is very slight, after the construction phase which employs large numbers of men for a short time. Forward linkages to consumer and intermediate industries have been particularly slight, and the multiplier effects of the major investments are thus felt not in the region but in Caracas. Power is exported via hightension lines, and aluminium, paper and steel go to markets in the core region. Ciudad Guayana still has something of an enclave economy, more so than the older and smaller centre at Ciudad Bolivar, which ironically enough was never intended to form the growth pole of the region.

Rather than a regional development, Guayana may be seen as a national development project which happens to be sited in one of the peripheral regions, but whose function is still primarily national. It could well be argued that the focus of effort should have been placed in the Andean highlands, where the greatest combination of large population and great poverty is to be found, or in the poor area of the northern Oriente, once a land of cocoa plantations, but without any modern economic base. If the aim is to reduce the flows of migrants, capital and resources from these regions to the centre, some investment must be made in them. The Guayana region was poor but not densely peopled, and it has proved no solution to the problems of the poor regions on the other national peripheries.

Appendix I
GLOSSARY OF PORTUGUESE AND SPANISH TERMS

Portuguese

aldeia	Jesuit mission village
bandeirante	member of slave-catching, exploring, or cattle droving party: the *bandeira* was the flag carried at the head of the party; especially in São Paulo in the colonial period
caboclo	backwoodsman, farm labourer, peasant
cafuso	Indian–Negro racial mixture (Brazil)
capoeira	secondary growth, brush forest
cerrado	wooded savanna
chapada	upland surface, plateau; *chapadão* refers to a larger plateau
donatária	grant of land and rights by the Portuguese king, including powers of tax raising and slave dealing, to its recipient, a *donatário*
engenho	sugar mill, usually with plantation land
favela	slum, shanty town; especially Rio de Janeiro
fazenda	ranch, large farm, estate; cf. *hacienda* in Spanish
mameluco	white–Indian cross
mata	forest. More specifically the coastlands of the Nordeste, originally densely forested.
morro	an isolated hill or small mountain
roça	cleared land; the field used in shifting cultivation
seringueiro	rubber collector
sertão	wilderness, backcountry; plural — *sertões*
tugurio	central city slum
vaqueiro	cowboy, especially in the Nordeste; cf. Spanish *vaquero*
varzea	lowland, usually alluvial floodplain, providing the best soil

Spanish

andén	terrace, especially the Inca and other Indian artificial terraces for agriculture
barriada	shanty town
barrio	suburb; shanty town (Venezuela)
cabildo	municipal authorities; town hall
callampa	shanty town (literally a mushroom) in Chile
charqui	dried or jerked beef
cimarrón	wild cattle; the descendants of escaped domestic cattle
comunidad	community, especially the Peruvian communities set up after agrarian reform and replacing older communities
conuco	shifting cultivation of forest areas, or plot of land under such cultivation. The *conuquero* is farmer of the *conuco*
criollo	local, native; more specifically, persons of Spanish extract but born in the New World. Sometimes translated into English as *creole*

estancia	a ranch or cattle farm of the Pampas region, owned by an *estanciero*
feria	a fair or market
frigorífico	meat freezing and chilling plant or factory
fundo	large farm, especially in Chile
gaucho	cowboy in Argentina, Uruguay, Rio Grande do Sul. Elsewhere the term *vaquero* (Portuguese *vaqueiro*) is used
hacendado	owner of *hacienda*
hacienda	large farm or estate
hato	large farm or ranch, Venezuelan Llanos
hoya	enclosed basin among hills
ingenio	sugar mill and plantation attached; cf. *engenho*, Portuguese
inquilino	tenant; more specifically in Chile, landless small farmer with rights of usufruct of a small plot
latifundio	large and underused estate
merced	grant of land by Spanish crown
minga	voluntary collective work of village (Quechua)
mestizo	European–Indian racial mixture
minifundio	excessively small and intensively used farm
mita	forced labour service to landlord (Quechua, Peru)
mulato	white–Negro mixture
nudo	mountain knot
oficina	nitrate works (Chile)
pampero	strong, dry, south wind of Argentine Pampas
páramo	high-level bunch-grass region above forest line. More generally, a deserted or desert area
rancho	hut or precarious urban dwelling
reducción	Jesuit mission village
salar	salt flat
selva	tropical rain forest
sindicato	trade union, union
templada	temperate, as in *tierra templada;* above it lies the *tierra fría* and *páramos*, below is the *tierra caliente*
tugurio	shanty town (Colombia)
yerba mate	mate tea

ABBREVIATIONS

C	temperature, degrees Celsius (centigrade)
ECLA	United Nations Economic Commission for Latin America
EEC	European Economic Community
GDP	Gross Domestic Product; the total value of all goods produced ignoring foreign trade
GNP	Gross National Product, value of all goods produced including foreign trade
ha	hectare
HEP	hydroelectric power
km	kilometre (m metre, cm centimetre, mm millimetre)
LAFTA	Latin American Free Trade Association

Note

Foreign words are generally italicized and given accentuation marks, which provide an indication of which syllable is stressed in pronunciation in Portuguese and Spanish. Town populations are given in some cases; these refer to the latest available figures where the date is not given. Measurements are in metric units.

Appendix II
BIBLIOGRAPHY

The following list tries to do several things. It covers most of the topics treated in any detail within the book, and is indeed often the basis for that treatment; it cites a few Spanish and Portuguese language sources, especially where English language writing is scarce; and it tries to be eclectic, using old as well as new sources, and varied viewpoints. The journals of most value will be apparent from the bibliographic entries, but apart from those regularly cited, some periodicals with special concern for the Latin American region are: *Americas*, published in English, Portuguese and Spanish by the Pan American Union, Washington, D.C. (monthly); *America Latina*, mostly in Spanish and Portuguese, from the Latin American Centre for Research in Social Sciences, Rio de Janerio (quarterly); *Economic Development and Cultural Change,* quarterly from the University of Chicago Press; the *Journal of Latin American Studies,* Cambridge, England (biannual); and *Revista Geografica,* mostly in English, from the Geography Commission of the Panamerican Institute of Geography and History, Mexico City, (triannual).

Useful annuals are the *South American Handbook*, edited by John Brooks and published by Trade and Travel Publications, Bath, England (a travellers' guide but with much background information), the *Economic Survey of Latin America*, from the UN Economic Commission for Latin America, and *Economic and Social Progress in Latin America*, from the Inter-American Development Bank, Washington, D.C. A unique publication is the annual series of Proceedings of the Conference of Latin American Geographers (CLAG), published since 1971 and available from the Department of Geography, Ball State University, Muncie, Indiana. A statistical source, apart from the regular United Nations yearbooks, with coverage of the whole region, is *Statistical*

Abstract of Latin America, from the University of California, Los Angeles, Latin American Center Publications, edited by J.W. Wilkie.

Place of publication is London unless indicated.

General works

Blakemore, H. and Smith, C.T., (eds.), *Latin America: Geographical Perspectives,* 2nd edition, Methuen, 1983

Bromley, Rosemary and Bromley, Ray, *South American Development; a geographical introduction*, London and New York, Cambridge Univ. Press, 1982

Cole, J.P., *Latin America, an Economic and Social Geography*, 3rd. edn., Butterworths, 1976

Cunill, P., *L'Amérique Andine*, translated from the Spanish by H. Lecomte de Martonne, Paris, Presses Universitaires, 1966

James, P.E., *Latin America*, New York, Odyssey Press, 5th edn., 1975

Martinson, T.L. and Elbow G., *Geographic Research on Latin America; Benchmark 1980,* Muncie, Indiana, Vol. 8 CLAG Proceedings, 1981

Niedergang, M., *The Twenty Latin Americas*, 2 vols., Penguin 1971

Odell, P.R. and Preston, D.A., *Economies and Societies in Latin America*, Wiley, 2nd. edn., 1978

Renner, J. (ed) *Source Book on South American Geography,* 2nd edition, Wellington, New Zealand, Hicks Smith, 1976

Webb, K.E., *Geography of Latin America*, Englewood Cliffs, N.J., Prentice-Hall, 1972

Physical

Allen, R.N., 'The Anchicaya hydroelectric project in Colombia; design and sedimentation problems', pp. 318–42 in M.T. Farvar and J.P. Milton, *The Careless Society,* London, Tom Stacey, 1973

Barker, Mary L., 'National parks, conservation and agrarian reform in Peru', *Geog. Review, 70* (1980), pp. 1–18

Barrett, S.W., 'Conservation in Amazonia', *Biological Conservation* 18 (1980), pp. 209–35

Bockh, A., 'Consequences of uncontrolled human activities in the Valencia Lake Basin,' pp. 301–17 in M.T. Farvar and J.P. Milton (eds), *The Careless Society* London, Tom Stacey, 1973

Caviedes, Cesar, 'El Nino 1972: its climatic, ecological, human and economic implications', *Geographical Review* 65/4 (1975), pp. 493–509

Caviedes, Cesar, 'Natural Hazards in Latin America: a survey and discussion', pp. 280–94, in T.L. Martinson and G. Elbow (eds), *Geographical Research on Latin America: Benchmark 1980,* Vol. 8 CLAG Proceedings, Muncie, Indiana, 1981

Caufield, Catherine, *In the Rainforest,* London, Heineman, 1984

Cole, M.M., 'Cerrado, Caatinga and Pantanal: the distribution and origin of the savanna vegetation of Brazil', *Geog. Journal,* **126** (1960), pp. 168–79

Dickinson, J.C., 'Alternatives to monoculture in the humid tropics of Latin America', *Professional Geographer* 24/3 (1972), pp. 217–22

Eden, Michael J., 'Ecology and land development: the case of the Amazonian rainforest', *Transactions Inst. Brit. Geog.*, N.S. 3/4 (1978), pp. 444–64

Fearnside, P.M. and Rankin, J.M., 'Jari and development in the Brazilian Amazon', *Interciencia* 5/3 (1980), pp. 146–56

Fittkau, E.J., Illies, J, *et al.*, *Biogeography and Ecology in South America*, The Hague, W. Junk, 1968, 2 volumes

Goodland, R., *The Savanna Controversy: Background Information on the Brazilian Cerrado Vegetation*, Savanna Research Series No. 15, Montreal, McGill University, 1970

Goodland, R.J.A. and Irwin, H.S., *Amazon Jungle: Green Hell to Red Desert?* Amsterdam, Elsevier, 1975

Harris, D.R., Human Ecology in Savanna Environments, Academic Press (1980), 'Europeanization of the savanna lands of North South America', pp. 267–289

Hemming, J. (ed), *Amazon development,* Manchester, Manchester Univ. Press (2 vols), 1985

Jenks, William F., *Handbook of South American Geology: an explanation of the geologic map of South America,* New York, Geological Society of America, Memoir No 65, 1956

Mountain Research and Development 2/1 (1982), 'Human Population and Biosphere Interactions in the Central Andes', volume editor Paul T. Baker

Nelson, J.G., Needham, R.D., and Mann, D.L.,

International Experience with National Parks and Related Reserves, Department of Geography, Publication Series No. 12, University of Waterloo, Waterloo, Ontario, (1978).

Paper 7 — 'Colombian National Parks and Related Reserves: research needs and management', Wetterberg, G.B., and Meganek, R.A., pp. 175–232

Parsons, J.J., 'The Northern Andean environment', *Mountain Research and Development* 2/3, (1982), pp. 253–62

Rudolph, William E., 'Catastrophe in Chile', *Geographical Review* 50 (1960), pp. 578–81

Scholten, J.J., 'Vegetation', pp. 21–42 in FAO-UNESCO, *Soil Map of the World, Vol. 4, South America,* Rome, FAO 1971

Schwerdtfeger, W. (ed.), 'Climates of Central and South America', in *World Survey of Climatology,* Vol. 12, Oxford, Elsevier Scientific Publishing Co. 1976

Smith, M.J.H., 'Caimans, Capybaras, Otters, Manatees and Man in Amazonia', *Biological Conservation* 1973 (1981), pp. 177–88

Trewartha, G.L., *The World's Problem Climates*, Ch. 1, Madison, Wisconsin, University of Wisconsin Press, 1962

Tricart, J., *Landforms of the Humid Tropics, Savannas and Forests,* (translated C.J.K. de Yonge), Longman, 1972

White, S., 'Relations of subsistence of the vegetation mosaic of Vilcabamba, Southern Peruvian Andes', *CLAG Yearbook No. 11* (1985), pp 3–10

History

Borah, W., *Early Colonial Trade and Navigation between Mexico and Peru*, Los Angeles, Univ. of California, Ibero-American Series, 1954

Camacho, G., *Latin America*, Penguin, 1973

Cobb, G., 'Supply and transportation for the Potosi mines 1545–1640', *Hispanic American Historical Review, 29* (1949), pp. 25–45

Conde, R. Cortes, *The First Stages of Modernization in Spanish America,* translated by Tony Talbot, New York, Harper and Row, 1974

Denevan, William M., *The native population of the Americas in 1492,* Madison, Univ. of Wisconsin, 1976

Hanke, L., *History of Latin American Civilization*, Vol. 1, *The Colonial Experience*, Methuen, 1969

Hennessy, Alistair, *The Frontier in Latin American History*, Edward Arnold, 1978

MacNeish, R.S., 'The origins of New World civilization', Ch. 16, pp. 155–63 in *New World Archaeology*, readings from *Scientific American*, San Francisco, W.H. Freeman, 1974

Philip A. Means, *Ancient civilizations of the Andes,* New York and London, Scribners 1931

Moseley, M.E. and Day, K.C., *Chan Chan: Andean*

Desert City, Albuquerque, Univ. of Arizona, 1982

Pendle, G.A., *A History of Latin America*, Penguin, 1963

Sanders, W.T. and Marino, J., *New World Prehistory*, Englewood Cliffs, N.J., Prentice-Hall, 1970

Sauer, C.O., *The Early Spanish Main*, Berkeley, Univ. of California, 1966

Agriculture

Burke, M., 'Land reform and its effects upon production and productivity in the Lake Titicaca region', *Econ. Devt. and Cultural Change, 18* (1970), pp. 410–50

Castillo, L. and Lehmann, D., 'Chile's three agrarian reforms: the inheritors', *Bulletin of Latin American Research* 1/2 (1982), pp. 21–43

Clark, R.J., 'Land reform and peasant participation on the northern highlands of Bolivia', *Land Economics, 44* (1968), pp. 153–72

De Janvry, A., *The agrarian question and reformism in Latin America,* Baltimore, Johns Hopkins Univ. Press, 1981

Dorner, P., *Land Reform and Economic Development*, Penguin, 1972

Dozier, C.L., *Land Development and Colonization in Latin America*, New York, Praeger, 1969

Hiraoka, M. and Yamamoto, S., 'Agricultural development in the upper Amazon of Ecuador', *Geog. Review,* **70**/4, (1980) pp. 423–45

Jones, David M., 'The Green Revolution in Latin America; success or failure?', CLAG Publications Vol. 6, pp. 55–64, Ball State Univ. Muncie, Indiana (1977)

Kay, C., 'Achievements and contradictions of the Peruvian agrarian reform', *Journal of Development Studies* 18/2 (1982), pp. 141–70

Nelson, Michael, *The Development of Tropical Lands: Policy Issues in Latin America*, Baltimore, Johns Hopkins Press, 1973

Ruddle, K., *The Yukpa Cultivation System: a study of shifting cultivation in Colombia and Venezuela*, Los Angeles, Univ. of California Press, Ibero-Americana Series No. 52, 1974

Wilkie, J.W., *Measuring Land Reform, Supplement to the Statistical Abstract of Latin America,* Los Angeles, UCLA, Latin American Centre, 1974

Industry

Brown, R.T., *Transport and the Economic Integration of South America*, Washington D.C., Brookings Inst., 1966

Fox, D.J., *Tin and the Bolivian Economy*, Latin American Publications Fund, 1970

Gilbert, Alan, 'Industrial location theory: its relevance to an industrializing nation', Ch. 14, pp. 271–89, in B.S. Hoyle, (ed.), *Spatial Aspects of Development*, Wiley, 1974

Gwynne, R. N., 'Location theory and the centralization of industry in Latin America', TESG 73/2 (1982), pp. 80–93

Gwynne, R. N., *Industrialization and Urbanization in Latin America,* London and Sydney, Croom Helm, 1985

Lagarde, Pierre, *La Politique de l'édition du livre en Argentine,* Toulouse, Univ. de Toulouse — Le Mirail, 1980

Niering, F., *et al., Latin American and Caribbean Oil Report*, Petroleum Economist, London, 1979

Odell, P.R., 'The oil industry in Latin America', in Penrose, E., *The Large International Firm in Developing Countries*, Cass, 1968

Stokes, C.J., *Transportation and Economic Development in Latin America*, New York, Praeger, 1968

U.N. Industrial Development Organization, *Technology Exports from Developing Countries; Argentina and Portugal,* New York, United Nations, 1983

World Bank, *Brazil: industrial policies and manufactured exports,* Washington, D.C., World Bank, 1983

Social and demographic patterns

Amato, P.W., 'Elitism and settlement patterns in the Latin American city', *Journal Amer. Inst. of Planners*, **36** (1970), pp. 96–105

Breton, F., 'Working and living conditions of migrant workers in S. America', *International Labour Review*, **144**/3 (1976), pp. 339–54

Bromley, Rosemary, and Bromley, R.D.F., 'Defining central place systems through the analysis of bus services: the case of Ecuador', *Geog. Journal*, **145**/3 (1979), pp. 416–36

Butterworth, D. and Chance, J. K., *Latin American Urbanization,* Cambridge, Cambridge Univ. Press, 1981

Cardona R. and Simmons A., 'Towards a model of migration in Latin America', pp. 19–48, in B.M. Du Toit and H.T. Safa, *Migration and Urbanization,* Paris Mouton, 1975

Gilbert, A. G., 'Planning for urban primacy and large cities in Latin America: a critique of the literature', in *Actes du 42ème Congrès International des Américanistes,* (1976) Paris, pp. 339–49

Gilbert, A. 'Pirates and invaders: land acquisition in urban Colombia and Venezuela', *World Development* Vol. 9/7 (1981), pp. 657–78

Graham, D.H., 'Divergent and convergent regional economic growth and internal migration in Brazil 1940–60', *Econ. Devt. and Cultural Change*, **18** (1970), pp. 362–82

Griffin, Ernst and Ford, Larry, 'A model of Latin American City Structure', *Geographical Review*

70/4 (1980), pp 397–422

Griffin, Ernst and Williams L.S., 'Social implications of changing populations patterns: the case of rural depopulation in Colombia', pp. 17–25 in R.N. Thomas and J.M. Hunter, *Internal Migration Systems in the Developing World,* Cambridge, Mass., Schenkman, 1980

Hall, M. Françoise, 'Population growth: U.S. and Latin American views', *Population Studies,* **27** (1973), pp. 415–29

Hardoy, J.E., *Urbanization in Latin America: approaches and issues,* New York, Anchor-Doubleday, 1975

Havens A.E. and Flinn, W.L., *Internal Colonialism and Structure Change in Colombia,* New York, Praeger, 1970

Morris, A.S., 'Urban growth patterns in Latin America, with illustrations from Caracas', *Urban Studies,* **15** (1978), pp. 299–312

Portes, A. and Browning, H.L., *Current Perspectives in Latin American Urban Research,* Austin, Univ, of Texas, 1976

Sanchez-Albornoz, Nicolás, *The population of Latin America; a history,* Berkeley, Univ. of California, 1974

Schnore, L.F., 'On the spatial structure of cities in the two Americas' Ch. 10, pp 347–399 in P.M. Hauser and L.F. Schnore (eds), *The study of Urbanization,* New York, Wiley, 1965

Steward, J.H. and Faron, L.C., *Native Peoples of South America,* New York, McGraw-Hill, 1959

Thomas, R.N. and Mulvihill, J.L., 'Temporal attributes of stage migration in Guatemala', pp. 51–61 in Thomas and Hunter, *Internal Migration Systems in the Developing World,* Cambridge, Mass., Schenkman, 1980

Politics and territory

Burgin, M., *The economic aspects of Argentine Federalism 1820-52,* Cambridge, Mass., 1946

Kasza, G.J., 'Regional conflict in Ecuador; Quito and Guayaquil', *Inter-American Economic Affairs,* 35/2, (1981), pp 3–41

Latin American Bureau, *Falklands/Malvinas: whose crisis?,* London, L.A.B., 1982

Love, J.L., *Rio Grande do Sul and Brazilian Regionalism 1882-1930,* Stanford, Stanford Univ. Press, 1971

Medina, Maria Elena 'Treaty for Amazonian Cooperation; general analysis', pp. 58–71 in F. Barbira-Scazzocchio, *Land, People and Planning in Contemporary Amazonia,* Cambridge Univ. Press, Centre for Latin American Studies Occasional Paper No. 3, 1980

Nickson, R.A. 'The Itaıpu hydro-electric project: the Paraguayan perspective', *Bulletin of Latin American Research* 2/1 (1982), pp 1–20.

Rivière d'Arc, Hélène 'L'Armée, aménageur et entrepreneur en Bolivie; le cas du département de Santa Cruz', *L'Espace Geographique* 8/2 (1979), pp. 93–103

Lord Shackleton, *Falkland Islands Economic Study 1982,* London, H.M.S.O., 1982

National and regional development

Brookfield, H., *Interdependent Development,* Methuen, 1975

Conroy, M.E., 'Rejection of growth center strategy in Latin American regional development planning', *Land Economics,* **49**/4 (1973), pp. 371–80

Frank, A.G., *Latin America: Underdevelopment or Revolution,* New York, Monthly Review Press, 1969

Friedmann, J. and Weaver, C., *Territory and Function: the Evolution of Regional Planning,* Edward Arnold, London 1979

Furtado, C., *Economic Development of Latin America,* Cambridge, Cambridge Univ. Press, 1970

Gilbert, A., *Latin American Development: a Geographical Perspective,* Penguin, 1974

Gilbert, A., 'The state and regional income disparity in Latin America', *Bulletin, Society for Latin American Sutdies,* No. 29 (1978), pp. 5–30

Gonzalez Casanova, P., 'Internal colonialism and national development', in I.L. Horowitz, J. de Castro and J. Gerassi, *Latin American Radicalism,* New York, Vintage Books, 1969

Grenier, P., *L'aménagement du térritoire en Amérique Latine,* Grenoble, Presses Universitaires, 1984

Griffin, K., *Underdevelopment in Spanish America,* Allen and Unwin, 1969

Hill, A. David, *Latin American Development Issues,* CLAG, No. 3, Muncie, Ind., Ball State Univ., 1971

Morris, A.S., 'The Argentine Colorado — Interprovincial rivalries over water resources', *Scottish Geog. Magazine,* **94** (1978), pp. 169–80

Morris, A.S., *Regional Development and Differentiation in Latin America,* Hutchinson, 1981

Pedersen, P.O., *Urban–Regional Development in South America: a Process of Diffusion and Integration,* UNRISD Regional Planning Series Vol 10, The Hague, Mouton, 1975

Prebisch, R., *Change and Development: Latin America's Great Task,* New York, Praeger, 1971

Richardson, H. W., 'The relevance of growth centre strategies to Latin America', *Econ. Geography,* **51** (1975), pp. 163–78

Slater, D., 'Underdevelopment and spatial inequality; approaches to the problems of regional planning in the Third World', *Progress in Planning,* **4**/2 (1975), pp. 97–167

Urquidi, V.L. and Thorp, R. (eds.), *Latin America in the International Economy*, Macmillan, 1973

Wionczek, M.S. (ed.), *Latin American Economic Integration*, New York, Praeger, 1966

Peru

Chapman, J.B. *Évolution portuair dans les pays en voie de développement: l'exemple du système portuaire péruvien*, Paris, Institut des Hautes Études de l'Amérique Latine, 1979

Cole, J.P., and Mather, P.M., 'Peru province level factor analysis', *Revista Geográfica*, **77** (1972), pp. 7-37

Collin Delavaud, Claude, 'Agrarian reform in Peru', Ch. 2, pp. 37–52 in Preston, D.A. (ed.), *Environment, Society and rural change in Latin America*, Chichester, Wiley, 1980

Coull, J.R., 'The development of the fishing industry in Peru', *Geography*, **39** (1974), pp. 322–32

Dickinson, J.C., 'The Eucalypt in the Sierra of Southern Peru', *Annals A.A.G.*, **59**/2 (1969), pp. 294–307

Hemming, J., *The Conquest of the Incas*, Macmillan, 1970

Lowenthal, A.F., *The Peruvian Experiment*, Princeton, Princeton Univ. Press, 1975

Reid, M., *Peru: paths to poverty*, London, Latin America Bureau, 1985

Reparaz, G., 'La zone aride du Pérou', *Geografiska Annaler* (1958), pp. 1–61

Rowe, J.H., 'The distribution of Indians and Indian languages in Peru', *Geog. Review*, **37** (1947), pp. 202–15

Smith, C.T., 'Problems of regional development in Peru', *Geography*, **53** (1968), pp. 260–81

White, Stuart, 'Cedar and mahogany logging in eastern Peru', *Geographical Review*, 68 (1978), pp. 394–415

Winterhalder, ·Bruce P. and Brooks, T.R., *Geoecology of Southern Highland Peru*, Boulder, Inst. of Arctic and Alpine Research, Univ. of Colorado, Occasional Paper No. 27, 1978

Bolivia

Alexander, R.J., *Bolivia*, New York, Praeger, 1982

Carter, W.E., *Aymara communities and the Bolivian Agrarian Reform*, Gainesville, Univ. of Florida Monographs, Social Sciences No. 24, 1964

Crossley, J.C., 'Santa Cruz at the cross-roads; a study of development in eastern Bolivia', *Tijdschrift voor Econ. en Soc. Geografie*, **52** (1971), pp. 197–296 and 230–41

Denevan, W.M., *The aboriginal cultural geography of the Llanos de Mojos of Bolivia*, Berkeley, Univ. of California, Ibero-Americana Series, 1966

Fifer, J.V., *Bolivia: Land, Location and Politics Since 1825*, Cambridge Univ. Press, 1972

Hanke, L., *The Imperial City of Potosí*, The Hague, Martinus Nijhoff, 1956

Heath, D.B. *et al.*, *Land Reform and Social Revolution in Bolivia*, New York, Pall Mall Press, 1969

Preston, D.A., 'New towns: a major change in the settlement pattern of highland Bolivia', *Journal Lat. Amer. Studies*, **2** (1970), pp. 1–27

Preston, D.A., 'Land tenure and agricultural development in the central Altiplano, Bolivia', Ch. 12, pp. 231–51 in B.S. Hoyle (ed.), *Spatial Aspects of Development*, Chichester, Wiley, 1974

South, R., 'Coca in Bolivia', *Geographical Review* 67, (1977), pp. 22–33

Argentina

Eidt, R.C., 'Japanese agricultural colonization; a new attempt at land opening in Argentina', *Econ. Geog.*, **44** (1968), pp. 1–20

Eidt, R.C., *Pioneer Settlement in Northeast Argentina*, Madison, Univ. of Wisconsin Press, 1971

Ferns, H.S., *Argentina*, Benn, 1969

Fitzgibbon, R.H., *Argentina*, New York, Oceana, 1974

Jefferson, M., *Peopling the Argentine Pampa*, New York, Amer. Geog. Society, 1926

Morris, A.S., 'The irrigation economy of Mendoza, Argentina', *Annals, A.A.G.*, **59** (1969), pp. 97–115

Morris, A.S., 'The regional problem in Argentine economic development', *Geography*, **57** (1972), pp. 289–306

Morris, A.S., 'The failure of small farmer settlement in Buenos Aires province', *Revista Geográfica*, **85** (1977), pp. 63–77

Reinoso, Marta O. and Ruthsatz, Barbara, 'Environment, human settlement and agriculture in the Puna de Jujuy, Argentina', *Mountain Research and Development* 2/1 (1982), pp 111–26

Scobie, J.R., *Revolution on the Pampas*, Austin, Texas, Univ. of Texas Press, 1967

Scobie, J.R., *Argentina: a City and a Nation*, Oxford Univ. Press, 1964

Sternberg, Rolf, 'Occupance of the humid Pampa: 1856–1914', *Revista Geográfica*, **76** (1972), pp. 61–102

Taylor, C.C., *Rural Life in Argentina*, Baton Rouge, La., Louisiana State Univ. Press, 1948

Uruguay

Alisky, M., *Uruguay*, New York, Praeger, 1969

Brannon, R.H., *Uruguay: Portrait of a Democracy*, Allen and Unwin, 1956

Griffin, E., 'Testing the von Thünen theory in Uruguay', *Geog. Review*, **63** (1973), pp. 500–16

Kleinpenning, J. M. G., 'Uruguay: the rise and fall of a welfare state seen against a background of dependency theory', *Revista Geografica* 93, (1981), pp. 101–17

Lamas, J. Martinez, *Riqueza y Pobreza del Uruguay*, Montevideo, Palacio del Libro, 1930

Snyder, D.E., 'The metropolitan nodality of Montevideo', *Econ. Geography*, **38** (1962), pp. 95–112

Paraguay

Gillespie, Fran, 'Comprehending the slow pace of urbanisation in Paraguay between 1950 and 1972', *Econ. Development and Cultural Change* 31/2 (1983), pp. 355–76

Gillespie, Fran and Browning, H., 'The effect of emigration upon socio-economic structure; the case of Paraguay', *International Migration Review* 1333 (1979), pp. 502–18

Hopkins, E.A., Crist, R.E. and Snow, W.P., *Paraguay*, New York, American Geographical Society, Occasional Publication No. 2, 1968

Kleinpenning, J.M.G., 'Rural development policy in Paraguay since 1960', *TESG* 75/3 (1984), pp. 164–76

Kohlhepp, G., 'Colonizacion y desarrollo dependiente en el oriente Paraguayo', *Revista Geografica* 99 (1984), pp. 5–33

Latin America Bureau, *Paraguay: Power Game*, London, Latin America Bureau, 1980

Nickson, R. A., 'The Itaipu hydroelectric project: the Paraguayan perspective', *Bulletin of Latin American Research* 2/1 (1982), pp. 1–20

Service, Elman R. and Service, Helen S., *Tobati, Paraguayan Town*, Chicago, Univ. of Chicago Press, 1954

Chile

Butland, G.J., *The Human Geography of Southern Chile*, Inst. Brit. Geographers, Publication No. 24, 1957

CORFO, *Geografía Económica de Chile*, Santiago, Editorial Universitaria, 1965

Cunill, P., *Geografía de Chile*, Santiago, Editorial Universitaria, 2nd edn., 1976

Fried, J. and Bianchi, J., 'Small-scale forestry enterprise in three zones of southern Chile', *Tijdschrift voor Econ. en Soc. Geografie*, **61** (1970), pp. 223–31

Gwynne, R.N., 'Government planning and the location of the motor vehicle industry in Chile', *Tijdschrift voor Econ. en Soc. Geografie*, **69** (1978), pp. 130–40

Jefferies, A., 'Agrarian reform in Chile', *Geography*, **56** (1971), pp. 221–30

Johnson, L.J., 'Problems of import substitution: the Chilean auto industry', *Econ. Devt. and Cult. Change*, **15** (1967), pp. 202–16

Larrain, M.A., 'A Chilean regional development policy', *Latin American Urban Research*, **5** (1975), pp. 143–50

MacBride, G.M., *Chile: Land and Society*, New York, Amer. Geog. Society, 1936

Rudolph, W. E., *Vanishing Trails of Atacama,* New York, Amer. Geographical Society, 1963

Brazil

Baer, W., *The Development of the Brazilian Steel Industry*, Nashville, Tenn., Vanderbilt Univ. Press, 1969

Barbira-Scazzocchio, F. (ed.), *Land, People and Planning in Contemporary Amazonia,* Cambridge, Univ. of Cambridge, Centre of Latin American Studies No. 3, 1980

Bourne, R., *Assault on the Amazon,* London, Gollancz (1978)

Brooks, R.H., 'Human response to recurrent drought in northeast Brazil', *Professional Geographer*, **23** (1971), pp. 40–44

Brooks, R.H., 'Drought and public policy in Northeast Brazil: alternatives to starvation', *Professional Geographer*, **25** (1973), pp. 338–46

Campbell, G., *Brazil Struggles for Development*, Charles Knight, 1972

Castro, J. de, *Death in the Northeast*, New York, Vintage Books, 1969

Cunha, Euclides de, *Rebellion in the Backlands*, Chicago, Univ. of Chicago Press, 1944

Dickenson, John P., *Brazil: Studies in Industrial Geography*, Folkestone, Dawson, 1978

Dickenson, J.P., *Brazil, The World's Landscape* Series, London, Longman, 1982

Dickenson, John P., 'Innovations for regional development in north east Brazil', *Third World Planning Review*, **2**/1 (1980), pp. 57–74

Epstein, D.G., *Brasília, Plan and Reality*, Berkeley, Univ. of California Press, 1973

Freyre, G., *The Masters and the Slaves*, translated by S. Putnam, New York, Alfred Knopf, 1956

Furneaux, R., *The Amazon*, Hamish Hamilton, 1969

Haller, A.O., 'A socio-economic regionalization of Brazil', *Geographical Review* 72/4 (1982), pp. 450–64

Henshall, J.D., and Momsen, R.P., *A Geography of Brazilian Development*, Bell, 1974

Johnson, A.W., *Sharecroppers of the Sertao*, Stanford, Calif., Stanford Univ. Press, 1971

Katzmann, M., 'Regional development policy in Brazil: the role of growth poles and development highways in Goias', *Econ. Devt. and Cult. Change,* **24** (1975–76), pp. 75–107

Katzmann, M.T., *Cities and Frontiers in Brazil: regional dimensions of economic development,* Cambridge, Mass. and London, Harvard, 1977

Kleinpenning, J.M.G., 'Objectives and results of the development policy in Northeast Brazil', *Tijdschrift voor Econ. en Soc. Geografie*, **62** (1971), pp. 271–84

Kleinpenning, J.M.G., 'A further evaluation of the policy for the integration of the Amazon Region', *Tijdschrift voor Econ. en Soc. Geografie*, **69** (1978), pp. 78–85

Moran, E.F., *Developing the Amazon,* Bloomington, Indiana Univ. Press, 1981

Sanders, J.H., and Bain, F.L., 'Agricultural development on the Brazilian frontier; southern Mato Grosso', *Econ. Devt. and Cultural Change*, **24** (1975), pp. 593–610

Simonsen, R.C., *História Económica do Brasil 1500–1810*, Sao Paulo, Editôra Nacional, 4th edn., 1962

Taylor, J. A., 'Current problems in Brazilian coffee production', *Geografisch Tijdschrift* 8/1 (1974), pp. 40–46

The Guianas
Auty, R.M., 'Transforming mineral enclaves; Caribbean bauxite in the nineteen-seventies', *Tijdschrift voor Econ. en Soc. Geografie*, **71** (1980), pp. 169–79

Dudler, H.J., Hurst, E., Hardon, M., and Lambert, M.H., 'The economy of Surinam', *International Monetary Fund Staff Papers* Nov. 1971, pp. 668–705

Goslinga, C. Ch., *A short history of the Netherlands Antilles and Surinam*, Martinus Nijhoff, The Hague, 1979

Smith, R.T., *British Guiana*, New York, Oxford University Press, 1962

Strachan, A.J., 'Water control in Guyana', *Geography,* **65**/4 (1980), pp. 297–304

Ecuador
Bromley, R.J., 'Agricultural colonization in the upper Amazon Basin', *Tijdschrift voor Econ. en Soc. Geografie*, **63** (1972), pp. 278–94

Bromley, R.J., *Development and Planning in Ecuador*, Latin Amer. Publications Fund 1977

Collin Delavaud, Anne, 'From colonization to agricultural development: the case of coastal Ecuador', Ch. 5, pp. 67–81, in Preston, D.A., (ed.), *Environment, Society and Rural Change in Latin America*, Chichester, Wiley, 1980

Morris, A.S., 'Forestry and land-use conflicts in Cuenca, Ecuador', *Mountain Research and Development* 5/2, 1985, pp. 183–96

Preston, D.A., 'Negro, Mestizo and Indian in an Andean environment', *Geog. Journal*, **131** (1965), pp. 220–34

Redclift, M.R., and Preston, D.A., 'Agrarian reform and rural change in Ecuador', Ch. 4, pp. 53–63, in Preston, D.A. (ed.), *Environment, Society and Rural Change in Latin America*, Chichester, Wiley, 1980

Zuvekas, C., 'Agrarian reform in Ecuador's Guayas River Basin', *Land Economics*, **52**/3 (1976), pp. 314–29

Colombia
Eidt., R.C., 'Aboriginal Chibcha settlement in Colombia', *Annals A.A.G.*, **49** (1959), pp. 374–92

Hagen, V.W. von, *The Golden Man: the quest for El Dorado*, Farnborough, Saxon House, 1974

McGreevey, W.P., *An Economic History of Colombia, 1845–1930*, Cambridge Univ. Press, 1971

Parsons, J.J., *Antioqueño Colonization in Western Colombia*, Berkeley, Univ. of California Press, Ibero-Americana Series, revised edn. 1968

Posada, A.J., and Posada, J. de, *The C.V.C.; challenge to underdevelopment and traditionalism*, Bogotá, Ediciones Tercer Mundo, 1966

Ridler, Neil B., 'Development through urbanization: a partial evaluation of the Colombian experiment', *International Journal of Urban and Regional Research*, 3/1 (1979), pp. 49–59

Townsend, Janet, 'Magdalena river of Colombia', *Scottish Geographical Magazine* 97/1 (1981), pp. 37–49

West, R.C., *The Pacific Lowlands of Colombia*, Baton Rouge, La., Louisiana State Univ. Press, 1957

Williams, L. S. and Griffin E. C., 'Rural and small-town depopulation in Colombia', *Geographical Review* 68 (1978), pp. 13–30

Venezuela
Eden, M.J., 'Irrigation systems and the development of peasant agriculture in Venezuela', *Tijdschrift voor Econ. en Soc. Geografie*, **65** (1974), pp. 48–54

Eidt, Robert C., 'Agrarian reform and the growth of new rural settlements in Venezuela', *Erdkunde*, **29**/2 (1975), pp. 118–33

Friedmann, J., *Regional Development Policy: a Case study of Venezuela*, Cambridge, Mass, MIT, 1966

Levy, D.F., *Economic Planning in Venezuela*, New York, Praeger, 1968

Lynch, E., 'Propositions for planning new towns in Venezuela', *Journal of Developing Areas*, **7** (1973)

Penfold, A., 'Caracas: urban growth and transportation', *Town Planning Review*, **41** (1970), pp. 103–20

Rodwin, L. and associates, *Planning urban growth and regional development: the experience of the Guayana program of Venezuela*, Cambridge, Mass., MIT, 1969

Turner, A. and Smulian J., 'New cities in Venezuela', *Town Planning Review*, **42** (1971), pp. 3–27

Index